Fodor's 05

NEW ORLEANS

Where to Stay and Eat
for All Budgets

Must-See Sights
and Local Secrets

Ratings You Can Trust

Fodor's Travel Publications   New York, Toronto, London, Sydney, Auckland
www.fodors.com

FODOR'S NEW ORLEANS 2005
EDITOR: William Travis

Editorial Contributors: Collin Campbell, Sharon Donovan, Paul A. Greenberg, Baty Landis, Sara Roahen
Editorial Production: Tom Holton
Maps: David Lindroth Inc., *cartographer;* Rebecca Baer and Bob Blake, *map editors*
Design: Fabrizio La Rocca, *creative director;* Moon Sun Kim, *cover designer;* Guido Caroti, *art director;* Melanie Marin, *senior picture editor*
Production/Manufacturing: Angela L. McLean
Cover Photo (horsedrawn carriage, French Quarter): Ken Reid/Taxi/Getty Images

ISBN 1–4000–1418–2

ISSN 0743–9385

SPECIAL SALES
This book is available for special discounts for bulk purchases for sales promotions or premiums. Special editions, including personalized covers, excerpts of existing books, and corporate imprints, can be created in large quantities for special needs. For more information, write to Special Markets/Premium Sales, 1745 Broadway, MD 6-2, New York, New York 10019 or e-mail specialmarkets@ randomhouse.com.

AN IMPORTANT TIP & AN INVITATION
Although all prices, opening times, and other details in this book are based on information supplied to us at press time, changes occur all the time in the travel world, and Fodor's cannot accept responsibility for facts that become outdated or for inadvertent errors or omissions. So **always confirm information when it matters,** especially if you're making a detour to visit a specific place. Your experiences—positive and negative—matter to us. If we have missed or misstated something, **please write to us.** We follow up on all suggestions. Contact the New Orleans editor at editors@fodors.com or c/o Fodor's at 1745 Broadway, New York, New York 10019.

PRINTED IN THE UNITED STATES OF AMERICA

10 9 8 7 6 5 4 3 2 1

DESTINATION NEW ORLEANS

D ay in and day out, New Orleans may be the most festive city in the world. Many destinations have a single celebratory season—Rio its Carnival, Edinburgh its Festival—but when the party's over, life reverts to a workaday pace. In New Orleans, the party is never quite over. Official celebrations fill up the calendar, from the most famous, Mardi Gras, to the less so—try the Great French Market Tomato Festival. And even when there's no official fete in the works, New Orleans parties on, to the beat of some of the best music in the world. Down here when they say, *"Laissez les bons temps rouler!"* they're not kidding. When you visit New Orleans, be ready to let the good times roll!

Tim Jarrell, Publisher

CONTENTS

ABOUT THIS BOOK

The best source for travel advice is a like-minded friend who's just been where you're headed. But with or without that friend, you'll be in great shape to find your way around your destination once you learn to find your way around your Fodor's guide.

SELECTION

Our goal is to cover the best properties, sights, and activities in their category, as well as the most interesting communities to visit. We make a point of including local food-lovers' hot spots as well as neighborhood options, and we avoid all that's touristy unless it's really worth your time. You can go on the assumption that everything in this book is recommended wholeheartedly by our writers and editors. Flip to On the Road with Fodor's to learn more about who they are. It goes without saying that no property pays to be included.

RATINGS

Orange stars ★ denote sights and properties that our editors and writers consider the very best in the area covered by the entire book. These, the best of the best, are listed in the Fodor's Choice section in the front of the book. Black stars ★ highlight the sights and properties we deem Highly Recommended, the don't-miss sights within any region. In cities, sights pinpointed with numbered map bullets ❶ in the margins tend to be more important than those without bullets.

SPECIAL SPOTS

Pleasures & Pastimes and text on chapter-title pages focus on experiences that reveal the spirit of the destination. Also watch for Off the Beaten Path sights. Some are out of the way, some are quirky, and all are worthwhile. When the munchies hit, look for Need a Break? suggestions.

TIME IT RIGHT

Check On the Calendar up front and chapters' Timing sections for weather and crowd overviews and best days and times to visit.

SEE IT ALL

Use Fodor's exclusive Great Itineraries as a model for your trip. Good Walks guide you to important sights in each neighborhood; ➤ indicates the starting points of walks and itineraries in the text and on the map.

BUDGET WELL

In the hotel and restaurant price categories, from ¢ to $$$$, we provide a balanced selection for every budget. For attractions, we always give standard adult admission fees; reductions are usually available for children, students, and senior citizens. Look in Discounts & Deals in Smart Travel Tips for information on destination-wide ticket schemes. Want to pay with plastic? AE, D, DC, MC, V following restaurant and hotel listings indicate whether American Express, Discover, Diner's Club, MasterCard, or Visa are accepted.

BASIC INFO

Smart Travel Tips lists travel essentials for the entire area covered by the book. To find the best way to get around, see the transportation section; see individual modes of travel ("Car Travel," "Train Travel") for details.

ON THE MAPS	Maps throughout the book show you what's where and help you find your way around. Black and orange numbered bullets ❶❷ in the text correlate to bullets on maps.
BACKGROUND	We give background information within the chapters in the course of explaining sights as well as in CloseUp boxes and in Understanding New Orleans at the end of the book. To get in the mood, review the Books & Movies section. The glossary can be invaluable.
FIND IT FAST	Within the Exploring New Orleans chapter, sights are grouped by neighborhood. Where to Eat and Where to Stay are also organized by neighborhood—Where to Eat is further divided by cuisine type. The Nightlife & the Arts chapter is arranged alphabetically by type. Within Shopping, a description of the city's main shopping districts is followed by a list of specialty shops grouped according to their focus. The Side Trips chapter explores Plantation Country and Cajun Country. These sections are subdivided by town. Heads at the top of each page help you find what you need within a chapter.
DON'T FORGET	Restaurants are open for lunch and dinner daily unless we state otherwise; we mention dress only when there's a specific requirement and reservations only when they're essential or not accepted—it's always best to book ahead. Hotels have private baths, phone, TVs, and air-conditioning and operate on the European Plan (a.k.a. EP, meaning without meals). We always list facilities but not whether you'll be charged extra to use them, so when pricing accommodations, find out what's included.
SYMBOLS	

Many Listings
- ★ Fodor's Choice
- ★ Highly recommended
- ⊠ Physical address
- ✛ Directions
- ⬧ Mailing address
- ☎ Telephone
- 🖷 Fax
- ⊕ On the Web
- ✉ E-mail
- 🎫 Admission fee
- ☉ Open/closed times
- ► Start of walk/itinerary
- Ⓜ Metro stations
- ▭ Credit cards

Outdoors
- 🏌 Golf
- ⛺ Camping

Hotels & Restaurants
- 🏨 Hotel
- ⇋ Number of rooms
- ⟲ Facilities
- ⦿ Meal plans
- ✕ Restaurant
- ⦿ Reservations
- 🏛 Dress code
- ⦆ Smoking
- ⦅⦆ BYOB
- ✕🏨 Hotel with restaurant that warrants a visit

Other
- ℭ Family-friendly
- 🛈 Contact information
- ⇨ See also
- ⊠ Branch address
- ☞ Take note

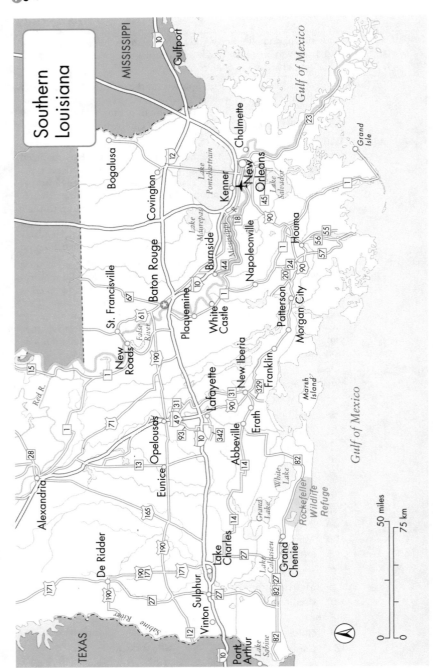

Southern Louisiana

TEXAS

MISSISSIPPI

Gulf of Mexico

Gulf of Mexico

Gulfport

Bogalusa

Covington

Lake Pontchartrain

Lake Maurepas

New Orleans

Kenner

Chalmette

Grand Isle

Baton Rouge

Burnside

Napoleonville

Houma

St. Francisville

White Castle

Plaquemine

Patterson

Morgan City

New Roads

False River

New Iberia

Franklin

Marsh Island

Lafayette

Erath

Abbeville

Opelousas

Eunice

White Lake

Grand Lake

Alexandria

Red R.

Rockefeller Wildlife Refuge

De Ridder

Lake Charles

Grand Chenier

Lake Calcasieu

Sulphur

Vinton

Port Arthur

Lake Sabine

Sabine River

Lake Salvador

50 miles

75 km

ON THE ROAD WITH FODOR'S

A trip takes you out of yourself. Concerns of life at home completely disappear, driven away by more immediate thoughts—about, say, what marvels will beguile the next day, or where you'll have dinner. That's where Fodor's comes in. We make sure that you know all your options, so that you don't miss something that's around the next bend just because you didn't know it was there. Because the best memories of your trip might well have nothing to do with what you came to New Orleans to see, we guide you to sights large and small all over the region. You might set out for dinner in the Garden District, but back at home you find yourself unable to forget strolling through the Faubourg Marigny or hearing some funky rhythm and blues in an Uptown music club. With Fodor's at your side, serendipitous discoveries are never far away.

Our success in showing you every corner of New Orleans is a credit to our extraordinary writers. Although there's no substitute for travel advice from a good friend who knows your style, our contributors are the next best thing—the kind of people you would poll for travel advice if you knew them.

Sharon Donovan is an intrepid traveler, especially within New Orleans, where she has lived for years. She writes about the city, as well as other exotic adventurous spots for a number of magazines, newspapers, and wire services. She has taught fledgling reporters how to pinpoint the essence of their travel pieces in a grain of sand and consulted with travel and tour operators on how to endear themselves to travelers.

A native New Orleanian, Baty Landis used her discerning knowledge of her home city for the Exploring, Mardi Gras & Jazz Fest, Nightlife & the Arts, and Side Trips chapters. She currently lives in the Faubourg Marigny and is working on a dissertation toward a Ph.D. in music.

Paul A. Greenberg, who revised the Where to Stay chapter, is a New Orleans writer with more than 20 years' experience writing about the City That Care Forgot. A perfect day in his life? Breakfast at Brennan's, shopping in the French Quarter, lunch at Commander's Palace, an ice-cold martini at the Polo Lounge at the Windsor Court, dinner at Mr. B's, and a concert by the Louisiana Philharmonic.

Where to Eat contributor Sara Roahen writes about food and restaurants in New Orleans, where she is the restaurant critic and a regular features contributor for *Gambit Weekly*. Her work has also appeared in *Gourmet, Tin House,* and *Wine & Spirits* magazines.

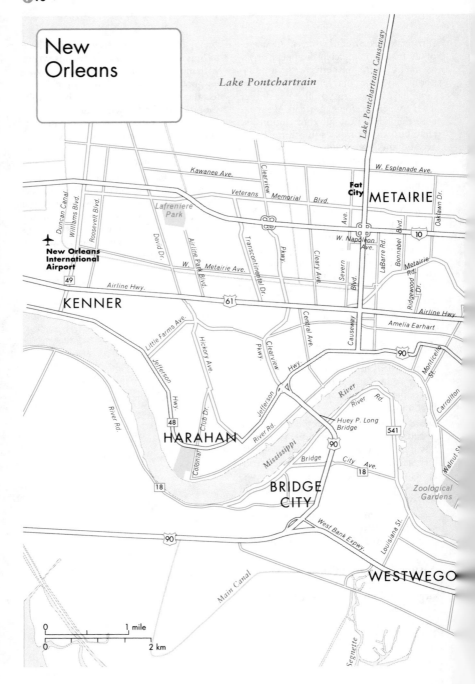

New
Orleans

Lake Pontchartrain

Lake Pontchartrain Causeway

Kawanee Ave.

Clearview

W. Esplanade Ave.

Veterans   Memorial   Blvd.

Fat
City   METAIRIE

Lafreniere
Park

Duncan Canal

Williams Blvd.

Roosevelt Blvd.

David Dr.

Airline Park Blvd.

W. Metairie Ave.

Transcontinental Dr.

Pkwy.

Ave.

Cleary Ave.

W. Napoleon
Ave.

Severn

Blvd.

LaBarre Rd.

Bonnabel Blvd.

Metairie
Rd.

Oaklawn Dr.

10

New Orleans
International
Airport

49

Airline Hwy.

61

Ridgewood
Dr.

Airline Hwy.

KENNER

Amelia Earhart

Little Farms Ave.

Hickory Ave.

Clearview

Pkwy.

Central Ave.

Causeway

90

Monticello St.

Jefferson   Hwy.

River   Rd.

River   Rd.

Carrollton

River Rd.

Club Dr.

River Rd.

Jefferson   Hwy.

Huey P. Long
Bridge

541

Walnut St.

48

HARAHAN

Colonial Dr.

Mississippi

Bridge

90

City   Ave.

18

Zoological
Gardens

18

BRIDGE
CITY

West Bank Expwy.

Louisiana St.

90

WESTWEGO

Main Canal

Segnette

0   1 mile

0   2 km

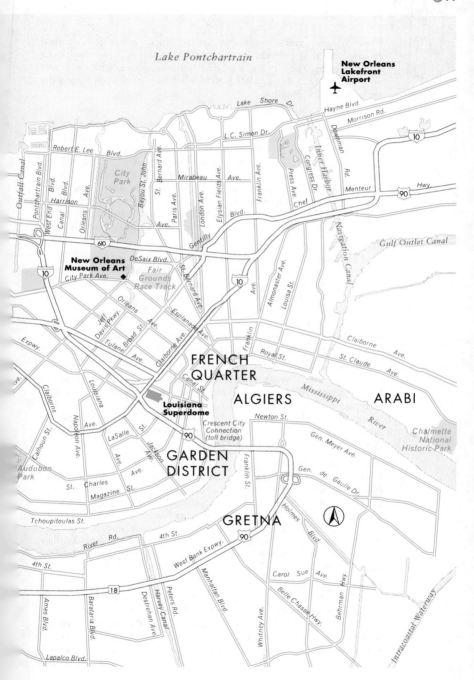

Lake Pontchartrain

New Orleans
Lakefront
Airport

Lake Shore Dr.
Hayne Blvd.
Morrison Rd.
10

L.C. Simon Dr.

Robert E. Lee Blvd.

City Park

Pontchartrain Blvd.
West End Blvd.
Canal Blvd.
Harrison Ave.
Orleans Ave.

Outfall Canal

Bayou St. John
St. Bernard Ave.
Mirabeau
Paris Ave.
London Ave.
Elysian Fields Ave.
Franklin Ave.
Press Ave.
Congress Dr.
Downman Rd.
Menteur
90 Hwy.

Inner Harbor
Chef

Gentilly Blvd.
Ave.

610

Gulf Outlet Canal

DeSaix Blvd.
New Orleans
Museum of Art
City Park Ave.
Fair
Grounds
Race Track

10

Orleans Ave.
Jeff Davis Pkwy.
Broad St.
Tulane Ave.
Esplanade Ave.
St. Bernard Ave.
Claiborne Ave.

Navigation Canal
Almonaster Ave.
Louisa St.

10
Ave.

Franklin
Claiborne Ave.

Expwy.
Claiborne Ave.
Louisiana Ave.
Napoleon Ave.
Calhoun St.

FRENCH
QUARTER

Canal St.

Royal St.
St. Claude Ave.

Mississippi River

ALGIERS

ARABI

Louisiana
Superdome

90
Crescent City
Connection
(toll bridge)

Newton St.

Chalmette
National
Historic Park

Audubon
Park

LaSalle St.
Jackson Ave.

GARDEN
DISTRICT

St. Charles Ave.
Magazine St.

Franklin St.
Gen. Meyer Ave.

Gen. de Gaulle Dr.

Tchoupitoulas St.

GRETNA

Holmes Blvd.

River Rd.
4th St.
90
West Bank Expwy.

4th St.
18
Peters Rd.
Destrehan Ave.
Harvey Canal
Manhattan Blvd.
Carol Sue Ave.
Belle Chasse Hwy.
Behrman Hwy.

Ames Blvd.
Barataria Blvd.
Whitney Ave.

Lapalco Blvd.

Intracoastal Waterway

New Orleans covers approximately 365 square mi of flat, drained swampland that extends between the Mississippi River and Lake Pontchartrain. The city has a small-town atmosphere, with neighborhoods in many cases populated by families who have lived within the same blocks for decades.

The French Quarter

The French Quarter, or Vieux Carré, a 6-by-12-block rectangle along the Mississippi River where the city was first established by the French in 1718, draws the most visitors. This area is both a residential and a business district, with streets lined with historic landmarks, beautifully restored residences, shops, restaurants, and offices. Except for Bourbon Street, a world-famous entertainment strip, the French Quarter has no neon signs, and its buildings conform to the architectural styles of the late 18th to mid-19th centuries. Artists, musicians, and street performers gravitate to Jackson Square, a landscaped park that is the heart of the Vieux Carré.

Faubourg Marigny & Bywater

Predominantly residential, the area downtown from the French Quarter has become a haven to artists, musicians, and bohemians. Colorful low-lying cottages and sprawling warehouses—some converted, some abandoned—compose its cityscape. The area has perked up considerably since the opening of the beautiful campus of the New Orleans Center for the Creative Arts (NOCCA). Although bars, scenic walks, and local color are the mainstays of a foray here, a growing number of galleries and ever-increasing cultural activity are promising diversions.

Central Business District (CBD)

Upriver from the French Quarter, this neighborhood, often called the CBD, encompasses impressive office buildings, courthouses, hotels, shopping malls, and the Louisiana Superdome, home to the New Orleans Saints football team. The CBD extends to the foot of Canal Street, home of the Aquarium of the Americas, the ferry across the river to Algiers Point, and Harrah's New Orleans casino.

Warehouse District

Once an industrial district serving the Port of New Orleans, today's Warehouse District is a trendy destination for loft-style living, museum and gallery hopping, shopping, and fine dining. Julia Street is the center, the site of monthly gallery openings and Emeril Lagasse's flagship restaurant. A cluster of quality museums around Lee Circle, including the National D-Day Museum and the Contemporary Arts Center, form another focal point. The Warehouse District's riverfront property is claimed by the Riverwalk, a half-mile marketplace of more than 200 shops.

The Garden District

The Garden District, which begins where St. Charles Avenue crosses Jackson Avenue, was settled by Americans who built their fortunes in New Orleans after the 1803 Louisiana Purchase. This wealthy neighborhood is renowned for its sumptuous antebellum homes (many in the Greek Revival style with lovely ironwork), surrounded by beautifully landscaped gardens. The Garden District is bordered on the south by the Magazine

Street shopping area and claims one of New Orleans's grandest contemporary Creole restaurants, Commander's Palace.

Uptown

Southwest of the French Quarter and the CBD, this area stretches from the Garden District past the Tulane and Loyola university neighborhoods, all the way to the end of the St. Charles Avenue streetcar line, which stops at Carrollton and Claiborne avenues. Uptown has mansions, several good music venues for everything from jazz to zydeco, and the Riverbend shopping area. Across from the universities is Audubon Park, a former plantation that now includes a world-class zoo, a golf course, winding lagoons, and miles of walking trails.

Mid-City

This working-class neighborhood north of the French Quarter and south of Lake Pontchartrain is mostly residential, but it also contains several sights of interest to visitors. The Fair Grounds is the third-oldest racetrack in the country and the site of the annual New Orleans Jazz & Heritage Festival. The West Indies–style Pitot House is the only plantation home in New Orleans open to visitors, and one of the oldest in the region. City Park, once a sugar plantation belonging to Louis Allard in the late 1700s, today holds the New Orleans Museum of Art, the enchanting Botanical Garden, Storyland amusement park, a turn-of-the-20th-century carousel, and plenty of picnic areas.

Lakefront

If you have a car, it's worth heading to Lakeshore Drive on the northern edge of the city for views of Lake Pontchartrain, especially around sunset. Lakeshore Drive is a favorite spot for boating, fishing, picnicking, and walking. Within the lakefront area are Lakeview, a residential neighborhood with modern ranch-style homes; a public and private marina; and several casual seafood joints.

Side Trips

Three areas within driving distance of New Orleans are worth investigating if you have the time. East and west of the Mississippi, the Great River Road extends between New Orleans and Baton Rouge and passes beautifully restored antebellum plantation homes furnished with period antiques. River Road is also called LA or Route 44 and 75 on the east bank, and LA or Route 18 on the west bank. Standouts among the plantations are Oak Alley, named for the 28 gnarled oak trees on the grounds; the Greek Revival mansions Houmas House and Madewood; and Nottoway, the South's largest plantation home, a white Greek Revival–Italianate castle with 64 rooms. Another region to explore is Cajun Country. The best way to become acquainted with Cajun life and lore is to visit the city of Lafayette (128 mi west of New Orleans on I–10), where you can tour recreations of early-19th-century bayou settlements, including examples of Acadian architecture, furnishings, and tools. From Lafayette you can head for a number of nearby tiny towns and villages with historic buildings and antiques shops. Visitors to Cajun Country will want to sample the region's rich, spicy cuisine and celebratory, foot-stomping music.

GREAT ITINERARIES

New Orleans in 5 Days

New Orleans is a city to savor at a leisurely pace, mostly on foot and with an eye for the unusual and even outrageous. Children find it as fascinating as their parents do. Five days is time enough to capture the essence of the city and its environs. *So that you don't show up somewhere and find the doors locked, shuffle the itinerary segments with closing days in mind.*

DAY 1

Think French Quarter, the heart of the city since its founding in 1718. The traditional breakfast of café au lait and beignets at Café du Monde on Jackson Square is a must. Walk through the Quarter's old streets and peek into intimate courtyards, galleries, and antiques shops on Chartres and Royal streets. Tour one of the house museums or the Cabildo. For lunch have a po'boy sandwich or muffuletta, both classics. A carriage ride through the narrow streets gives you a bird's-eye view and a colorful local guide. Bourbon Street is jumping at night. Try a spicy seafood dish to the hot sounds of jazz or blues, and of course a Hurricane drink at Pat O'Brien's is de rigueur. *This is fine any day but Monday, when many of the historic buildings are closed.*

DAY 2

The streetcar is your ticket to uptown and the Garden District with its antebellum mansions and live oak trees. Take the St. Charles Avenue streetcar from the CBD, getting off at Washington Avenue for the Garden District houses. Lunch at Commander's Palace is straight out of an Anne Rice novel. After you eat, take the streetcar to Audubon Park. A six-block walk through the park brings you to Audubon Zoo, one of the country's best. Magazine Street begins just in front of the Zoo; hop the Magazine Street Shuttle for a tour of this extended commercial strip, where you'll find lots of collectibles in the shops and galleries. After dinner at a bistro on Magazine Street, take in some live music at the legendary clubs uptown like Tipitina's or the Maple Leaf. *Don't do this on Sunday if you want to see Lafayette Cemetery. The House of Broel's Victorian Mansion and Doll House Museum are closed Monday.*

DAY 3

It's back to nature in bayou country. Schedule a bus tour that takes you to a plantation upriver in the morning and on a swamp tour in the afternoon. Lunch is included. The plantation homes are beautifully restored to give you that *Gone With the Wind* feeling. From the boat in the swamp you'll learn about the birds, fish, and fauna—watch out for those alligators! Back in town extend the rural feel with lively Cajun and zydeco music into the early morning hours downtown at Mulate's or Michaul's; you can grab a late dinner at either. *This won't work on Sunday if you're exploring on your own with a view toward stopping at one of the restaurants listed in Cajun Country, because many of them are closed then. If you are taking an escorted tour of the plantations and swamps, food will be provided, so any day will do.*

DAY 4

Spend the day on the riverfront of the mighty Mississippi. Check out the Aquarium of the Americas and its IMAX theater. Then ride the ferry across the Mississippi for lunch on the other side in Algiers Point. The narrow streets of Victorian houses, most lovingly restored, invite an after-lunch stroll. A tour of Blaine Kern's Mardi Gras World lets you see how Carnival is done. A photo of you inside an elaborate costume is a great souvenir. Take the ferry back across the river for a front-seat view of the sunset and have dinner at the Riverwalk Marketplace. The evening can be capped with a run on the slot machines at Harrah's New Orleans casino or a return to Bourbon Street in the French Quarter nearby. *These suggestions are good for any day of the week.*

DAY 5

Art and Lake Pontchartrain beckon. Start the day with a tour of the New Orleans Museum of Art and the Botanical Garden, both in City Park. Hire a taxi to drive out along Lake Pontchartrain. You can pack a picnic lunch or try one of the seafood restaurants in Bucktown. For the afternoon, venture into the Warehouse District and cruise the galleries along Julia Street. A tour of the National D-Day Museum or Ogden Museum of Southern Art, both off Lee Circle, rounds out the day. Several excellent restaurants in the area are open for dinner. *Don't do this on a Monday, when the New Orleans Museum of Art, Botanical Garden, and Ogden Museum are closed. The drive along Lake Pontchartrain is easier on weekdays, when two-way travel is allowed along Lakeshore Drive.*

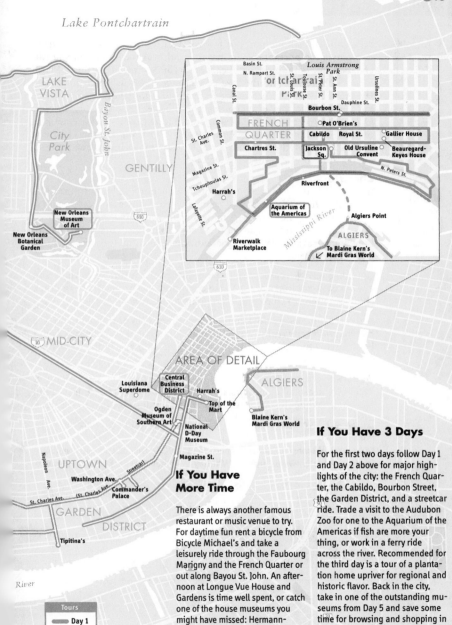

Lake Pontchartrain

LAKE VISTA

City Park

GENTILLY

New Orleans Museum of Art

New Orleans Botanical Garden

Louis Armstrong Park

Basin St.
N. Rampart St.

Canal St.

Bourbon St.

Dauphine St.
St. Ann St.
Ursulines St.

FRENCH QUARTER

Pat O'Brien's

St. Charles Ave.
Common St.

Cabildo Royal St. Gallier House

Chartres St. Jackson Sq. Old Ursuline Convent Beauregard-Keyes House

Magazine St.

Tchoupitoulas St.

Harrah's

N. Peters St.

Riverfront

Aquarium of the Americas

Algiers Point

Mississippi River

ALGIERS

Riverwalk Marketplace

To Blaine Kern's Mardi Gras World

MID-CITY

AREA OF DETAIL

ALGIERS

Louisiana Superdome

Central Business District

Harrah's

Top of the Mart

Ogden Museum of Southern Art

Blaine Kern's Mardi Gras World

National D-Day Museum

Magazine St.

UPTOWN

Washington Ave.

Commander's Palace

Streetcar

St. Charles Ave. (St. Charles Ave.)

GARDEN DISTRICT

Tipitina's

Napoleon Ave.

River

If You Have More Time

There is always another famous restaurant or music venue to try. For daytime fun rent a bicycle from Bicycle Michael's and take a leisurely ride through the Faubourg Marigny and the French Quarter or out along Bayou St. John. An afternoon at Longue Vue House and Gardens is time well spent, or catch one of the house museums you might have missed: Hermann-Grima House, Gallier House, Beauregard-Keyes House, or Pitot House, or a specialty museum such as the Old Ursuline Convent.

If You Have 3 Days

For the first two days follow Day 1 and Day 2 above for major highlights of the city: the French Quarter, the Cabildo, Bourbon Street, the Garden District, and a streetcar ride. Trade a visit to the Audubon Zoo for one to the Aquarium of the Americas if fish are more your thing, or work in a ferry ride across the river. Recommended for the third day is a tour of a plantation home upriver for regional and historic flavor. Back in the city, take in one of the outstanding museums from Day 5 and save some time for browsing and shopping in the Warehouse District and on Magazine Street. Don't miss hearing some jazz, R&B, Cajun, or zydeco music.

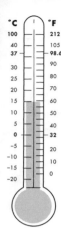

New Orleans is nothing if not festive. It's no surprise, then, that festivals play an important role in the city's cultural and entertainment calendars. Some of the more significant events include the Sugar Bowl, Mardi Gras celebrations, and the Jazz & Heritage Festival, which runs from late April to early May. Smaller festivals may not be quite as showy as Fat Tuesday, but they often give visitors a better understanding of New Orleans than the better-publicized, star-studded events. Some examples of these are the Tennessee Williams–New Orleans Literary Festival, held each March; the French Quarter Festival, in April; and Swamp Fest, held in Audubon Zoo in early October.

Climate

In New Orleans, May through September is hot and humid. Just mustering the energy to raise a mint julep to your lips may cause exhaustion. These long hot summers may explain why things are less hurried down here. If you visit during these sticky months, you'll find that all hotels and restaurants are air-conditioned and, in July and August, hotel prices are lower.

June through November are the months to watch for heavy rains and even occasional hurricanes. These conditions occur mainly with quick changes in temperature that accompany cold fronts.

Although winters are mild compared with those in northern climes, the high humidity can really put a chill in the air December–February. Don't be surprised to see women wearing fur coats in many of the city's finer establishments.

Perhaps the best time to visit the city is early spring. Days are pleasant, except for seasonal cloudbursts, and nights are cool. The azaleas are in full bloom while the city bustles from one outdoor festival to the next.

Below are average daily maximum and minimum temperatures for New Orleans.

Forecasts Weather Channel Connection ☎ 900/932-8437 [95¢ per min from Touch-Tone phone] ⊕ www.weather.com. **Whitney Weather Forecast** ☎ 504/828-4000.

Jan.	62F	17C	May	83F	28C	Sept.	86F	30C
	47	8		68	20		73	23
Feb.	65F	18C	June	88F	31C	Oct.	79F	26C
	50	10		74	23		64	18
Mar.	71F	22C	July	90F	32C	Nov.	70F	21C
	55	13		76	24		55	13
Apr.	77F	25C	Aug.	90F	32C	Dec.	64F	18C
	61	16		76	24		48	9

As rich as New Orleans's history are the events that celebrate it. Festivals and processions fill the city's timetable. If you want your visit to coincide with one of these occasions, be sure to plan well in advance.

WINTER

Dec.	**A New Orleans Christmas** (✉ French Quarter Festival, 400 N. Peters St., 70130 ☎ 504/522–5730), held December 5–January 5, includes tree lighting, teas, caroling, parades, and open houses. Many downtown restaurants celebrate New Year's Eve with special fixed-price menus. Special hotel rates are available December 5–25.
Dec.	Around Christmas, **bonfires** are lighted on the levee at various points along the Mississippi from below New Orleans up into Cajun Country. The bonfires, legend says, originally were lit by the early settlers to help Papa Noël (the Cajun Santa Claus) find his way to their new homes. Residents begin gathering wood for these huge pyres on Thanksgiving. **New Orleans Paddle Wheel** (☎ 866/596–2599 or 504/524–0814) and **New Orleans Steamboat Company** (☎ 800/233–2628 or 504/586–8777) run boats up the muddy Mississippi for this blazing festival.
Dec. 31	**Countdown** is a huge, televised New Year's Eve celebration in Jackson Square. This is *the place* to ring in the year.
Dec. & Jan.	The **Sugar Bowl Classic** (✉ 1500 Sugar Bowl Dr., 70112 ☎ 504/525–8573 ⊕ www.nokiasugarbowl.com), the city's oldest annual sporting event, includes not only one of the biggest college football games of the year but also tennis, basketball, sailing, running, and flag football championship events. Soccer, swimming, basketball, and even a regatta have been added to the festival, making the Sugar Bowl Classic one of the most extensive athletic events in the United States.
Feb. or early Mar.	**Mardi Gras** is rollicking, raucous, and ritualistic. Expect street celebrations, parades, and formal masked balls. For information, *see* Chapter 2.
Mid-Mar.	Two St. Patrick's Day Parades mark the Irish holiday. A downtown parade begins at **Molly's at the Market** (✉ 1107 Decatur St., 70116 ☎ 504/525–5169). It takes place on a weekend night around St. Patrick's Day and covers the French Quarter. Uptowners can catch a daytime parade on Magazine Street, where paraders throw potatoes, carrots, and onions instead of the usual beads and trinkets. Why? So they can go home and fix themselves a mess of Irish stew, of course.
Late Mar.	**Earth Fest** (✉ Audubon Zoo ☎ 504/581–4629 ⊕ www.auduboninstitute.org) is a fun-filled educational celebration with exhibits, shows, and nationally known entertainers, all with an eye on the environment.

Late Mar.	The Tennessee Williams–New Orleans Literary Festival and Writer's Conference (☎ 504/581–1144 ⊕ www.tennesseewilliams.net) began as a forum for writers and scholars to talk about literature—particularly the work of Tennessee Williams. Over the years, the focus of the festival has steadily expanded to include a broad range of New Orleans–based authors and writings. Now, attendees of the weekend-long festival are just as likely to see stagings of Williams's plays (especially his more obscure gems) as they are panel discussions of the southern gothic novel and lectures by notable literary figures. Everyone's favorite event? The Stanley and Stella screaming match that takes place in Jackson Square. And don't miss the walking tour of the Quarter; you'll get to visit some of Williams's favorite haunts.

SPRING

Late Mar.–mid-Apr.	The Spring Fiesta (✉ 826 St. Ann St., 70112 ☎ 504/581–1367) spotlights some of the city's most beautiful historic homes and includes a parade through the French Quarter and the coronation of a queen.
Mid-Apr.	The Crescent City Classic (✆ Box 13587, 70185 ☎ 504/861–8686 ⊕ www.ccc10k.com) is a very popular 10K footrace culminating in a huge party in City Park.
Apr.	The French Quarter Festival (✉ 400 N. Peters St., 70130 ☎ 504/522–5730 ⊕ www.frenchquarterfestival.com) is a weekend of free music and entertainment for all ages in Woldenberg Riverfront Park. It includes fireworks as well as the world's largest jazz brunch.
Late Apr.–early May	The New Orleans Jazz & Heritage Festival (✉ 1205 N. Rampart St., 70116 ☎ 504/522–4786 ⊕ www.nojazzfest.com) at the Fair Grounds involves more than 4,000 musicians. For information, *see* Chapter 2.
Late May	The Greek Festival (✉ 1200 Robert E. Lee Blvd., 70122 ☎ 504/282–0259 ⊕ www.greekfestnola.com) fills the Hellenic Cultural Center with Greek music, food, and crafts. Ouzo and baklava are plentiful.
Late May	New Orleans Wine & Food Experience (✆ Box 70514, 70172 ☎ 504/529–9463 ⊕ www.nowfe.com), held each Memorial Day weekend, is a chance to match the cuisine of the best local chefs with wines from around the world. Held at the Ernest N. Morial Convention Center, the event features more than 350 wines and 80 restaurants.
June	The French Market Tomato Festival (☎ 504/522–2621) includes cooking demonstrations and tastings at the French Market.

SUMMER

July 4	The Fourth of July is celebrated in grand style during Go 4th on the River (☎ 504/528–9994 ⊕ www.go4thontheriver.com), a daylong

series of music, food, and entertainment events along the riverfront and in Woldenberg Park. A spectacular fireworks display completes the day.

The African-American-oriented Essence Music Festival (☎ 504/410–4100) is held over the Fourth of July weekend in downtown New Orleans. Speakers and empowerment seminars fill the days in the Ernest N. Morial Convention Center. At night, a musical extravaganza fills the Louisiana Superdome, with headliners drawn from the hottest hip-hop and R&B stars, and smaller "Superlounges" featuring local acts and more intimate jazz.

Early Aug.	White Linen Night (☎ 504/528–3805), held the first Saturday in August, fills Julia Street with a contemporary arts gala, featuring food, wine, art openings, and music.
Early Sept.	Southern Decadence (✉ 828-A Bourbon St., 70116 ☎ 504/522–8047 ⊕ www.southerndecadence.com), the city's largest gay and lesbian event, is held Labor Day weekend. For information, contact *Ambush* magazine. One highlight is a parade of elaborately costumed drag queens.

FALL

Late Sept.	Words and Music Festival (✉ 632 Pirate's Alley, at Royal St., 70116 ☎ 504/586–1609 ⊕ www.wordsandmusic.org), an annual event celebrating the birthday of author William Faulkner, is presented by the Pirate's Alley Faulkner Society. It includes panels, seminars, and readings by famous actors, writers, and musicians.
Early to mid-Oct.	Art for Art's Sake is a street art festival marking the opening of the arts season. Galleries throughout the city, and especially in the Warehouse District, showcase their own artists, and a small celebratory parade runs down Julia Street. New Orleans Film and Video Festival (✉ 843 Carondelet S, No. 1, 70130 ☎ 504/523–3818 ⊕ www.neworleansfilmfest.com), hosted in mid-month by the New Orleans Film and Video Society, showcases local, regional, and international films, with visits from actors, writers, and other industry professionals. The Swamp Festival (☎ 504/581–4629 ⊕ www.auduboninstitute.org/swampfest) brings Cajun food, music, and crafts to Audubon Zoo the first two weekends of October.
Late Nov.– Dec.	From Thanksgiving through December, thousands of tree lights surround Storyland and the Carousel Gardens for the evening Celebration in the Oaks (✉ 1 Dreyfous Ave., at City Park, 70122 ☎ 504/483–9415 ⊕ www.neworleanscitypark.com). For many New Orleanians, Christmas just isn't Christmas without the mandatory drive through City Park with its dazzling and dramatic assortment of lights.

PLEASURES & PASTIMES

Architecture The distinctive architecture of New Orleans is part Deep South, part Caribbean French colonial, with a dash of local quirkiness thrown in. A trip from the French Quarter along St. Charles Avenue, traveling uptown, showcases this blend of styles in chronological order. The 18th-century, Spanish-inspired aesthetic of lavish town houses with lacy ironwork stacked one against another and vying for attention characterizes much of the French Quarter. In the Garden District, 19th-century Greek Revival homes on large plots create complete little worlds of domesticity, entertaining, and the outdoors, all in an urban setting. Continuing uptown, the houses become progressively more modern until you reach Carrollton Avenue, where an appetite for greenery endures despite a diminished scale of homes; the canopies of centuries-old live oak trees lend a beauty that is no less striking than elaborate wrought iron. Elsewhere, the architectural innovations of the semitropical West Indies predominate around Bayou St. John, in Mid-City. Pitot House, a former plantation home, is the highlight of this area and will whet your appetite for a day trip along the Great River Road, where majestic plantation homes such as Destrehan, Oak Alley, Laura, and Houmas House dot the landscape.

Dining New Orleans–style cooking reflects a blend of ethnic culinary influences, with contributions from Africans, Spaniards, French, Choctaw Native Americans, and Acadians. Creole, the traditional New Orleans cuisine, blends French, Spanish, Caribbean, and African cooking styles. Cajun is a kind of cooking derived from Acadiana, a southwestern Louisiana region of coastal prairie, bayous, and marshlands. Cajun dishes tend to be more heavily spiced and more rustic in presentation than Creole entrées, which favor generous filets of meat or fish in cream- and butter-based sauces. Besides these two cuisines, which are sometimes blended together at some newer establishments, visitors have many other international restaurants from which to choose, including French, Italian, Chinese, Mexican, Greek, Spanish, and even Lebanese eateries. Beyond the first-class restaurants, casual diners, bistros, and seafood houses, food-lovers can also celebrate at cafés, coffeehouses, and pastry shops, where they can stuff themselves with beignets and pralines, as well as at sandwich shops serving hearty po'boys and muffulettas (ham, salami, and mozzarella topped with olive salad).

Music Many visitors come to New Orleans just to hear music. In addition to Louis Armstrong, New Orleans has produced such notable musicians as Dr. John, Professor Longhair, Harry Connick Jr., and the Marsalis and Neville clans. Every night of the week you can find a place to hear jazz, rhythm and blues, gospel, salsa and Latin rhythms, Cajun music and zydeco, rock and roll, and more. The largest number of music clubs is concentrated in the French Quarter, with many of them clustered on Bourbon and Decatur streets. Preservation Hall on St. Peter Street is world renowned for its traditional jazz performers. More music clubs and bars with music are scattered throughout the CBD, the Warehouse District, Faubourg Marigny, and uptown, which has several clubs featuring rhythm and blues and Cajun music.

Jazz Fest As if the music festival New Orleans offers nightly weren't enough, once a year, in late April and early May, the city pulls out all the stops. Thousands of performers—and hundreds of thousands of fans—converge on the Fair Grounds Race Track for the annual New Orleans Jazz & Heritage Festival. Great jazz can be heard, but so can just about every other kind of music known in America, on no fewer than a dozen stages. Big names are everywhere at Jazz Fest, but an even greater treat is hearing a talented headliner-to-be, or just enjoying a small-town band. Crafts and food stalls round out the festival, so you can eat well and do a bit of shopping between sets.

Mardi Gras At no time is New Orleans exactly a button-down town, but every year in February or March it outdoes itself, throwing America's greatest street party, Mardi Gras. Balls and general merriment go on for days, and private clubs called krewes stage fantastic parades through the Garden District, uptown, and the Central Business District past landmarks like Gallier Hall. Elaborately costumed participants ride on glittering floats and toss trinkets to the crowds. Black neighborhood groups known as Mardi Gras Indians roam the city in feathered finery. The climax comes on Fat Tuesday, when the parades kick off a day of abandon that can make *Animal House* seem like high tea. The next day is Ash Wednesday, the first day of Lent, a time of abstinence and reflection. (A massive hangover can produce the same effect.) But this is New Orleans, after all. And when penance has been paid and the pounding headache eases up a bit, the French Quarter beckons anew.

Walking New Orleans has delightful areas for those who like to walk. The French Quarter, with its carefully restored 18th- and 19th-century buildings, is a good place to start. Free 90-minute walking tours of the neighborhood are conducted daily by park rangers of Jean Lafitte National Park, who also provide daily tours of the wealthy Garden District. Moon Walk is a landscaped promenade facing the river in front of Jackson Square; sit on a bench and enjoy the activities of ships, tugboats, and paddle wheelers. Moon Walk is linked to Woldenberg Riverfront Park, a 16-acre attractively landscaped stretch along the river, between Jackson Brewery and the Aquarium of the Americas. The Garden District and uptown are residential districts with quiet, beautiful sidewalks for strolling. Walkers can stroll along Lake Pontchartrain, with miles of seawall for relaxation. New Orleans has two excellent parks with walking trails, City Park and Audubon Park.

FODOR'S CHOICE

Fodor'sChoice ★	The sights, restaurants, hotels, and other travel experiences on these pages are our editors' top picks—our Fodor's Choices. They're the best of their type in the area covered by the book—not to be missed and always worth your time. In the chapters that follow, you will find all the details.

LODGING

$$$–$$$$	**Windsor Court Hotel,** CBD. One of the city's top places to stay, this exquisite, eminently civilized lodging has remarkably large rooms with plush carpeting, canopy and four-poster beds, marble vanities, and oversize mirrors.
$$$–$$$$	**Omni Royal Orleans Hotel,** French Quarter. One of the standard bearers for local hotel excellence occupies a full block in the center of the French Quarter. From the gleaming lobby to the sheer southern elegance of the guest rooms, no other hotel in town has quite the same charm.
$$$–$$$$	**Soniat House,** French Quarter. Antiques and fine fabrics from every continent enhance the natural splendor of the two historic mansions that make up this supremely comfortable small hotel.
$$–$$$$	**Fairmont Hotel,** CBD. A full measure of gracious southern hospitality unfolds at this meticulously maintained grande dame, more than a century old. The public areas evoke Victorian splendor, and each room is uniquely designed and appointed.
$$–$$$$	**Monteleone Hotel,** French Quarter. For the authentic French Quarter experience, stay here on historic Royal Street. The service is consistently outstanding, and even though you're in the heart of one of the busiest areas of the city, the rooms are quiet and serene.
$$$	**Hotel Maison de Ville,** French Quarter. You can escape the contemporary bustle of the French Quarter at this small, antiques-furnished gem with a romantic 19th-century ambience. Hideaway seekers can stay in the private Audubon Cottages.
$$–$$$	**Maison des Amis,** Breaux Bridge. Comfort and relaxation are the themes of this 19th-century house on the bank of Bayou Teche. A pier and gazebo are perfect for watching moonlight over the bayou.
$–$$	**Chimes Bed and Breakfast,** uptown. This uptown residence provides the comforts of home and conveniences of large hotels. High ceilings, hardwood or slate floors, and an airy dining room add to the charm.

RESTAURANTS

$$$–$$$$	**Commander's Palace,** Garden District. The worldwide reputation of this Garden District institution stems from its hospitality and its

kitchen's imaginative uses of traditional ingredients. A refurbished Garden Room and courtyard have added to its many enticements.

$$-$$$ **August,** CBD. Underneath the chandelier prisms, thick brocade fabrics, and glossy woods, chef John Besh creates dazzling beef and lamb dishes, all paired with a hefty, affordable wine list.

$$-$$$ **Gautreau's,** Uptown. Modest in size but ambitious in its cooking, this haven of sophistication serves an ever-changing menu in a quiet, leafy residential neighborhood.

$$-$$$ **Peristyle,** French Quarter. Chef Anne Kearney takes a thoroughly modern and personal approach to Continental cooking in the kitchen of this little restaurant on the French Quarter's edge.

$$-$$$ **Cuvée,** CBD. Cuisine here blends French inspirations with distinctively New Orleans flavors, all served in a soaring space defined by exposed brick and gilt-framed paintings in several styles.

$-$$$ **Galatoire's,** French Quarter. At this old-style French-Creole bistro you can savor time-tested dishes. Purists prefer the old downstairs room, lit with glittering brass chandeliers and bordered with white-frame mirrored panels.

$-$$ **Herbsaint,** CBD. Although the interior is modern and perfunctory, the cooking can be exciting and filled with rich and robust flavors—as in creamy shrimp bisque, a textbook version of steak frites, and a first-rate charcuterie plate.

$-$$ **Jacques-Imo's Cafe,** Uptown. Although the wait is long, food at this Oak Street cafe is worth it, especially for the innovative takes on deep-fried roast-beef po'boys, alligator sausage cheesecake, Cajun bouillabaisse, and panéed duck.

¢-$$ **Acme Oyster and Seafood Restaurant,** French Quarter. Don't expect coddling at this no-nonsense eatery, where you can get raw oysters on the half shell, red beans and rice, and great shrimp, oyster, and roast-beef po'boys.

¢-$ **Liuzza's by the Track,** Mid-City. Seafood Gumbo and the barbecue shrimp po'boy highlight this barroom near the racetrack and Jazz Fest grounds.

AFTER HOURS

Columns Hotel, uptown. An evening cocktail on the expansive front porch here, shaded by centuries-old oak trees, is one of the more romantic New Orleans experiences.

Lafitte's Blacksmith Shop, French Quarter. You won't feel like you're on Bourbon Street at this rustic 18th-century cottage.

The Maple Leaf, uptown. A funky uptown spot, reliable for quality live music any night of the week.

The Spotted Cat, Faubourg Marigny. Rattan furniture in the storefront window makes a perfect perch for an afternoon libation.

FOR KIDS

Carousel Gardens. Adults and children alike love riding this exquisitely refurbished 1906 carousel, replete with authentic wooden flying horses, giraffes, zebras, and other exotic creatures.

HISTORIC HOUSES

Hermann-Grima House. One of the largest and best-preserved examples of American architecture in the Quarter, this house has the best docents in the biz.

Laura Plantation. Nowhere else on River Road will you get a more intimate, well-documented presentation of Creole plantation life than at this 1805 Creole-style house.

Nottoway. Built in 1859, the South's largest plantation house is a gem of Italianate and Greek Revival style. You can stay here overnight, and a formal restaurant serves three meals daily.

Pitot House. Built in French West Indies style and beautifully maintained, this house sits in irresistible charm on the bank of Bayou St. John. It's the only plantation home in the city open to visitors.

MUSEUMS

National D-Day Museum. This modern museum tells the story of the Second World War through artifacts, video, and audio clips and a replica of the *Higgins* boat troop landing craft, built in New Orleans and crucial to the D-Day invasion of Normandy.

The Presbytère Mardi Gras exhibit. New Orleans's most famous tradition is vividly explored in video, photographs, artifacts, and engaging explanations. Even if you're here for the real thing, an informative hour at this museum will enrich your trip.

PARKS & GARDENS

City Park. Rent a four-seat paddleboat for an intimate view of the swampy lagoons in this 1,500-acre park, which also has the largest number of mature live oak trees in the world.

QUINTESSENTIAL NEW ORLEANS

Bacchus Parade, Mardi Gras. On Sunday night before Mardi Gras, this parade unveils spectacular floats with celebrity monarchs. Throws pour plentifully from the floats.

Gospel Tent, Jazz Fest. Always lively, the tent hosts large choruses and smaller groups alike that commonly rouse the crowd to its feet.

St. Charles Avenue streetcar. The most fun way to explore the CBD, the Garden District, and uptown is to take a ride on one of the historic city streetcars that run along St. Charles Avenue.

Upper Garden District Walk. Surround yourself with beautifully landscaped gardens surrounding elegant antebellum homes with a walk through this historical district.

SHOPPING

Bush Antiques, uptown. Beds are the favorite here, including French, sleigh, day, and canopy.

Faulkner House Books, French Quarter. In the 1920s, William Faulkner lived and wrote here; now it's stocked with rare and out-of-print books by southern authors.

Fifi Mahony's, French Quarter. It's a drag-queen's heaven, with custom wigs and wild accessories.

A Gallery for Fine Photography, French Quarter. Vintage, modern, and fine-art photography from such pioneers such as E. J. Belloq, Ansel Adams, and Julia Margaret Cameron are on display.

Hové Parfumeur, Ltd, French Quarter. Fine fragrances for men and women, such as oils, soaps, sachets, and potpourri, are made to order on the premises.

Laura's Candies, French Quarter. The shop has been turning out mouthwatering pralines and confections since 1913.

Little Shop of Fantasy, French Quarter. Come here for a variety of masks, from fun dress-up to works of art.

Louisiana Music Factory, French Quarter. The best source for New Orleans and regional music, new and old, is right here, with a huge selection of records, tapes, CDs, books, and memorabilia.

TASTE OF CAJUN COUNTRY

Savoy Music Center and Accordion Factory. On Saturday morning, accordion players and other instrumentalists tune up during jam sessions in the music store. Musicians from all over the area drop in.

WHERE ART COMES FIRST

New Orleans Center for Creative Arts, Bywater. This modern facility hosts consistently top-notch performances of dance, music, and theater.

WILDLIFE

Aquarium of the Americas. You can feel part of the watery worlds with close-up encounters of more than 7,000 inhabitants who swim in this spectacular aquarium.

SMART TRAVEL TIPS

Finding out about your destination before you leave home means you won't squander time organizing everyday minutiae once you've arrived. You'll be more streetwise when you hit the ground as well, better prepared to explore the aspects of New Orleans that drew you here in the first place. The organizations in this section can provide information to supplement this guide; contact them for up-to-the-minute details, and consult the A to Z sections that end the Side Trips chapter for facts on the various topics as they relate to the areas around New Orleans. Happy landings!

ADDRESSES

New Orleans fills an 8-mi stretch between the Mississippi River and Lake Pontchartrain. Downtown includes the Vieux Carré (Old Square), or the French Quarter; the Central Business District (CBD) and Warehouse District; Tremé; and the Faubourg Marigny. Addresses in a city that bases its compass on the bends of the river can be confusing. Canal Street, a long avenue that runs from the river to the lake, divides the city roughly into uptown and downtown sections (though the CBD and Warehouse District, considered part of downtown, actually lie just upriver from Canal). Locals will give directions using the terms "uptown," "downtown," "lakeside," and "riverside." Rarely will you hear the words "north," "south," "east," or "west" used with their conventional meanings. Streets to the north of Canal are named North and run downtown; those to the south of Canal are named South and run uptown. Addresses begin at 100 on either side of Canal Street. Only the French Quarter is laid out in a grid pattern. Within the French Quarter, street names are different downtown from Canal than uptown, so you will suddenly find that a street name has changed once you pass the boundaries of the Quarter. Addresses begin at 400 in the Quarter on the river side. Street signs may be weathered, oddly placed, or just plain missing. It's helpful to keep a map handy.

AIR TRAVEL TO & FROM NEW ORLEANS

BOOKING

When you book, look for nonstop flights and remember that "direct" flights stop at least once. Try to avoid connecting flights, which require a change of plane. Two airlines may operate a connecting flight jointly, so ask whether your airline operates every segment of the trip; you may find that the carrier you prefer flies you only part of the way. To find more booking tips and to check prices and make online flight reservations, log on to www.fodors.com.

CARRIERS

🛂 Major Airlines **AirTran** 📞 800/825-8538 or 770/994-8258. **America West** 📞 800/235-9292. **American** 📞 800/433-7300. **Continental** 📞 800/525-0280. **Delta** 📞 800/221-1212. **JetBlue** 📞 800/538-2583. **Northwest** 📞 800/225-2525. **Southwest** 📞 800/435-9792. **United** 📞 800/241-6522. **US Airways** 📞 800/428-4322.

🛂 For direct flights from the U.K. **American** 📞 0845/778-9789 via Chicago or Miami. **British Airways** 📞 0845/722-2111 via Dallas. **Delta** 📞 0800/414767 via Atlanta or Cincinnati. **United** 📞 0845/844-4777 via Washington or Chicago. **Virgin Atlantic** 📞 01293/747747 via Newark or Washington.

CHECK-IN & BOARDING

Always **find out your carrier's check-in policy.** Plan to arrive at the airport about 2 hours before your scheduled departure time for domestic flights and 2½ to 3 hours before international flights. You may need to arrive earlier if you're flying from one of the busier airports or during peak air-traffic times. To avoid delays at airport-security checkpoints, try not to wear any metal. Jewelry, belt and other buckles, steel-toe shoes, barrettes, and underwire bras are among the items that can set off detectors.

Assuming that not everyone with a ticket will show up, airlines routinely overbook planes. When everyone does, airlines ask for volunteers to give up their seats. In return, these volunteers usually get a several-hundred-dollar flight voucher, which can be used toward the purchase of another

ticket, and are rebooked on the next flight out. If there are not enough volunteers, the airline must choose who will be denied boarding. The first to get bumped are passengers who checked in late and those flying on discounted tickets, so get to the gate and check in as early as possible, especially during peak periods.

Always **bring a government-issued photo ID** to the airport; even when it's not required, a passport is best.

CUTTING COSTS

The least-expensive airfares to New Orleans on most airlines are priced for round-trip travel and must usually be purchased in advance. JetBlue and Southwest Airlines have low one-way fares, with shorter advance purchase requirements. Airlines generally allow you to change your flight dates for a fee; most low-fare tickets, however, are nonrefundable. It's smart to call a number of airlines and check the Internet; when you are quoted a good price, book it on the spot—the same fare may not be available the next day, or even the next hour. Always check different routings and look into using alternate airports. Also, price off-peak flights, which may be significantly less expensive than others. Travel agents, especially low-fare specialists (⇨ Discounts & Deals), are helpful.

Consolidators are another good source. They buy tickets for scheduled flights at reduced rates from the airlines, then sell them at prices that beat the best fare available directly from the airlines. (Many also offer reduced car-rental and hotel rates.) Sometimes you can even get your money back if you need to return the ticket. Carefully read the fine print detailing penalties for changes and cancellations, purchase the ticket with a credit card, and confirm your consolidator reservation with the airline.

When you fly as a courier, you trade your checked-luggage space for a ticket deeply subsidized by a courier service. There are restrictions on when you can book and how long you can stay. Some courier companies list with membership organizations, such as the Air Courier Association and the International Association of Air Travel Couriers; these require you to become a member before you can book a flight.

📁 Consolidators **AirlineConsolidator.com** ☎ 888/468-5385 ⊕ www.airlineconsolidator.com; for international tickets. **Best Fares** ☎ 800/880-1234 or 800/576-8255 ⊕ www.bestfares.com; $59.90 annual membership. **Cheap Tickets** ☎ 800/377-1000 or 800/652-4327 ⊕ www.cheaptickets.com. **Expedia** ☎ 800/397-3342 or 404/728-8787 ⊕ www.expedia.com. **Hotwire** ☎ 866/468-9473 or 920/330-9418 ⊕ www.hotwire.com. **Now Voyager Travel** ✉ 45 W. 21st St., Suite 5A, New York, NY 10010 ☎ 212/459-1616 🖷 212/243-2711 ⊕ www.nowvoyagertravel.com. **Onetravel.com** ⊕ www.onetravel.com. **Orbitz** ☎ 888/656-4546 ⊕ www.orbitz.com. **Priceline.com** ⊕ www.priceline.com. **Travelocity** ☎ 888/709-5983, 877/282-2925 in Canada, 0870/876-3876 in the U.K. ⊕ www.travelocity.com.

📁 Courier Resources **Air Courier Association/Cheaptrips.com** ☎ 800/280-5973 or 800/282-1202 ⊕ www.aircourier.org or www.cheaptrips.com; $34 annual membership. **International Association of Air Travel Couriers** ☎ 308/632-3273 ⊕ www.courier.org; $45 annual membership. **Now Voyager Travel** ✉ 45 W. 21st St., Suite 5A, New York, NY 10010 ☎ 212/459-1616 🖷 212/243-2711 ⊕ www.nowvoyagertravel.com.

ENJOYING THE FLIGHT

State your seat preference when purchasing your ticket, and then repeat it when you confirm and when you check in. For more legroom, you can request one of the few emergency-aisle seats at check-in, if you're capable of moving obstacles comparable in weight to an airplane exit door (usually between 35 pounds and 60 pounds)—a Federal Aviation Administration requirement of passengers in these seats. Seats behind a bulkhead also offer more legroom, but they don't have underseat storage. Don't sit in the row in front of the emergency aisle or in front of a bulkhead, where seats may not recline.

Ask the airline whether a snack or meal is served on the flight. If you have dietary concerns, request special meals when booking. These can be vegetarian, low-cholesterol, or kosher, for example. It's a

good idea to pack some healthful snacks and a small (plastic) bottle of water in your carry-on bag. On long flights, try to maintain a normal routine, to help fight jet lag. At night, get some sleep. By day, eat light meals, drink water (not alcohol), and **move around the cabin** to stretch your legs. For additional jet-lag tips consult *Fodor's FYI: Travel Fit & Healthy* (available at bookstores everywhere).

Smoking policies vary from carrier to carrier. Many airlines prohibit smoking on all of their flights; others allow smoking only on certain routes or certain departures. Ask your carrier about its policy.

FLYING TIMES

Flying time is 2½ hours from New York, 2¼ hours from Chicago, 1¼ hours from Dallas, 4½ hours from Los Angeles, 4¼ hours from San Francisco, 9¼ hours from London, and 18 hours from Sydney.

HOW TO COMPLAIN

If your baggage goes astray or your flight goes awry, complain right away. Most carriers require that you **file a claim immediately.** The Aviation Consumer Protection Division of the Department of Transportation publishes *Fly-Rights*, which discusses airlines and consumer issues and is available online. You can also find articles and information on mytravelrights.com, the Web site of the nonprofit Consumer Travel Rights Center.

📁 Airline Complaints **Aviation Consumer Protection Division** ✉ U.S. Department of Transportation, Office of Aviation Enforcement and Proceedings, C-75, Room 4107, 400 7th St. SW, Washington, DC 20590 ☎ 202/366-2220 ⊕ airconsumer.ost.dot.gov. **Federal Aviation Administration Consumer Hotline** ✉ For inquiries: FAA, 800 Independence Ave. SW, Washington, DC 20591 ☎ 800/322-7873 ⊕ www.faa.gov.

RECONFIRMING

Check the status of your flight before you leave for the airport. You can do this on your carrier's Web site, by linking to a flight-status checker (many Web booking services offer these), or by calling your carrier or travel agent.

AIRPORTS & TRANSFERS

The major gateway to New Orleans is Louis Armstrong New Orleans International Airport (MSY), 15 mi west of the city in Kenner. There's an Airport exit off I–10. An alternative route is Airline Drive, which will take you directly to the airport from Tulane Avenue or the Earhart Expressway. Be prepared for many stoplights. 🔲 Airport Information **Louis Armstrong New Orleans International Airport** ✉ 900 Airline Dr., Kenner ☎ 504/464-0831.

AIRPORT TRANSFERS

Shuttle-bus service to and from the airport and downtown hotels, as well as local hospitals and the uptown college campuses, is available through New Orleans Tours Airport Shuttle. Buses leave regularly from the ground-floor level near the baggage claim. To return to the airport, call 24 hours in advance of flight time. The cost one-way is $13 per person, and the trip takes about 40 minutes.

Louisiana Transit also runs a bus between the airport, the CBD, and Mid-City. The trip costs $1.60 in exact change ($1.10 from Carrollton and Tulane avenues) and takes about 45 minutes. Departures for the airport are every 10 to 20 minutes from Elks Place and Tulane Avenue across from the main branch of the New Orleans Public Library, and from the corner of Tulane and Carrollton avenues. The last bus leaves at 7:40 PM from Tulane and Elks Place, 11:45 PM from Tulane and Carrollton.

A cab ride to or from the airport from uptown or downtown New Orleans costs $28 for the first two passengers, then $12 for each additional passenger. Pick-up is on the lower level, outside the baggage-claim area. There may be an additional charge for extra baggage.

By car, take the I–10 Expressway (from the CBD, go west to the Airport exit). Allow an hour for the drive during afternoon rush hour; without traffic, the drive takes a half hour. 🔲 Taxis & Shuttles **Louisiana Transit** ☎ 504/818-1077. **New Orleans Tours Airport Shuttle** ☎ 504/522-3500.

BOAT & FERRY TRAVEL

The ferry ride across the river to a part of New Orleans called Algiers is an experience in itself, offering great views of the river and the New Orleans skyline as well as the heady feeling of being on one of the largest and most powerful rivers in the world. Pedestrians climb the stairs (there is a ramp for wheelchair access) near the Spanish Plaza and the Riverwalk shopping area and board the Canal Street Ferry from above, while bicycles and cars board from below on the left of the terminal. The trip takes about 10 minutes; ferries leave on the hour and half hour from the east bank and on the :15 and :45 of every hour on the west bank. and run from 5:45 AM to midnight. Hours at night may vary, so be sure to check with the attendants if you are crossing in the evening—it is no fun to be stranded on the other side. There are handicap-accessible restrooms on the ferry.

FARES & SCHEDULES

🔲 Boat & Ferry Information **Canal Street Ferry** ✉ Foot of Canal ☎ 504/376-8100, $1 cash round-trip per car, free for pedestrians.

BUS TRAVEL TO & FROM NEW ORLEANS

Greyhound has one terminal in the city, in the Union Passenger Terminal in the CBD. Ask about special travel passes. Check with your local Greyhound ticket office for prices and schedules. 🔲 Bus Information **Greyhound** Union Passenger Terminal, ✉ 1001 Loyola Ave. ☎ 800/231-2222 ⊕ www.greyhound.com.

BUS TRAVEL WITHIN NEW ORLEANS

Within New Orleans, the Regional Transit Authority (RTA) operates a public bus and streetcar transportation system with interconnecting lines throughout the city. The buses are generally clean and on time. Bus and streetcar service runs 24 hours a day, though wait times can be as long as an hour or more in the morning's earliest hours. Smoking, eating, and drinking are not permitted on RTA vehicles. Those who violate this rule can find themselves paying a hefty fine in Municipal Court or, worse, pulled off the bus and arrested. Buses are wheelchair accessible; streetcars are not.

FARES & SCHEDULES

Bus and streetcar fare is $1.25 exact change plus 25¢ for transfers. Visiting senior citizens 65 or over who have a valid Medicare ID card may ride public transit for only 50¢. Unlimited passes cost $5 for one day, $12 for three days of unlimited rides, and $55 for a month. The daily passes are available from streetcar and bus operators; three-day passes are available at many hotels; monthly passes must be purchased from official vendors, including all local Whitney Banks.

☎ Bus & Streetcar Information **RTA** ☎ 504/248-3900, 504/242-2600 automated information ⊕ www.norta.com.

BUSINESS HOURS

BANKS & OFFICES

Banks are open weekdays 9–4, and in most cases in the morning on Saturday. Drive-through windows keep longer hours but often restrict transactions to local customers. ATMs are abundant, however. Business offices are typically open weekdays 8–5.

MUSEUMS & SIGHTS

Many museums are closed Monday, and some are not open Sunday as well. Very few have evening hours. Hours of sights and attractions are denoted in the book by the clock icon, ☉.

PHARMACIES

Pharmacies generally open daily at 8 or 9 AM and close between 5 and 9 PM. The national chains offer 24-hour prescription service at selected locations.

SHOPS

Store hours are generally from 10 to 5:30 or 6 Monday through Saturday, with shorter hours—from noon to 5—on Sunday. In areas with active nightlife, such as the French Quarter and at shopping malls, many stores stay open until 7 PM and beyond.

CAMERAS & PHOTOGRAPHY

Although New Orleans welcomes cameras in most places, **you cannot use flashes in churches and art museums.** Many people will want a photo of Jackson Square and the distinctive wrought iron that decorates many buildings in the French Quarter; the St. Charles Avenue streetcar and the riverfront are other distinctive sights. The *Kodak Guide to Shooting Great Travel Pictures* (available at bookstores everywhere) is loaded with tips.

☎ Photo Help **Kodak Information Center** ☎ 800/242-2424 ⊕ www.kodak.com.

EQUIPMENT PRECAUTIONS

Don't pack film or equipment in checked luggage, where it is much more susceptible to damage. X-ray machines used to view checked luggage are extremely powerful and therefore are likely to ruin your film. Try to ask for hand inspection of film, which becomes clouded after repeated exposure to airport X-ray machines, and keep videotapes and computer disks away from metal detectors. Always keep film, tape, and computer disks out of the sun. Carry an extra supply of batteries, and be prepared to turn on your camera, camcorder, or laptop to prove to airport security personnel that the device is real.

CAR RENTAL

Rates in New Orleans begin at around $20 per day and $130 per week for an economy car with air-conditioning, an automatic transmission, and unlimited mileage. This does not include tax on car rentals, which is 11%–12%, or other surcharges, which can add another 10%–15%.

☎ Major Agencies **Alamo** ☎ 800/327-9633 ⊕ www.alamo.com. **Avis** ☎ 800/331-1212, 800/879-2847 or 800/272-5871 in Canada, 0870/606-0100 in the U.K., 02/9353-9000 in Australia, 09/526-2847 in New Zealand ⊕ www.avis.com. **Budget** ☎ 800/527-0700, 0870/156-5656 in the U.K. ⊕ www.budget.com. **Dollar** ☎ 800/800-4000, 0800/085-4578 in the U.K. ⊕ www.dollar.com. **Hertz** ☎ 800/654-3131, 800/263-0600 in Canada, 0870/844-8844 in the U.K., 02/9669-2444 in Australia, 09/256-8690 in New Zealand ⊕ www.hertz.com. **National Car Rental** ☎ 800/227-7368, 0870/600-6666 in the U.K. ⊕ www.nationalcar.com.

CUTTING COSTS

For a good deal, book through a travel agent who will shop around. Also, price local car-rental companies—whose prices may be lower still, although their service and maintenance may not be as good as those of major rental agencies—and research rates on the Internet. Consolidators that specialize in air travel can offer good rates on cars as well (⇨ Air Travel to & from New Orleans). Remember to ask about required deposits, cancellation penalties, and drop-off charges if you're planning to pick up the car in one city and leave it in another. If you're traveling during a holiday period, also make sure that a confirmed reservation guarantees you a car.

INSURANCE

When driving a rented car you are generally responsible for any damage to or loss of the vehicle. You also may be liable for any property damage or personal injury that you may cause while driving. Before you rent, see what coverage you already have under the terms of your personal auto-insurance policy and credit cards.

For about $9 to $25 a day, rental companies sell protection, known as a collision- or loss-damage waiver (CDW or LDW), that eliminates your liability for damage to the car; it's always optional and should never be automatically added to your bill.In most states you don't need a CDW if you have personal auto insurance or other liability insurance. However, **make sure you have enough coverage to pay for the car.** If you do not have auto insurance or an umbrella policy that covers damage to third parties, purchasing liability insurance and a CDW or LDW is highly recommended.

REQUIREMENTS & RESTRICTIONS

In Louisiana you must be 21 to rent a car. Some agencies won't rent to you if you're under the age of 25.

SURCHARGES

Before you pick up a car in one city and leave it in another, ask about drop-off charges or one-way service fees, which can be substantial. Also inquire about early-return policies; some rental agencies charge extra if you return the car before the time specified in your contract while others give

you a refund for the days not used. To avoid a hefty refueling fee, fill the tank just before you turn in the car, but be aware that gas stations near the rental outlet may overcharge. It's almost never a deal to buy the tank of gas that's in the car when you rent it; the understanding is that you'll return it empty, but some fuel usually remains. Surcharges may apply if you're under 25 or if you take the car outside the area approved by the rental agency. You'll pay extra for child seats (about $8 a day), which are compulsory for children under 5, and usually for additional drivers (up to $25 a day, depending on location).

CAR TRAVEL

Having a car in New Orleans is no problem—except at Mardi Gras and during other special events, including the Sugar Bowl (around New Year's) and the Bayou Classic (Thanksgiving weekend). During these times some or most of the French Quarter is closed to traffic, and cars parked illegally—especially those on Mardi Gras parade routes—get whisked away. At all times of the year, carefully read street signs in the French Quarter and CBD; tickets are quickly written, and towings are frequent. A car is not needed for sightseeing around the most-visited areas of the city, however. You can get around many popular areas on foot or by streetcar or taxi. For excursions to surrounding areas, cars are advisable.

I–10 runs from Florida to California and passes directly through the city. To get to the CBD, exit at Poydras Street near the Louisiana Superdome. For the French Quarter, look for the Orleans Avenue/ Vieux Carré exit.

Gas stations are not plentiful within the city of New Orleans. The downtown area is particularly short on stations. Head for Lee Circle if you need gas while in the downtown area. Most stations in the city and suburbs are open 24 hours. Some all-night stations are available.

PARKING

Finding a parking space is fairly easy in most of the city, except for the French Quarter, where meter maids are plentiful and tow trucks eager. If in doubt about a space, pass it up and pay to use a parking lot. Avoid parking spaces at corners and curbs: less than 15 feet between your car and the corner will result in a ticket. Watch for temporary NO PARKING signs, which pop up along parade routes and film shoots.

CHILDREN IN NEW ORLEANS

Be sure to plan ahead and **involve your youngsters** as you outline your trip. When packing, include things to keep them busy en route. On sightseeing days try to schedule activities of special interest to your children. The *Times-Picayune,* the city's daily, publishes a "Kidstuff" column every Monday that lists upcoming events for families and kids. The Louisiana Children's Museum is an excellent resource for activities that are both educational and fun.

If you are renting a car, don't forget to arrange for a car seat when you reserve. For general advice about traveling with children, consult *Fodor's FYI: Travel with Your Baby* (available in bookstores everywhere).

Local Information **Louisiana Children's Museum** ✉ 420 Julia St., Warehouse District, 70112 ☎ 504/523-1357 ⊕ www.lcm.org. **New Orleans Convention and Visitors Bureau** ✉ 2020 St. Charles Ave.,, Garden District 70112 ☎ 800/672-6124 or 504/566-5011 ⊕ www.visitneworleans.info.

BABYSITTING

Accent on Arrangements arranges individual babysitters for hotel guests and group care. Dependable Kid Care arranges child care for hotels and residences.

Agencies **Accent on Arrangements** ☎ 504/524-1227 ⊕ www.accentoca.com. **Dependable Kid Care** ☎ 504/486-4001 ⊕ www.dependablekidcare.com.

FLYING

Experts agree that it's a good idea to use safety seats aloft for children weighing less than 40 pounds. Airlines set their own policies: if you use a safety seat, U.S. carriers usually require that the child be ticketed, even if he or she is young enough to ride free, because the seats must be strapped into regular seats. And even if you pay the full adult fare for the seat, it may be worth it, especially on longer trips. Do **check your airline's policy about using safety seats during takeoff and landing.** Safety seats are not allowed everywhere in the plane, so get your seat assignments as early as possible.

When reserving, request children's meals or a freestanding bassinet (not available at all airlines) if you need them. But note that bulkhead seats, where you must sit to use the bassinet, may lack an overhead bin or storage space on the floor.

LODGING

Most hotels in New Orleans allow children under a certain age to stay in their parents' room at no extra charge, but others charge for them as extra adults; be sure to find out the cutoff age for children's discounts.

SIGHTS & ATTRACTIONS

Places that are especially appealing to children are indicated by a rubber-duckie icon (🦆) in the margin.

CONCIERGES

Concierges, found in many hotels, can help you with theater tickets and dinner reservations: a good one with connections may be able to get you seats for a hot show or prime-time dinner reservations at the restaurant of the moment. You can also turn to your hotel's concierge for help with travel arrangements, sightseeing plans, services ranging from aromatherapy to zipper repair, and emergencies. **Always tip** a concierge who has been of assistance (⇨ Tipping).

CONSUMER PROTECTION

Whether you're shopping for gifts or purchasing travel services, **pay with a major credit card** whenever possible, so you can cancel payment or get reimbursed if there's a problem (and you can provide documentation). If you're doing business with a particular company for the first time, contact your local Better Business Bureau and the attorney general's offices in your state and (for U.S. businesses) the company's home state as well. Have any complaints been filed? Finally, if you're buying a package or tour, always consider travel in-

surance that includes default coverage
(⇨ Insurance).

🔲 BBBs **Council of Better Business Bureaus**
✉ 4200 Wilson Blvd., Suite 800, Arlington, VA
22203 ☎ 703/276-0100 🖷 703/525-8277 ⊕ www.
bbb.org.

CRUISE TRAVEL

The *Delta Queen* Steamboat Company offers 3- to 11-night excursions up the Big
Muddy and environs aboard the *Delta
Queen*, a National Historic Landmark
built in the 1920s; the *Mississippi Queen,*
built in 1976; or the *American Queen*, the
largest paddle wheeler ever built. Cruises
up the Mississippi focus on the river's effect on history and historic onshore sites
such as antebellum plantation houses,
Vicksburg, and Natchez. Founded in
1890, the company operates one of an
enormous and efficient waterfront terminal complex adjacent to the Ernest N. Morial Convention Center. Carnival Cruise
Lines departs from New Orleans.

To learn how to plan, choose, and book a
cruise-ship voyage, consult *Fodor's FYI:
Plan & Enjoy Your Cruise* (available in
bookstores everywhere).

🔲 Cruise Lines **Carnival Cruise Lines** ✉ Carnival
Pl., 3655 N.W. 87th Ave., Miami, FL 33178 ☎ 800/
227-6482 ⊕ www.carnival.com. **Delta Queen
Steamboat Company** ✉ Robin St. Wharf ☎ 800/
543-1949 or 504/586-0631 ⊕ www.deltaqueen.com.

CUSTOMS & DUTIES

IN AUSTRALIA

Australian residents who are 18 or older
may bring home A$400 worth of sou-
venirs and gifts (including jewelry), 250
cigarettes or 250 grams of cigars or other
tobacco products, and 1,125 ml of alcohol
(including wine, beer, and spirits). Residents under 18 may bring back A$200
worth of goods. Members of the same
family traveling together may pool their
allowances. Prohibited items include meat
products. Seeds, plants, and fruits need to
be declared upon arrival.

🔲 **Australian Customs Service** ⌖ Regional Director, Box 8, Sydney, NSW 2001 ☎ 02/9213-2000 or
1300/363263, 02/9364-7222 or 1800/020-504 quar-
antine-inquiry line 🖷 02/9213-4043 ⊕ www.
customs.gov.au.

IN CANADA

Canadian residents who have been out of
Canada for at least seven days may bring
in C$750 worth of goods duty-free. If
you've been away fewer than seven days
but more than 48 hours, the duty-free allowance drops to C$200. If your trip lasts
24 to 48 hours, the allowance is C$50.
You may not pool allowances with family
members. Goods claimed under the C$750
exemption may follow you by mail; those
claimed under the lesser exemptions must
accompany you. Alcohol and tobacco
products may be included in the seven-day
and 48-hour exemptions but not in the 24-
hour exemption. If you meet the age requirements of the province or territory
through which you reenter Canada, you
may bring in, duty-free, 1.5 liters of wine
or 1.14 liters (40 imperial ounces) of
liquor *or* 24 12-ounce cans or bottles of
beer or ale. Also, if you meet the local age
requirement for tobacco products, you
may bring in, duty-free, 200 cigarettes and
50 cigars. Check ahead of time with the
Canada Customs and Revenue Agency or
the Department of Agriculture for policies
regarding meat products, seeds, plants,
and fruits.

You may send an unlimited number of
gifts (only one gift per recipient, however)
worth up to C$60 each duty-free to
Canada. Label the package UNSOLICITED
GIFT—VALUE UNDER $60. Alcohol and to-
bacco are excluded.

🔲 **Canada Customs and Revenue Agency** ✉ 2265
St. Laurent Blvd., Ottawa, Ontario K1G 4K3 ☎ 800/
461-9999 in Canada, 204/983-3500, 506/636-5064
⊕ www.ccra.gc.ca.

IN NEW ZEALAND

All homeward-bound residents may bring
back NZ$700 worth of souvenirs and
gifts; passengers may not pool their allowances, and children can claim only the
concession on goods intended for their
own use. For those 17 or older, the duty-
free allowance also includes 4.5 liters of
wine or beer; one 1,125-ml bottle of spirits; and either 200 cigarettes, 250 grams
of tobacco, 50 cigars, *or* a combination
of the three up to 250 grams. Meat products, seeds, plants, and fruits must be de-

clared upon arrival to the Agricultural Services Department.

🔳 **New Zealand Customs** ⊠ Head office: The Customhouse, 17–21 Whitmore St., Box 2218, Wellington ☎ 09/300-5399 or 0800/428-786 ⊕ www.customs.govt.nz.

IN THE U.K.

From countries outside the European Union, including the United States, you may bring home, duty-free, 200 cigarettes, 50 cigars, 100 cigarillos, or 250 grams of tobacco; 1 liter of spirits or 2 liters of fortified or sparkling wine or liqueurs; 2 liters of still table wine; 60 ml of perfume; 250 ml of toilet water; plus £145 worth of other goods, including gifts and souvenirs. Prohibited items include meat and dairy products, seeds, plants, and fruits.

🔳 **HM Customs and Excise** ⊠ Portcullis House, 21 Cowbridge Rd. E, Cardiff CF11 9SS ☎ 0845/010-9000 or 0208/929-0152 advice service, 0208/929-6731 or 0208/910-3602 complaints ⊕ www.hmce.gov.uk.

DISABILITIES & ACCESSIBILITY

Curbs are cut on most corners in the French Quarter and CBD. In the Garden District the terrain is flat, but not all curbs are cut and the sidewalks are badly cracked by the roots of the many live oaks. Audubon Zoo, the Aquarium of the Americas, riverboats, and swamp boats are all accessible. Gray Line (⇨ Sightseeing Tours) has tour buses that accommodate visitors with mobility, hearing, and visual impairments.

🔳 Local Resources **Advocacy Center for the Elderly and Disabled** ⊠ 225 Baronne St., Suite 2112, 70112 ☎ 800/960-7705 [also TTY], 504/522-2337 [also TTY]. **Easter Seals Society of Louisiana for Children and Adults with Disabilities** ⊠ 305 Baronne St., 4th fl., Box 8245, 70112 ☎ 800/695-7325 [also TTY], 504/523-7325 [also TTY].

LODGING

Despite the Americans with Disabilities Act, the definition of accessibility seems to differ from hotel to hotel. Some properties may be accessible by ADA standards for people with mobility problems but not for people with hearing or vision impairments, for example.

If you have mobility problems, ask for the lowest floor on which accessible services are offered. If you have a hearing impairment, check whether the hotel has devices to alert you visually to the ring of the telephone, a knock at the door, and a fire/emergency alarm. Some hotels provide these devices without charge. Discuss your needs with hotel personnel if this equipment isn't available, so that a staff member can personally alert you in the event of an emergency.

If you're bringing a guide dog, get authorization ahead of time and write down the name of the person with whom you spoke.

RESERVATIONS

When discussing accessibility with an operator or reservations agent, ask hard questions. Are there any stairs, inside *or* out? Are there grab bars next to the toilet *and* in the shower/tub? How wide is the doorway to the room? To the bathroom? For the most extensive facilities meeting the latest legal specifications, opt for newer accommodations. If you reserve through a toll-free number, consider also calling the hotel's local number to confirm the information from the central reservations office. Get confirmation in writing when you can.

TRANSPORTATION

🔳 Complaints **Aviation Consumer Protection Division** (⇨ Air Travel to & from New Orleans) for airline-related problems. **Departmental Office of Civil Rights** ⊠ For general inquiries: U.S. Department of Transportation, S-30, 400 7th St. SW, Room 10215, Washington, DC 20590 ☎ 202/366-4648 🖷 202/366-9371 ⊕ www.dot.gov/ost/docr/index.htm. **Disability Rights Section** ⊠ NYAV, U.S. Department of Justice, Civil Rights Division, 950 Pennsylvania Ave. NW, Washington, DC 20530 ☎ 800/514-0301, 800/514-0383 TTY, 202/514-0301 ADA information line, 202/514-0383 TTY ⊕ www.ada.gov. **U.S. Department of Transportation Hotline** ☎ 800/778-4838 or 800/455-9880 TTY for disability-related air-travel problems.

TRAVEL AGENCIES

In the United States, the Americans with Disabilities Act requires that travel firms serve the needs of all travelers. Some agencies specialize in working with people with disabilities.

🔃 Travelers with Mobility Problems **Access Adventures/B. Roberts Travel** ✉ 206 Chestnut Ridge Rd., Scottsville, NY 14624 ☎ 585/889-9096 ⊕ www.brobertstravel.com ✎ dltravel@prodigy. net, run by a former physical-rehabilitation counselor. **Accessible Vans of America** ✉ 9 Spielman Rd., Fairfield, NJ 07004 ☎ 877/282-8267, 888/282-8267, 973/808-9709 reservations ⊞ 973/808-9713 ⊕ www.accessiblevans.com. **CareVacations** ✉ No. 5, 5110-50 Ave., Leduc, Alberta T9E 6V4 Canada ☎ 877/478-7827 or 780/986-6404 ⊞ 780/986-8332 ⊕ www.carevacations.com, for group tours and cruise vacations. **Flying Wheels Travel** ✉ 143 W. Bridge St., Box 382, Owatonna, MN 55060 ☎ 507/451-5005 ⊞ 507/451-1685 ⊕ www. flyingwheelstravel.com.

🔃 Travelers with Developmental Disabilities **Sprout** ✉ 893 Amsterdam Ave., New York, NY 10025 ☎ 888/222-9575 or 212/222-9575 ⊞ 212/222-9768 ⊕ www.gosprout.org.

DISCOUNTS & DEALS
Be a smart shopper and compare all your options before making decisions. A plane ticket bought with a promotional coupon from travel clubs, coupon books, and direct-mail offers or purchased on the Internet may not be cheaper than the least-expensive fare from a discount ticket agency. And always keep in mind that what you get is just as important as what you save.

DISCOUNT RESERVATIONS
To save money, look into discount reservations services with Web sites and toll-free numbers, which use their buying power to get a better price on hotels, airline tickets (⇨ Air Travel to & from New Orleans), even car rentals. When booking a room, always **call the hotel's local toll-free number** (if one is available) rather than the central reservations number—you'll often get a better price. Always ask about special packages or corporate rates.

🔃 Airline Tickets **Air 4 Less** ☎ 800/AIR4LESS; low-fare specialist.

🔃 Hotel Rooms **Accommodations Express** ☎ 800/444-7666 or 800/277-1064 ⊕ www.acex. net. **Hotels.com** ☎ 800/246-8357 ⊕ www.hotels. com. **Quikbook** ☎ 800/789-9887 ⊕ www.

quikbook.com. **Steigenberger Reservation Service** ☎ 800/223-5652 ⊕ www.srs-worldhotels. com. **Turbotrip.com** ☎ 800/473-7829 ⊕ www. turbotrip.com.

PACKAGE DEALS
Don't confuse packages and guided tours. When you buy a package, you travel on your own, just as though you had planned the trip yourself. Fly/drive packages, which combine airfare and car rental, are often a good deal. In cities, ask the local visitor's bureau about hotel and local transportation packages that include tickets to major museum exhibits or other special events.

EMERGENCIES
🔃 Doctors & Dentists **Charity Hospital & Medical Center of Louisiana** provides 24-hour dental emergency treatment (⇨ Hospitals).For referrals, contact the **New Orleans Dental Association** ✉ 3101 W. Napoleon St., Suite 119, Metairie ☎ 504/834-6449 ⊕ www.nodental.org. **Touro Infirmary** ☎ 504/ 897-7777, has a physician-referral service available weekdays 8-5 (⇨ Hospitals).

🔃 Hospitals **Charity Hospital & Medical Center of Louisiana** ✉ 1532 Tulane Ave. ☎ 504/903-3000. **Touro Infirmary** ✉ 1401 Foucher St. ☎ 504/897-7011 or 504/897-8250. **Tulane University Medical Center** ✉ 1415 Tulane Ave. ☎ 504/588-5711.

🔃 Pharmacies **Rite-Aid** ✉ 2669 Canal St., Mid-City ☎ 504/827-1400. **Royal Pharmacy** ✉ 1101 Royal St., French Quarter ☎ 504/523-5401. **Walgreens** ✉ 900 Canal St., French Quarter ☎ 504/ 568-1271 ✉ 3311 Canal St., Mid-City ☎ 504/822-8073 ✉ 1801 St. Charles Ave. [24-hr pharmacy], Garden District ☎ 504/561-8458.

GAY & LESBIAN TRAVEL
New Orleans has a large gay and lesbian population spread throughout the metropolitan area. The most gay-friendly neighborhood is the French Quarter, followed by the Faubourg Marigny, just outside the Quarter. Most bars for gay men are within these neighborhoods; lesbians may have to venture farther, to Mid-City or Metairie. Robert Spatzen leads a 2½-hour Gay Heritage Tour through the French Quarter and environs on Wednesday and Saturday at 1 PM. Call ahead for a reservation; he needs at least four people signed up an hour before starting time

to guarantee a tour. Throughout the year a number of festivals (➪ When to Go) celebrate gay culture. The city also has gay-friendly guesthouses and bed-and-breakfasts, particularly along Esplanade Avenue. *Impact* and *Ambush,* local bi-weekly newspapers, provide lists of current events in addition to news and reviews. *Impact* also publishes a slick glossy called *Eclipse* with all its nightlife coverage. These publications are found in many gay bars and in the Faubourg Marigny Bookstore. For full information about services, accommodations, and events, contact the Gay and Lesbian Community Center.

For details about the gay and lesbian scene, consult *Fodor's Gay Guide to the USA* (available in bookstores everywhere). ◨ Gay- & Lesbian-Friendly Travel Agencies **Different Roads Travel** ✉ 8383 Wilshire Blvd., Suite 520, Beverly Hills, CA 90211 ☎ 800/429–8747 or 323/651–5557 [Ext. 14 for both] 🖷 323/651–5454 ✍ lgernert@tzell.com. **Kennedy Travel** ✉ 130 W. 42nd St., Suite 401, New York, NY 10036 ☎ 800/237–7433 or 212/840–8659 🖷 212/730–2269 ⊕ www.kennedytravel.com. **Now, Voyager** ✉ 4406 18th St., San Francisco, CA 94114 ☎ 800/255–6951 or 415/626–1169 🖷 415/626–8626 ⊕ www.nowvoyager.com. **Skylink Travel and Tour/Flying Dutchmen Travel** ✉ 1455 N. Dutton Ave., Suite A, Santa Rosa, CA 95401 ☎ 800/225–5759 or 707/546–9888 🖷 707/636–0951; serving lesbian travelers. ◨ Local Sources **Faubourg Marigny Bookstore** ✉ 600 Frenchmen St. ☎ 504/947–3700. **Gay and Lesbian Community Center** ✉ 2114 Decatur St., 70116 ☎ 504/945–1103 ⊕ www.lgccno.net.

Robert Spatzen ✉ 909 Bourbon St. ☎ 504/945–6789 ✍ nolabienville@aol.com.

HEALTH

The intense heat and humidity of New Orleans in the height of summer can be a concern for anyone unused to a semitropical climate. Pace yourself to avoid problems such as dehydration. Pollen levels can be extremely high, especially in April and May. Walk at a reasonable pace, stop frequently, and drink plenty of water. Know your own limits and select indoor activities in the middle of the day; you'll find the locals doing the same thing.

HOLIDAYS

Major national holidays are New Year's Day (January 1); Martin Luther King Day (third Monday in January); Presidents' Day (third Monday in February); Memorial Day (last Monday in May); Independence Day (July 4); Labor Day (first Monday in September); Columbus Day (second Monday in October); Thanksgiving Day (fourth Thursday in November); Christmas Eve and Christmas Day (December 24 and 25); and New Year's Eve (December 31).

In New Orleans, of course, Mardi Gras is a major holiday where no serious business is conducted and just about everything is closed. For the actual date, check a calendar for Ash Wednesday; Fat Tuesday is the day before.

INSURANCE

The most useful travel-insurance plan is a comprehensive policy that includes coverage for trip cancellation and interruption, default, trip delay, and medical expenses (with a waiver for preexisting conditions).

Without insurance you'll lose all or most of your money if you cancel your trip, regardless of the reason. Default insurance covers you if your tour operator, airline, or cruise line goes out of business—the chances of which have been increasing. Trip-delay covers expenses that arise because of bad weather or mechanical delays. Study the fine print when comparing policies.

U.K. residents can buy a travel-insurance policy valid for most vacations taken during the year in which it's purchased (but check preexisting-condition coverage).

Always **buy travel policies directly from the insurance company;** if you buy them from a cruise line, airline, or tour operator that goes out of business you probably won't be covered for the agency or operator's default, a major risk. Before making any purchase, review your existing health and home-owner's policies to find what they cover away from home. ◨ Travel Insurers In the United States: **Access America** ✉ 2805 N. Parham Rd., Richmond, VA 23294 ☎ 800/284–8300 🖷 800/346–9265 or 804/

673-1491 ⊕ www.accessamerica.com. **Travel Guard International** ✉ 1145 Clark St., Stevens Point, WI 54481 ☎ 800/826-1300 or 715/345-0505 🖷 800/955-8785 ⊕ www.travelguard.com.

INTERNATIONAL TRAVELERS

For information on customs restrictions, *see* Customs & Duties.

CAR RENTAL

When picking up a rental car, non-U.S. residents need a reservation voucher for any prepaid reservations that were made in the traveler's home country, a passport, a driver's license, and a travel policy that covers each driver.

CAR TRAVEL

Driving in the United States is on the right. Do **obey speed limits** posted along roads and highways. Watch for lower limits in small towns and on back roads. In New Orleans, on weekdays between 6 and 9 AM and again between 4 and 6 PM **expect heavy traffic.**

Bookstores, gas stations, convenience stores, and rest stops sell maps (about $3) and multiregion road atlases (about $10).

The fastest routes are interstate highways—limited-access, multilane highways whose numbers are prefixed by "I–." Interstates with three-digit numbers encircle urban areas, which may have other limited-access expressways, freeways, and parkways as well. Tolls may be levied on limited-access highways. So-called U.S. highways and state highways are not necessarily limited-access but may have several lanes.

Along larger highways, roadside stops with restrooms, fast-food restaurants, and sundries stores are well spaced. State police and tow trucks patrol major highways and lend assistance. If your car breaks down on an interstate, pull onto the shoulder and wait for help, or have your passengers wait while you walk to an emergency phone. If you carry a cell phone, dial *55, noting your location on the small, green, roadside mileage markers.

CURRENCY

The dollar is the basic unit of U.S. currency. It has 100 cents. Coins are the cop-

per penny (1¢); the silvery nickel (5¢), dime (10¢), quarter (25¢), and half-dollar (50¢); and the golden $1 coin, replacing a now-rare silver dollar. Bills are denominated $1, $5, $10, $20, $50, and $100, all mostly green and identical in size; designs and background tints vary. In addition, you may come across a $2 bill, but the chances are slim.

ELECTRICITY

The U.S. standard is AC, 110 volts/60 cycles. Plugs have two flat pins set parallel to each other.

EMERGENCIES

For police, fire, or ambulance, **dial 911** (0 in rural areas).

INSURANCE

Britons and Australians need extra medical coverage when traveling overseas. 🛈 Insurance Information In Australia: **Insurance Council of Australia** ✉ Insurance Enquiries and Complaints, Level 12, Box 561, Collins St. W, Melbourne, VIC 8007 ☎ 1300/780808 or 03/9629-4109 🖷 03/9621-2060 ⊕ www.iecltd.com.au.

In Canada: **RBC Insurance** ✉ 6880 Financial Dr., Mississauga, Ontario L5N 7Y5 ☎ 800/668-4342 or 905/816-2400 🖷 905/813-4704 ⊕ www.rbcinsurance.com.

In New Zealand: **Insurance Council of New Zealand** ✉ Level 7, 111-115 Customhouse Quay, Box 474, Wellington ☎ 04/472-5230 🖷 04/473-3011 ⊕ www.icnz.org.nz.

In the United Kingdom: **Association of British Insurers** ✉ 51 Gresham St., London EC2V 7HQ ☎ 020/7600-3333 🖷 020/7696-8999 ⊕ www.abi.org.uk.

MAIL & SHIPPING

You can buy stamps and aerograms and send letters and parcels in post offices. Stamp-dispensing machines can occasionally be found in airports, bus and train stations, office buildings, drugstores, and the like. You can also deposit mail in the stout, dark-blue, steel bins at strategic locations everywhere and in the mail chutes of large buildings; pick-up schedules are posted. You can deposit packages at public collection boxes as long as the parcels are affixed with proper postage and weigh less than 1 pound. Packages weighing 1 pound or more must be taken to a post office or handed to a postal carrier.

For mail sent within the United States, you need a 37¢ stamp for first-class letters weighing up to 1 ounce (23¢ for each additional ounce) and 23¢ for postcards. You pay 80¢ for 1-ounce airmail letters and 70¢ for airmail postcards to most other countries; to Canada and Mexico, you need a 60¢ stamp for a 1-ounce letter and 50¢ for a postcard. An aerogram—a single sheet of lightweight blue paper that folds into its own envelope, stamped for overseas airmail—costs 70¢.

To receive mail on the road, have it sent c/o General Delivery at your destination's main post office (use the correct five-digit zip code). You must pick up mail in person within 30 days and show a driver's license or passport.

PASSPORTS & VISAS

When traveling internationally, carry your passport even if you don't need one (it's always the best form of ID) and **make two photocopies of the data page** (one for someone at home and another for you, carried separately from your passport). If you lose your passport, promptly call the nearest embassy or consulate and the local police.

Visitor visas aren't necessary for Canadian or European Union citizens, or for citizens of Australia who are staying fewer than 90 days.

🔂 Australian Citizens **Passports Australia** ☎ 131-232 ⊕ www.passports.gov.au. **United States Consulate General** ✉ MLC Centre, Level 59, 19–29 Martin Pl., Sydney, NSW 2000 ☎ 02/9373-9200, 1902/941-641 fee-based visa-inquiry line ⊕ usembassy-australia.state.gov/sydney.

🔂 Canadian Citizens **Passport Office** ✉ To mail in applications: 200 Promenade du Portage, Hull, Québec J8X 4B7 ☎ 800/567-6868, 866/255-7655 TTY, 819/994-3500 ⊕ www.ppt.gc.ca.

🔂 New Zealand Citizens **New Zealand Passports Office** ✉ For applications and information: Level 3, Boulcott House, 47 Boulcott St., Wellington ☎ 0800/22-5050 or 04/474-8100 ⊕ www.passports.govt.nz. **Embassy of the United States** ✉ 29 Fitzherbert Terr., Thorndon, Wellington

☎ 04/462-6000 ⊕ usembassy.org.nz. **U.S. Consulate General** ✉ Citibank Bldg., 3rd fl., 23 Customs St. E, Auckland ☎ 09/303-2724 ⊕ usembassy.org.nz.

🔂 U.K. Citizens **U.K. Passport Service** ☎ 0870/521-0410 ⊕ www.passport.gov.uk. **American Consulate General** ✉ Danesfort House, 223 Stranmillis Rd., Belfast, Northern Ireland BT9 5GR ☎ 028/9032-8239 ⏚ 028/9024-8482 ⊕ usembassy.org.uk. **American Embassy** ✉ For visa and immigration information or to submit a visa application via mail (enclose an SASE): Consular Information Unit, 24 Grosvenor Sq., London W1 1AE ☎ 09055/444-546 for visa information [per-min charges], 0207/499-9000 main switchboard ⊕ usembassy.org.uk.

TELEPHONES

All U.S. telephone numbers consist of a three-digit area code and a seven-digit local number. Within many local calling areas, you dial only the seven-digit number. Within some area codes, you must dial "1" first for calls outside the local area. To call between area-code regions, dial "1" then all 10 digits; the same goes for calls to numbers prefixed by "800," "888," "866," and "877"—all toll free. For calls to numbers preceded by "900" you must pay—usually dearly.

For international calls, dial "011" followed by the country code and the local number. For help, dial "0" and ask for an overseas operator. The country code is 61 for Australia, 64 for New Zealand, 44 for the United Kingdom. Calling Canada is the same as calling within the United States. Most local phone books list country codes and U.S. area codes. The country code for the United States is 1.

For operator assistance, dial "0." To obtain someone's phone number, call directory assistance at 555–1212 or occasionally 411 (free at many public phones). To have the person you're calling foot the bill, phone collect; dial "0" instead of "1" before the 10-digit number.

At pay phones, instructions often are posted. Usually you insert coins in a slot (usually 25¢–50¢ for local calls) and wait for a steady tone before dialing. When you call long-distance, the operator tells you how much to insert; prepaid phone cards, widely available in various denominations, are easier. Call the number on the back, punch in the card's personal identification number when prompted, then dial your number.

MAIL & SHIPPING
P Post Offices **Main post office** ✉ 701 Loyola Ave. ☎ 504/589–1706. **Post office in French Quarter** ✉ 1022 Iberville St. ☎ 504/525–4896 **French Quarter Postal Emporium** ✉ 1000 Bourbon St. ☎ 504/525–6651.

MEDIA

NEWSPAPERS & MAGAZINES
The local daily newspaper is the Newhouse-owned *Times-Picayune,* (⊕ www.timespicayune.com), which has won Pulitzer prizes for investigative reporting and editorial cartooning. *Gambit* (⊕ www.bestofneworleans.com), a locally owned weekly paper, is free around town and covers local issues as well as arts, entertainment, and dining. *OffBeat* (⊕ www.offbeat.com) is a free monthly publication that explores the music scene in depth. *CityBusiness* (⊕ www.neworleanscitybusiness.com) is the city's weekly publication about commerce and local economic issues. *New Orleans Magazine* (⊕ www.neworleansmagazine.com) is a glossy monthly publication about local culture and attractions.

RADIO & TELEVISION
AM radio stations include WWL 870 (news, talk, country music late at night), WYLD 940 (gospel), WQUE 1280 (sports), and WSMB 1350 (talk). FM stations include WWNO 89.9 (classical, National Public Radio), WWOZ 90.7 (regional music and jazz), WTUL 91.5 (Tulane University student-operated, various formats, mainly rock and alternative music), WCKW 92.3 (rock), WQUE 93.3 (hip-hop and rap), WNOE 101.1 (country), WLMG 101.9 (easy listening), and KMEZ 102.9 (old-school R&B).

The network television stations are WWL (UHF 4, Cable 3, CBS), WDSU (UHF 6, Cable 7, NBC), WVUE (UHF 8, Cable 9, Fox), WGNO (UHF 26, Cable 11, ABC), and WNOL (38, Cable 13, Warner Bros.).

The public television stations are WYES (UHF and Cable 12) and WLAE (UHF 32, Cable 14). Channel 7 (Cable 6) is the locally run government channel.

MONEY MATTERS
Prices throughout this guide are given for adults. Substantially reduced fees are almost always available for children, students, and senior citizens. For information on taxes, *see* Taxes.

ATMS
ATMs are readily available throughout New Orleans. Most accept American Express, MasterCard, and Visa with an affiliated PIN. Practically all pharmacies, groceries, gas stations, and banks provide ATMs. Fees run from free to $3 to $18, depending on the service provider. It is wise to use caution when accessing ATMs; choose a well-lighted, secure machine. Exact locations of ATMs that will accept your card can be obtained from your bank before leaving home.

CREDIT CARDS
Throughout this guide, the following abbreviations are used: **AE,** American Express; **D,** Discover; **DC,** Diners Club; **MC,** MasterCard; and **V,** Visa.
P Reporting Lost Cards **American Express** ☎ 800/992–3404. **Diners Club** ☎ 800/234–6377. **Discover** ☎ 800/347–2683. **MasterCard** ☎ 800/622–7747. **Visa** ☎ 800/847–2911.

PACKING
New Orleans is casual during the day and casual to slightly dressy at night. A number of restaurants in the French Quarter require men to wear a jacket and tie. For sightseeing, pack walking shorts, sundresses, cotton slacks or jeans, T-shirts, and a light sweater. In winter you'll want a coat or warm jacket, especially for evenings, which can be downright cold. In summer pack for hot, sticky weather, but **be prepared for air-conditioning bordering on glacial, and bring an umbrella in case of sudden thunderstorms; leave the plastic raincoats behind** (they're extremely uncomfortable in the high humidity). In addition, **pack a sun hat and sunscreen lotion,** even for strolls in the city, because the sun

can be fierce. Insect repellent will also come in handy if you plan to be outdoors on a swamp cruise or in the city dining alfresco, because mosquitoes come out in full force after sunset in hot weather.

In your carry-on luggage, pack an extra pair of eyeglasses or contact lenses and enough of any medication you take to last a few days longer than the entire trip. You may also ask your doctor to write a spare prescription using the drug's generic name, as brand names may vary from country to country. In luggage to be checked, **never pack prescription drugs, valuables, or undeveloped film.** And don't forget to carry with you the addresses of offices that handle refunds of lost traveler's checks. Check *Fodor's How to Pack* (available at online retailers and bookstores everywhere) for more tips.

To avoid customs and security delays, carry medications in their original packaging. Don't pack any sharp objects in your carry-on luggage, including knives of any size or material, scissors, nail clippers, and corkscrews, or anything else that might arouse suspicion.

To avoid having your checked luggage chosen for hand inspection, don't cram bags full. The U.S. Transportation Security Administration suggests packing shoes on top and placing personal items you don't want touched in clear plastic bags.

CHECKING LUGGAGE

You're allowed to carry aboard one bag and one personal article, such as a purse or a laptop computer. Make sure what you carry on fits under your seat or in the overhead bin. Get to the gate early, so you can board as soon as possible, before the overhead bins fill up.

Baggage allowances vary by carrier, destination, and ticket class. On international flights, you're usually allowed to check two bags weighing up to 70 pounds (32 kilograms) each, although a few airlines allow checked bags of up to 88 pounds (40 kilograms) in first class. Some international carriers don't allow more than 66 pounds (30 kilograms) per bag in business class and 44 pounds (20 kilograms) in

economy. On domestic flights, the limit is usually 50 to 70 pounds (23 to 32 kilograms) per bag. In general, carry-on bags shouldn't exceed 40 pounds (18 kilograms). Most airlines won't accept bags that weigh more than 100 pounds (45 kilograms) on domestic or international flights. Expect to pay a fee for baggage that exceeds weight limits. Check baggage restrictions with your carrier before you pack.

Airline liability for baggage is limited to $2,500 per person on flights within the United States. On international flights it amounts to $9.07 per pound or $20 per kilogram for checked baggage (roughly $640 per 70-pound bag), with a maximum of $634.90 per piece, and $400 per passenger for unchecked baggage. You can buy additional coverage at check-in for about $10 per $1,000 of coverage, but it often excludes a rather extensive list of items, shown on your airline ticket.

Before departure, itemize your bags' contents and their worth, and label the bags with your name, address, and phone number. (If you use your home address, cover it so potential thieves can't see it readily.) Include a label inside each bag and **pack a copy of your itinerary.** At check-in, make sure each bag is correctly tagged with the destination airport's three-letter code. Because some checked bags will be opened for hand inspection, the U.S. Transportation Security Administration recommends that you leave luggage unlocked or use the plastic locks offered at check-in. TSA screeners place an inspection notice inside searched bags, which are resealed with a special lock.

If your bag has been searched and contents are missing or damaged, file a claim with the TSA Consumer Response Center as soon as possible. If your bags arrive damaged or fail to arrive at all, file a written report with the airline before leaving the airport.

🚩 Complaints **U.S. Transportation Security Administration Contact Center** ☎ 866/289-9673 ⊕ www.tsa.gov.

SAFETY

New Orleans has long drawn unwelcome attention for its high crime rate. Tourists are seldom the target of major crimes but can, like other citizens, be the target of pickpockets and purse-snatchers. The New Orleans Police Department regularly patrols the French Quarter. Still, common sense is invaluable, so keep a couple of things in mind. Know where you're going or ask someone, preferably the concierge at your hotel. In the French Quarter, particularly if you are on foot, stay on streets that are heavily populated. After dark, walk with a sense of purpose; night is not the time for obvious sightseeing. In other, less populated, areas of the city it is always advisable to drive. High-end neighborhoods and slums back up to one another throughout New Orleans, making aimless strolling a bad idea outside the Quarter. Try to stick to the recommended walks and areas in this book, and be aware of your surroundings. Take a taxi late at night or when the distance is too great to walk; this is even more important if you've been drinking.

SENIOR-CITIZEN TRAVEL

To qualify for age-related discounts, mention your senior-citizen status up front when booking hotel reservations (not when checking out) and before you're seated in restaurants (not when paying the bill). Be sure to have identification on hand. When renting a car, ask about promotional car-rental discounts, which can be cheaper than senior-citizen rates.

🔢 **Educational Programs Elderhostel** ✉ 11 Ave. de Lafayette, Boston, MA 02111-1746 ☎ 877/426-8056, 877/426-2167 TTY, 978/323-4141 international callers 🖷 877/426-2166 ⊕ www.elderhostel.org. **Interhostel** ✉ University of New Hampshire, 6 Garrison Ave., Durham, NH 03824 ☎ 800/733-9753 or 603/862-1147 🖷 603/862-1113 ⊕ www.learn. unh.edu.

SIGHTSEEING TOURS

BUS TOURS

Gray Line conducts city, plantation, walking, and combination bus–paddle wheeler tours. Le'Ob's Tours runs a three-hour daily bus tour and, for groups, swamp and plantation tours. Their tours are multicultural and focus particularly on the contributions of African-Americans. New Orleans Tours leads city, swamp, and plantation tours and combination city–paddle wheeler outings, and runs a Magazine Street Shopping Shuttle. Tours by Isabelle runs city, swamp, plantation, and combination swamp-and-plantation tours. Steppin' Out Tours is a smaller operation that runs minivan tours through New Orleans and to the plantations.

🔢 **Fees and Schedules Gray Line** ☎ 800/535-7786 or 504/587-0861 ⊕ www.graylineneworleans. com. **Le'Ob's Tours** ☎ 504/288-3478 ⊕ www. leobstours.com. **New Orleans Tours** ☎ 866/596-2698 or 504/212-5925 ⊕ www.notours.com. **Steppin' Out Tours** ☎ 888/557-7465 or 504/246-1006 ⊕ www.steppinouttours.com. **Tours by Isabelle** ☎ 877/665-8687 or 504/391-3544 ⊕ www. toursbyisabelle.com.

ORIENTATION TOURS

Several local tour companies give three- to four-hour city tours by bus that include the French Quarter, the Garden District, uptown New Orleans, and the lakefront. Prices range from $25 to $40 per person. Both Gray Line and New Orleans Tours offer a longer, seven-hour city tour by bus that includes a steamboat ride on the Mississippi River. Gray Line also operates a narrated loop tour by bus with 13 drop-off and pick-up points around the city.

🔢 **Tour Operators Gray Line** ☎ 800/535-7786 or 504/587-0861 ⊕ www.graylineneworleans.com. **New Orleans Tours** ☎ 866/596-2698 or 504/ 212-5925 ⊕ www.notours.com. **Steppin' Out Tours** ☎ 888/557-7465 or 504/246-1006 ⊕ www.steppinouttours.com. **Tours by Isabelle** ☎ 877/665-8687 or 504/391-3544 ⊕ www. toursbyisabelle.com.

RIVERBOAT CRUISES

The New Orleans Steamboat Company offers narrated riverboat cruises and evening jazz cruises up and down the Mississippi on the steamboat *Natchez,* an authentic paddle wheeler. The same company operates the *John James Audubon* paddle wheeler, which makes several trips daily between the Aquarium of the Americas and the Audubon Zoo. Ticket sales and departures for the *Natchez* are at the Toulouse Street Wharf behind Jackson Brewery. The *John James Audubon* operates from in front of the aquarium and a dock at the levee behind the zoo. New Orleans Paddle Wheel has a river-plantation and battlefield cruise twice daily departing from the Riverwalk. There is also an evening jazz dinner cruise from 8 to 10 (boarding at 7 PM); tickets are available for the dinner and cruise or just the cruise and live music. The ticket office is at the Poydras Street Wharf near the Riverwalk and at the Aquarium on Canal Street.

🚢 Cruise Operators **New Orleans Paddle Wheel** 🕾 504/524-0814. **New Orleans Steamboat Company** 🕾 800/233-2628 or 504/586-8777 ⊕ www.steamboatnatchez.com.

SPECIAL-INTEREST TOURS

Full-day plantation tours by bus from New Orleans, which include guided tours through two antebellum plantation homes along the Mississippi River and a stop for lunch in a Cajun-Creole restaurant outside the city, are offered by Gray Line and New Orleans Tours. Tours by Isabelle includes lunch in its full-day plantation package that traces the history of the Cajun people. Also available is the Grand Tour: a full-day minibus tour that includes a visit to one plantation, lunch in a Cajun restaurant, and a 1½-hour boat tour in the swamps with a Cajun trapper.

Other special-interests tours focus on popular activities. Le'Ob's Tours leads jazz history tours, complete with club recommendations for the week of your visit. You can also take cooking classes or arrange a shopping tour. Magic Walking Tours offer a special culinary tour of the French Quarter.

A visit to the Audubon Zoo or Aquarium of the Americas (⇨ French Quarter *in* Chapter 1) can be combined with a ride on the riverboat *John James Audubon,* a ship that can accommodate 600. The 7-mi ride takes 30 minutes. Tickets for such package tours are available in kiosks at both the zoo and the aquarium. Prices vary depending on whether you choose

only the cruise or combine it with zoo and aquarium admissions.

Exploring an exotic Louisiana swamp and traveling into Cajun country is an adventure not to be missed. Dozens of swamp-tour companies are available. You can check at your hotel or the visitor center for a complete listing. Many do not provide transportation from downtown hotels; those listed below do. Full-day tours often include visiting a plantation home.

For highlights of African-American history and culture, contact Le'Ob's Tours.

🚢 African-American Tours **Le'Ob's Tours** 🕾 504/288-3478 ⊕ www.leobstours.com.

🚢 Antiques Shopping **Macon Riddle** 🕾 504/899-3027 ⊕ www.neworleansantiquing.com.

🚢 Cooking Classes **Cookin' Cajun** ✉ Riverwalk 🕾 800/786-0941 or 504/523-8832 ⊕ www.cookincajun.com. **New Orleans School of Cooking** ✉ 524 St. Louis St. 🕾 800/237-4841 or 504/525-2665 ⊕ www.thelouisianageneralstore.com. **Savvy Gourmet School of Cooking** 🕾 504/482-3726 ⊕ www.savvy-gourmet.com.

🚢 Nightlife **Le'Ob's Tours** 🕾 504/288-3478 ⊕ www.leobstours.com.

🚢 Plantations & Swamps **Gray Line** 🕾 800/535-7786 or 504/587-0861 ⊕ www.graylineneworleans.com. **New Orleans Tours** 🕾 866/596-2698 or 504/212-5925 ⊕ www.notours.com. **Tours by Isabelle** 🕾 877/665-8687 or 504/391-3544 ⊕ www.toursbyisabelle.com.

🚢 Swamp Tours **Cypress Swamp Tours** 🕾 504/581-4501 ⊕ www.cypressswamp.com. **Chacahoula Tours** 🕾 504/436-2640 ⊕ www.mulates.com/homeinswamp.htm.**Gray Line** 🕾 800/535-7786 or 504/587-0861 ⊕ www.graylineneworleans.com. **Honey Island Swamp Tours** 🕾 985/641-1769 ⊕ www.honeyislandswamp.com. **Tours by Isabelle** 🕾 877/665-8687 or 504/391-3544 ⊕ www.toursbyisabelle.com.

WALKING TOURS

Free 1½-hour, general history tours of the French Quarter are given daily at 9:30 AM by rangers of the Jean Lafitte National Park. Each visitor may procure a ticket for either tour at the Park Service office at the National Park Visitor Center after 9 AM on the morning of the tour. Tickets are free, but tours are limited to 25 people. Two-hour, general history tours, beginning at the 1850 House on Jackson Square, are given daily at 10 and 1:30 by Friends of the Cabildo (on Monday only the afternoon tour is offered). The tour price includes admission to the 1850 House and Madame John's Legacy.

Several specialized walking tours conducted by knowledgeable guides on specific aspects of the French Quarter are also available. Because some of these tours accommodate as few as two people, be sure to make advance reservations. Heritage Tours leads a general literary tour and others focusing on either William Faulkner or Tennessee Williams. A Garden District walking tour is given several times a week at 2 and 3:30 PM by Jean Lafitte National Park rangers. You must pick up a free ticket in person the morning of the tour at the Jean Lafitte Visitor Center in the French Quarter.

The cemeteries of New Orleans fascinate many people because of their unique aboveground tombs. The most famous, St. Louis Cemetery No. 1, is just outside the French Quarter; Magic Walking Tours, Hidden Treasures Tours, and Save Our Cemeteries conduct guided walking tours. Reservations are generally required.
🔁 French Quarter **Friends of the Cabildo** 🕿 504/523-3939.
🔁 French Quarter & Garden District **Gray Line** 🕿 800/535-7786 or 504/587-0861 🌐 www.graylineneworleans.com. **Hidden Treasures Tours** 🕿 504/529-4507. **Jean Lafitte National Park** ✉ 419 Decatur St. French Quarter 🕿 504/589-2636.
🔁 Literary **Heritage Tours** 🕿 504/949-9805.
🔁 Voodoo, Ghosts, Vampires & Cemeteries **Haunted History Tours** 🕿 888/644-6787 or 504/861-2727 🌐 www.hauntedhistorytours.com. **Historic New Orleans Walking Tours** 🕿 504/947-2120 🌐 www.tourneworleans.com. **Magic Walking Tours** 🕿 504/588-9693 🌐 www.neworleansmagicwalkingtours.com. **New Orleans Spirit Tours** 🕿 504/566-9877. **Save Our Cemeteries** 🕿 888/721-7493 or 504/525-3377 🌐 www.saveourcemeteries.org.

OTHER TOURS
Limousine services make arrangements for personal interests and private guides;

rentals vary. Southern Seaplane will fly you over the city and its surrounding areas.
🔁 By Limousine **Bonomolo Limousines** 🕿 800/451-9258 or 504/522-0892. **New Orleans Limousine Service** 🕿 800/214-0133 or 504/529-5226.
🔁 By Seaplane **Southern Seaplane** 🕿 504/394-5633.

STREETCARS
The riverfront streetcar covers a 2-mi route along the Mississippi River, connecting major sights from the end of the French Quarter (Esplanade Avenue) to the New Orleans Convention Center (Julia Street). Eight stops en route include the French Market, Jackson Brewery, Canal Place, the World Trade Center, the Riverwalk, and the Hilton Hotel. This streetcar operates 7 AM until midnight, passing each stop every 20 minutes. Unlike the historic St. Charles Avenue streetcar, the newer riverfront streetcars are wheelchair accessible. The St. Charles Avenue streetcar runs the 5 mi from the CBD to Carrollton Avenue 24 hours a day, about every 10 minutes 7 AM–8 PM, every half hour 8 PM–midnight, and every hour midnight–7 AM. It's a great way to explore areas like the Garden District. A third streetcar line runs along Canal Street several blocks from the river to City Park.

FARES & SCHEDULES
One-way fare is $1.25 (exact change); one-day and three-day visitor passes are available at $5 and $12, respectively, for unlimited rides on both the St. Charles Avenue and riverfront streetcar lines. Visitor passes apply to buses as well as streetcars. The one-day pass is available from streetcar operators. For information on other visitor passes and schedules, check information centers at hotels and retail centers or call the RTA.
🔁 Streetcar Information **RTA** 🕿 504/248-3900, 504/242-2600 automated information 🌐 www.norta.com.

STUDENTS IN NEW ORLEANS
🔁 IDs & Services **STA Travel** ✉ 10 Downing St., New York, NY 10014 🕿 800/777-0112 24-hr service center, 212/627-3111 🖷 212/627-3387 🌐 www.sta.com. **Travel Cuts** ✉ 187 College St., Toronto, On-

tario M5T 1P7 Canada ☎ 800/592-2887 in the U.S., 866/246-9762 in Canada, 416/979-2406 🖷 416/979-8167 ⊕ www.travelcuts.com.

TAXES

SALES TAX
A local sales tax of 9% applies to all goods and services purchased in Orleans Parish, including food. Taxes outside Orleans Parish vary and are slightly lower.

TAX REFUNDS
Louisiana is the only state that grants a sales-tax rebate to shoppers from other countries who are in the country for no more than 90 days. Look for shops, restaurants, and hotels that display the distinctive tax-free sign and ask for a voucher for the 9% sales tax tacked on to the price of many products and services. Present the vouchers with your plane ticket at the tax rebate office at the Louis Armstrong New Orleans International Airport and receive up to $500 in cash back. If the amount redeemable is more than $500, a check for the difference will be mailed to your home address. Call the airport refund office (☎ 504/467–0723) for complete information.

TAXIS
Cabs are metered at $2.50 minimum for two passengers, plus $1 for each additional passenger and $1.60 per mile. You can either hail cabs in some of the busier areas or call one.

🚖 Taxi Companies **Checker Yellow Cabs** ☎ 504/943-2411. **United Cabs** ☎ 504/522-9771.

TIME
New Orleans is in the Central Time Zone, the same as Chicago. It's one hour behind New York and two hours ahead of Los Angeles.

TIPPING
Tips should be given for good service. The standard is 15% (20% for outstanding service) for waiters. And, because New Orleans is a service-based city, keep a few dollar bills handy. They'll go a long way with bellhops, doormen, and valet parking attendants. As always, use your discretion when tipping.

If you use the services of the concierge, a tip of $5 to $10 is appropriate, with an additional gratuity for special services or favors.

TOURS & PACKAGES
Because everything is prearranged on a prepackaged tour or independent vacation, you spend less time planning—and often get it all at a good price.

BOOKING WITH AN AGENT
Travel agents are excellent resources. But it's a good idea to collect brochures from several agencies, as some agents' suggestions may be influenced by relationships with tour and package firms that reward them for volume sales. If you have a special interest, find an agent with expertise in that area; the American Society of Travel Agents (ASTA; ⇨ Travel Agencies) has a database of specialists worldwide. You can log on to the group's Web site to find an ASTA travel agent in your neighborhood.

Make sure your travel agent knows the accommodations and other services of the place being recommended. Ask about the hotel's location, room size, beds, and whether it has a pool, room service, or programs for children, if you care about these. Has your agent been there in person or sent others whom you can contact?

Do some homework on your own, too: local tourism boards can provide information about lesser-known and small-niche operators, some of which may sell only direct.

BUYER BEWARE
Each year consumers are stranded or lose their money when tour operators—even large ones with excellent reputations—go out of business. So check out the operator. Ask several travel agents about its reputation, and try to **book with a company that has a consumer-protection program.** (Look for information in the company's brochure.) In the United States, members of the United States Tour Operators Association are required to set aside funds ($1 million) to help eligible customers cover payments and travel arrangements in the

event that the company defaults. It's also a good idea to choose a company that participates in the American Society of Travel Agents' Tour Operator Program; ASTA will act as mediator in any disputes between you and your tour operator.

Remember that the more your package or tour includes, the better you can predict the ultimate cost of your vacation. Make sure you know exactly what is covered, and beware of hidden costs. Are taxes, tips, and transfers included? Entertainment and excursions? These can add up.

Tour-Operator Recommendations American Society of Travel Agents (➪ Travel Agencies). **National Tour Association (NTA)** ✉ 546 E. Main St., Lexington, KY 40508 ☎ 800/682-8886 or 859/226-4444 🖷 859/226-4404 ⊕ www.ntaonline.com. **United States Tour Operators Association (USTOA)** ✉ 275 Madison Ave., Suite 2014, New York, NY 10016 ☎ 212/599-6599 🖷 212/599-6744 ⊕ www.ustoa.com.

TRAIN TRAVEL

Three major Amtrak lines arrive at and depart from New Orleans's Union Passenger Terminal. The *Crescent* makes daily runs from New York to New Orleans by way of Washington, D.C. The *City of New Orleans* runs daily between New Orleans and Chicago. The *Sunset Limited* makes the two-day trip from Los Angeles to New Orleans en route to Orlando. It departs from New Orleans traveling westward on Monday, Wednesday, and Saturday and leaves Los Angeles on Sunday, Wednesday, and Friday. Some routes may change with cutbacks in Amtrak funding. Trains arrive at and depart from New Orleans's Union Passenger Terminal in the heart of the CBD.

Train Information Amtrak ☎ 800/872-7245 ⊕ www.amtrak.com. **Union Passenger Terminal** ✉ 1001 Loyola Ave. ☎ 504/524-7571.

TRAVEL AGENCIES

A good travel agent puts your needs first. Look for an agency that has been in business at least five years, emphasizes customer service, and has someone on staff who specializes in your destination. In addition, **make sure the agency belongs to a**

professional trade organization. The American Society of Travel Agents (ASTA)—the largest and most influential in the field with more than 20,000 members in some 140 countries—maintains and enforces a strict code of ethics and will step in to help mediate any agent-client disputes involving ASTA members if necessary. ASTA (whose motto is "Without a travel agent, you're on your own") also maintains a Web site that includes a directory of agents. (If a travel agency is also acting as your tour operator, *see* Buyer Beware *in* Tours & Packages.)

Local Agent Referrals American Society of Travel Agents (ASTA) ✉ 1101 King St., Suite 200, Alexandria, VA 22314 ☎ 800/965-2782 24-hr hotline, 703/739-2782 🖷 703/684-8319 ⊕ www.astanet.com. **Association of British Travel Agents** ✉ 68-71 Newman St., London W1T 3AH ☎ 020/7637-2444 🖷 020/7637-0713 ⊕ www.abta.com. **Association of Canadian Travel Agencies** ✉ 130 Albert St., Suite 1705, Ottawa, Ontario K1P 5G4 ☎ 613/237-3657 🖷 613/237-7052 ⊕ www.acta.ca. **Australian Federation of Travel Agents** ✉ Level 3, 309 Pitt St., Sydney, NSW 2000 ☎ 02/9264-3299 or 1300/363416 🖷 02/9264-1085 ⊕ www.afta.com.au. **Travel Agents' Association of New Zealand** ✉ Level 5, Tourism and Travel House, 79 Boulcott St., Box 1888, Wellington 6001 ☎ 04/499-0104 🖷 04/499-0786 ⊕ www.taanz.org.nz.

VISITOR INFORMATION

For general information and brochures contact the city and state tourism bureaus below. The New Orleans Multicultural Tourism Network produces a variety of multicultural heritage directories.

Tourist Information Louisiana Office of Tourism ✉ Box 94291, Baton Rouge, LA 70804-9291 ☎ 800/633-6970 🖷 225/342-8390 ⊕ www.louisianatravel.com. **New Orleans and River Region Chamber of Commerce** ✉ 601 Poydras St., 70190 ☎ 504/527-6900 🖷 504/527-6970. **New Orleans Convention & Visitors Bureau** ✉ 2020 St. Charles Ave., 70112 ☎ 800/672-6124 or 504/566-5011 🖷 504/566-5021 ⊕ www.visitneworleans.info ✉ in the U.K.: ✉ 33 Market Pl., Hitchin, Hertfordshire SG5 1DY ☎ 146/245-8696 🖷 208/466-9205. **New Orleans Multicultural Tourism Network** ✉ 1520 Sugar Bowl Dr., 70112 ☎ 800/725-5652 or 504/523-5652 🖷 504/522-0785 ⊕ www.soulofneworleans.com.

WEB SITES

Do check out the World Wide Web when planning your trip. You'll find everything from weather forecasts to virtual tours of famous cities. Be sure to visit Fodors.com (⊕ www.fodors.com), a complete travel-planning site. You can research prices and book plane tickets, hotel rooms, rental cars, vacation packages, and more. In addition, you can post your pressing questions in the Travel Talk section. Other planning tools include a currency converter and weather reports, and there are loads of links to travel resources.

🔁 New Orleans Web Sites ⊕ **www.crt.state.la. us;** ⊕ **www.neworleansonline.com;** ⊕ **www. new-orleans.la.us** the city's official site; ⊕ **www. nojazzfest.com** the site of the New Orleans Jazz and Heritage Festival; ⊕ **www.nolalive.com;** ⊕ **www. offbeat.com** site of *OffBeat* magazine, with music coverage.

EXPLORING
NEW ORLEANS

(1)

Updated by
Baty Landis

SOMETIME DURING YOUR VISIT TO NEW ORLEANS, find a wrought-iron balcony or an oak-shaded courtyard or a columned front porch and sit quietly, favorite beverage in hand, at 6 AM. At this hour, when the moist air sits most heavily on the streets, New Orleans is a city of mesmerizing tranquillity. By noon, early-morning calm confronts big-city chaos: with all there is to see and hear and eat and drink and do, the old, mystical, weighty spirit in the city's air can at times be frustrating, seeming to prevent you and everyone around you from accomplishing anything too quickly or efficiently. But when it also keeps you from really caring, then you have found the true secret of New Orleans.

The spiritual and cultural heart of New Orleans is the French Quarter, where the city was originally settled by the French in 1718. You can easily spend several days visiting museums, shops, and eateries in this area. Yet the rest of the city's neighborhoods, radiating out from this focal point, also make for rewarding rambling. The mansion-lined streets of the Garden District and uptown, the aboveground cemeteries that dot the city, and the open air along Lake Pontchartrain provide a nice balance to the frenzy of the Quarter. Despite its sprawling size, residents treat New Orleans like a small town, or perhaps like a collection of small towns. Families have lived in the same neighborhoods for generations; red beans and rice is served throughout the city on Monday; people visit the tombs of their departed on All Saints' Day; and from the smartest office to the most down-home local bar, New Orleanians are ready to celebrate anything at the drop of a hat.

To experience this fun-filled city, you can begin with the usual tourist attractions, but you must go beyond them to linger in a corner grocery store, sip a cold drink in a local joint, or chat with a stoop-sitter. New Orleanians, for all their gripes and grumbling, love their city. They treasure custom and tradition, take in stride the heat and humidity of a semitropical climate, and face life with a laid-back attitude.

Getting Your Bearings

The city occupies an 8-mi stretch between the Mississippi River and Lake Pontchartrain, covering roughly 365 square mi of flat, swamp-drained land. The heart of the city, downtown, includes the famous old area called the Vieux Carré (Old Square), or the French Quarter; the historic African-American district of Tremé; the Central Business District (CBD); and the Warehouse District. Across the river from downtown is an extension of New Orleans known as the Westbank, which includes the neighborhood of Algiers Point.

Downriver from the sight-packed French Quarter are the Faubourg Marigny and the Bywater districts, neighborhoods developed in the early 1800s. The mainly residential area is also home to eateries, cafés, music clubs, and collectibles shops. Across Rampart Street, next to the French Quarter, lies Tremé. A couple of small museums add to the allure of this mainly residential area.

Canal Street divides the French Quarter from the "American Sector," as it was designated in the early days following the Louisiana Purchase. Americans built their homes in increasing extravagance as they began to make money in the city and moved farther upriver. Eventually, a business district overtook what had been the residential blocks just uptown from Canal, and now the lawyers and artists of the CBD and Warehouse District share the area, taking advantage of the bars, clubs, and loft apartment buildings in this burgeoning neighborhood.

Canal Street itself is undergoing a revival, and a historic streetcar once again runs down the center of the street after a hiatus of more than 20 years. The foot of Canal Street, where the French Quarter, the CBD, the Warehouse District, and the Mississippi River converge, is the site of major attractions such as the Aquarium of the Americas, Woldenberg Riverfront Park, Harrah's New Orleans casino, and the Riverwalk shopping-and-entertainment complex.

The St. Charles Avenue streetcar parallels the Mississippi River on a route several blocks inland along St. Charles Avenue, home to antebellum mansions, the Garden District, and the university sector uptown. It's easy to get off the streetcar en route to take in the art and history museums around Lee Circle, stroll around the lush Garden District, or visit the neo-Gothic uptown campus of Tulane University, but you will have to pay the fare again when you reboard.

Mid-City, Metairie, and the lakefront are accessible primarily by automobile. City Park, within Mid-City, covers a vast area that includes the New Orleans Museum of Art, the Botanical Garden, and Storyland, an entertainment area for children, plus miles of lagoons, golf courses, and recreation areas. Along the lakefront, a seawall with steps invites sitters, and open spaces welcome pickup sports and picnicking.

The Mississippi River dominates New Orleans, even passing through one corner of it. The corner across the river from downtown is called Algiers, which was settled in the late 1800s and remained fairly isolated until a modern bridge and regularly scheduled ferries connected it with the east bank in the 1960s. Algiers continues to maintain a small-town flavor, with pocket parks surrounded by Victorian cottages and oak-canopied streets.

Outlying areas include such attractions as the Chalmette Battlefield and National Cemetery some 5 mi south of New Orleans. Kenner, a suburb 15 mi to the west, includes the New Orleans International Airport and a cluster of museums detailing such aspects of local heritage as the railroads, the Saints football team, Mardi Gras, and space exploration.

Directions in a city that bases its compass on the curve of the river can be hopelessly confusing. Canal Street, a long avenue that runs from the river to the lake, divides the city roughly into uptown and downtown sections. Streets to the north of Canal are named North and run downtown; those to the south of Canal are named South and run uptown. Only the French Quarter is laid out in a grid pattern. Ask a New Orleanian for directions and you are likely to hear about so many blocks downtown or uptown and on the lake or river side. The best advice is to keep a map handy at all times.

New Orleans's housing patterns are very mixed. It is not uncommon to find mansions on one block and run-down tenements on the next, or nearby. You should be alert to conditions around you, taking precautions not to wander alone on deserted streets or in questionable areas. New Orleans has a high crime rate. If in doubt about the safety of sights to visit, ask hotel personnel for advice, tour areas in groups when possible, and take a cab at night. (Areas requiring special precautions are noted throughout this chapter.)

Downtown, the Garden District, and Algiers are best explored on foot, because sites are near one another and should be experienced at a slow pace. For other areas, biking, driving, or riding the streetcar is recommended because of the long distances covered.

THE FRENCH QUARTER

The French Quarter lives up to all you've heard: it's alive with the sights, sounds, odors, and experiences of a major entertainment hub. However, it's also a residential neighborhood, where locals meet on street corners to discuss the weather, run to warn one another when a tow truck is coming, and glare suspiciously at wayfaring visitors. In a city of contradictions, the French Quarter holds its own. Along historic, carefully arranged blocks ornamented with wrought iron, rebellious greenery seems to sprout from every crevice. To top it off, the architecture here is largely Spanish rather than French; a disastrous fire in 1794 wiped out almost every structure in the area, and the old center was rebuilt by the then-Spanish government.

A statue of French-Canadian Jean-Baptiste le Moyne, sieur de Bienville, sits near the spot where Bienville landed and founded the French settlement. It was here in the French Quarter that the original French settlers and the Creoles (children born in the colony to French and Spanish settlers) built their stately town houses, churches, marketplaces, opera houses, and theaters. And here, served by African slaves, they developed one of the most sophisticated styles of living in North America. Much of this old-world opulence began to fade when, in 1803, the Louisiana Purchase was signed and the Americans, who were predominantly Anglo-Saxon, moved into power. The Civil War in the 1860s put an end to the golden age of antebellum New Orleans, and the French Quarter went through years of decline and neglect. Only since the mid-20th century has restoration begun in earnest.

The Vieux Carré Commission, formed in 1936 to preserve the historic integrity of the Quarter, controls all renovation and rebuilding with strict codes. Notice that with the exception of those on Bourbon Street there are few neon signs or garish flashing lights, and buildings throughout the Quarter conform to the architectural style of the late 1700s to mid-1800s. Although the commission enforces codes that preserve the authenticity of exteriors, modernization is allowed inside.

The French Quarter is strictly delineated by the Mississippi River to the south (roughly), Rampart Street to the north, Esplanade Avenue to the east (downriver), and Canal Street to the west (upriver). The streets running parallel to the river carry distinct personas: Decatur Street is a strip of tourist shops and hotels uptown from Jackson Square; downtown from the Square, it becomes an alternative hangout for leather-clad regulars drawn to shadowy bars and ethnic shops. Chartres Street is a relatively calm stretch of inviting shops and eateries. Royal Street is the address of sophisticated antiques shops and many of the Quarter's finest homes. Bourbon Street claims the sex shops, extravagant cocktails, and music clubs filmmakers love to feature. Dauphine and Burgundy streets are more residential, with just a few restaurants and bars serving as local retreats.

The French Quarter is the only section of New Orleans in which you will find an easily navigable grid pattern to the streets, so take advantage of it. The city curves with the river, so locals generally describe locations based on relative proximity to the river or the lake and to uptown or downtown. Thus, "it's on the downtown, lake corner" of a given intersection indicates that a destination is more or less on the northeast corner. As local directions also often refer to the number block that a site is on (as in the 500 block of Royal Street), block numbers are included in the French Quarter blocks of the French Quarter and Faubourg Marigny map. The numbers across the top of the map are applicable to all the streets parallel to North Rampart Street. Those streets in the French Quarter that are perpendicular to North Rampart Street all start at 500 at Decatur Street and progress at increments of 100 at each block in the direction of North Rampart.

Numbers in the text correspond to numbers in the margin and on the French Quarter and Faubourg Marigny map.

Inside the Vieux Carré

The only way to see all the sights in the Quarter is to crisscross systematically up and down every street, a tour totaling approximately 12 mi. The following walk will take you past most of the major sights, but veer off the beaten path when a particularly stunning balcony or courtyard catches your eye. Plaques throughout the Quarter will reward your explorations with historical tidbits.

To see the highlights, begin in **Jackson Square** ❶ ▶, the military, political, and spiritual heart of the old French colony. Exit the square by following St. Ann St. to Royal St., where en route you'll pass the Werlein House, former home of early preservationist Elizabeth Werlein and the site of the first Louisiana School (1725), now the Hotel Place d'Armes. Turning right on Royal St., you'll come to Dumaine Street; to your left is the **New Orleans Historic Voodoo Museum** ❷, which displays and sells artifacts used in rituals. Back across Royal Street on Dumaine stands **Madame John's Legacy** ❸, a West Indies–style house (now a state museum) named for a fictitious free woman of color. The **Miltenberger Houses** ❹, in the next block on Royal Street, are historic homes of the 1830s. The cornstalk-and-morning-glory design of an iron fence across the street shows the intricacy of cast-iron work in the late 1800s.

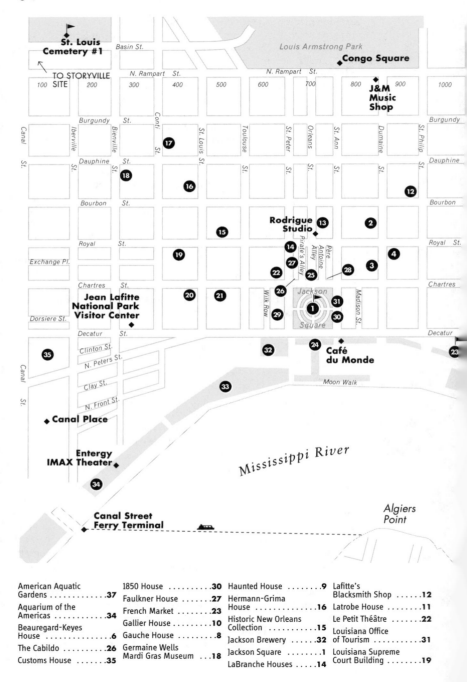

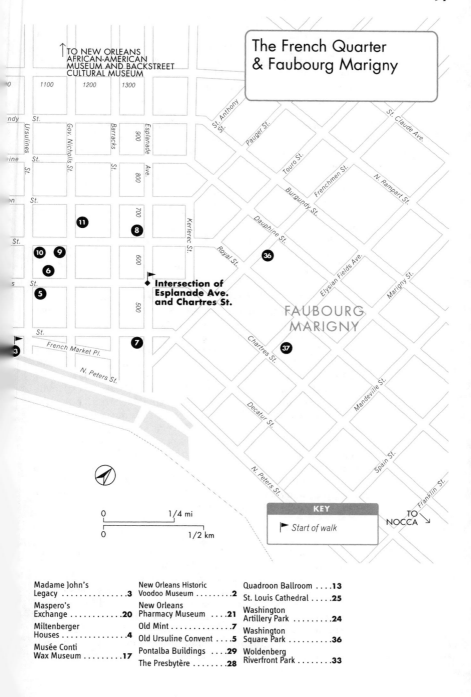

The French Quarter & Faubourg Marigny

TO NEW ORLEANS
AFRICAN-AMERICAN
MUSEUM AND BACKSTREET
CULTURAL MUSEUM

1100   1200   1300

ndy   St.

Ursulines   St.

ine   St.

Gov. Nichols St.

on   St.

Barracks   St.

St.

Esplanade   Ave.

900

800

700

600

500

Kerlerec St.

St. Anthony St.

Pauger St.

Touro St.

Burgundy St.

Frenchmen St.

Dauphine St.

Royal St.

N. Rampart St.

St. Claude Ave.

Elysian Fields Ave.

Marigny St.

11

8

10 **9**

6

5

◆ **Intersection of
Esplanade Ave.
and Chartres St.**

36

FAUBOURG
MARIGNY

St.

French Market Pl.

N. Peters St.

7

Chartres St.

37

Decatur St.

Mandeville St.

N. Peters St.

Spain St.

Franklin St.

3

0   1/4 mi

0   1/2 km

KEY
► *Start of walk*

TO
NOCCA ↘

As you continue down Royal, the large red edifice at St. Philip Street is McDonough 15 public school, one of dozens of city schools founded by 19th-century philanthropist John McDonough. At the next corner is the Royal Pharmacy, an old-time drugstore and soda fountain in continuous operation since the 19th century. Turn right onto Ursulines Street, where you will pass the Croissant d'Or Patisserie, a former Italian ice-cream parlor, on your way to the **Old Ursuline Convent** ❺, the oldest building in the Quarter. Across the street from the Convent, the **Beauregard-Keyes House** ❻ has a lovely formal garden. Continuing down Ursulines Street will land you in the midst of the **French Market** (⇨ Sights to See, Jackson Square & the Riverfront), filled with fresh produce and local souvenirs. Turn left and follow the French Market downtown to the **Old Mint** ❼, a former working mint that now houses a jazz history exhibit and other holdings of the Louisiana State Museum. Even if you do not plan to visit the Mint's exhibits now, pass through the building; the front door spills you onto Esplanade Avenue, which was once the most fashionable street in town and remains the address of many stunning old homes. Exiting the Mint, take a left and stroll along Esplanade away from the river; emerging on your left at the corner of Royal Street is the **Gauche House** ❽, a particularly extravagant example of Esplanade's architecturally lavish residences.

Turn left onto Royal and delve into the heart of the Quarter. At the corner Governor Nicholls and Royal streets is the **Haunted House** ❾, which locals believe still harbors the spirit of the scandalous Madame Lalaurie. A few doors down from the Haunted House stands **Gallier House** ❿, creation and final residence of architect James Gallier, who designed many homes and buildings in mid-19th-century New Orleans. Turn right onto Governor Nicholls off Royal. Ahead on your right, the **Latrobe House** ⓫, built in 1814, is considered the oldest example of Greek Revival architecture in New Orleans. When you reach Dauphine Street, look right: the park that claims much of this block comprises the center of a relatively calm, residential pocket of the French Quarter. Turn left onto Dauphine to appreciate the beauty of this peaceful area for a few blocks. Turn left onto Ursulines, then right onto the residential part of Bourbon Street. As you look up ahead, increasing lights and crowds signal the more notorious portion of the strip. At the corner of St. Philip and Royal streets, **Lafitte's Blacksmith Shop** ⓬, now a wonderfully rustic bar, was the reputed front for Jean Lafitte's pirating operations.

Get a taste for the Bourbon Street madness by continuing to Orleans Street and then turning left, where you encounter a striking view of St. Louis Cathedral from the rear. On the left-hand side of Orleans Street, in what is now a hotel, is the former **Quadroon Ballroom** ⓭, where dashing French and Creole men once sought mistresses from among the lovely free women of color who danced with them there. A few steps further is the studio of Cajun artist George Rodrigue. Turn right onto Royal and take a moment to admire the intricate wrought iron that marks the **LaBranche Houses** ⓮. Continue along Royal Street. Antiques enthusiasts may want to stop in at M. S. Rau Antiques, on your left, which has one of the most impressive collections in the city. A bit farther along on your right is the **Historic New Orleans Collection** ⑮, part research center, part exhibition space. Turn right onto St. Louis Street; the block on your right is dominated by the grand old Antoine's restaurant, run by the same family since 1840. Recross Bourbon Street. Ahead on the left is the **Hermann-Grima House** ⑯. Turn left onto Dauphine Street and follow it to Bienville Street, looking right at Conti Street to catch sight of the **Musée Conti Wax Museum** ⑰, a good family sight.

Turning left onto Bienville will lead you past Arnaud's restaurant and, within it, the small but fascinating **Germaine Wells Mardi Gras Museum** ⑱. Continue to Royal Street and turn left, where you will see more of this street's many antiques dealers. The yellow, Greek Revival structure at the corner of Conti and Royal was originally the Bank of Louisiana; today it is the Eighth Precinct police station. Venture into the lobby for a better look at the building and to gather visitor pamphlets. Government also claims the next block along Royal: the imposing white edifice commanding the entire block is the **Louisiana Supreme Court Building** ⑲. Turn right onto St. Louis Street for further perspectives on this heavily ornamented structure. Across Chartres at the next corner are two smaller buildings of historical significance: **Maspero's Exchange** ⑳, once a slave-trading hub, and the Napoleon House Bar and Cafe, so named in an unsuccessful attempt to lure a certain emperor into exile here. Turn left onto Chartres Street, and on your right the **New Orleans Pharmacy Museum** ㉑ promises a trip back in medical time.

Continue along Chartres toward Jackson Square (the cathedral is easily visible from here), where you'll pass Wilkenson Row, a short, picturesque street to your right. Whiff the square, turning left onto St. Peter Street. The first block of St. Peter provides a reasonable chance to sight southern belles old and new. The historic **Le Petit Théâtre** ㉒ often presents works by southern playwrights, including Tennessee Williams, who lived down the block at No. 632 while writing *A Streetcar Named Desire*. Beside Le Petit Théâtre is the Le Petit Salon, a literary club that draws a loyal crowd from uptown. Two icons occupy the next block of St. Peter: Preservation Hall, revered site of nightly traditional New Orleans jazz; and Pat O'Brien's, home of the notorious Hurricane cocktail. Pick your reward.

TIMING   The walk alone takes about two hours. Adding a sight or two and a break quickly turns it into a full day's journey at least. If you have time, make a note along the way of sights you want to return to for fuller treatment on another day, and allow for leisure time to browse in shops, tour museums, snack at cafés, and listen to a street musician or watch a portrait artist at work. A tour of a home or museum usually takes an hour; allow more time for the Old Mint.

Sights to See

❻ **Beauregard-Keyes House.** This stately 19th-century mansion with period furnishings was the temporary home of Confederate general P. G. T. Beauregard. The house and grounds had severely deteriorated by the 1940s, when the well-known novelist Frances Parkinson Keyes moved in and helped restore it. Her studio at the back of the large courtyard remains intact, complete with family photos, original manuscripts, and her doll and teapot collections. Keyes wrote 40 novels in this studio, all in longhand, among them the local favorite, *Dinner at Antoine's*. If you do not have time to tour the house, take a peek through the gates at the beautiful walled garden at the corner of Chartres and Ursulines streets, or enter the garden through the driveway alongside the house, where you will find the gate unlocked during open hours. Landscaped in the same sun pattern as Jackson Square, the garden is in bloom throughout the year. ⊠ *1113 Chartres St., French Quarter* ☎ *504/523–7257* 💰 *$5* ☉ *Mon.–Sat. 10–3, tours on the hr.*

Bourbon Street. Ignore your better judgment and take a stroll down Bourbon Street, past the bars, restaurants, music clubs, and novelty shops that have given this strip its reputation as the playground of the South. The noise, raucous crowds, and bawdy sights are not family fare; if you go with children, do so before sundown. Although the street is usually well patrolled, it is wise to stay alert to your surroundings. The street is blocked to make a pedestrian mall at night; often the area is shoulder-to-shoulder, especially during major sports events and Mardi Gras.

At Toulouse Street is the former site of the **French Opera House,** once one of New Orleans's most opulent public buildings, which burned down in 1919. There is probably a Lucky Dog vendor nearby, with a vending cart shaped like a hot dog. These carts were immortalized by John Kennedy Toole in his Pulitzer prize–winning novel about New Orleans, *A Confederacy of Dunces*. St. Ann Street marks the beginning of a strip of gay bars.

⑩ Gallier House. Famous New Orleans architect James Gallier designed this as his family home in 1857. Today it contains an excellent collection of early Victorian furnishings. The tour includes the house, servants' quarters, and a gift shop. ⊠ *1132 Royal St., French Quarter* ☎ *504/ 525–5661* 💰 *$6, combination ticket with Hermann-Grima House $10* ☉ *Tours Mon.–Sat. 10–4.*

❽ Gauche House. One of the most distinctive houses in the French Quarter, this mansion and its service buildings date from 1856. The cherub design of the effusive ironwork is the only one of its kind. It was once the estate of businessman John Gauche and is still privately owned. This house is not open to the public. ⊠ *704 Esplanade Ave., French Quarter.*

⑱ Germaine Wells Mardi Gras Museum. During a 31-year period (1937–68), Germaine Cazenave Wells, daughter of Arnaud's restaurant founder Arnaud Cazenave, was queen of Carnival balls a record 22 times for 17 different krewes, or organizations. Many of her ball gowns, in addition to costumes worn by other family members, are on display in this dim, quirky one-room museum above Arnaud's restaurant. ⊠ *Arnaud's restaurant, 813 Bienville St., 2nd fl. (enter through restaurant), French Quarter* ☎ *504/523–5433* 💰 *Free* ☉ *Daily 10–2 and 6–10.*

need a break? **Napoleon House Bar and Cafe** (⊠ 500 Chartres St., French Quarter ☎ 504/524–9752 ⊕ www.napoleonhouse.com) is a favorite gathering place for local characters, who favor such romantic drinks as the Pimm's Cup and the Sazerac. Snack on a muffuletta sandwich (ham, salami, mozzarella, and olive salad on seeded bread) or a cheese plate, and enjoy the surroundings. Napoléon never made it to Louisiana, but he would have felt right at home here in the building intended for him in exile.

❾ Haunted House. Locals agree that this is the most haunted house in a generally haunted neighborhood. Most blame the spooks on Madame Lalaurie, a wealthy but ill-fated socialite who lost both parents as a child, then two husbands before finding a third and moving with him into this mansion on Royal Street. Madame Lalaurie fell out with society when a fire in her attic exposed atrocious treatment of her slaves: according to newspaper reports, well-wishing neighbors who rushed into the house found seven mutilated slaves in one of the apartments. Madame Lalaurie fled town that night, but occupants of the house have told of hauntings ever since. One tour guide claims that when clients faint from the heat, it is always by this house and that cameras often mysteriously refuse to function when pointed at the house, which is not open to the public. ⊠ *1140 Royal St., French Quarter.*

⟳ ⓰ Hermann-Grima House. One of the largest and best-preserved examples
Fodor'sChoice   of American architecture in the Quarter, this Georgian-style house has
★   the only restored private stable and the only working 1830s Creole kitchen in the Quarter. American architect William Brand built the house in 1831. Cooking demonstrations on the open hearth are held here all day Thursday from October through May. You'll want to check the gift shop, which has many local crafts and books. ⊠ *820 St. Louis St., French Quarter* ☎ *504/525–5661* ⊕ *www.gnofn.org~hggh* 🎫 *$6, combination ticket with the Gallier House $10* ⊙ *Tours weekdays 10–4.*

★ ⓯ Historic New Orleans Collection. This private archive and exhibit complex, with thousands of historic photos, documents, and books, is one of the finest research centers in the South. It occupies the 19th-century town house of General Kemper Williams and the 1792 Merrieult House. Changing exhibits focus on aspects of local history; history tours and home tours of the houses, grounds, and archives are offered several times daily. A museum shop sells books, prints, and gifts. Children under 12 are not admitted. ⊠ *533 Royal St., French Quarter* ☎ *504/523–4662* ⊕ *www.hnoc.org* 🎫 *Exhibit at 533 Royal St. and use of research library at 410 Chartres St. free, tour of houses or archive galleries $4* ⊙ *Tues.–Sat. 10–4:30.*

★ ⟳ ⌐ ❶ Jackson Square. Surrounded by historic buildings and filled with plenty of the city's atmospheric street life, the heart of the French Quarter is today a beautifully landscaped park. Originally called the Place d'Armes, the square was founded in 1718 as a military parade ground. It was also the site of public executions carried out in various styles, including burning at the stake, beheading, breaking on the wheel, and hanging. A **statue of Andrew Jackson,** victorious leader of the Battle of New Orleans in the War of 1812, commands the center of the square; the park was renamed for him in the 1850s. The words carved in the base on the cathedral side of the statue—"The Union must and shall be preserved"—

are a lasting reminder of the federal troops who occupied New Orleans during the Civil War and who inscribed them.

Among the notable buildings around the square is **St. Louis Cathedral** and **Faulkner House.** Two Spanish colonial–style buildings, the **Cabildo** and the **Presbytère,** flank the cathedral. The handsome rows of brick apartments on either side of the square are the **Pontalba Buildings.** The park is landscaped in a sun pattern, with walkways set like rays streaming out from the center, a popular garden design in the royal court of King Louis XIV, the Sun King. In the daytime, dozens of artists hang their paintings on the park fence and set up outdoor studios where they work on canvases or offer to draw portraits of passersby. These artists are easy to engage in conversation and are knowledgeable about many aspects of the Quarter and New Orleans. You can also be entertained by musicians, mimes, tarot-card readers, and magicians who perform on the flagstone pedestrian mall surrounding the square, many of them day and night. ⊠ *French Quarter* ⊙ *Park daily 8–at least 6 PM; flagstone paths on park's periphery open 24 hrs.*

★ **Jean Lafitte National Park Visitor Center.** This center has free visual and sound exhibits on the customs of various communities throughout in the state, as well as information-rich daily history tours of the French Quarter. The one-hour tours leave at 9:30 AM and are free; tickets are handed out one per person (you must be present to get a ticket), beginning at 9 AM, for that day's tours only. Arrive at least 15 minutes before tour time to be sure of a spot. The office also supervises and provides information on Jean Lafitte National Park Barataria Unit across the river from New Orleans, and the Chalmette Battlefield, where the Battle of New Orleans was fought in the War of 1812. ⊠ *419 Decatur St., French Quarter* ☎ *504/589–2636* ⊙ *Daily 9–5.*

⑭ **LaBranche Houses.** This complex of lovely town houses, built in the 1830s by Widow LaBranche, fills the half block between Pirate's Alley and Royal and St. Peter streets behind the **Cabildo.** The house on the corner of Royal and St. Peter streets, with its elaborate, rounded cast-iron balconies, is the most photographed residence in the French Quarter. The **Royal Café** restaurant (⇨ Dining, French Quarter) has seating on the second-floor curve of the balcony. ⊠ *French Quarter.*

⑫ **Lafitte's Blacksmith Shop.** The striking anvil no longer sounds in this ancient weathered building. You'll hear only the clinking of glasses at this favorite local bar for patrons from all walks of life. Legend has it that the pirate Jean Lafitte and his cronies operated a blacksmith shop here as a front for their vast illicit trade in contraband. The building, dating from 1772 and thus a rare survivor of the 18th-century French Quarter fires, is interesting as one of the few surviving examples of soft bricks reinforced with timber, a construction form used by early settlers. ⊠ *941 Bourbon St., French Quarter* ☎ *504/522–9397.*

⑪ **Latrobe House.** The young New Orleans architect Henry Latrobe designed this modest house with Arsene Latour in 1814. Its smooth lines and porticoes started a passion for Greek Revival architecture in Louisiana, evidenced later in many plantation houses upriver as well as in a significant number of buildings in New Orleans. This house, believed to be the earliest example of Greek Revival in the city, is not open to the public. ⊠ *721 Governor Nicholls St., French Quarter.*

㉒ Le Petit Théâtre. Since 1916 this community-based theater group has entertained the Quarter with plays, musicals, and variety shows. The organization was originally housed in one of the Pontalba apartments on Jackson Square, but it quickly outgrew that space and moved to this building in 1922. Hosting the Tennessee Williams Festival every spring, Le Petit Théâtre attracts national attention. The flagstone patio with its fountain is postcard-perfect. The building next door is **Le Petit Salon** (⊠ 620 St. Peter St. French Quarter), headquarters of a ladies' literary club since 1925. The house was originally built for a pair of French newlyweds in 1838; the wrought-iron staircase leads to the formal, second-floor entrance. ⊠ *616 St. Peter St., French Quarter* ☎ *504/522–2081* ⊕ *www.lepetittheatre.com.*

⓱ Louisiana Supreme Court Building. This imposing Victorian building that takes up the whole block of Royal Street between St. Louis and Conti streets is the Old New Orleans Court, erected in 1908. After years of vacancy and neglect, this magnificent edifice is being partially restored as the elegant home of the Louisiana Supreme Court. ⊠ *French Quarter.*

★ ❸ Madame John's Legacy. Now a state museum, this is the only example in the French Quarter of West Indies architecture and early Creole-colonial home design. The large, dark rooms of the main living space occupy the second story, while a porch (called a gallery) runs along the front and back of the house, providing ventilation for the steamy summers and protection from both sun and rain. The current building was constructed in 1789, following the 1788 fire that took out much of the Quarter. The house has a colorful past. The first owner, Jean Pascal, a French sea captain, was killed by Natchez Indians. The name "Madame John's Legacy" was adopted in the late 1800s from a short story by New Orleans writer George Washington Cable. The popular tale was about Madame John, a "free woman of color" who, like many mulatto women at that time, became the mistress of a Frenchman. Having never married, the Frenchman, John (Jean), bequeathed his house and estate to her on his deathbed. Wander through the house and enjoy displays of archaeological finds from the site, exhibits on the architecture of the house, local folk art, and rotating art exhibits. ⊠ *632 Dumaine St., French Quarter* ☎ *504/568–6968* ⊠ *$3* ⊙ *Tues.–Sun. 9–5.*

⓴ Maspero's Exchange. This restaurant was once a slave auction house and for many years thereafter the Exchange Coffeehouse, where the city's notable Creoles gathered. From the outside, the building appears to have only two floors, whereas inside, a middle floor, called an entresol, is in the area above the window arch. This low middle floor was used for storage. ⊠ *440 Chartres St., French Quarter.*

❹ Miltenberger Houses. The widow Amelie Miltenberger built this row of three brick town houses in the 1830s for her three sons. Two generations later, her daughter Alice Heine became famous for wedding Prince Albert of Monaco. Although the marriage ended childless and in divorce,

Princess Alice was a sensation in New Orleans. ⊠ *900, 906, and 910 Royal St., French Quarter.*

☾ ⑰ **Musée Conti Wax Museum.** The history of New Orleans and Louisiana unfolds in colorful vignettes in this fun museum. Local legends are captured life-size at seminal moments: Madame Lalaurie discovered torturing her slaves; Napoléon leaping out of the bathtub at news of the Louisiana Purchase; Marie Laveau selling gris-gris to downtown customers; the Duke and Duchess of Windsor attending a Mardi Gras ball. Written and audio explanations supplement the visual scenes. A miniature Mardi Gras parade fills one corridor. The museum is an enjoyable way to acquaint yourself and your children with New Orleans history, although the history depicted here tends toward the sensational and the occasionally unsubstantiated. ⊠ *917 Conti St., French Quarter* ☎ *504/581–1993 or 800/233–5405* ⊕ *www.get-waxed.com* ⊡ *$6.75* ☉ *Mon.–Sat. 10–5, Sun. noon–5.*

❷ **New Orleans Historic Voodoo Museum.** A large collection of artifacts and information on voodoo as it was—and still is—practiced in New Orleans is here in a two-room, rather homegrown museum. Items on display include portraits by and of voodoo legends, African artifacts believed to have influenced the development of the religion, a video discussing voodoo, and lots of gris-gris. The gift shop sells gris-gris potions and voodoo dolls. ⊠ *724 Dumaine St., French Quarter* ☎ *504/234–2096* ⊡ *Museum $7* ☉ *Daily 10–6.*

㉑ **New Orleans Pharmacy Museum.** This building was the apothecary shop and residence of Louis J. Dufilho, America's first licensed pharmacist with his own shop, in the 1820s. His botanical and herbal gardens are still cultivated in the courtyard. To tour the musty shop is to step back into 19th-century medicine. Even the window display, with its enormous leech jar and other antiquated paraphernalia, is fascinating. Watch for free 19th-century seasonal health tips posted in the front window. ⊠ *514 Chartres St., French Quarter* ☎ *504/565–8027* ⊕ *www.pharmacymuseum.org* ⊡ *$2* ☉ *Tues.–Sun. 10–5.*

★ ❼ **Old Mint.** Minting began in 1838 in this ambitious, Ionic structure, a project of President Andrew Jackson. The New Orleans mint was to provide currency for the South and the West, which it did until the Confederacy began minting its own currency here in 1861. When supplies ran out, the building served as a barracks, then a prison, for Confederate soldiers; the production of U.S. coins recommenced only in 1879. It stopped again, for good, in 1909. After years of neglect, the federal government handed the Old Mint over to Louisiana in 1966; the state now uses the quarters to exhibit collections of the Louisiana State Museum. The principal exhibit here is the **New Orleans Jazz Collection,** a brief but evocative tour through the history of traditional New Orleans jazz. In addition to informative written explanations, a wealth of artifacts movingly tells the story of the emergent art form. Among the gems are the soprano saxophone owned by Sidney Bechet, the trumpets of Pops Celestin and Dizzy Gillespie, and the cornet given to Louis Armstrong at the juvenile home where he spent much of his youth. Sheet music, biographies, personal effects, and photos round out the displays. Across the hall from the jazz exhibit are a few rooms filled with the beautiful and locally treasured Newcomb pottery. This school of pottery was developed by teachers and students at Newcomb Women's College in uptown New Orleans during the late 19th and early 20th centuries, and it subtly reflects the art-nouveau movement. The **Louisiana Historical Center**, which holds the French and Spanish Louisiana archives, is open free to researchers by appointment. At the Barracks Street entrance, notice the one remaining sample of the mint's old walls—it'll give you an idea of the building's deterioration before its restoration. ✉ *400 Esplanade Ave., French Quarter* ☎ *504/568–6968* 💰 *$5* ☉ *Tues.–Sun. 9–5.*

❺ **Old Ursuline Convent.** The Ursulines were the first of many orders of religious women who came to New Orleans and founded schools, orphanages, and asylums and ministered to the needs of the poor. Their original convent was built in 1734 and is now the oldest French-colonial building in the Mississippi valley, having survived the disastrous 18th-century fires that destroyed the rest of the Quarter. **St. Mary's Church,** adjoining the convent, was added in 1845. The original tract of land for a convent, school, and gardens covered several French Quarter blocks. Now an archive for the archdiocese, the convent was used by the Ursulines for 90 years. The formal gardens, church, and first floor of the old convent are open for guided tours. You'll want to see the herb gardens, which inspired one of the nuns to become the first pharmacist in the United States: she was never licensed, but she published a list of herbs that cured various maladies. The Ursuline Academy, the convent's girls' school founded in 1727, is now uptown on State Street, where the newer convent and chapel were built. The academy is the oldest girls' school in the country. ✉ *1100 Chartres St., French Quarter* ☎ *504/529–2651* 💰 *$5* ☉ *Tours Tues.–Fri. at 10, 11, 1, 2, and 3; weekends at 11:15, 1, and 2.*

⓭ **Quadroon Ballroom.** In the early 1800s the wooden-rail balcony extending over Orleans Street was linked to a ballroom where free women of color met their French suitors, as Madame John of **Madame John's Legacy** is said to have done. The quadroons (technically, people whose racial makeup was one-quarter African) who met here were young unmarried women of legendary beauty. A gentleman would select a favorite beauty and, with her mother's approval, buy her a house and support her as his mistress. The children of these unions, which were generally maintained in addition to legal marriages with French women, were often sent to France to be educated. The Quadroon Ballroom later became part of a convent and school for the Sisters of the Holy Family, a religious order founded in New Orleans in 1842 by the daughter of a quadroon to educate and care for African-American women. ✉ *Bourbon Orleans Hotel, 717 Orleans St., 2nd fl., French Quarter.*

Rodrigue Studio. Cajun artist George Rodrigue started painting blue dogs in 1984, spurred by the spirit of his deceased pet Tiffany. Since then, the blue dog has found thousands of manifestations in various settings in the cult artist's paintings. Of late, Rodrigue has ventured a few non-blue-dog works, which after nearly two decades of singular focus seems like a radical move. Rodrigue's principal gallery, a single room rather eerily lined almost entirely with paintings of the blue dog (and her evil red twin), sits directly behind St. Louis Cathedral. ⊠ *721 Royal St., French Quarter* ☎ *504/581–4244* ⊕ *www.georgerodrigue.com* ⊙ *Mon.–Sat. 10–6, Sun. noon–5.*

need a break?

A great favorite among pensive French Quarter intellectuals, the tiny **Pirates Alley Café** (⊠ 622 Pirates Alley, French Quarter ☎ 504/ 524–9332) is an ideal setting for espresso, wine, or a light salad or sandwich alongside St. Louis Cathedral.

Jackson Square & the Riverfront

Old Man River, having rolled his long journey down through the United States, makes his last major appearance in New Orleans before emptying into the Gulf of Mexico, and a trip to the city is not quite complete without paying homage to this mighty body of water. In addition to being a powerful economic force, the Mississippi is the repository of endless myths, legends, and Americana; the thoroughfare of Huckleberry Finn; the main artery of the blues circuit; and the romance-tinged route of paddle wheelers and steamships that still ply the waters, tracing and retracing the steps of generations. A subtly landscaped park and path line the portion of the Mississippi that borders the French Quarter, providing expansive views of the curves that inspired the nickname "Crescent City."

A Good Walk

Begin your walk along the river at the **French Market** ❷, at Ursulines Street. Around the bushes at the flood wall, near the market's arcaded entry, follow the ramp beyond the flood wall over the train tracks (watch for streetcars!). Take the ramp up to the river's edge, where a walkway begins to your right at Governor Nicholls Street. As you face the river, to your left extends a series of wharves, and in the distance you can spot the towers of the Industrial Canal drawbridge, unofficial border of the Ninth Ward, a colorful working-class district. To your right the river curves under the twin spans of the Crescent City Connection bridge and beyond, toward uptown. The buildings directly across the river belong to the sleepy community of Algiers Point: the towers in plain sight are those of the town library and the old courthouse.

With your back to the water, the impressive red edifice of the Old Mint rises above the oaks to your right, and the French and domestic flags of the Place de France are directly in front of you. As you begin walking along the river away from the Governor Nicholls Wharf, look back after about 20 paces to see the colorful campus of the New Orleans Center for Creative Arts (NOCCA), back in the Bywater District. At Dumaine Street the broad riverfront windows belong to Bella Luna restaurant, one of the French Quarter's more romantic eateries, particularly during a full moon. Past Bella Luna, the French Market continues (you're likely to hear live jazz emanating from this stretch during the afternoon), culminating in Café du Monde, marked by green-and-white-stripe awnings. The riverfront scene gathers intensity here: benches, lampposts, and flower boxes begin to appear along the side of the path, the foot traffic increases, and performers in various media stake out their individual grass stages.

Soon you find yourself opposite **Jackson Square** (⇨ Sights to See, Inside the Vieux Carré) and before a view familiar from countless New Orleans postcards. Wooden stairs lead right down to the river's edge here, with the current lapping the bottom steps. This section of the walkway is known as the Moon Walk, named for former Mayor Moon Landrieu. Walk away from the river and onto the concrete **Washington Artillery Park** ㉔, which honors a Louisiana National Guard unit formed in 1838, for a closer view over the square. You will often encounter a crowd here, cheering on some street performer or other.

Jackson Square, like the main squares found in most French towns, has a church, a seat of government, and major shops. **St. Louis Cathedral** ㉕, where Pope John Paul II has given a service, dominates the square. Two Spanish colonial–style buildings, now museums, flank the cathedral: to the left, the **Cabildo** ㉖, the seat of the Spanish government in the 1700s; down Pirate's Alley is **Faulkner House** ㉗, where the young William Faulkner once lived and wrote his first novel (behind the cathedral is St. Anthony's Garden, which is not open to the public; the statue of the Sacred Heart of Jesus, however, casts an imposing shadow at nighttime); to your right, the **Presbytère** ㉘, which has an excellent exhibit on Mardi Gras. The handsome rows of brick apartments on either side of the square are the **Pontalba Buildings** ㉙, built in 1850. In the row on the right (as you face the cathedral), the **1850 House** ㉚ is open for tours. A few doors away in the same row is the **Louisiana Office of Tourism** ㉛. Café du Monde is down the ramp on your right; the large Euro-hybrid structure on your left is the **Jackson Brewery** ㉜ mall (often referred to simply as "Jax," the name of the beer formerly brewed here), filled with souvenirs, clothing, and crafts shops and a Virgin Megastore.

As you return to the Moon Walk and continue past Jax, the commercial town houses of Decatur Street become visible opposite the Riverboat *Natchez* dock. Past the dock, look right to spot the distinguished roofline of the Louisiana Supreme Court Building, rising in the midst of the Quarter. A Hard Rock Cafe on your right occupies an extension of Jax. Follow the riverfront path around a small Greek theater to reach **Woldenberg Riverfront Park** ㉝, occupied by horn players, skateboarders, and a handful of sculptures and monuments. The Holocaust Memorial, completed in 2003, emerges at the far edge of the park's lawn.

Finally you reach the large riverfront structure housing the Entergy IMAX Theater and **Aquarium of the Americas** ㉞ and marking the end of Woldenberg Park. As you circle around the aquarium and toward Canal Street, the historical divide between the French and American parts of town, the bricks underfoot bear the names of Audubon Institute sponsors. Spilling onto Canal Street, you encounter a bevy of sights and attractions: the upscale Canal Place shopping center to your right, and beyond it the **Customs House** ㉟; Harrah's New Orleans casino lies straight ahead. The World Trade Center is on your left; and behind that, back up on the river, the Riverwalk shopping center. Your options from here are many: venture left to enter the Warehouse District; hop the riverfront streetcar to carry you back toward the French Market; walk a few blocks down Canal Street to catch the St. Charles Avenue streetcar at Royal Street, or to cut back into the heart of the French Quarter; or simply turn back along the Mississippi River for a reverse perspective on the worlds of activity it engenders.

TIMING   A leisurely stroll along the riverfront takes about 30 minutes. Allow two extra hours if you plan to visit the Aquarium of the Americas and the Mardi Gras exhibit in the Presbytère. Woldenberg Park is also a nice place for a riverfront picnic, which can stretch the stroll into an afternoon journey.

Sights to See

🐾 ㉞   **Aquarium of the Americas.** In this marvelous family attraction more than
Fodor$Choice   7,000 aquatic creatures swim in 60 displays ranging from 500 to 500,000
★   gallons of water. Each of the four major exhibit areas—the Amazon Rain Forest, the Caribbean Reef, the Mississippi River, and the Gulf Coast—has fish and animals native to that environment. A fun exhibit called Beyond Green houses more than 25 different frog species and includes informative displays. The aquarium's spectacular design allows you to feel part of the watery worlds by providing close-up encounters with the inhabitants. A gift shop and café are on the premises.

Woldenberg Riverfront Park, which surrounds the aquarium, is a tranquil spot with a view of the Mississippi. Package tickets for the aquarium and a river cruise are available outside the aquarium. You can also combine tickets for the aquarium and the **Entergy IMAX Theater,** a river cruise, and the **Audubon Zoo** in a package, or take the river cruise by itself. Note that the zoo cruise halts operation for several weeks around December each year for maintenance. ⊠ *1 Canal St., French Quarter* ☎ *504/581–4629 or 800/774–7394* ⊕ *www.audoboninstitute.org* ⌨*Aquarium $14; combination ticket with IMAX $18; combination ticket for aquarium, zoo, and round-trip cruise $32.50* ☉ *Aquarium Sun.–Thurs. 9:30–6 (last ticket sold at 5), Fri. and Sat. 9:30–7 (last ticket sold at 6).*

㉖   **The Cabildo.** Dating from 1799, this Spanish colonial–style building is named for the Spanish council—or *cabildo*—that met there. The transfer of Louisiana to the United States was made in 1803 in the front room on the second floor overlooking the square. The Cabildo later served as the city hall and then the Supreme Court. Three floors of multicultural exhibits recount Louisiana history—from the colonial period through Reconstruction—with countless artifacts, including the death mask of Napoléon Bonaparte. In 1988 the building suffered terrible damage from a four-alarm fire. Most of the historic pieces inside were saved, but the top floor, roof, and cupola had to be replaced. The Cabildo is almost a twin to the **Presbytère** on the other side of the cathedral. ⊠ *Jackson Sq., French Quarter* ☎ *504/568–6968* ⌨ *$5* ☉ *Tues.–Sun. 9–5.*

need a break?   Open 24 hours, **Café du Monde** (⊠ 800 Decatur St., French Quarter ☎ 504/525–4544 ⊕ www.cafedumonde.com) serves up café au lait and beignets (and not much else) in a style that has not varied for more than a century. Don't miss it.

Canal Place. In addition to such tony stores as Saks Fifth Avenue, Brooks Brothers, Gucci, and local jeweler Mignon Faget, this upscale shopping and office complex contains **Canal Place Cinema,** the only location in this area that screens first-run movies. The four theaters and the concession stand have artwork based on local novelist Walker Percy's *The Moviegoer.* The **Southern Repertory Theater,** on the third floor, specializes in plays by local artists or of local interest. Nearby, **Rhino Gallery** sells arts and crafts by top local artists. The **Wyndham New Orleans at Canal Place** tops the complex; its dining rooms and lobby have fantastic river views. ⊠ *333 Canal St., French Quarter* ☎ *504/522–9200* ⏱ *Mon.–Sat. 10–7, Sun. noon–6.*

Canal Street. Canal Street, 170 feet wide, is the widest main street in the United States and one of the liveliest. It was once scheduled to be made into a canal; plans changed, but the name remains. In the early 1800s, after the Louisiana Purchase, the French Creoles residing in the French Quarter were segregated from the Americans who settled upriver from Canal Street. The communities had separate governments and police systems, and what is now Canal Street—and, most specifically, the central median running down Canal Street—was neutral ground between them. Today animosities between these two groups are history, but the term "neutral ground" has survived as the name for all medians throughout the city.

Some of the grand buildings that once lined Canal Street remain, many of them former department stores and other businesses now serving as hotels, restaurants, or souvenir shops. The Werlein Building (605 Canal St.), once a multilevel music store, is now the Palace Café restaurant. The former home of Maison Blanche (921 Canal St.), once the most elegant of the downtown department stores, is now a Ritz-Carlton hotel, with a ground floor devoted to an upscale mini-mall. One building still serving its original purpose is Adler's (722 Canal St.), the city's most elite jewelry and gift store. For the most part, these buildings are faithfully restored, so you can still appreciate the grandeur that once reigned on this fabled strip.

③⑤ Customs House. Since it was built in 1849, this massive building has served as the customs house for the Port of New Orleans. It occupies an entire city block and replaces what had been Fort St. Louis, which guarded the old French city. The building has identical entrances on all four sides, because at the time it was completed no decision had been made as to which side would be the main entrance. You are welcome to look around, but no tours of the building are given. ⊠ *423 Canal St., French Quarter.*

③⓪ 1850 House. A docent leads you through this well-preserved town house and courtyard, part of the **Pontalba Buildings** and furnished in the style of 1850, when the buildings were built as upscale residences and retail space. Notice the ornate ironwork on the balconies of the apartments: the original owner, Baroness Micaela Pontalba, introduced cast (or molded) iron with these buildings, and it eventually replaced much of the old hand-wrought ironwork in the French Quarter. The initials for her families, *A* and *P*—Almonester and Pontalba—are worked into the design. A gift shop and bookstore run by Friends of the Cabildo is downstairs. ✉ *523 St. Ann St., on Jackson Sq., French Quarter* ☎ *504/568–6968* 💲 *$3* 🕐 *Tues.–Sun. 9–5.*

🔄 **Entergy IMAX Theater.** This cinema along the river and adjacent to the **Aquarium of the Americas** has an 11,500-watt digital sound system and a screen 5½ stories tall. The theater shows classic IMAX fare—high-quality nature films related to the sea, Earth, and outer space that are suitable for everyone in the family. ✉ *1 Canal St., French Quarter* ☎ *504/581–4629* 🌐 *www.auduboninstitute.org* 🎫 *Theater $8, combination ticket with aquarium $18* 🕐 *Shows Sun.–Thurs. 10–6, Fri. and Sat. 10–8; arrive 30 mins before any showtime.*

27 **Faulkner House.** The young novelist William Faulkner lived and wrote his first book, *Soldier's Pay,* here in the 1920s. He later returned to his native Oxford, Mississippi, and became a Pulitzer prize–winning writer. The house is not open for tours, but accommodates **Faulkner House Books** (⇨ Shopping, French Quarter) and the literary group **Pirate's Alley Faulkner Society,** which specializes in local and southern writers. ✉ *624 Pirate's Alley, French Quarter* ☎ *504/524–2940* 🕐 *Daily 10–6.*

▶ **23** **French Market.** The sounds, colors, and smells here are alluring: street performers, ships' horns on the river, pralines, muffulettas, sugarcane, and Creole tomatoes. Originally a Native American trading post, later a bustling open-air market under the French and Spanish, the French Market historically began at Café du Monde and stretched along Decatur and North Peters streets all the way to the downtown edge of the Quarter. Today the market's graceful arcades have been mostly enclosed and filled with shops and eateries, while the fresh market has been pushed several blocks downriver, under sheds built in 1936 as part of a Works Progress Administration project. Since then, farmers from the New Orleans area have pulled their trucks up to the loading bays here to sell their produce. The market begins at Ursulines Street; after a block or so, the fresh produce and local goods give way to a **flea market,** filled with bargain collectibles, jewelry, posters, records, and the occasional quality craftsperson. Street performers and musicians often enliven the market's outdoor areas.

Latrobe Park, a small recreational area at the uptown end of the fresh market, honors Benjamin Latrobe, designer of the city's first waterworks. A modern fountain evoking a waterworks marks the spot where Latrobe's invention once stood. Sunken seating, fountains, and greenery make this a lovely spot to relax with a drink served from a kiosk nearby. 🕐 *Daily 7–7; hrs may vary depending on season and weather* ✉ *Decatur St., French Quarter.*

32 **Jackson Brewery.** Also called Jax Brewery, this former brewery was remodeled in the 1980s to house a three-section shopping-and-entertainment complex. Outside are multilevel terraces facing the river, and inside are more than 50 shops (including the monumental Virgin Megastore) and galleries plus a food court and restaurants. The **Hard Rock Cafe** is in a separate building. ✉ *620 Decatur St., French Quarter* ☎ *504/566–7245* 🌐 *www.jacksonbrewery.com* 🕐 *Mon.–Sat. 9–8, Sun. 10–7.*

㉛ **Louisiana Office of Tourism.** In addition to maps and hundreds of brochures about sights in the city and its environs, this information center has guides who can answer questions. ✉ *529 St. Ann St., French Quarter* ☎ *504/568–5661* ☉ *Daily 9–5.*

Mississippi River. When facing the river, you see to the right the **Crescent City Connection,** a twin-span bridge between downtown New Orleans and the Westbank, and a ferry that crosses the river every 30 minutes. The river flows to the left downstream for another 100 mi until it merges with the Gulf of Mexico. Directly across the river are the ferry landing and a ship-repair dry dock in a neighborhood called **Algiers Point.** The river is always active with steamboats carrying tour groups, tugboats pushing enormous barges, and oceangoing ships. Sometimes a dredge is visible, dredging the river's bottom of silt to keep the channel open for large ships.

㉙ **Pontalba Buildings.** Baroness Micaela Pontalba built these twin sets of town houses, one on each side of Jackson Square, in the late 1840s; they are known for their ornate cast-iron balcony railings. Baroness Pontalba's father was Don Almonester, who sponsored the rebuilding of St. Louis Cathedral in 1788. The strong-willed Miss Almonester also helped fund the landscaping of the square and the erection of the Andrew Jackson statue in its center. She later moved to Paris, where she is buried. The Pontalba Buildings are publicly owned; the side to the right of the cathedral, on St. Ann Street, is owned by the state, and the other side, on St. Peter Street, by the city. In the state-owned side is the **1850 House,** and at 540-B St. Peter Street on the city-owned side is a plaque marking this apartment as that of Sherwood Anderson, writer and mentor to William Faulkner. ✉ *French Quarter.*

㉘ **The Presbytère.** One of twin Spanish colonial–style buildings flanking
Fodor'sChoice   St. Louis Cathedral, this one, on the right, now holds an outstanding
★   exhibit on Mardi Gras. The building was originally designed to house the priests of the cathedral; instead, it served as a courthouse under the Spanish and later under the Americans. The Mardi Gras exhibit fills the first two floors with hundreds of pieces of Carnival memorabilia, including elaborate costumes and jewelry. Interactive displays and videos illustrate the history of Mardi Gras in New Orleans and other parts of the state. ✉ *Jackson Sq., French Quarter* ☎ *504/568–6968* 💲 *$5* ☉ *Tues.–Sun. 9–5.*

㉕ **St. Louis Cathedral.** The oldest active cathedral in the United States, this church at the heart of the Old City is named for the 13th-century French king who led two crusades. The current building, which replaced two former structures destroyed by fire, dates from 1794, although it was remodeled and enlarged in 1851. The austere interior is brightened by murals covering the ceiling and stained-glass windows along the first floor. A tour guide is on hand to answer questions and lead complete tours. Pope John Paul II held a prayer service for clergy here during his New Orleans visit in 1987; to honor the occasion, the pedestrian mall in front of the cathedral was renamed Place Jean Paul Deux. Nearly every evening in December brings a free concert held inside the cathedral. The

CloseUp

MICAELA PONTALBA

EVERY LIFE HAS ITS LITTLE DRAMAS, but how many of us can claim lives dramatic enough to inspire an opera? The Baroness Micaela Almonester de Pontalba is in that rarefied number, albeit posthumously.

In 2003, on the 200th anniversary of the Louisiana Purchase, the New Orleans Opera Association commissioned an opera based on Pontalba's life and the mark she left on New Orleans. Although you can encounter Pontalba's legacy most readily in the Pontalba Buildings, those elegant brick apartment buildings lining Jackson Square, few are aware of the energies, efforts, and sagas that led from the time of the Louisiana Purchase to the eventual completion of these buildings, in 1851.

Micaela Almonaster was of Spanish stock, the daughter of the wealthy entrepreneur and developer Don Andres Almonester, who was instrumental in the creation of the Cabildo and Prebytère. Don Almonester died while Micaela was still young, but not before passing on to his daughter a passion for building and urban design. The rest of her life became a tale of the impact a single will can have upon an urban environment, as well as a tragedy-torn drama of international scope.

At the time of the Louisiana Purchase, in 1803, New Orleans was in cultural upheaval. Following a period under Spanish rule during the late 18th century, the French had re-acquired the colony— but only in time to sell it to the Americans. The blending of French and Spanish society was further complicated by the anticipated imposition of American laws and mores, so foreign to the population of New Orleans. Micaela Almonester was right in the middle of the confusion: daughter of Spanish gentry, she fell in love and married a Frenchman, who took her to Paris with his family to avoid coming under American rule in New Orleans.

Far from her New Orleans roots, the Baroness Pontalba found herself severely oppressed by her new family, and particularly her father-in-law, who took what he could of her wealth and tormented her with blame that she could not give him more. She lived for many years in extremely tense conditions, comforted only by her children. Her father-in-law's finances deteriorated, and in frustration he actually shot Micaela, four times, lodging two bullets in her chest but not killing her. When he turned the gun on himself (with more finite results), Micaela's life changed. She was able to re-access her inheritance and turn it to the building projects she had always dreamt of. In addition to New Orleans's Pontalba Buildings, she built the Hotel Pontalba in Paris, which today is the residence of the American Ambassador to France.

Micaela finally returned to New Orleans in the 1840s, in order to direct construction of the elegant apartment buildings that would complete the square her father had been so instrumental in developing during the previous century. The Pontalba Buildings, designed by James Gallier in the French style favored by Micaela, were dedicated in 1851 to great fanfare. Each building (one along each side of Jackson Square) contained 16 grand and lavishly detailed apartments; today you can gain an idea of the living style the residences afforded by visiting the 1850 House.

Somewhat incredibly, following the dedication of the buildings, Pontalba returned to France. She had been living in Paris for nearly 50 years by now, her children had grown up there, and it had become her home. Yet the pilgrimage she had made to New Orleans, in order to complete a dream in the name of her father's memory, hints that her heart had never really left her childhood home.

statue of the Sacred Heart of Jesus dominates **St. Anthony's Garden,** which extends behind the rectory to Royal Street. The garden is also the site of a monument to 30 members of a French ship who died in a yellow fever epidemic in 1857. ⊠*615 Père Antoine Alley, French Quarter* ☎*504/ 525–9585* 💳 *Free* ☉ *Tours Mon.–Sat. 9–4:30, Sun. 1–4:30.*

❷❹ **Washington Artillery Park.** This raised concrete area on the river side of Decatur Street, directly across from Jackson Square, is a great spot to photograph the square and the barges and paddle wheelers on the Mississippi. The cannon mounted in the center and pointing toward the river is a model 1861 Parrot Rifle used in the Civil War. This monument honors the local 141st Field Artillery of the Louisiana National Guard that saw action from the Civil War through World War II. Marble tablets at the base give the history of the group, represented today by the Washington Artillery Association. ⊠ *Decatur St. between St. Peter and St. Ann Sts., French Quarter.*

❸❸ **Woldenberg Riverfront Park.** This stretch of green from Canal Street to Esplanade Avenue overlooks the Mississippi River as it curves around New Orleans, giving the city the name the Crescent City. The wooden promenade section in front of Jackson Square is called **Moon Walk,** named for Mayor Moon Landrieu, under whose administration in the 1970s the riverfront beyond the flood wall was first opened to public view. Erected in 2003, the modest **Holocaust Memorial** has a spiral walkway clad in Jerusalem stone. At the center of the spiral are nine sculptures by Jewish artist Yaacov Agam. Woldenberg Park is named for its benefactor, local businessman Malcolm Woldenberg, whose statue is in the park. *Ocean Song,* a large kinetic sculpture near the statue of Woldenberg, was created by local artist John T. Scott. ⊠ *French Quarter.*

FAUBOURG MARIGNY & BYWATER

The Faubourg Marigny, across Esplanade Avenue from the French Quarter, was developed in the early 1800s by wealthy planter Bernard de Marigny. With architectural styles ranging from classic Creole cottage to Victorian mansion, the Marigny is in effect a residential extension of the Quarter. The streets are more peaceful and the rents a bit cheaper, attracting musicians, artists, and other downtown types. Frenchmen Street is the main strip here, lined with music clubs, shops, coffeehouses, and restaurants. All the streets in the Marigny are narrow and intersect at odd angles; look for street names in inlaid tiles at corners. The Bywater, a crumbling yet beautiful old neighborhood across Elysian Fields, is a haven to those musicians and artists who find even the Marigny too expensive and overrun. The New Orleans Center for Creative Arts (NOCCA) occupies a beautiful campus of renovated warehouses here. Although you won't find the head-swiveling density of sights here that you will in the French Quarter, a tour through the Faubourg Marigny and especially the Bywater gives you a feel for New Orleans as it lives day to day, in a colorful, overgrown, slightly sleepy cityscape reminiscent of island communities and tinged with a sense of perpetual decay.

Numbers in the text correspond to numbers in the margin and on the French Quarter and Faubourg Marigny map.

a good walk

Begin at the intersection of **Esplanade Avenue and Chartres Street** ☛. Enter the Faubourg Marigny along Chartres, veering right at Kerlerec Street. The next corner, Chartres and Frenchmen streets, is the hub of the Marigny, shared by Café Brasil, a hip music club, and the Praline Connection, a purveyor of popular soul food. Ahead on Chartres, the studio of popular local artist Michalopoulos provides a glimpse of his recent work in the front windows, although the interior is not open to the public. Turn left onto Frenchmen Street and watch for local institutions including Bicycle Michael's, essential stop for biking enthusiasts looking for advice, and the famed Snug Harbor, where top-notch jazz acts headline nightly. A smattering of bars and clubs and a local coffee shop round out the scene.

As you cross Royal Street, you come under the influence of the broad **Washington Square Park** ➌, especially popular among dogs and their owners. Continue down Frenchmen and turn left onto Burgundy Street. Halfway down the block on your left is Sun Oak, a brick-between-post cottage dating from 1806, when this neighborhood was Bernard de Marigny's plantation. Fresh bright red, yellow, and blue paint highlight the building's structure. The distinguished brick edifice on your right at the next corner is the former Canal Commercial Trust Savings Bank, now a studio space for artists. Across the street, faded lettering above the entrance to a long-closed shop called shoppers of old to "Shop at Blaise's." The bank and Blaise's hint at the commercial activity that once animated this residential district. Turn left onto Touro Street, past Blaise's. Coming up on your right, a small corner cottage houses La Peniche, early-morning restaurant of choice among club-hoppers and musicians on their way home from gigs. Turn left again, onto Dauphine Street, and follow it back past Washington Square Park and across Elysian Fields Avenue.

The neighborhood you are now entering is the Lower Marigny, quieter and less polished than its counterpart across Elysian Fields. Halfway down the first block on your left, the tiny, whitewashed Beacon Baptist Church looms over the sidewalk. Two blocks farther, a crumbling old factory has been turning out Hubig's pies since 1922. Once popular throughout the South, the New Orleans factory is today the last remaining trace of the grand visions of founder Simon Hubig.

Continue on Dauphine Street to Spain Street and turn right to encounter more candy-color cottages. Turn left onto Chartres Street; one block ahead is Franklin Street, the commercial hub of the Lower Marigny. Beyond Franklin Street, Chartres leads you past a hip new coffee shop before arriving at the fabulous modern campus of the **New Orleans Center for the Creative Arts (NOCCA)**. During school hours, you can enter the red gateway on facing Chartres and tour the impressive grounds and buildings, adapted from old warehouses. Just outside NOCCA, working railroad tracks testify to the industrial heritage of this area and mark the official border of the Bywater District. Continuing along Chartres, **Dr. Bob's** studio and shop is just beyond Montegut Street, through a broad dirt lot on the left. Turn away from the river on Montegut Street to visit the gallery and active studio of **Studio Inferno Glassworks.** Leaving Studio Inferno, those who are charmed by the Bywater and want to see more should head right on Royal. You will soon encounter the barbecue joints, Irish pubs, and local shops that cater to this diverse neighborhood—not to mention increasingly colorful cottages and shotgun houses. Dauphine Street near Louisa Street is especially active.

When you are ready to start your return trip, head left on Royal outside Studio Inferno. As you recross the railroad tracks, the steeple off to your right belongs to the now-abandoned Holy Trinity Church, founded in 1847 to serve the German immigrants who peopled this district. You will pass Flora's Coffee—a bohemian favorite—as you cross Franklin Street. Ahead on Royal, Nos. 2438 and 2446, now a welcoming guesthouse, were once a palatial private residence (No. 2438) and a corner grocery (No. 2446). Arriving back at Elysian Fields, peer through the fence at the lovely **American Aquatic Gardens** ❸❼ on your left. The entrance is around the corner, on Elysian Fields.

TIMING   You can walk the Marigny in an hour. The Bywater is far more spread out; either bike it or limit your rambling to the blocks around NOCCA. The entire walk will take more than two hours. If you're planning to club-hop with the locals, Frenchmen Street clubs come alive after 10 PM.

Sights to See

❸❼ **American Aquatic Gardens.** A commercial nursery and boutique gift shop, this small but wonderfully relaxing garden invites walks past grasses, reeds, flowers, and sculptures. Dozens of artistic fountains add pleasant water sounds. You're not pressured to buy anything. ✉ *621 Elysian Fields, Faubourg Marigny* ☎ *504/944–0410* ⊕ *www. americanaquaticgardens.com* ⊙ *Daily 9–5.*

need a break?   **Sound Cafe** (✉ 2700 Chartres St., Faubourg Marigny ☎ 504/947–8358), a new addition to the Marigny/Bywater arts scene, serves coffee, tea, and snacks under the gaze of local artworks. The building dates to 1835 and for many years was a grocery store.

Christopher Porché-West Galerie. This working studio and exhibit space holds the assemblages and other creations of Porché-West and, occasionally, other local artists. The atmosphere depends on the current vigor of Porché-West's activities: sometimes it is more work oriented, sometimes more formally set up for exhibits. The gallery occupies an old pharmacy storefront, and it is open whenever the artist happens to be in, or by appointment. ✉ *3201 Burgundy St., Bywater* ☎ *504/947–3880* ⊕ *www.porche-west.com.*

Dr. Bob. This small compound of artists' and furniture-makers' studios includes the headquarters of Dr. Bob, beloved local folk artist. His shop is chock-full of original furniture, colorful signs, and unidentifiable objects of artistic fancy. A raised interior patio affords a beautiful view of the river. Bring a cup of coffee and have a seat at the window. The sign outside advertises the open hours: "By chance or appointment." ✉ *3027 Chartres St., Bywater* ☎ *504/945–2225.*

off the
beaten
path

JELLY ROLL MORTON HOUSE – Jazz enthusiasts will want to follow Frenchmen Street beyond the borders of the Marigny to pay homage to Jelly Roll Morton at the pianist and composer's modest former home, now a private residence with nary a plaque to suggest its import. Morton was a Creole of color (free African-American of mixed race), a clear distinction from darker blacks in those days; Morton himself always explained his roots as French. Though rather affluent when Morton lived here, the neighborhood has since declined; plan to take a car or taxi here. ⊠ *1443 Frenchmen St.*

Mercury Injection Studio Arts. Glassworks, mirrors, and paintings fill this tiny studio of artist Michael Cain. Don't be discouraged if the doors are closed: knock, and if Michael is around you're in for a show as he blows his fanciful pieces into existence. Visits by appointment are also available. ⊠ *727 Louisa St., Bywater* ☎ *504/723–6397* ⊕ *www. michaelcainarts.com* ☜ *Free.*

Fodor'sChoice **New Orleans Center for Creative Arts (NOCCA).** Many of New Orleans's
★ most talented young musicians, artists, and writers pass through this high-school arts program, where the faculty includes professional artists from around the country. Although the school covers all major artistic disciplines, the music program has been particularly successful: well-known alums include Donald Harrison, Terence Blanchard, Harry Connick Jr., and four or five Marsalises. The capacious modern campus, derived from abandoned 19th-century riverside warehouses, was completed in 2000. At one point, this conglomeration of structures served as a freight terminal for cotton; today it's filled with state-of-the-art equipment and surrounded by industrial chic. During school hours, you can wander the welcoming grounds. With luck, you might happen upon a free performance or art showing. ⊠ *2800 Chartres St., Faubourg Marigny* ☎ *504/ 940–2800* ⊕ *www.nocca.com.*

need a
break?

Café Rose Nicaud (⊠ 634 Frenchmen St., Faubourg Marigny ☎ 504/949–3300 ⊕ www.pjscoffee.com) is a neighborhood hangout that serves hot and iced coffee or tea, sandwiches, salads, and pastries. It is also a good place to people-watch from sidewalk tables.

Studio Inferno Glassworks. This working studio gives demonstrations of glassblowing and glass casting and sells the results in its gallery. The whole operation occupies a spacious red warehouse in the heart of the Bywater. ⊠ *3000 Royal St., Bywater* ☎ *504/945–1878* ☜ *Free* ☉ *Weekdays 9–5, Sat. 10–5.*

③⑥ **Washington Square Park.** This park provides a large green space in which to play Frisbee or catch some sun. The far side of the park borders Elysian Fields, named for Paris's Champs-Élysées. Though it never achieved the grandeur of its French counterpart, Elysian Fields is a major thoroughfare. Small-scale festivals or events sometimes take place here. ⊠ *Bordered by Royal, Dauphine, and Frenchmen Sts. and Elysian Fields, Faubourg Marigny.*

TREMÉ

Across Rampart Street from the French Quarter, the neighborhood of Tremé (pronounced truh-*may*) claims to be the oldest African-American neighborhood in the country. Once the site of the Claude Tremé plantation, it became home to many free people of color during the late 18th and early 19th centuries. Today Tremé is a vibrant and developing area, not exactly tailor-made for the tour bus but rewarding for the adventurous, who will find cottages in every color of the rainbow, small and large churches, Armstrong Park, and a couple of small museums. This is not a heavily touristed area. For the sake of safety, visit only during the day and follow the recommended walk.

a good walk

Begin at **St. Louis Cemetery No. 1** ➤, on Basin Street between Conti and St. Louis streets. You can get a feel for the cemetery during daylight by exploring the first few rows of tombs; avoid venturing too deep into the cemetery without a tour, as muggings are common. Housing projects line two sides of the cemetery; although the well-intentioned, town house–inspired design lends the projects a pleasant exterior, you should not explore more closely. Basin Street was the main drag of **Storyville,** the notorious red-light district of the early 20th century. Most structures were destroyed when Storyville was outlawed in 1917, but a few remain. Lulu White, one of Storyville's most famous madams, had her headquarters and saloon at 237 Basin Street; next door, at 1214 Bienville Street, Tony Jackson composed the classic Storyville song "Pretty Baby" at Frank Early's Saloon. The broad "neutral ground" (median) of Basin Street is graced by statues of Central American heroes Francisco Morazan and Benito Juarez.

Exiting the cemetery, turn left. One block dead ahead are the Municipal Auditorium, site of many Carnival balls, and the surrounding **Louis Armstrong Park.** Veer right with the road around the police station, and turn left onto Rampart Street. This was the raucous strip most readily evoked by the designation "Back o' Town" during the early jazz years. Though unmarked, the buildings on the far side of Rampart are of historical interest to the jazz buff. Cosimo Matassa's studio, where New Orleans R&B was born at the hands of Irma Thomas, Allen Toussaint, Dave Bartholemew, and Fats Domino, among others, was at 840 North Rampart Street. According to legend, Buddy Bolden worked at a barbershop on Rampart. Most addresses in this row saw a jazz-friendly nightclub come and go at some point. Two of the best spots to hear jazz today, the Funky Butt at Congo Square (named after Bolden's tune) and Donna's Bar & Grill (➪ Nightlife in Chapter 5), are at the corners of Orleans and St. Ann, respectively.

Louis Armstrong Park itself is rather undermaintained. However, if you want to set foot on the former site of Congo Square, where slaves once spent their precious Sunday afternoons of relative freedom, enter at St. Ann Street. The park also holds a number of memorials to local jazz artists, including Sidney Bechet and Jelly Roll Morton, as well as a former Masonic lodge, which dates from 1810. Work your way through the park toward the collection of small buildings on the downtown side; the structure housing the studios of WWOZ 90.7 FM, the local jazz and heritage radio station, once held the kitchen for the Masonic lodge. Beyond the OZ studio, a gateway deposits you onto St. Philip Street.

If you choose to bypass the park, turn left onto St. Philip Street from Rampart Street. From St. Philip you can see I–10, which was controversially planted in the middle of this neighborhood some decades ago. Head down St. Claude Street (the first street parallel to Rampart; street signs are scarce) away from the park; immediately you will notice that looser restrictions apply to this neighborhood than to the more heavily touristed French Quarter; the houses are painted in shades shocking to a cautious preservationist.

On the following block sit the small but bountiful **Backstreet Cultural Museum** and **St. Augustine Catholic Church.** Turn left onto Governor Nicholls Street to reach the lovely grounds of the **New Orleans African-American Museum,** a few blocks down. Returning back along Governor Nicholls from the museum, turn left onto Tremé Street and right onto Barracks Street to find one of the prettiest residential stretches in the neighborhood. Little People's Place is a tiny shack of a bar at number 1226—a neighborhood staple. As you reach Rampart Street again, you will see the sharp spire of the **Center of Jesus the Lord.** From here, turn along any street to reenter the French Quarter.

TIMING Plan an hour for the walk itself. Winding through St. Louis Cemetery, however, can easily consume another hour. If you plan to visit any of the small museums, allow a half hour for each.

Sights to See

★ **Backstreet Cultural Museum.** Local photographer and self-made historian Sylvester Francis is an enthusiastic guide through his own rich collection of Mardi Gras Indian costumes and other musical artifacts tied to the street traditions of New Orleans. Sylvester is also an excellent source for current musical goings-on in Tremé and throughout town. ⊠ *1116 St. Claude St., Tremé* ☎ *504/522–4806* ⊕ *www.backstreetculturalmuseum. com* ⊠ *$5* ☉ *Tues.–Sat. 10–5.*

Center of Jesus the Lord. This compound was a Carmelite cloister until 1975; nuns who entered the order never left the grounds of the monastery. Today it serves a Catholic-charismatic community, whose services include speaking in tongues. The beautiful jewel box of a chapel is adorned with stained glass honoring the Virgin and many patrons of the Carmelites, including Jacques Telesphore Roman, who built Oak Alley Plantation. The chapel can be viewed by passing through the courtyard and ringing the doorbell, or by attending one of the weekly services. ⊠ *1236 N. Rampart St., Tremé* ☎ *504/529–1636.*

J&M Music Shop. A plaque on this 1835 building marks it as the former site of the recording studio that launched the rock-and-roll careers of such greats as Fats Domino, Jerry Lee Lewis, Little Richard, and Ray Charles. It's one of the most significant musical landmarks in New Orleans. Owned by Cosimo Matassa, the studio operated from 1945 to 1955. ⊠ *840 N. Rampart St., Tremé.*

Louis Armstrong Park. This large park with its grassy knolls and lagoons is named for native son and world-famous musician Louis Armstrong (1900–71), whose statue by Elizabeth Catlett is near the brightly lighted entrance on the outer boundary of the French Quarter. To the left inside the park is **Congo Square,** marked by an inlaid-stone space where slaves in the 18th and early 19th centuries gathered on Sunday, the only time they were permitted to play their music openly. The weekly meetings held here have been immortalized in the travelogues of visitors, leaving invaluable insight into the earliest stages of free musical practices by Africans in America and African-Americans. Neighborhood musicians still congregate here at times for percussion jams, and it is difficult not to think of the musical spirit of ancestors hovering over them. Marie Laveau, the greatly feared and respected voodoo queen of antebellum New Orleans, had her home a block away on St. Ann Street, and is reported to have held voodoo rituals here regularly.

Behind Congo Square is a large gray building, the **Morris F. X. Jeff Municipal Auditorium,** and to the right behind the auditorium is the **Mahalia Jackson Center for the Performing Arts.** The complex of smaller buildings near the center of the park houses WWOZ, an FM radio station that broadcasts only New Orleans music and close relatives. The park is patrolled by a security detail, but be very careful when wandering, and do not visit after dark. ✉ *N. Rampart St. between St. Philip and St. Peter Sts., Tremé* ☺ *Auditorium and performing arts center open by event; check local newspapers for listings.*

New Orleans African-American Museum. Set in a historic villa surrounded by a lovely small park, this museum is a prime example of the West Indies–style, French-colonial architecture that used to fill much of the French Quarter. It was built in 1829 by Simon Meilleur, a prosperous brick maker: the main house was constructed with Meilleur's bricks, and the brick patio behind it bears imprints identifying the original manufacture. Inside, temporary exhibits spotlight African and African diaspora art and artists. ✉ *1418 Governor Nicholls St., Tremé* ☎ *504/565–7497* ⊕ *www. noaam.org* ▨ *$5* ☺ *Tues.–Fri. 9–5, Sat. 10-4.*

St. Augustine Catholic Church. Ursuline nuns donated the land for this church in 1841. Upon its completion in 1842, St. Augustine's became an integrated place of worship, with slaves relegated to the side pews but free blacks claiming just as much right to center pews as whites. The architect, J. N. B. de Pouilly, attended the École des Beaux-Arts in Paris and was known for his idiosyncratic style, which borrowed freely from a variety of traditions and resisted classification. Some of the ornamentation in his original drawings had to be eliminated when money ran out, but effusive pink-and-gold paint inside brightens the austere structure. The church is ordinarily locked outside service hours, but venture around the right side of the edifice and ring the rectory bell: if the lively and informative pastor Father LeDoux is around he will gladly bring you inside the church for a look. The Sunday-morning Mass, often of over two hours' duration, is a musical and spiritual treat. ✉ *1210 Governor Nicholls St., Tremé* ☎ *504/525–5934.*

A MUSIC HISTORY TOUR

THE BIRTHPLACE OF JAZZ IS A BANNER NEW ORLEANS WEARS WITH PRIDE. *In fact, it's hard to visit the city without seeing and hearing signs of the rich musical heritage that resonates through every street in town. Many of the city's most popular sights concern music, but other spots important to jazz history remain unmarked, and largely unvisited. The following list combines sights both on and off the beaten track.*

Backstreet Cultural Museum. *This tiny but fabulous museum brings together artifacts from the Mardi Gras Indian, brass band, and second line traditions.* ⊠ 1116 St. Claude Ave., Treme ☎ 504/522–4806. **Buddy Bolden's House.** *The most mysterious figure of early jazz, cornetist Buddy Bolden is the legendary originator of the "hot" sound that came to be associated with jazz. He lived and played across St. Charles Avenue from the Garden District.* ⊠ 2309 and 2527 First St., Uptown. **Congo Square.** *There is no single spot in New Orleans that argues as strongly for the link between this city and jazz as Congo Square. Louis Armstrong Park, on the northern edge of the French Quarter, now contains this zone that, during the 1700s and 1800s, was reserved on Sunday for slaves seeking entertainment on their day off. Sharing a common language of music, rhythm, and dance, they helped linked African tribal drumming rituals to jazz.* ⊠ N. Rampart St., between St. Philip and St. Peter Sts. Treme. **Jazz National Historic Park.** *A major, permanent exhibit on the history of jazz is underway in Louis Armstrong Park. Until the permanent quarters are ready, this temporary office shows informational videos, sells books and some recordings, and hosts small concerts on Saturday afternoons.* ⊠ 916 N. Peters St., French Quarter ☎ 504/589–4841. **Jelly Roll Morton's House.** *The legendary pianist, who blurred the line between ragtime and jazz, lived in a mixed-race neighborhood. A "Creole of color," Morton always described his roots as French.* ⊠ 1443 Frenchmen St. **Lincoln Park and Johnson Park.** *Buddy Bolden, his rival John Robichaux, and countless other important early jazzmen played at these contiguous recreational areas popular with African-Americans at the turn of the 20th century. No structures or markers indicate the rich history here, but true aficionados will want to set foot on the hallowed ground. The site of the parks is Uptown, in a low-income neighborhood known as Gert Town.* ⊠ Bounded by S. Carrollton Ave., Forshey St., Fern St., and Oleander St. **Louis Armstrong's birthplace.** *The man who would bring jazz to the world was born in the poorest of circumstances, in a neighborhood now consumed by the Orleans Parish Prison and associated buildings. The house itself has been long since demolished, but the legendary address still draws fans and historians to the area where it once stood.* ⊠ 723 Jane Alley, Mid-City. **Old Mint.** *A small but rich exhibit on the evolution of New Orleans jazz is housed upstairs and includes the original instruments of many jazz greats.* ⊠ 400 Esplanade Ave. French Quarter ☎ 504/568–6968. **Old Algiers.** *During the early jazz era, many musicians lived in this quiet neighborhood across the Mississippi River from the French Quarter, crossing the river by boat for downtown gigs. You can pick up a complete list of musician residences and other landmarks at the Algiers Library.* **Perdido Street.** *Perdido Street, above South Rampart, was the hotspot for clubs and shops at the turn of the 20th century. Buddy Bolden, Buck Johnson, and Louis Armstrong all frequented this area as they were coming up. The Odd Fellows and Masonic Hall (1116 Perdido St.), at the corner of Rampart, was the site of many dances in the early 20th century.*

➤ **St. Louis Cemetery No. 1.** New Orleans's "cities of the dead," with rows of crypts like little houses, are some of the city's most enduring images. This cemetery, the oldest in the city, is an example of the aboveground burial practices of the French and Spanish. Because of the high water table, it was difficult to bury bodies underground without having the coffin float to the surface after the first hard rain. Modern-day burial methods permit underground interment, but many people prefer these ornate family tombs and vaults, which have figured in several movies, among them *Easy Rider*. Buried here are such notables as Etienne Boré, father of the sugar industry; Homer Plessy of the *Plessy v. Ferguson* 1892 U.S. Supreme Court decision establishing the separate but equal "Jim Crow" laws for African-Americans and whites in the South (he was baptized and married in nearby St. Augustine Church); and Marie Laveau, voodoo queen. Her tomb is marked with Xs freshly chalked by those who still believe in her supernatural powers.

A second Marie Laveau, believed to be her daughter, is buried in **St. Louis Cemetery No. 2,** four blocks beyond this cemetery, on Claiborne Avenue. **St. Louis Cemetery No. 3** is at the end of Esplanade Avenue, a good drive from here (⇨ Bayou St. John and Mid-City). Although these cemeteries are open to the public, it is dangerous to enter them alone because of frequent muggings inside; group tours are a rational option. **Save Our Cemeteries** (☎ 504/525–3377) leads tours every Sunday at 10 AM or by group appointment, departing from Royal Blend Coffee House at 621 Royal Street. Tickets are $12; reserve by Friday afternoon to be sure of a spot on the tour. ⊠ *Cemetery No. 1: Basin and Conti Sts., Tremé* ⊙ *Daily 9–3.*

Storyville. The legitimized red-light district that lasted from 1897 to 1917 has been destroyed, and in its place stands a public housing project. Storyville spawned splendid Victorian homes that served as brothels and provided a venue for the raw sounds of ragtime and early jazz; an extremely young Louis Armstrong cut his teeth in some of the clubs here. The world's first electrically lighted saloon, Tom Anderson's House of Diamonds, was at the corner of Basin and Bienville streets, and the whole area has been the subject of many novels, songs, and films. In 1917, after several incidents involving naval officers, the government ordered the district shut down. Some buildings were razed almost overnight; the housing project was built in the 1930s. Only a historical marker on the "neutral ground" (median) of Basin Street remains to mark alderman Sidney Story's experiment in legalized prostitution. ⊠ *Basin St. next to St. Louis Cemetery No. 1, Tremé.*

CBD & WAREHOUSE DISTRICT

The Warehouse District is one of the most rewarding areas of the city for visitors. Bordered by the river, St. Charles Avenue, Poydras Street, and Andrew Higgins Drive and filled with former factories and warehouse buildings, the area has exploded over the past decade. In 1984 the city hosted the World's Fair on this site. Old abandoned warehouse buildings were renovated to match the fair, and consequently set the scene for future development. Today, the neighborhood is dotted with modern renovations of historic buildings, excellent eateries, a growing number of bars and music clubs, and a host of contemporary art galleries as well as the National D-Day Museum, the Ogden Museum of Southern Art, and the Contemporary Arts Center. These larger museums sit outside the neighborhood's original center of activity, farther from the river and near Lee Circle, but the Warehouse District's borders have expanded to accommodate its growing influence and spirit while managing to hold on to that feeling of decay so peculiarly charming in New Orleans.

The Central Business District (CBD) covers the ground between Canal Street and Poydras Avenue, with some spillover into the Warehouse District's official territory. Some of the old government and office buildings, especially those around Lafayette Square, are quite beautiful.

Numbers in the text correspond to numbers in the margin and on the CBD & Warehouse District map.

a good walk

Start at the foot of Poydras Street, site of the Riverwalk shopping mall, the World Trade Center, and Harrah's New Orleans casino. Walk three blocks up Poydras and turn left onto South Peters Street to enter the heart of the Warehouse District. In the first block on your right is the **American Italian Renaissance Foundation Museum and Library ❶** ▶, an important force in the local Italian-American community. Ernst Cafe, the appealing bar with the wraparound balcony at the next corner, has been serving libations since 1905.

Turning right onto Lafayette Street, you can get a peek at the **Piazza d'Italia ❷**, a seminal, if crumbling, work of modernist architecture, which backs onto the American-Italian Renaissance Foundation. As you cross Tchoupitoulas Street, look to your right: the diner at the corner of Poydras is Mother's, a local favorite for po'boys. A block farther along, Lafayette Street lands you in the midst of government buildings and law offices. Directly ahead is the imposing **John Minor Wisdom United States Court of Appeals Building ❸**. Walk along the right side of this Italianate building to reach Lafayette Square, a park named for the French and American Revolutionary hero. A block to your left is **St. Patrick's Church ❹**, built in the early 19th century to serve the Irish-American community. Stroll across Lafayette Square to admire **Gallier Hall ❺**, perhaps the finest example of Greek Revival architecture in the city. Immediately after Christmas, bleachers go up along the Gallier Hall edge of the park, blocking access to the street—this is in anticipation of the Mardi Gras parades, many of which pass Gallier Hall and stop here to toast the mayor. Turn left onto St. Charles Avenue. Several blocks directly ahead is the commanding statue of General Robert E. Lee, standing high above the **Lee Circle ❻** traffic roundabout.

Two blocks ahead is Julia Street, the main gallery strip in the neighborhood. Turn left and walk to the 600 block, which is dominated by the Thirteen Sisters—13 redbrick row houses. Peer into these and the buildings across the street to find specialty galleries and shops. A detour to your right at Camp Street will take you to a rich group of mu-

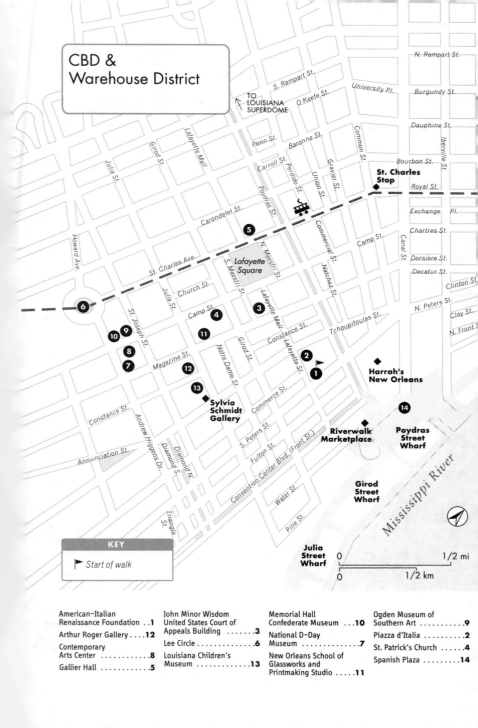

CBD & Warehouse District

TO
LOUISIANA
SUPERDOME

N. Rampart St.

S. Rampart St.

University Pl.

Burgundy St.

Penn St.

O. Keefe St.

Baronne St.

Common St.

Dauphine St.

Girod St.

Lafayette Mall

Carroll St.

Perdido St.

Gravier St.

Bourbon St.

Iberville St.

St. Charles
Stop

Royal St.

Julia St.

Poydras St.

Union St.

Exchange Pl.

Carondelet St.

⑤

N. Maestri St.

Commercial St.

Camp St.

Chartres St.

Canal St.

Dorsiere St.

Howard Ave.

St. Charles Ave.

Lafayette
Square

S. Maestri St.

Natchez St.

Decatur St.

Clinton St.

Church St.

Julia St.

⑥

Camp St.

④

③

Lafayette Mall

Constance St.

N. Peters St.

Clay St.

N. Front St.

St. Joseph St.

⑩ ⑨

⑪

Notre Dame St.

Girod St.

Tchoupitoulas St.

⑧

⑦

Magazine St.

⑫

Lafayette St.

②

①

Harrah's
New Orleans

Constance St.

Andrew Higgins Dr.

⑬

Sylvia
Schmidt
Gallery

Commerce St.

Diamond N.

Diamond S.

Annunciation St.

S. Peters St.

Fulton St.

Convention Center Blvd. (Front St.)

Riverwalk
Marketplace

Poydras
Street
Wharf

⑭

Spanish Plaza

Water St.

Girod
Street
Wharf

Mississippi River

Triangle St.

Pilie St.

Julia
Street
Wharf

0   1/2 mi

0   1/2 km

KEY

▶ Start of walk

American-Italian
Renaissance Foundation ..**1**

Arthur Roger Gallery **12**

Contemporary
Arts Center **8**

Gallier Hall **5**

John Minor Wisdom
United States Court of
Appeals Building **3**

Lee Circle **6**

Louisiana Children's
Museum **13**

Memorial Hall
Confederate Museum ...**10**

National D-Day
Museum **7**

New Orleans School of
Glassworks and
Printmaking Studio **11**

Ogden Museum of
Southern Art **9**

Piazza d'Italia **2**

St. Patrick's Church **4**

Spanish Plaza **14**

seums around Lee Circle, including the **National D-Day Museum ❼**, the **Contemporary Arts Center ❽**, the **Ogden Museum of Southern Art ❾**, and the **Memorial Hall Confederate Museum ❿**. As you continue along Julia Street you pass some of the city's finest contemporary art galleries. At Magazine Street, the **New Orleans School of Glassworks and Printmaking Studio ⓫** is a few doors to your left. The **Arthur Roger Gallery ⓬**, the **Louisiana Children's Museum ⓭**, and the Sylvia Schmidt Gallery occupy the 400 block of Julia. At the next corner stands celebrity chef Emeril Lagasse's flagship restaurant, Emeril's; stop in for a drink or a sampling of his imaginative neo-Creole cuisine.

To your right at South Peters Street, the Howlin' Wolf music club shares a block-long stretch of warehouses filled with eateries and drinking holes. After another two blocks, Julia Street ends at Convention Center Boulevard; the mammoth structure to your right is the Ernest N. Morial Convention Center. Cross Convention Center Boulevard and follow the footpath to the uptown end of the Riverwalk shopping center, which you can follow back to **Spanish Plaza ⓮** and the World Trade Center. An outdoor promenade, which bypasses some of the shops, affords a pleasant stroll and an intimate view of river culture. You can also return to Spanish Plaza along Convention Center Boulevard.

TIMING   The Warehouse District covers 47 blocks; unlike those in the French Quarter, sights in this area are fairly spread out. If you plan to tour entirely on foot, you should invest a full day. The D-Day Museum will take two hours; the Contemporary Arts Center and other Lee Circle museums each take a bit less time, depending on your level of interest. Be sure to allow time to browse in the smaller galleries and to enjoy the broad, spacious layout of streets imposed by the warehouses themselves.

Sights to See

► ❶ **American-Italian Renaissance Foundation Museum and Library.** Italian–New Orleans customs are explained and artifacts exhibited in this small, carefully curated museum. The research library includes records of the large local Italian immigrant community. ☒ *537 S. Peters St., Warehouse District* ☎ *504/522-7294* ⊕ *www.airf.org* ☜ *Free* ☉ *Wed.–Fri. 10–3, Sat. 10–2.*

❶❷ **Arthur Roger Gallery.** A highlight among Julia Street galleries, this gallery showcases quality contemporary art, primarily by local and regional artists. ☒ *432 Julia St., Warehouse District* ☎ *504/522-1999* ⊕ *www.artroger. com* ☉ *Tues.–Sat. 10–5.*

❽ **Contemporary Arts Center.** Founded in 1976, the center has endured long, hard years of economic and cultural stagnation, and it takes great satisfaction in the Warehouse District gallery scene it has helped to spawn. The center showcases temporary exhibits, often featuring local or regional artists but also welcoming the work of national and international talent. The CAC theater hosts experimental and conventional concerts, films, dance, plays, and lectures. ☒ *900 Camp St., Warehouse District* ☎ *504/528-3805, 504/528-3800 theater box office* ⊕ *www. cacno.org* ☜ *$5, free Thurs.* ☉ *Tues.–Sun. 11–5.*

need a
break? In the Contemporary Arts Center, the modernistic cybercafé **N. O. Net Cafe** (✉ 900 Camp St., Warehouse District ☎ 504/523–0990) mixes lunch and cocktails with the usual coffee fare.

❺ Gallier Hall. This Greek Revival building, modeled on the Erectheum of Athens, was built in 1845 by architect James Gallier Sr. It served as City Hall in the mid-20th century. Today it hosts special events and is the mayor's official perch during Mardi Gras parades; the kings and queens of many parades stop here to be toasted by the mayor and dignitaries and to receive the key to the city. The grand rooms inside the hall are adorned with portraits and decorative details ordered by Gallier from Paris. ✉ *545 St. Charles Ave. (entrance on the side at 705 Lafayette St.), CBD* ☎ *504/565–7457 or 504/565–6023* ☉ *Weekdays 9:30–noon and 2–5; visits by appointment.*

Harrah's New Orleans. The only land-based casino in Louisiana, Harrah's contains 175,000 square feet of space divided into five areas, each with a New Orleans theme: Jazz Court, Court of Good Fortune, Smugglers Court, Mardi Gras Court, and Court of the Mansion. ✉ *512 S. Peters St., CBD* ☎ *504/533–6000 or 800/427–7247* ⊕ *www.harrahs. com/our_casinos/nor* ☉ *Daily 24 hrs.*

❸ John Minor Wisdom United States Court of Appeals Building. New York architect James Gamble Rogers was summoned to design this three-story granite structure as a post office and court building in 1909. By the 1960s the post office had moved to larger digs, and McDonough No. 35 High School found refuge here after Hurricane Betsy in 1965. Today the Renaissance Revival building houses the Fifth Circuit Court of Appeals in an elaborately paneled and ornamented series of courtrooms. The dark, cool corridors of the ground floor have an arcaded, bronzed ceiling. As you enter the building and pass security, turn left and continue around the corner to find the library, where you can pick up information on the courthouse. Outside, a repeating sculpture of four women stands on each corner of the building: the four ladies represent History, Agriculture, Industry, and the Arts. The building is named for Judge John Minor Wisdom, the New Orleans native who was instrumental in dismantling the segregation laws of the South. Judge Wisdom received the Presidential Medal of Freedom in 1993. ✉ *600 Camp St., CBD* ☎ *504/ 310–7777* ☉ *Weekdays 8–5.*

Julia Street. Contemporary art dealers have adopted this strip in the Warehouse District as their own. The street is lined with galleries, flower shops, and modern apartment buildings. The first Saturday evening of each month gallery owners throw open their doors to show off new exhibits, to the accompaniment of wine, music, and general merriment.

❻ Lee Circle. At the northern edge of the Warehouse District, a bronze statue of Civil War general Robert E. Lee stands high above the city on a white marble column in a traffic circle. Lee faces due north, as he has since 1884. Recent extensive renovation and new construction have greatly improved the area immediately around the circle, which now includes the **Contemporary Arts Center**, the **Ogden Museum of**

Southern Art, the National D-Day Museum, and the **Memorial Hall Confederate Museum.**

🐾 **⑬** **Louisiana Children's Museum.** An invaluable resource for anyone traveling with kids, the top-notch Children's Museum is fun and educational. Favorite activities include a mini–grocery store, with both carts and registers manned by visitors, and a giant bubble station. A welcoming environment is provided for children with disabilities: most exhibits are accessible, and some are aimed directly at increasing healthy children's awareness of the disabilities of others. Art teachers lead classes daily; a theater hosts morning programs; and special activities such as jewelry making and storytelling are held each week. A special indoor playground is reserved for toddlers age three and under. There's also a mini–fitness center with a kid-size stationary bicycle and rock-climbing wall. ✉ *420 Julia St., Warehouse District* ☎ *504/523–1357* ⊕ *www. lcm.org* 🖾 *$6* ⊗ *Late Aug.–early June, Tues.–Sat. 9:30–4:30, Sun. noon–4:30; early June–late Aug., Mon.–Sat. 9:30–4:30, Sun. noon–4:30 (last ticket sold at 4).*

off the beaten path

LOUISIANA SUPERDOME – A national sports facility, the site of many Sugar Bowls and a number of Super Bowls, and home to the New Orleans Saints football team, the Superdome seats up to 100,000 people and is one of the largest buildings of its kind in the world. Built in 1975, it has a 166,000-square-foot playing field and a roof that covers almost 8 acres at a height of 27 stories. The bronze statue on the Poydras Street side is the Vietnam Veterans Memorial. The New Orleans Arena, behind the Superdome, is home to the NBA New Orleans Hornets, the New Orleans Brass minor-league hockey team, and Tulane University's basketball team. Across from the Superdome on Poydras Street is a large abstract sculpture called the *Krewe of Poydras.* The sculptor, Ida Kohlmeyer, meant to evoke the frivolity and zany spirit of Mardi Gras. A good walk (six long blocks) down Poydras Street from St. Charles Avenue brings you to the Superdome. Along the way you will pass the Bloch Cancer Survivors Monument, a block-long walkway of whimsical columns, figures, and a triumphal arch in the median of Loyola Avenue at its intersection with Poydras Street. The streets around the Superdome and Civic Center are usually busy during business hours, but at night and on weekends, except during a game, this area should not be explored alone. ✉ *1 Sugar Bowl Dr., CBD* ☎ *504/587–3663* ⊕ *www.superdome.com.*

need a break?

Louisiana Products Deli and Grocery (✉ 618 Julia St., Warehouse District ☎ 504/529–1666), a sweet, old-fashioned grocery store in the midst of the galleries, sells inexpensive coffee and sandwiches and has a few small tables at which to enjoy them.

The brightly decorated bar and dining room inside **Lucy's Retired Surfers Restaurant and Bar** (✉ 701 Tchoupitoulas St., Warehouse District ☎ 504/523–8995 ⊕ www.lucysretiredsurfers.com), open from 11 AM until late, provide a nice spot for a beer, a cup of coffee, or a southwestern snack. During happy hour the bar fills up with young lawyers and paralegals who work in the area.

🔟 **Memorial Hall Confederate Museum.** This ponderous stone building at Lee Circle was built in 1891 to house a collection of artifacts from the Civil War, making it the oldest museum in the state. The displays include uniforms, flags, and soldiers' personal effects. ☒ *929 Camp St., Warehouse District* ☎ *504/523–4522* ⊕ *www.confederatemuseum.com* 🎟 *$5* ⊘ *Mon.–Sat. 10–4.*

⑦ National D-Day Museum. The brainchild of historian and writer Dr.
Fodor'sChoice Stephen Ambrose, who taught for many years at the University of New
★ Orleans until his death in 2002, this moving, well-executed examination of World War II covers far more ground than simply the 1944 D-Day invasion of Normandy. The seminal moments are re-created through propaganda posters and radio clips from the period; biographical sketches of the military personnel involved; a number of short documentary films (including one bitterly sad film on the Holocaust, featuring interviews with survivors); and collections of weapons, personal items, and other artifacts from the war. The exhibits occupy a series of galleries spread through the interior of a huge warehouse space. One spotlighted exhibit, in a large, open portion of the warehouse near the entrance, is a replica of the Higgins boat troop landing craft, which were manufactured in New Orleans. ☒ *925 Magazine St. (main entrance on Andrew Higgins Dr.), Warehouse District* ☎ *504/527–6012* ⊕ *www. ddaymuseum.org* 🎟 *$10* ⊘ *Daily 9–5.*

⊙ ⑪ **New Orleans School of Glassworks and Printmaking Studio.** A fun family stop, the School of Glassworks gives demonstrations of all stages of glassmaking and design, printmaking, and silver alchemy in a large warehouse space. A shop and gallery up front displays and sells the finished products. ☒ *727 Magazine St., Warehouse District* ☎ *504/529–7277* ⊕ *www.neworleansglassworks.com* ⊘ *June–Aug., weekdays 11–5; Sept.–May, Mon.–Sat. 11–5.*

⑨ **Ogden Museum of Southern Art.** The very premise behind this exciting new addition to the Warehouse District arts scene, and the latest among the superb cluster of museums just off Lee Circle, begs the question: what is southern art? The answer lies inside, where art by southerners, art made in the South, art about the South, artistic explorations into southern themes, and more fill this elegant new building. More than 1,200 works collected by local developer Roger Ogden since the 1960s are on display. A central stair hall filters natural light through the series of galleries, and a rooftop patio affords lovely views of the surrounding area. The gift shop sells crafts by local artists. ☒ *925 Camp St., Warehouse District* ☎ *504/539–9600* ⊕ *www.ogdenmuseum.org* 🎟 *$10* ⊘ *Tues.–Sun. 9:30–5:30 (Thurs. until 8:30).*

❷ **Piazza d'Italia.** This modern plaza by architect Charles Moore is a gathering place for the large Italian community on St. Joseph's Day and Columbus Day. Its postmodern style is reminiscent of a Roman ruin. On the South Peters Street side of the piazza is the **American-Italian Museum.**

Riverwalk Marketplace. This three-block-long shopping-and-entertainment center with 140 shops and eateries is laid out in three tiers and lined in places by a promenade along the river's edge. Plaques along the walkway relate bits of the Mississippi River's history and folklore. Nearby at the Poydras Street streetcar stop is a grand splash of color, a 200-foot-long Mexican mural on the flood wall. The tropical motifs were created by Julio Quintanilla, and the mural is a gift to New Orleans from Mérida, Mexico, the artist's native city. Various cruise ships leave from the Julia Street Wharf slightly upriver; you can often see them from the front of the Riverwalk. ⊠ *1 Poydras St., Warehouse District* ☎ *504/522–1555* ⊕ *www.riverwalkmarketplace.com* ⊙ *Mon.–Sat. 10–9, Sun. 11–7.*

❹ **St. Patrick's Church.** A stark exterior gives way to a far more ornate, richly painted interior in this first church built in the American sector of New Orleans, intended to provide the city's Irish Catholics with a place of worship as distinguished as the French St. Louis Cathedral. The vaulted interior was completed in 1838 by local architect James Gallier, who moved here from Ireland in 1834 in order to work on the cathedral. High stained-glass windows and huge murals, painted in 1841, enrich the interior. ⊠ *724 Camp St., Warehouse District* ☎ *504/525–4413.*

> **need a break?**
>
> **True Brew Café** (⊠ 200 Julia St., Warehouse District ☎ 504/524–8441) is a comfortable, low-key coffeehouse popular with locals, serving hearty sandwiches and breakfast dishes along with premium coffees and cocktails.
>
> **P. J.'s Coffee and Teas** (⊠ 644 Camp St., CBD ☎ 504/529–3658 ⊕ www.pjscoffee.com), a local chain serving delicious, cold-brewed iced coffee, has a small but pleasant location just off Lafayette Square.

❶❹ **Spanish Plaza.** For a terrific view of the river and a place to relax, go behind the **World Trade Center** at 2 Canal Street to Spanish Plaza, a large, sunken space with beautiful inlaid tiles and a magnificent fountain. The plaza was a gift from Spain in the mid-1970s; you can hear occasional live music played here and you can purchase tickets for riverboat cruises in the offices that face the river.

Sylvia Schmidt Gallery. The contemporary shows are always strong at this gallery, which hosts exhibits by both local and national artists. ⊠ *400A Julia St., Warehouse District* ☎ *504/522–2000* ⊙ *Tues.–Sat. 11–5.*

World Trade Center. Dozens of foreign consulates and many international trade offices are housed in this 33-floor building facing the river. 360° (☎ 504/595–8900), on the top floor, is a revolving nightclub that provides a great view of the city and river. Children under 21 are not admitted. The building is surrounded by statues and plazas: Winston Churchill is memorialized in a bronze statue in **British Park Place,** also known as Winston's Circle, where the stone-inlaid street curves in front of the Riverfront Hilton to the right; and a bronze equestrian statue of Bernardo de Galvez, Spanish governor of Louisiana in the 1780s, guards

the entrance of the **Spanish Plaza** behind the World Trade Center. ✉ 2
Canal St., CBD ☎ *504/529–1601.*

GARDEN DISTRICT

With its beautifully landscaped gardens surrounding elegant antebellum
homes, the Garden District lives up to its name. Very few buildings in
the neighborhood are open to the public on a regular basis, but the occupants do not mind your enjoying the sights from outside the cast-iron
fences surrounding their magnificent estates. What cannot be appreci-
ated from the outside of these mansions are the sumptuous, carefully
preserved interiors: ceilings as high as 22 feet, crystal chandeliers, hand-
painted murals, Italianate marble mantels and fireplaces, pine floors, spiral staircases, mahogany window and door frames, handmade
windowpanes, and elaborate carved moldings.

The area, originally the vast Livaudais Plantation, was laid out in
streets and blocks in the late 1820s. It remained part of the separate
city of Lafayette until incorporated into New Orleans in 1852. The district attracted wealthy Americans who were not welcome in the Creole sections of the city. Here they constructed homes in three basic
architectural styles: the three-bay, London-parlor, Greek Revival design;
the center-hall, columnar Greek Revival; and the raised cottage. Surrounding the houses were English-style landscaped gardens. As the Americans developed their own social life, the raised cottage and Greek Revival
prototypes were more elaborately expanded to provide for entertainment and ostentation.

The Garden District is divided into two sections by Jackson Avenue. Upriver from Jackson is the wealthy **Upper Garden District,** where the homes
are meticulously kept up. Below Jackson, the Lower Garden District is
considerably rougher, though the homes here are often structurally just
as beautiful. The streets are also less well patrolled; wander cautiously.
Magazine Street, lined with antiques shops and coffeehouses (ritzier along
the Upper Garden District, hipper along the Lower Garden District),
serves as a southern border to the Garden District. St. Charles Avenue
forms the northern border, and the **St. Charles Avenue streetcar** is a convenient way to get here from downtown. A number of companies offer
walking tours (⇨ Sightseeing Tours *in* Smart Travel Tips A to Z).

*Numbers in the text correspond to numbers in the margin and on the
Garden District map.*

Upper Garden District

One block from the streetcar stop at the intersection of Washington Avenue and Prytania Street is the **Rink ①** ►, a small shopping complex that
was once a roller-skating rink. Across Washington Avenue is the impressive
facade of the **Behrman Gym ②**. Walk down Washington Avenue toward
Coliseum Street: the 1600 block, on your right, is taken up by the
white-walled **Lafayette Cemetery No. 1 ③**. One of the grandest restaurants in New Orleans is Commander's Palace, across from the ceme-

*a good
walk*

Fodor'sChoice
★

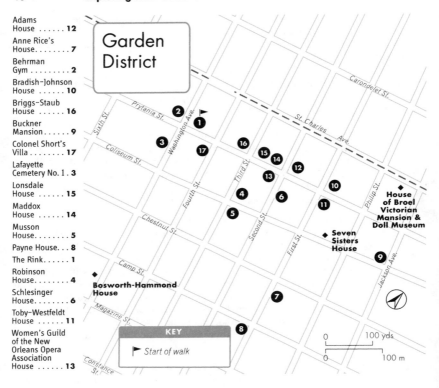

tery. Farther along Washington Avenue is the Bosworth-Hammond House, or "Bow-front Mansion."

Next, a stroll down Coliseum Street toward Jackson Avenue takes you past some of the most beautiful and historic homes in the South. At Coliseum and 3rd streets are the extravagant **Robinson House** ❹ and the **Musson House** ❺. The **Schlesinger House** ❻, to your left at 2nd Street, is a classic Greek Revival. Continuing along Coliseum, turn right and walk down 1st Street to see **Anne Rice's House** ❼ and the **Payne House** ❽, where Confederate president Jefferson Davis died. Returning to Coliseum Street, look toward Jackson Avenue to glimpse the triple ballroom of the **Buckner Mansion** ❾.

The blocks along both Philip and 1st streets, between Prytania and Coliseum, have many noteworthy homes. At First and Prytania streets you will find both the regal **Bradish-Johnson House** ❿, now a private girls' school, and the relatively modest **Toby-Westfeldt House** ⓫. At the corner of Second and Prytania is the predominantly Greek Revival **Adams House** ⓬, as well as the hybrid **Women's Guild of the New Orleans Opera Association House** ⓭, with its distinctive octagonal turret. The **Maddox House** ⓮, across the street, is an excellent example of the five-bay expansion of the basic Greek Revival model. Venture to your left down

Prytania Street, the main artery of the district. No expense was spared in the construction of the **Lonsdale House** ⓯, at Prytania and 3rd streets. Across 3rd, the **Briggs-Staub House** ⓰ is one of the few Gothic Revival houses in the city. Cross Prytania Street at the corner of 4th Street to **Colonel Short's Villa** ⓱, best known for its cornstalk fence.

To conclude the Garden District tour, walk down 4th Street to St. Charles Avenue, board the streetcar on the far side of the neutral ground (median), and continue up the avenue. Many more mansions along the route are of the same style and magnitude as those of the Garden District.

TIMING   You have so many beautiful things to observe along this walk that you should allow plenty of time for strolling and enjoying it all. Plan 1½ hours for the tour and another half hour for a refreshment stop. The streetcar ride from Canal Street takes approximately 25 minutes.

Sights to See

⓬ **Adams House.** The curved gallery on the left side of this circa-1860 house is a twist on the raised cottage theme. Greek Revival influence is evident in the columns and the windows. ⊠ *2423 Prytania St., Garden District.*

❼ **Anne Rice's House.** The famous novelist's elegant Garden District home is a three-bay Greek Revival, extended over a luxurious side yard. At the time of writing, she had moved and the house is up for sale. ⊠ *1239 1st St., Garden District.*

❷ **Behrman Gym.** This gym had the first indoor pool in the South, and was where John L. Sullivan trained when he fought "Gentleman Jim" Corbett. It dates from the turn of the 20th century, when it was the Southern Athletic Club. Today only the distinctive wooden facade remains. ⊠ *1500 Washington Ave., Garden District.*

Bosworth-Hammond House. Ice magnate A. J. Bosworth, who shipped ice to New Orleans from Maine, clearly embraced the competitive spirit among the local well-to-do when he built this house in 1859. It elaborates on the ubiquitous Greek Revival prototype by expanding the facade to five bays and two stories, as well as extending the front porch forward. This last detail earned Bosworth's house the nickname "Bow-front Mansion." Architect Thomas Wharton, who was also responsible for the Customs House downtown, laid out the house in an L shape, reportedly creating the first home in the city with juxtaposed dining room and kitchen. After nearly being condemned a few years back, the house is currently undergoing a painstaking restoration. ⊠ *1126 Washington St., Garden District.*

⓾ **Bradish-Johnson House.** A private girls' school since 1929, this regal building served as a residence when it was built in 1872. Though based on the common five-bay Garden District plan, this was the first house in the district to embrace the French Second Empire style, visible in the mansard roof and superficial ornamental details. ⊠ *2343 Prytania St., Garden District.*

⓰ **Briggs-Staub House.** The only Gothic Revival house in the district was built around 1849 and has undergone several restorations. Garden District Americans typically shunned the Gothic Revival style as linked to Creole-Catholic tradition, but Londoner Charles Briggs ignored decorum and had James Gallier Sr. design this anomaly, described at the time as a "Gothic cottage." The interior departed from a strict Gothic breakup of rooms, thus becoming better suited for entertaining, but Gothic detailing is prevalent both inside and out. ⊠ *2605 Prytania St., Garden District.*

❾ Buckner Mansion. This 1856 home was built by cotton factor Henry S. Buckner in overt competition with the famous Stanton Hall in Natchez, built by Buckner's former partner. Among the luxurious details are 48 fluted cypress columns and a rare honeysuckle-design cast-iron fence. The generously proportioned triple ballroom, visible from Coliseum Street, answered 19th-century New Orleans's entertaining needs and until recently was used by debutantes practicing their walks and curtsies. Now privately owned, the house served as the campus of Soulé College from 1923 to 1975. ⊠ *1410 Jackson Ave., Garden District.*

off the beaten path

BUDDY BOLDEN NEIGHBORHOOD – Semi-mythical, turn-of-the-20th-century cornetist Buddy Bolden, remembered by many first-generation jazz players as "the first jazzman," lived with his mother and sister at two addresses on 1st Street, on the lake side of St. Charles Avenue: No. 2309 from the mid-1880s to 1905, and No. 2527 from 1906. Bolden was committed to an asylum shortly after the move to the second location. He took his first cornet lessons around the corner, at 2212 South Liberty, attended church at the 1st Street Baptist Church, 2432 1st Street, and played dances at Providence Hall, 2241 South Liberty. Jelly Roll Morton recalled seeing Bolden play at 2059 Jackson Avenue. All these spots are within a block or two of each other, but you should drive or take a cab here, as the neighborhood is not safe. ⊠ *Garden District.*

⓱ Colonel Short's Villa. A dining-room wing is tacked onto the Greek Revival layout of this home; the two-story galleries around the wing, railed with cast iron rather than wood, were influential in the ornamental use of cast iron throughout the neighborhood. The cast-iron fence, with a pattern of morning glories intertwining with cornstalks, was ordered from a Philadelphia catalog and is certainly the most famous example of cast iron in the Garden District. Legend has it that Colonel Short purchased the fence for his wife, who was homesick for Kentucky. Another cornstalk fence similar to this one appears in the French Quarter at 915 Royal Street. ⊠ *1448 4th St., Garden District.*

House of Broel's Victorian Mansion and Dollhouse Museum. Antique furnishings fill this restored antebellum home. The dollhouse collection, owned by Bonnie Broel, includes beautiful miniatures of Victorian, Tudor, and plantation-style houses. The home also houses a wedding store; several of the rooms are devoted to gowns and other wedding necessities. ⊠ *2220 St. Charles Ave., Garden District* ☎ *504/522–2220* ⊕ *www.houseofbroel. com* ▣ *Mansion and museum $10* ☉ *Mon.–Sat. 10–5.*

★ ❸ Lafayette Cemetery No. 1. Begun around 1833, this was the first planned cemetery in the city, with symmetrical rows, roadways for funeral vehicles, and lavish aboveground vaults and tombs for the wealthy families who built the surrounding mansions. In 1852, 2,000 yellow fever victims were buried here. The cemetery and environs figure in Anne Rice's popular series *The Vampire Chronicles,* and movies such as *Interview with the Vampire* have used this walled cemetery for its eerie beauty. You can wander the grounds on your own or take an organized tour. One guided tour is arranged by **Save Our Cemeteries** (☎ 504/525–3377). ⊠ *1400 block of Washington Ave., Garden District* ☒ *Cemetery free, tour $6* ⊙ *Weekdays 7–2:30, Sat. 7–noon; tours Mon., Wed., Fri., and Sat. at 10:30.*

⑮ Lonsdale House. As a 16-year-old immigrant working in the New Orleans shipyards, Henry Lonsdale noticed how many damaged goods were arriving from upriver. Spotting a need for more protective shipping materials, Lonsdale developed the burlap bag (clued in by his parents, who had picked up a sample in India). He made a fortune in burlap, only to lose it all in the 1837 depression. Lonsdale next turned to coffee importing, an industry that ran into problems during the Civil War: the Union blocked imports from Brazil, the major supplier of coffee to New Orleans. Lonsdale hit upon the fateful idea of cutting the limited coffee grinds with chicory, a bitter root, and New Orleanians have been drinking the coffee and chicory blend ever since. The house, built with his entrepreneurial dollars, displays many fine details, including the intricate cast-iron work on the galleries and the marble entrance hall. ⊠ *2523 Prytania St., Garden District.*

⑭ Maddox House. Built in 1852, this house exemplifies the five-bay, center-hall extension of the Greek Revival style—notice the Ionic and Corinthian columns that support the broadened galleries. Inside is a magnificent gold ballroom decorated by a Viennese artist for the original owners. ⊠ *2507 Prytania St., Garden District.*

⑤ Musson House. This Italianate house was built by impressionist painter Edgar Degas's maternal uncle, Michel Musson—a rare Creole inhabitant of the predominantly American Garden District. A later owner added the famous "lace" galleries, named for their elaborate cast-iron work. ⊠ *1331 3rd St., Garden District.*

⑧ Payne House. Confederate president Jefferson Davis died here on December 6, 1889; a monument out front outlines his active political and military careers. The two-story galleries overlook the side yard. Cast iron ornaments the capitals of the Ionic columns, each embossed with the date (1848) and place (New York) of manufacture. ⊠ *1134 1st St., Garden District.*

▶ **❶ The Rink.** This small collection of specialty shops was once the South's first roller-skating rink, built in the 1880s. Locals can be found here browsing in the **Garden District Book Shop,** which stocks regional, rare, and old books. Cult novelist Anne Rice has a large store on the mezzanine, filled with character dolls and other merchandise related to the author and her work. ⊠ *Washington Ave. and Prytania St., Garden District.*

need a break?	A pleasant place to relax is outdoors on the deck of **Still Perkin'** (⊠ 2727 Prytania St., Garden District ☎ 504/899–0335) at the Rink. Gourmet coffees and teas and baked goods are served.

❹ Robinson House. Styled after an Italian villa, this home built in the late 1850s is one of the largest in the district. Doric and Corinthian columns support the rounded galleries. It is believed to be the first house in New Orleans with "waterworks," as indoor plumbing was called then. At the time of writing, the house is undergoing a major renovation based on the original plans. ⊠ *1415 3rd St., Garden District.*

❻ Schlesinger House. The columns and the simple lines in the framing of doors and windows stand out here. This house is a classic example of the Greek Revival style popular in the 1850s, which was used in many plantation homes upriver, as well. Its lovely ironwork was added to the front gallery in the 1930s. ⊠ *1427 2nd St., Garden District.*

Seven Sisters Houses. Legend has it that the seven nearly identical shotgun houses occupying the 2300 block of Coliseum Street were built for seven sisters. In fact they were the first speculation houses in the city, and some of the first in the United States. Though renovations have blurred the family resemblance, the homes are structurally distinguished only by the front galleries: some are Greek Revival, some Italianate. ⊠ *2300 Coliseum St., Garden District.*

⓫ Toby-Westfeldt House. Dating from the 1830s, this unpretentious French-colonial home sits amid a large, plantation-like garden, surrounded by a copy of the original white picket fence. Thomas Toby, a Philadelphia businessman, moved to New Orleans and had this house built well above the ground to protect it from flooding. The house is thought to be the oldest in this part of the Garden District. ⊠ *2340 Prytania St., Garden District.*

⓭ Women's Guild of the New Orleans Opera Association House. This fundamentally Greek Revival house, built in 1858, has a distinctive Italianate octagonal turret, added in the late 19th century. The last private owner, Nettie Seebold, willed the estate to the Women's Guild of the New Orleans Opera upon her death in 1955. It is now furnished with period pieces and used for receptions and private parties. This is one of the few houses in the area open to the public, but only on Monday afternoons or for groups with advance reservations. ⊠ *2504 Prytania St., Garden District* ☎ *504/899–1945* ⊠ *$5* ☼ *Tours Mon. 1–4.*

Lower Garden District

a good walk

Part of what appeals in the Lower Garden District is that it is proving slow to gentrify. This means that crumbling and spruced-up mansions and cottages share the same blocks, and old junk stores sit alongside pristine antiques shops. Remain cautious when visiting this area.

As you cross Jackson Avenue heading downtown on Prytania, you can't miss the imposing **Harris-Maginnis House** ▶, an oversize adaptation of the basic Creole cottage design. At the next corner, look to your left: across St. Charles Avenue from one another on Josephine Street sit the grand old **Pontchartrain Hotel** and the gaudy **Eiffel Tower Building.** Continue along Prytania and turn right onto Felicity Street, which leads you into the heart of the Lower Garden District. At Felicity and Chestnut Sts., the

United Felicity Methodist Church has stood since 1888. Take a right onto Sophie Wright Place to find antiques, crafts, and records stores, along with shops and cafés. After visiting the shops and galleries surrounding tiny Sophie Wright park, head downtown on Magazine Street to view the **St. Vincent's Guesthouse** and enjoy an iced coffee at **Rue de la Course** café; its name is French for Race Street, which runs along its side.

Turn left on Race Street: one block down brings you to Coliseum Square, a large park lined with some of the finest old homes in town, though many of them are in disrepair. To walk around the entire park takes a half hour; if you have less time, limit your explorations to the first few blocks on the uptown end. Of special note is the **Goodrich-Stanley House,** a meticulously restored Creole cottage at 1729 Coliseum. When you are ready, walk to St. Charles Avenue to catch the streetcar or to Prytania or Magazine Street to walk back to the Upper Garden District.

TIMING   You can get a good feel for the Lower Garden District in an hour. Allow an extra hour if you plan to visit St. Vincent's and any of the numerous shops and galleries along Magazine Street.

Sights to See

Derby Pottery. Fragments of wrought ironwork and other architectural details form the inspiration for many of Mark Derby's beautiful mugs, vases, and tiles. ⊠ *2029 Magazine St., Lower Garden District* ☎ *504/ 586–9003* ⊕ *www.derbypottery.com* ☉ *Mon.–Sat. 10–5.*

Eiffel Tower Building. This building, one of the more unusual in the city, occupies the intersection of Josephine Street and St. Charles Avenue. Each piece of the original restaurant inside the Eiffel Tower in Paris was shipped here and carefully reassembled in 1986. ⊠ *2040 St. Charles Ave., Lower Garden District.*

Goodrich-Stanley House. This restored Creole cottage is an excellent example of the modest prototype for much of the far more elaborate architecture of the surrounding Garden District. The scale of the Creole cottage, derived from the climate-conscious design prevalent in the West Indies, made it easily adaptable to the higher pretensions of the Greek Revival look, as well as the slightly more reserved Colonial Revival. Built in 1837, the house has had one famous occupant: John Rowlands, who was adopted by Henry Hope Stanley, owner of the house. Rowlands changed his name to Henry Morton Stanley and became a renowned explorer of Africa and founder of the Congo Free States. Perhaps most notoriously, he uttered the phrase "Dr. Livingstone, I presume" upon encountering the long-lost Scottish missionary. ⊠ *1729 Coliseum St., Lower Garden District.*

▶ **Harris-Maginnis House.** This oversize Creole cottage is notable for the unusually deep portico stretching over the front garden and the 11 carved Corinthian columns. The interior is filled with lavish woodwork, though this is hidden from public view. ⊠ *2127 Prytania St., Lower Garden District.*

St. Alphonsus Art and Cultural Center. Though no longer an active church, this lovely building dates from the mid-19th century and is sometimes open to visitors. It was founded for the Irish sector of Redemptorist Parish; the church across the street served the German community, and a third church down the street (no longer standing) served the French community. The frescoed, weathered interior has been preserved in its original form; admission includes a cassette tour. A small museum displays artifacts and memorabilia from the area, including personal effects of local bishops, scrapbooks, and yearbooks. A block toward the river from Magazine, St. Alphonsus is in a high-crime area; use caution if you plan to walk here. ⊠ *2045 Constance St., Lower Garden District* 🕾 *504/524–8116* ⊕ *www. stalphonsus.org* 🖾 *$3, $5 with tour* ⊙ *Tues., Thurs., and Sat. 10–2.*

St. Vincent's Guesthouse. This large, brick structure was once an orphanage and home for unwed mothers. Today most of St. Vincent's has been converted into guest rooms, but the rather grand downstairs is open for public admiration. ⊠ *1507 Magazine St., Lower Garden District* 🕾 *504/523–3411* ⊕ *www.stvincentsguesthouse.com.*

Thomas Mann Gallery. Imaginative furniture design and sculptural forays fill this small gallery. Thomas Mann also showcases jewelry by other local artists. ⊠ *1804 Magazine St., Lower Garden District* 🕾 *504/ 581–2113* ⊕ *www.thomasmann.com* ⊙ *Mon.–Sat. 11–6.*

UPTOWN

Lying west of the Garden District, uptown is the residential area on both sides of St. Charles Avenue along the streetcar route, upriver from Louisiana Avenue. It includes many mansions as sumptuous as those in the Garden District, as well as Loyola and Tulane universities and a large urban park named for John James Audubon. Traveling along the avenue from downtown to uptown provides something of a historical narrative: the city's development unfolded upriver, and the houses grow discernibly more modern the farther uptown you go.

FodorśChoice ★ The **St. Charles Avenue streetcar** provides a wonderful way to take in this neighborhood. In the early 1900s streetcars were the most prominent mode of public transit and ran on many streets, but today they operate only along the riverfront, Canal Street, Carrollton Avenue, and St. Charles Avenue. Avoid rush hours—from 7 to 9 and 3 to 6—or you may have to stand much of the way and will not be able to enjoy the scenery or sights.

Numbers in the text correspond to numbers in the margin and on the St. Charles Avenue Uptown map.

a good ride Board the streetcar at Washington Avenue to catch some Garden District sights not covered on the walking tour. **Christ Church Cathedral** ⓲ ➤, a beautiful Gothic Revival Episcopal church, is on your right on St. Charles Avenue between 6th and 7th streets. The **Elms Mansion** ⓳, down the block from the cathedral, was built around 1869 and is open for tours. It has marble fireplaces, stained-glass windows, and original tapestries. Louisiana Avenue forms the boundary between the Garden District and uptown. As you approach Louisiana Avenue, the **Bultman Funeral Home** ⓴ is the huge white mansion on your left at the intersection.

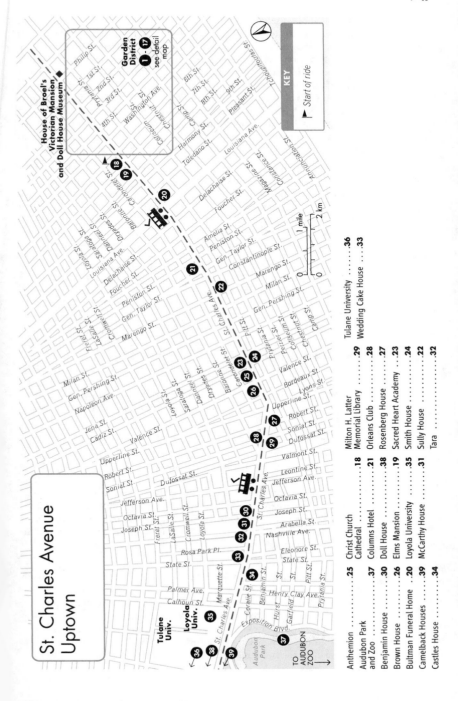

St. Charles Avenue
Uptown

KEY

▲ *Start of ride*

House of Broel's
Victorian Mansion
and Doll House Museum ◆

Garden
District
❶ · ❶
see detail
map

Unity Temple, the circular building on the left at Peniston Street, was built in 1960 by a student of Frank Lloyd Wright. Its harmonious and simple design reflects Wright's influence. The **Columns Hotel** ㉑, which certainly deserves its name, is on the right after Peniston Street. The Rayne Memorial Methodist Church, built in 1875 and notable for its Gothic-style gables and arched windows, is on the next block up from the Columns Hotel, on the left. The 1887 Queen Anne–style Grant House, up the block from the Rayne Memorial Church, has a decorative porch and balcony balustrades. Popular local architect Thomas Sully is credited with its design. The **Sully House** ㉒, the family home of the famous architect himself, is in the middle of the next block, before Marengo Street.

The large avenue intersecting at the next stop is Napoleon Avenue, the starting point for the many Mardi Gras parades that wind their way down St. Charles Avenue to Canal Street. Copeland's Restaurant, on the corner to the left, is named for its proprietor, Al Copeland, the founder of Popeye's Famous Fried Chicken. Dominating the opposite corner, also on the left, is the interdenominational Watson Memorial Teaching Ministry, built in the early 1900s in Colonial Revival style.

The spectacular **Sacred Heart Academy** ㉓, a private girls' school, is on the right in the next block, past Jena Street. Across the street, the Mediterranean **Smith House** ㉔ claims one of the most picturesque settings on the avenue. On the left past Cadiz Street, St. George's Episcopal Church, dating from 1900, is in the Romanesque style, with softly curved arches. The oldest house on St. Charles Avenue (circa 1850s) is the 4621 St. Charles House on the right, before Valence Street. Next door, **Anthemion** ㉕ is an early example of the Colonial Revival movement. The **Brown House** ㉖, on the right before Bordeaux Street, is the largest mansion on St. Charles Avenue. The Hernandez House, in the next block past the Brown House, to the right, is a showcase home illustrating the Second Empire style. Mansard roofs like this one are relatively rare in New Orleans.

Several houses in the next block past the Hernandez House are turn-of-the-20th-century buildings, though they artfully re-create an antebellum style. On the left, the neighboring **Rosenberg House** ㉗ and Stirling House provide a study in contrasting Colonial and Classical Revival. The Tudor style, with its steep gables, Gothic arches, and half timbering, was popular when banana magnate Joseph Vaccaro built the Vaccaro House, on the left, in 1910. The **Orleans Club** ㉘, on the right at the corner of Robert Street, is an elegant ladies club. The **Milton H. Latter Memorial Library** ㉙, a beaux-arts mansion that is now a public library, is on the left at Soniat Street.

Several blocks ahead, the **Benjamin House** ㉚, between Octavia and Joseph streets, is a stunning mansion (circa 1912) made of limestone, an expensive and unusual building material for New Orleans. In the next block, past Joseph Street on the right, is the **McCarthy House** ㉛, a Colonial Revival home with ornate columns and flat-top doors and windows. Tara, the plantation home used in the film *Gone With the Wind*, was a set, but it inspired the columned New Orleans **Tara** ㉜, coming up on the right side of the avenue at the corner of Arabella.

As you cross Nashville Avenue, the Colonial Revival **Wedding Cake House** ㉝ is on the right. As you enter the university district, dominating the next block on the left is the neo-Gothic St. Charles Avenue Presbyterian Church.

Castles House ㉞, on the left after State Street, is another Colonial Revival similar to the Wedding Cake House. The St. Charles Avenue Christian Church, two blocks from Castles House, on the left, is 1923 Colonial Revival. On the right, across from the St. Charles Avenue Christian Church, is Temple Sinai, the first Reform Jewish congregation in New Orleans. This building dates from 1928; the annex on the corner was built in 1970.

Just beyond Calhoun Street, **Loyola University** ㉟, on the right, takes up the block past Temple Sinai. The Jesuit institution is well known for its communications, law, and music departments. **Tulane University** ㊱, founded in 1884, is directly beside Loyola and houses the wonderful Newcomb Art Gallery and the Middle American Research Institute and Gallery. Campuses for both universities extend back several blocks off the avenue. On the left, across the avenue from the two universities is **Audubon Park and Zoo** ㊲. Get off here to visit it.

Back on the St. Charles Avenue streetcar again, the heavy stone archway on the right just after Tulane University is the entrance to exclusive Audubon Place. Only residents and their guests can enter the two-block-long private drive, which has some of the most elegant mansions in the city. Zemurray House, the columned white mansion facing the archway, was built in 1907 by Sam Zemurray, president of the United Fruit Company. Zemurray's widow deeded the house to Tulane University, and it is now the official residence of the university's president.

The **Doll House** ㊳, a miniature house in the corner yard on the right at Broadway, stands at the next major intersection. At Broadway, to the left, is the Loyola University School of Law, an Italianate building that housed the Dominican sisters who operated Mary's Dominican College for Women here from the late 1800s, when this was rural countryside, until the 1980s. St. Charles Avenue continues several more stops past Broadway until it turns, just short of the levee. Especially interesting are two houses on the left, between Hillary and Adams streets, called the **Camelback Houses** ㊴.

As the streetcar makes the bend after Short Street, St. Charles turns into Carrollton Avenue. This turn used to mark the entrance to the town of Carrollton, a resort town at the end of the original rail line that opened in 1835 and ran the length of the road from the Vieux Carré. A service station now occupies the former site of a grand resort hotel. As you turn the bend, to the left in the distance is the green expanse of the levee, an artificial earthen wall built both to protect against floods and to keep the Mississippi River flowing in a set course. A paved path along the levee's rim affords opportunity for strolls, bike rides, and views over the river. Once around the turn, you're in the Riverbend neighborhood, where you'll have to look behind the shopping strip on the left facing Carrollton Avenue for a town square surrounded by Victorian cottages—most of which are now specialty shops and restaurants. The tour ends at the next stop, so prepare to leave the streetcar, unless you wish to stay aboard another 20 minutes to ride to the end of the line at Claiborne Avenue. Either way, you will have to pay a new fare to reboard the streetcar in the opposite direction, back downtown.

As you exit the streetcar at Riverbend, the large, stately columned building on your right that today is an elementary school was built in 1855 as the Old Carrollton Court House. Cross the tracks to spend some time browsing in the shops and eateries in Riverbend.

TIMING   The ride on the streetcar from Washington Avenue, in the center of the Garden District, or from Louisiana Avenue takes about 30 minutes (considerably more during rush hour). Plan a half day minimum for visiting the Audubon Zoo and enjoying the park that surrounds it.

Sights to See

②⑤ Anthemion. A fashion for Colonial Revival architecture in the late 19th century indicated local weariness with the excesses of the Greek Revival craze that had dominated the mid-century. Anthemion, built in 1896 and the headquarters of the Japanese consulate from 1938 to 1941, is an excellent example of this return to simplicity. ⊠ *4631 St. Charles Ave., Uptown.*

★ ☺ ③⑦ **Audubon Park.** Formerly the plantation of Etienne de Boré, the father of the granulated sugar industry in Louisiana, **Audubon Park** is a large, lush stretch of green between St. Charles Avenue and Magazine Street, continuing across Magazine Street to the river. Designed by John Charles Olmsted, nephew of Frederick Law Olmsted (who laid out New York City's Central Park), it contains the world-class **Audubon Zoo**; a 1.7-mi track for running, walking, or biking; picnic and play areas; a golf course; riding stables; a tennis court; and a river view. Calm lagoons wind through the park, harboring egrets, catfish, and other indigenous species. The park and zoo were named for the famous ornithologist and painter John James Audubon, who spent many years working in and around New Orleans. None of the original buildings from its former plantation days remain; in fact, none of the buildings that housed the 1884–85 World's Industrial and Cotton Centennial Exposition, which was held on these acres and gave New Orleans its first international publicity after the Civil War, has survived. The only reminder of this important event in New Orleans's history is Exposition Boulevard, the street address assigned to houses that front the park along the downtown side.

If time permits, you may want to venture beyond the zoo, cross the railroad tracks, and stroll along **Riverview Drive**, a long stretch of land behind the zoo that is part of Audubon Park, on the levee overlooking the Mississippi River. This area is referred to as "The Fly" by locals, after a butterfly-shape building that was torn down here some years ago, and it is a popular place for picnics and pickup sports. The river lookout includes Audubon Landing, where the *John James Audubon* cruise boat (nicknamed "the zoo cruise") docks, and a landscaped walkway. ⊠ *6500 Magazine St., Uptown* ☎ *504/586–8777* ⊕ *www.auduboninstitute.org* ⊠ *Park free; zoo cruise $16.50, combination ticket for cruise, zoo, and* *aquarium $32.50* ☉ *7-mi river ride to French Quarter and Canal St. daily at 11, 1, 3, and 5.*

★ ☾ **Audubon Zoo.** Animals roam and frolic in natural-habitat settings at this excellent zoo in **Audubon Park**. It harbors lions, tigers, bears, sea lions, and a family of extremely rare white (albino) alligators. The Louisiana Swamp exhibit re-creates the natural habitat of alligators, nutria (large swamp rodents), and catfish; alligator-feeding time is always well attended. Other highlights include the butterfly exhibit, the children's petting zoo, and white Bengal tigers. You can walk here from the streetcar line across Audubon Park (allow a half hour), or take the free shuttle that stops in front of the park's St. Charles entrance every 15 minutes daily 9:30–5. The Magazine Street bus also stops right at the zoo and can take you to and from Canal Street. ✉ *6500 Magazine St., Uptown* ☎ *504/ 581–4629* ⊕ *www.auduboninstitute.org* ✍ *$10, combination ticket for zoo and Aquarium of the Americas $18* ☉ *Daily 9:30–5; last ticket sold 1 hr before closing.*

③⓪ Benjamin House. This beaux-arts beauty, built in 1912 for cotton factor Emanuel Benjamin, shares the block with Danneel Park. It was constructed of expensive limestone, leaving Benjamin with a bill of $30,000—an outrageous sum at the time. ✉ *5531 St. Charles Ave., Uptown.*

②⑥ Brown House. Completed in 1904, the Brown House is the largest mansion on St. Charles Avenue. Its solid monumental look, Syrian arches, and steep gables make it a choice example of Romanesque Revival style. ✉ *4717 St. Charles Ave., Uptown.*

②⓪ Bultman Funeral Home. This huge white mansion with an enclosed garden is a working funeral home, one of the most elegant in the South. A balcony bears a wrought-iron motif of downward crossed arrows, a symbol of death. Tennessee Williams set his play *Suddenly Last Summer* here in the solarium, which is now open for occasional Sunday-afternoon concerts. If no funeral services are taking place, they might let you in for a peek at the gracious interior. ✉ *3338 St. Charles Ave., Garden District* ☎ *504/895–7766.*

③⑨ Camelback Houses. When these were built in the late 1800s, houses were taxed by the width and height of their facades: working-class homes were usually narrow and long. Sometimes a second floor was added to the back half of the house, giving it the architectural designation of "camelback." The camelback and the gingerbread-type decoration on porches were popular details at the turn of the 20th century. ✉ *7628–7630, 7632–7634, and 7820–7822 St. Charles Ave., Uptown.*

③④ Castles House. Local architect Thomas Sully designed this 1896 Colonial Revival house after the Longfellow House in Cambridge, Massachusetts. The interior has often appeared in the pages of design magazines. ✉ *6000 St. Charles Ave., Uptown.*

➤ **①⑧ Christ Church Cathedral.** This beautiful Gothic Revival Episcopal church completed in 1887 has steeply pitched gables, an architectural detail that was a precursor to the New Orleans Victorian style. The cathedral is the oldest non–Roman Catholic church in the Louisiana Purchase: the congregation was established in 1805, and this is the third building erected on the same site. It is the diocesan headquarters of the Episcopal Church in Louisiana. ⊠ *2919 St. Charles Ave., Garden District.*

㉑ Columns Hotel. In recent years this elegant white hotel, built in 1884 as a private home, has been the scene of TV ads and movies. The interior scenes of Louis Malle's *Pretty Baby* were filmed here. The Colonial Revival hotel has a popular bar and a grand veranda for sipping cocktails; there's live music some nights and during Sunday brunch. The grand rooms of the first floor are open to the public; note the stained-glass skylight topping the mahogany stairwell. ⊠ *3811 St. Charles Ave., Uptown* ☎ *504/899–9308 or 800/445–9308* ⊕ *www.thecolumns.com.*

㊳ Doll House. Designed in the same Tudor style as the main house beside it for the daughter of a former owner, this is the smallest house in New Orleans to have its own postal address. ⊠ *7209 St. Charles Ave., Uptown.*

⑲ Elms Mansion. Built in 1869, this elegant home with marble fireplaces and stained-glass windows saw the Confederate president Jefferson Davis as a frequent guest. The house, which has been carefully restored and furnished with period pieces, is the site of many receptions. Tours of the interior are conducted on weekdays; reservations are recommended in case of closures for special events. Highlights include a fantastic carved oak staircase and mantelpiece and 24-karat gilt moldings and sconces. ⊠ *3029 St. Charles Ave., Garden District* ☎ *504/895–5493* ⊞ *Tours $5 per person* ⊙ *Weekdays 10–2:30.*

㉟ Loyola University. The Jesuits built this complex facing the avenue in 1914. The modernistic Gothic-style building on the corner is the **Louis J. Roussel Building**, which houses the music department. The campus, with its dorms, recreational center, and library, extends for two blocks behind the **Church of the Holy Name of Jesus**, a masterfully constructed Gothic and Tudor edifice. The fourth floor of the neo-Gothic **library** holds a gallery with changing exhibits by students, faculty, and other regional artists. ⊠ *6363 St. Charles Ave., Uptown.*

㉛ McCarthy House. A deep front lawn emphasizes the perfect symmetry of this classic Colonial Revival, constructed in 1903. The brick veneer and Ionic columns are emblematic of the style. ⊠ *5603 St. Charles Ave., Uptown.*

Middle American Research Institute and Gallery. Way up on the fourth floor of a musty old academic building, this research institute and gallery at **Tulane University** has exhibits of pre-Columbian and Central and South American culture. Established in 1924, the institute has an extensive collection of pre-Columbian Mayan artifacts and one of the largest collections of Guatemalan textiles in the nation. Tulane's main library has an extensive collection of books on Latin American culture associated with the research institute. ⊠ *Dinwiddie Hall, 4th fl., Uptown* ☎ *504/865–5110* ⊞ *Free* ⊙ *Weekdays 8:30–4.*

㉙ Milton H. Latter Memorial Library. A former private home now serves as the most elegant public library in New Orleans. Built in 1907 and ornamenting its own beautifully landscaped block, this Italianate–beaux-arts mansion was once the home of silent-screen star Marguerite Clark, who lived here in the 1940s. It was then purchased by the Latter family and given to the city as a library in 1948 in memory of their son, who was killed in World War II. You can sit a spell and leaf through a copy of Walker Percy's *The Moviegoer* or Anne Rice's *The Vampire Lestat* (two popular novels set in New Orleans), or just relax in a wicker chair on the solarium. This is one of the few mansions on St. Charles Avenue open to the public. Local artisans contributed the murals and carved mantels. ✉ *5120 St. Charles Ave., Uptown* ☎ *504/596–2625* ⊕ *www.nutrias.org* ⊙ *Mon. and Wed. 10–8, Tues. and Thurs. 10–6, Sat. 10–5.*

❷❽ Orleans Club. This sumptuous mansion was built in 1868 as a wedding gift from Colonel William Lewis Wynn to his daughter. The dormer windows, typical of French Empire style, were added during a remodeling in 1909. The side building, on the uptown side of the main building, is an auditorium added in the 1950s. The house is closed to the public but serves as headquarters to a ladies' social club and hosts many debutante teas and wedding receptions. ✉ *5005 St. Charles Ave., Uptown.*

❷❼ Rosenberg House. The brick facade and Corinthian columns on this stately 1911 house mark it as Colonial Revival. Behind these traits, a modern, craftsman-style interior (not open to the public) suggests the progressive tastes of the Rosenbergs. The Stirling House, next door at number 4930, provides an interesting contrast, embodying as it does the Classical Revival characteristics of clean, white exterior and simple Doric columns. ✉ *4920 St. Charles Ave., Uptown.*

❷❸ Sacred Heart Academy. Unusual aspects of this building, a Catholic girls' school built in 1899, include wide, wraparound balconies (or galleries) and colonnades facing a large garden. The academy is exceptionally beautiful during the holidays, when the galleries are decked with wreaths and garlands. ✉ *4521 St. Charles Ave., Uptown.*

❷❹ Smith House. This bucolic Mediterranean villa was built in 1906 for William Smith, president of the New Orleans Cotton Exchange. Smith himself planted the three live oak trees that have now grown to shade the expansive yard. The front porch is anchored by stone columns with capitals in the Greek honeysuckle-and-palmette pattern. ✉ *4534 St. Charles Ave., Uptown.*

❷❷ Sully House. This was the family home of local architect Thomas Sully, who designed it around 1890. Sully was known for his use of deep shades of color and varied textures. Similar gables, towers, and gingerbread appear on many other homes in the vicinity. ✉ *4010 St. Charles Ave., Uptown.*

❸❷ Tara. A replica built from the plans of the movie set of *Gone With the Wind,* Tara seems almost dwarfed here by far more sumptuous houses. ✉ *5705 St. Charles Ave., Uptown.*

❸❻ Tulane University. The venerable university sits next to Loyola University on St. Charles Avenue. Three original buildings face the avenue: **Tilton Hall** (1901) on the left, **Gibson Hall** (1894) in the middle, and **Dinwiddie Hall** (1936) on the right. The Romanesque style, with its massive stone look and arched windows and doors, is repeated in the several buildings around a large quad behind these. Modern campus buildings extend another three blocks to the rear. Tulane is well known for its medical school, law school, and fine main library. The **Sophie H. Newcomb College for Women** shares part of the Tulane campus but has a separate dean and faculty. It is known for the **Newcomb College Center for Research on Women,** a fine women's resource center that brings in speakers, writers, and academics throughout the school year. Also here is the **Middle American Research Institute.** ⊠ *6823 St. Charles Ave., Uptown.*

㉝ Wedding Cake House. A portico and decorative balconies help this house outshine most other mansions on the avenue. Its key beauty is the beveled leaded glass in its front door, one of the most beautiful entryways in the city. ⊠ *5809 St. Charles Ave., Uptown.*

★ **Woldenberg Art Center and Newcomb Art Gallery.** The building where the renowned Newcomb pottery and bookbindings were produced in the late 19th and early 20th centuries has been lovingly restored with an eye to interior detail. Tiffany stained glass marks the entrance to the refurbished halls of the Newcomb Art Gallery, where excellent temporary exhibits, often of regional origin or interest, join works from the art school's own collection. ⊠ *Tulane University Campus, Willow St. entrance, Uptown* ☎ *504/865–5328* 🖃 *Free* ☉ *Weekdays 10–5, weekends noon–5.*

BAYOU ST. JOHN & MID-CITY

Above the French Quarter, below the lakefront, neither uptown nor quite downtown, Mid-City is an amorphous yet prideful territory embracing everything from the massive, lush City Park to gritty diners along Broad Street and Carrollton Avenue. It is a neighborhood of tremendous ethnic and economic diversity. Here are great restaurants, cultural landmarks such as Mid-City Bowling Lanes, restored former plantation homes, and crumbling inner-city neighborhoods. Actual sights are few and far between in Mid-City, but the area around Bayou St. John near City Park is one of the most picturesque in town and is fruitful for walks or bike rides.

Numbers in the text correspond to numbers in the margin and on the Bayou St. John–Lakefront map.

a good drive

Begin on Canal Street, the main avenue of downtown New Orleans, which connects the Mississippi River with Lake Pontchartrain, and head away from the river. As you cross under the Claiborne Avenue overpass you are entering Mid-City. Those interested in black Mardi Gras traditions should take a detour at Broad Street, turning right to visit the Zulu Social Aide and Pleasure Club. Approximately 1 mi farther along Canal, take a right onto North Jefferson Davis Parkway. Follow the parkway four blocks and over the railroad tracks. Directly ahead on the left begins a natural inlet of slow-moving water called **Bayou St. John ❶** ▶, which leads into **Lake Pontchartrain** about 5 mi out.

Continue straight for one block beyond the tracks; turn left onto Toulouse Street, then right onto Moss Street to follow the bayou. Across the bayou from Toulouse stands the American Can Company building, now filled with loft-style condos. You will then pass the Greek Revival **Blanc House** ❷ on your way to **Pitot House** ❸, a structure dating from the late 1700s that you can tour. After stopping at the Pitot House, take a walk around the quiet streets of the Bayou St. John area. During school hours you can walk through the parking lot next to Pitot House to reach Esplanade Avenue. Otherwise, stroll back along the bayou the way you came to Grand Route St. John, turning away from the bayou to reach Esplanade Avenue; the small triangular park at the intersection of Esplanade is **Alcee Fortier Park** ❹, named for the educator who founded Fortier High School uptown. Across Esplanade is a cluster of cafés, restaurants, and shops, forming a center of activity in this youthful neighborhood. Beyond these businesses lies the **Fair Grounds Race Course** ❺, one of the oldest in the country. A few blocks away from Alcee Fortier Park down this lovely stretch of Esplanade you'll find C. C.'s Coffee, a good spot for a break. The blocks along Esplanade toward City Park include the aboveground vaults of **St. Louis Cemetery No. 3** ❻, and **Cabrini High School and Mother Cabrini Shrine** ❼, which was originally an orphanage: you can still make out the name "Sacred Heart Orphan Asylum" over the entrance. Return to Pitot House via any of the small streets connecting Esplanade Avenue and Bayou St. John; the streets around Kennedy Place Park, on Ursulines Street, are especially scenic.

Back in the car, follow Moss Street as it curves with the bayou until it intersects with Esplanade Avenue. Turn left and cross the Esplanade Avenue Bridge; City Park lies just beyond Beauregard Circle, with the statue of General P. G. T. Beauregard in its center. The Civil War hero, mounted on his horse, is in full uniform and looks ready to charge down Esplanade Avenue.

As you enter the park, the **New Orleans Museum of Art** ❽ comes into view directly ahead on Lelong Avenue. Follow the half circle behind the museum, take a right onto Roosevelt Mall, cross the bridge, and take an immediate left onto Victory Avenue; the **New Orleans Botanical Garden** ❾ is on the right. Past the garden is **Storyland** ❿, a children's fantasy play area; next door in the **Carousel Gardens** ⓫ are several amusement rides, including a beautifully refurbished 1906 carousel.

As you drive away from the Carousel Gardens on Anseman Avenue, still inside the park, peer beyond the tennis courts on your left to view a grand entrance to the park and, across City Park Avenue, historic **Ralph's on the Park** ⓬ restaurant, where 19th-century downtowners would stop for refreshments on their way into the park. Turning left at the end of the courts, onto Dreyfous Drive, leads you to the City Park Peristyle, with its tall columns and cement lions overlooking the lagoon, a favorite spot for picnics and parties. Ahead on the right is the Timken Center, where you can pick up ice cream and other treats. Back on Dreyfous, drive across the narrow bridge; the museum will reemerge on your left. Follow the road to the stop sign, then turn right to exit the park onto Esplanade Avenue. Esplanade will lead you back to the French Quarter. As you cross Broad Street, watch to your left for the **Benachi-Torre House** ⓭, then to your right for the **Edgar Degas House** ⓮, just two of many beautiful old homes along the avenue.

Bayou St. John–
Lakefront

*Lake
Pontchartrain*

Breakwater Dr. ◆ **Lighthouse**

◆ **Orleans
Marina**

**Mardi Gras
Fountains** ◆

Lakeshore Dr.

*West
End
Park*

Lake Ave.

Robert E. Lee Blvd.

Live Oak St.

❶❺

W. Esplanade

Pontchartrain Blvd.

End Blvd.

Canal Blvd.

Marconi Dr.

Fillmore Ave.

Bayou St. John

St. Bernard Ave.

*City
Park*

Veterans

Mem.

Hwy.

[10]

[610]

Magnolia Dr.

Wisner Blvd.

DeSaix Blvd.

❶❶ ❶❶ ❾

Dreyfous Dr. ❽

❻

*Fair
Grounds*

Gentilly Blvd.

❶❻

Old Metairie Rd.

*Metairie
Cemetery*

City Park Ave.

❶❷

Metairie Rd.

[10]

Canal St.

Orleans Ave.

❼

❺

Esplanade Ave.

[61]

Carrollton Ave.

Moss St.

❶

❹

❷❸

❶❸

Monticello St.

Palmetto St.

S. Jeff Davis Pkwy.

Tulane Ave.

N. Broad St.

❶❹

Amelia Earhart Blvd.

Apple St.

Claiborne Ave.

◆ **Zulu Social
Aid and
Pleasure
Club**

0   1 mile
0   1 km

[10]

TIMING   The drive takes a half hour. Allow another two hours to visit Pitot House and the New Orleans Museum of Art, a bit more if you want to relax on the shores of the bayou or wander through the peaceful surrounding streets. City Park can take a half day or more, depending on how many activities you engage in.

Sights to See

4 **Alcee Fortier Park.** This tiny sliver of a park was named for philanthropist Alcee Fortier, who owned much of the surrounding area in the 19th century and founded a public school uptown. It forms a focal point of the Bayou St. John neighborhood, surrounded by hip restaurants and shops. ✉ *Esplanade Ave. and Ponce de Leon Blvd., Bayou St. John.*

► **1** **Bayou St. John.** A bayou is an inlet, a still, narrow waterway that emerges from the swamp at one end and normally joins a larger body of water at the other. This bayou—the only remaining bayou in New Orleans—borders City Park on the east and extends about 7 mi from Lake Pontchartrain to just past Orleans Avenue. It is named for John the Baptist, whose nativity (St. John's Eve, June 23), the most important day in the year for voodoo practitioners, was notoriously celebrated on the bayou's banks in the 1800s. The first European settlers in the area, believed to have been trappers, coexisted with Native Americans here beginning in 1704. Graceful old homes join more modern houses along picturesque **Moss Street**, along the section of the bayou nearest downtown. The small streets branching off from Moss Street make for scenic walks.

13 **Benachi-Torre House.** This elegant Greek Revival mansion was built in 1859 for the Greek consul in New Orleans. It earned the nickname "Rendezvous des Chasseurs" (meeting place of hunters) during the 19th century. The house is not open to the public. ✉ *2257 Bayou Rd., at Tonti St., Bayou St. John.*

2 **Blanc House.** Evariste Blanc built this house according to Greek Revival principles in 1834; his widow willed it to the Archdiocese of New Orleans to serve as a parish church. The building became a rectory instead, and a new structure was built, directly behind this one and facing Esplanade Avenue, to serve as the church. ✉ *1342 Moss St., Bayou St. John.*

need a break? Enjoy a cup of coffee or a pastry at **C. C.'s Coffee House** (✉ 2800 Esplanade Ave., Bayou St. John ☏ 504/482–9865 ⊕ www.ccscoffee. com), where sunny window seats look out onto a picturesque stretch of Esplanade Avenue. A few oak-shaded iron tables outside are a nice alternative in good weather.

7 **Cabrini High School and Mother Cabrini Shrine.** Mother Frances Cabrini, the first American-citizen saint (she was canonized in 1946), purchased the land between Esplanade Avenue and Bayou St. John near City Park in 1905 and built the Sacred Heart Orphan Asylum here. She stayed in the Pitot House, which was on her property until she gave it to the city during construction of the orphanage. In 1959 the institution was converted to a girls' high school in St. Cabrini's name. Her bedroom has been preserved as it was when she lived here, filled with personal effects and maintained as a shrine. Call ahead to arrange a tour, which includes the bedroom and the chapel where she prayed. ⊠ *3400 Esplanade Ave., Bayou St. John* ☎ *504/483–8690* ⊕ *www.cabrinihigh.com.*

🐾 ⑪ **Carousel Gardens.** This small amusement park has a New Orleans trea-
Fodor'sChoice sure as its centerpiece—a carousel from 1906 that is on the National
★ Register of Historic Places. The horses on one of the few remaining authentic carved wooden carousels in the country are periodically restored by artisans in Connecticut. Surrounding it are a roller coaster,
tilt-a-whirl, Ferris wheel, bumper cars, and other rides. A miniature train
takes adults and children throughout the area on its own track, and there
is a wading pool with bronze statuary. ⊠ *Victory Ave., City Park,
Bayou St. John* ☎ *504/482–4888* ⊕ *www.neworleanscitypark.com*
🎟 *General admission $2, unlimited-ride ticket $10* ◐ *During Celebration
in the Oaks, open evenings 5:30–10:30 PM; Mar.–May and Sept.–Nov.,
weekends only 10–4; June–Aug., daily 10–4.*

Fodor'sChoice **City Park.** Nineteenth-century French Quarter families used to spend en-
★ tire days in City Park, bringing their carriages down Esplanade Avenue
to enjoy the former sugar plantation that had been donated to the city
in 1850 by John McDonough, founder of numerous public schools. City
Park is one of the largest urban recreation areas in the country, a great
place to picnic, walk or jog, fish, feed the ducks, or just relax. The 1,500-
acre park has the largest number of mature live oak trees in the world;
more than 250 are registered with the Live Oak Society. Also included
within City Park's boundaries are the **Timken Center, New Orleans Botanical Garden, Storyland, Carousel Gardens, New Orleans Museum of Art,**
tennis courts, and a golf course. The artificial lagoons meandering
through the park are home to wild geese, ducks, and swans, and native
flora and fauna thrive among the moss-draped oaks. Art-deco benches,
fountains, bridges, and ironwork in the park are remnants of the 1930s
refurbishment by the Works Progress Administration. Around Christmas every year, the main area of the park dons thousands of Christmas
lights and decorations for the annual Celebration in the Oaks (walk-
through $5, drive-through $10). ⊠ *Bordered by City Park Ave., Robert
E. Lee Blvd., Marconi Dr., and Bayou St. John* ☎ *504/482–4888, 504/
483–9397 golf facilities* ⊕ *www.neworleanscitypark.com.*

⑭ **Edgar Degas House.** Impressionist painter Edgar Degas stayed with his
Musson cousins in this house during an 1872 visit to New Orleans, producing more than 70 works while here. Degas's mother and grandmother
were both born in New Orleans, and local lore makes much of the connection. Today this is a guesthouse, though public tours, which include
watching a film on Degas's family and their sojourn in New Orleans
and a discussion of the historic neighborhood, are arranged by appointment. ⊠ *2306 Esplanade Ave., Bayou St. John* ☎ *504/821–5009*
⊕ *www.degashouse.com* 🎟 *$10 suggested donation* ◐ *Tours by ap-
pointment weekdays 9–5, Sat. 9–3, Sun. 10–2.*

❺ **Fair Grounds Race Course.** The third-oldest racetrack in the country, and
one of the few remaining independent tracks, sits just off Esplanade Avenue, among the houses of Mid-City. Fire destroyed the historic old grandstand in the mid-1990s; the new facility is modern and comfortable,

complete with restaurant and snack bars. Pick up a serving of the corned beef hash, the house specialty. This is a fun place to spend a sunny afternoon on the bleachers or a rainy afternoon inside the grandstand. ⊠ *1751 Gentilly Blvd., Bayou St. John* ☎ *504/943–2200* ⊕ *www. fgno.com* ✉ *Grandstand $1, clubhouse $4* ⊙ *Thanksgiving–Mar., Thurs.–Mon. 1st post 12:30 PM.*

❾ New Orleans Botanical Garden. The very notion of a botanical garden might seem like gilding the lily in a city so uniformly lush with green, but horticulturists will enjoy this summary exhibit of indigenous flora and fauna. The peaceful 10-acre garden has a tropical conservatory, a water-lily pond, a formal rose garden, azalea and camellia gardens, and horticultural gardens, all decorated with fountains and sculptures by world-renowned local artist Enrique Alferez. Groups can take a guided tour (call ahead for times); otherwise, browse on your own through the grounds and the Pavilion of Two Sisters, a European-style orangery that houses a small horticultural library and a gift shop. ⊠ *Victory Ave., City Park, Bayou St. John* ☎ *504/483–9386* ⊕ *www.neworleanscitypark. com* ✉ *$5* ⊙ *Tues.–Sun. 10–4:30; hrs may vary by season.*

★ ❽ New Orleans Museum of Art (NOMA). Gracing the main entrance to City Park is this traditional fine arts museum, built in 1911. Modern wings, added to the original structure in the 1990s, bring light and space into the grand old building, which has a formal central staircase and many formal rooms as galleries. The jeweled treasures, particularly some of the famous eggs by Peter Carl Fabergé, are a favorite exhibit, along with European and American paintings, sculpture, drawings, prints, and photography. The museum holds one of the largest glass collections in the country and a large collection of Latin American colonial art. The comprehensive Asian art wing includes a good selection of Japanese painting of the Edo period; African, Oceanic, pre-Columbian, and Native American art are also represented. Temporary exhibits often favor local topics, such as Louis Armstrong or Edgar Degas (Degas's mother's family was from New Orleans, and Degas visited and painted here). The Courtyard Café in the museum looks out on a lovely sculpture garden. ⊠ *1 Collins Diboll Circle, City Park, Bayou St. John* ☎ *504/488–2631* ⊕ *www.noma.org* ✉ *$6, free Thurs. 10–noon for Louisiana residents* ⊙ *Tues.–Sun. 10–5.*

❸ Pitot House. One of the few surviving houses that lined the bayou in the late 1700s, and the only plantation house in the city open to the public, Pitot House is named for James Pitot, who bought the property in 1810 as a country home for his family. Pitot built one of the first cotton presses in New Orleans and served as the city's mayor from 1804 to 1805 and later as parish court judge. The Pitot House was restored and moved a block to its current location in the 1960s to make way for the expansion of Cabrini High School. It is noteworthy for its stucco-covered brick-between-post construction, an example of which is exposed on the second floor. The house is typical of the West Indies style brought to Louisiana by early planters, with galleries around the house that protect the interior from both rain and sunshine. No interior halls stifle ventilation, and opposing doors encourage a cross breeze. The house is furnished with period antiques from the United States, and particu-

FodorsChoice
★

larly Louisiana. ✉ *1440 Moss St., Bayou St. John* ☎ *504/482–0312* 💲*$5* ⊙ *Wed.–Sat. 10–3; last tour at 2.*

⓬ Ralph's on the Park. In 1860 Jean-Marie Saux opened a coffeehouse just outside the entrance to City Park, selling cold lemonades to the thirsty aristocrats who would venture out here from the French Quarter for the day. When Union troops set up camp in City Park during the Civil War, General Butler frequented Saux's establishment. Saux operated his coffee shop for 33 years before selling it to the Alciatore family, who also owned and operated Antoine's restaurant in the French Quarter (and still do). Since that time, the property has changed hands repeatedly, at one point serving as a favorite eatery among the prostitutes of Storyville. It has recently reopened for lunch and dinner; outside meal times, a bar menu is served. ✉ *900 City Park Ave., Bayou St. John* ☎ *504/486–3333* ⊕ *www.ralphsonthepark.com.*

➏ St. Louis Cemetery No. 3. Established in 1854, the St. Louis No. 3 is one block from the entrance to City Park, well paved and lined with elaborate aboveground crypts and mausoleums. ✉ *3428 Esplanade Ave., Bayou St. John.*

⟳ ⓾ Storyland. This is a whimsical and entertaining theme park for children, with 26 storybook exhibits built around fairy-tale characters. Children can climb, slide, and pretend to be Pinocchio, Captain Hook, or the Little Mermaid. Regular performances are staged in the Puppet Castle. ✉ *Victory Ave., City Park, Bayou St. John* ☎ *504/483–9381* ⊕ *www.neworleanscitypark.com* 💲 *$2* ⊙ *Weekends only; hrs vary by season (call ahead).*

Sydney and Walda Bestoff Sculpture Garden. In the shadow of the New Orleans Museum of Art is this lovely, peaceful garden, in which the contemporary sculpture collection donated by the Bestoff family is distributed along two banks of a small bayou. A docent is available to discuss the works with you at 11 AM and 2 PM, but the greatest pleasure the sculpture garden offers is a quiet stroll through the indigenously landscaped parcel of land. The sculptures themselves emerge in settings sometimes subtle, sometimes dramatic, and they include pieces by René Magritte, Barbara Hepworth, and Isamu Noguchi. ✉ *City Park, beside the New Orleans Museum of Art, Bayou St. John* ☎ *504/488–2631* ⊕ *www.noma.org* 💲 *Free* ⊙ *Tues.–Sun. 10–5.*

need a break? Built in 1913 as a casino, the **Timken Center** (✉ 1 Dreyfous Ave., City Park, Bayou St. John ☎ 504/483–9475), a Spanish mission–style building in City Park, has long served as a self-service restaurant, with public restrooms for park visitors. Po'boy sandwiches are standard fare, along with plate lunches; a Ben & Jerry's ice-cream counter dishes up dessert.

off the beaten path **ZULU SOCIAL AID AND PLEASURE CLUB –** Few institutions embody the local African-American heritage as well as this venerable club, home to the Mardi Gras krewe of the Zulus. Activities here are usually limited to members, but the lounge has an exuberant clientele that welcomes visitors, and the souvenir shop is open to anyone wishing to take home a bit of authentic New Orleans black history. The club is not in an area frequented by tourists; drive or take a taxi here. ⊠ *Lounge, 732 N. Broad St., Mid-City* ☎ *504/822–9850* ⊠ *Souvenir shop, 722 N. Broad St., Mid-City* ☎ *504/822–1559* ⊙ *Lounge daily around 3 PM, souvenir shop Mon.–Sat. 10–5:30; hrs of both may vary between Christmas and Mardi Gras.*

METAIRIE & THE LAKEFRONT

The neighborhood of Old Metairie is part of Orleans Parish and feels like much of uptown. The historic **Longue Vue House and Gardens,** tucked along what feels like a country road, is in the center of a particularly attractive area. Most of Metairie, however, has a modern, suburban feel. Metairie extends to the lakefront, an area buzzing with bikers, joggers, and especially boaters. On a pretty day, a picnic along the shore includes the spectacle of sailing extravaganzas.

Numbers in the text correspond to numbers in the margin and on the Bayou St. John–Lakefront map.

a good drive

From the French Quarter, drive away from the river on Esplanade Avenue until you hit City Park. Cross Bayou St. John, turn right onto Wisner Boulevard, and follow the bayou for another 3½ mi to the lakefront; City Park will be on the left most of the way. Private homes in every style line the bayou, often with canoes parked out front; especially striking are the richly modern homes on Park Island, at Harrison Avenue. On Saturday and Sunday you have to turn left onto Robert E. Lee Boulevard, then right onto Lakeshore Drive (after a mile), which will lead you to the Coast Guard lighthouse and link you back to the tour below. During the week, continue on Wisner Boulevard across Robert E. Lee Boulevard, and then go straight a few blocks until the road veers right, following a semicircle under an overpass; make a right turn onto Lakeshore Drive. The lake—not yet visible from behind the levee—is on the right. Keep right on Lakeshore Drive, along Lake Pontchartrain, for about 2 mi.

The sight of the lake, as it emerges from behind the levee, is impressive: it measures 24 mi across and stretches as far as the eye can see. The University of New Orleans lies about a mile behind you, and beyond that the Lakefront Airport (for small aircraft); neither is visible from here. In front of you, farther out, is the marina, and beyond that is Metairie. A cement seawall and walkway line the lake, with ample benches for picnicking or cuddling. A vigorous Save Our Lake program has helped revive the lake for fishing—a formerly dismal pursuit, owing to pollution—and you may see a number of fishermen taking advantage of the newly healthy waters. Soon after you cross the bayou, the colorful Mardi Gras Fountains, built to honor the many clubs that parade during the Mardi Gras season, appear on your left.

A short ride ahead, the United States Coast Guard has a headquarters and modest lighthouse; next door, Joe's Crab Shack, marked by the huge red EAT AT JOES sign, is more visually assertive and provides a pleasant deck overlooking the lake. The road curves sharply to the left here; beyond the curve, take your first right, onto Lake Avenue. A flood wall lines this road and blocks your view of the marina until you curve to the right, onto Roadway Drive. West End Park approaches on your right, lined by boathouses, marine service shops, and the Southern Yacht Club, the second-oldest yacht club in the country. On your left, opposite the park, is a handful of fresh seafood restaurants. The road continues out onto a breakwater, with boathouses lining the route. Some are modest homes, others elegant weekend getaways in disguise. All have boat docks beneath the upstairs living quarters and decks over the marina on the other side. When you reach the point of the breakwater, step out of the car to be enveloped by lake breezes. Across the harbor to your right is the Southern Yacht Club and the Coast Guard lighthouse; in every other direction are simply expanses of lake.

Return back along the breakwater, past West End Park, and along the flood wall back to the stoplight. Turn right onto West End Boulevard, and take another right at the first traffic light just beyond. Stay to the right as the road becomes the Metairie-Hammond Highway. After a mile or so you will reencounter the lake, marking your arrival in the Bucktown District of Metairie. Casual but good seafood joints abound, and here the lake is bounded by a levee that you can walk or bike along, called the **Linear Parkway** ⓕ. The path leads all the way to the Lake Pontchartrain Causeway, several miles away, making it popular for walking and biking.

Retrace your drive along the Metairie-Hammond Highway, and turn right at the second light onto Pontchartrain Boulevard. The road is separated by a large civil-defense air-raid shelter, a relic from the 1950s, which lies partially underground. Just past the shelter stands a large Celtic cross on a landscaped mound, which commemorates the thousands of Irish immigrants who built a canal—long since covered over—through this area in the 1830s. The boulevard eventually feeds onto I–10 East.

On I–10 going east, exit at the METAIRIE ROAD–CITY PARK sign. On the right is Metairie Cemetery, which you can drive through to observe lavish aboveground tombs and vaults. To reach the cemetery, continue to Metairie Road at the traffic light, turn left under the overpass, and left again to drive along the other side of the expressway. A sign will indicate where you should turn to enter the cemetery.

Leaving Metairie Cemetery, return on the feeder road beside the expressway, turning right at the traffic light onto Metairie Road. On the left are the grounds of the New Orleans Country Club. Turn left farther on at the sign for **Longue Vue House and Gardens** ⓖ, an English-style country estate. After the tour of Longue Vue, return to Metairie Road, turn right and go under the expressway overpass. At the next traffic light, turn right onto Canal Street, which will take you downtown and to the French Quarter.

The lakefront is patrolled by the levee police, but it is a vast area and can be isolated in spots. Although locals may be fishing and crabbing at night, it is not advisable to linger along the seawall or at the marina after sunset.

Sights to See

Lake Pontchartrain. This is a popular spot for fishing and boating: in good weather you may see lots of sailboats and windsurfers. Swimming, once very common, is slowly coming back into fashion thanks to pollution cleanup efforts. Lakeshore Drive, a road along Lake Pontchartrain, has many park and picnic areas that generally are filled on warm weekends and holidays. Many parking bays encourage you to stop and take a walk or sit on the seawall, the cement steps bordering the lake. The wall is a 5½-mi levee and seawall protection system, built by the Orleans Levee Board in the 1930s and leased to the U.S. government for a hospital and for Army and Navy installations during and after World War II. A Navy air station at Elysian Fields and Lakeshore Drive once stood at the present site of the University of New Orleans. The land around the seawall area (Lake Vista) was turned into private residential districts in the 1930s. This area is relatively safe during the day because of frequent police patrols. It's best, however, not to linger after sunset.

⑮ Linear Parkway. Along the south shore of Lake Pontchartrain is the Linear Parkway, a 7½-mi path for biking and hiking. This is a great place to see and hear local birds, watch the sun set over the lake, or chat with other walkers. You can plan a picnic for one of the informal rest stops along the way, but be prepared because there are no restrooms, water fountains, or concession stands anywhere nearby. Free parking is provided at both ends of the trail: in Bucktown and at the Williams Boulevard Boat Launch. Depending on the season, you can combine walking here with the **Bird-Watcher's Delight:** every evening at dusk from April through August, massive flocks of purple martin swallows gather near the Causeway bridge.

★ ℭ ⑯ Longue Vue House and Gardens. Eight acres of beautiful gardens embellished with fountains surround this city estate fashioned in the 1940s after the great country houses of England. The villa-style mansion is decorated with its original furnishings of English and American antiques, priceless tapestries, modern art, porcelain, and pottery. The fine millwork, special-ordered from New York, is mahogany and birch. You must visit the house by tour, but the wonderful gardens are open for independent exploration. They have various themes: the formal Spanish court, for instance, is modeled after a 14th-century Spanish garden, while a Discovery Garden introduces kids to the intricacies of horticulture. ⊠ 7 *Bamboo Rd., Metairie* ☎ *504/488–5488* ⊕ *www.longuevue.com* 🎫 *$10* ☉ *Mon.–Sat. 10–4:30, Sun. 1–5; last tour at 4.*

need a break? **Bruning's Restaurant** (⊠ 1922 West End Pkwy., Metairie ☎ 504/282–9395), overlooking Lake Pontchartrain, is a local institution, serving traditional New Orleans cuisine (including a whole fried flounder specialty). The original Bruning's was destroyed in Hurricane George and the owners are rebuilding. Meanwhile, they are running a smaller, but similar, restaurant next door.

ALGIERS POINT

Directly across the Mississippi River from the French Quarter and Canal Street, extending out into the river's curve, is the sleepy, historic neighborhood of Algiers Point. Settled at the turn of the 20th century, the community has quiet, tree-lined streets, quaint shops, and renovated Victorian houses, and has managed to remain somewhat isolated. In the early days of New Orleans, Algiers, named for the North African slave port, was a holding area for African slaves. The slaves were eventually ferried across the river to the French Quarter, where they were auctioned.

Algiers Point is best experienced by walking along its quiet streets, admiring the architecture, and savoring its small-town feel. However, because it is primarily residential and separated from the main part of the city by the river, it is isolated; you should take the usual precautions for personal safety. The big attraction here is Blaine Kern's Mardi Gras World, where Mardi Gras floats are made. A one-man Algiers Point welcoming and information service is provided by Russell Templet at his **Hair and Style Shop** (✉ 143 Delaronde St., Algiers Point ☎ 504/368–9417) a half block on the right from the ferry landing. Drop in and say hello.

Numbers in the text correspond to numbers in the margin and on the Algiers Point map.

a good walk

Blaine Kern's Mardi Gras World ❶ ➤, the main attraction on this side of the river, lies a five-minute drive upriver from the ferry landing. You can take a free shuttle (daily 9:30–4) or stroll the pedestrian path along the levee and then catch the shuttle back to the ferry. The ferry terminal is also the start of the neighborhood walk.

The following walk takes you around the historic renovation district that is bordered by Morgan Street, Patterson Road, Verret Street, Opelousas Avenue, and Powder Street. Note the various sizes and styles of homes, from ornate mansions to modest shotgun houses (in which all the doors open one behind another in a straight line, so you could fire a gun from the front step to a backyard wall without hitting a wall in between), a popular style of working-class architecture in New Orleans. Because these homes were all built around the early 1900s, they reflect the Victorian influence in vogue at that time.

From the ferry terminal, walk down on the left to Morgan Street. The Moorish-inspired Algiers Courthouse, built in 1896 and still in use, is on Morgan Street facing the levee. Its distinctive clock tower can be seen from the French Quarter. Bermuda Street, at the next corner, is lined with typical Victorian cottages, as are Pelican Avenue and Lavergne and Verret streets. No houses here are open to the public, but home owners are flattered when strollers stop to admire the many fine examples of historic preservation and restoration. Walk down Bermuda Street, take a left on Pelican Avenue, and follow it to Verret Street. At this corner is a vintage gas station, with its original Gulf sign intact.

Three blocks farther along Pelican Avenue is the **Algiers Point Library ❷**, an Italianate gift of Andrew Carnegie. Just beyond the library, turn right on Elmira Avenue, then right again on Alix Street. Confetti Park, a triangular playground, will be on your left a few blocks down, at Verret Street. It has a whimsical iron fence and walkways inlaid with marbles, doubloons, and shards of pottery. Across the street is a town square dominated by **Holy Name of Mary Church** ❸, a fine example of 1920s neo-Gothic architecture. Within the square, McDonough Memorial Park has small houses and shops lining its sides. An obelisk in the center honors local residents who died in various wars.

Two blocks beyond the park along Verret Street lies Opelousas Avenue, once as grand as St. Charles Avenue, but since fallen on hard times. Walk right on Opelousas and turn right again onto Bouny Street, lined with many lovely small homes. At 538 Bouny, stop to read the open hours painted onto the side of Daigle's Grocery: the entertaining testament, full of loopholes, makes you wonder if they ever open at all. Ahead you will pass the Crown and Anchor, an English pub that sometimes hosts live music. The ferry landing is directly ahead, just across from the Crown and Anchor.

Back on the ferry, Bollinger Algiers, Inc. is on your right. Oceangoing vessels are put into dry dock here for repairs and refurbishing, a reminder that New Orleans is a world-class port. Some work areas are visible from the ferry and levee.

TIMING Allot two to three hours for the ferry rides and the neighborhood walk. The ferry takes about 10 minutes each way, and you'll want at least an hour to wander along the streets of this small-town neighborhood. Count on another hour if you take in Mardi Gras World. The ferry ride is fine at night, but use caution if you do any walking on the Algiers side after dark.

Sights to See

❷ **Algiers Point Library.** This lovely Italianate library was built in 1907, a gift of Andrew Carnegie. A kiosk out front has a wealth of information on Algiers, including maps designating where various jazz artists, many of whom lived in Algiers, had homes. ⊠ *725 Pelican Ave., Algiers Point* ☏ *504/596–2640.*

☝ ▶ ❶ **Blaine Kern's Mardi Gras World.** Blaine Kern has for many years been the best-known artist and creator of Mardi Gras floats; he often personally conducts tours through this one-of-a-kind facility. You can watch the artists and builders at work, view a film about Mardi Gras, and buy Carnival memorabilia in the gift shop. A photo of yourself with one of the giant figures used on the floats makes a terrific souvenir, and there's a chest full of costumes for children to try on. A free shuttle van takes you from the ferry to Mardi Gras World; otherwise, an enjoyable 10-minute walk along the levee gets you here. ⊠ *233 Newton St., Algiers Point* ☏ *504/362–8211* ⊕ *www.mardigrasworld.com* 🎟 *$13.50 includes cake and coffee* ⊙ *Daily 9:30–4:30.*

❸ **Holy Name of Mary Church.** The largest church in Algiers, this redbrick building was constructed in 1929 to replace a former church from 1871. It is designed in English Gothic style and dominates the 400 block of Verret Street. ⊠ *Verret and Alix Sts.; church office at 500 Eliza St., Algiers Point* ☏ *504/362–5511.*

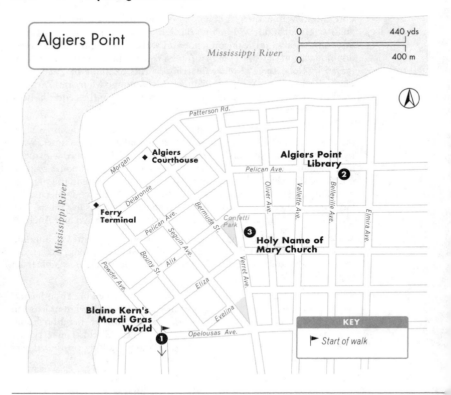

ELSEWHERE AROUND NEW ORLEANS

The Ninth Ward

The Ninth Ward is the largest of New Orleans's wards, or legislative districts, and one of the most colorful. Residents of this low- to middle-income area enthusiastically decorate for Christmas yet patronize lingerie nights at the corner bar without the slightest sense of irony. Figures such as Fats Domino, who could certainly move into tonier neighborhoods, stubbornly stick around. When asked where they live, residents will sooner crow "Ninth Ward" than "New Orleans." The area is also historically important: the Battle of New Orleans took place here in 1815, too late to affect the outcome of the War of 1812 but in time to pave the way for General Andrew Jackson's political career. The Ninth Ward is unsafe at night; visit the recommended sights only by car and during the day.

Leading away from the French Quarter, North Rampart Street joins with St. Claude Avenue, which extends into the Ninth Ward. This same road becomes St. Bernard Highway once you've crossed the Industrial Canal. All the following sights are within a few blocks of this main drag, and you should avoid venturing too far from it.

Boat Houses of Egania Street. Enclosed widow's walks and decorative, draped beading are among the striking details on these elegant houses just below the levee. Wraparound galleries add to the romance and reinforce the resemblance of these houses to old-fashioned steamships. To get here, turn right onto Reynes Street, just beyond the Industrial Canal. Veer left, with the levee, onto Douglass Street; the Boat Houses are several blocks ahead, at the corner of Egania and Douglass. The houses are closed to the public. ✉ *Egania and Douglass Sts., Ninth Ward.*

Chalmette Battlefield. The Battle of New Orleans, Andrew Jackson's vehicle to heroism, was fought on this site in 1815. The battle against British forces led by Major General Sir Edward Pakenham was fabulously successful—the British suffered some 2,000 casualties to the American 13—but belated: Jackson would later learn that peace had been declared two weeks earlier. The site is maintained by Jean Lafitte National Historical Park and includes the **Chalmette Cemetery,** resting place of soldiers from the Civil War through the Vietnam War; the **Chalmette Monument,** an obelisk commissioned to commemorate the 25th anniversary of the American victory under Jackson; and the **Malus-Beauregard House,** dating from the early 19th century. A visitor center is next to the monument, with historical exhibits, a diorama, and films about the battle. Ranger tours depart the visitor center twice daily. ✉ *8606 W. St. Bernard Hwy. (Rte. 46), 6 mi from downtown New Orleans, Ninth Ward* ☎ *504/281–0510 or 504/589–2636* ▨ *Free* ⊙ *Daily 9–5.*

Fats Domino's House. Turn left off St. Claude Avenue onto Caffin Street, at the second major intersection past the Industrial Canal; one block ahead is Antoine "Fats" Domino's unmistakable abode. The large "FD" on the facade of the colorful, one-story complex is one way to spot it. Domino, a rhythm-and-blues legend, rarely grants public performances or appearances these days, preferring to relax with his family in the Ninth Ward. In spite of the built-in advertising, the pink-detailed house is not open to the public. ✉ *1208 Caffin St., Ninth Ward.*

Jackson Barracks Military Museum. This is an indoor-outdoor display of aircraft and tanks used by Louisiana's Army National Guard and Air National Guard. Housed in the original Jackson Barracks powder magazine, which was built in 1837, the museum exhibits memorabilia, weaponry, and artifacts from all major U.S. wars through the Persian Gulf War. ✉ *6400 St. Claude Ave., Ninth Ward* ☎ *504/278–8242* ▨ *Free* ⊙ *Weekdays 8–4.*

New Orleans East

New Orleans East is pure suburbia, with the exception of the Bayou St. John Wildlife Refuge that sprawls across much of its acreage.

Audubon Louisiana Nature Center. The 86-acre Nature Center is a wonderful way to become acquainted with the natural environment surrounding New Orleans. Hiking trails, including 3 mi of raised boardwalk trails, reveal native flora and fauna; a hands-on museum, planetarium, and butterfly garden are educational and fun for kids. Special programs include animal presentations, trail hikes, and planetarium talks. School groups reserve much of the center on weekdays; weekends are oriented more toward visitors. ⊠ *5600 Read Blvd., at Nature Center Dr., Exit 244 off I–10* ☎ *504/246–5672* ⊕ *www.auduboninstitute.org* 🎟 *$5* ⊘ *Tues.–Fri. 9–5, Sat. 10–5, Sun. noon–5.*

⊙ **Six Flags New Orleans.** This 140-acre amusement park has dozens of rides and attractions for kids and adults. Highlights include a Batman inverted roller coaster, a children's village, and daily live music performances and stunt shows. Six Flags is about 12 mi from downtown. The hours and prices listed below are tentative; call ahead. ⊠ *12301 Lake Forest Blvd., junction of I–10 and I–510* ☎ *504/253–8000* ⊕ *www.sixflags. com* 🎟 *$40* ⊘ *Mid-Mar.–Memorial Day and mid-Aug.–Oct., Sat. 10–8, Sun. 11–7; Memorial Day–mid-Aug., Mon.–Thurs. 10–9, Fri. and Sat. 10–10, Sun. 11–8.*

Kenner

Kenner is a suburb 20 minutes from downtown New Orleans, home to New Orleans International Airport and to Rivertown, U.S.A., a historic district which has some small museums, many of them geared toward children. A statue marks the spot in Rivertown where the explorer La Salle first set foot in the region in 1682.

⊙ **Rivertown, U.S.A.** A collection of turn-of-the-20th-century Victorian cottages has been refurbished to house antiques shops, offices, and restaurants. Along the main stretch are numerous museums. A $15 pass is available for all museums; individually, the museums cost $3 each, except for the Space Station ($7). At the **Freeport–McMoran Daily Living Science Center, Planetarium, and Space Station** (⊠ 409A Williams Blvd., Kenner), a hands-on learning center focuses on science, health, and environmental issues. The planetarium in the Science Center has a high-powered telescope used to point out celestial seasonal wonders. Tickets for the Space Station are sold until 3:30. At the **Children's Castle** (⊠ 501 Williams Blvd., Kenner) kids can get involved in music, magic, mime, puppets, and storytelling. The **Louisiana Toy Train Museum** (⊠ 519 Williams Blvd., Kenner) is housed in a former train depot and depicts railroad history through photos, model trains, films, and slide shows. Native Americans demonstrate pirogue making, palmetto-hut building, dancing, beading, and storytelling at the **Louisiana Wildlife and Fisheries Museum** (⊠ 303 Williams Blvd., Kenner), which also displays 700 species of animals, some in their natural habitat. The **Mardi Gras Museum** (⊠ 421 Williams Blvd., Kenner) houses a lively, participatory simulation of Carnival, with live music, moving floats, and revelers tossing throws. Finally, the **Saints Hall of Fame Museum** (⊠ 409 Williams Blvd., Kenner) includes busts, memorabilia, and films of the popular home pro football team. Beyond all the museums, there is a beautiful overview of the Mississippi River at La Salle's Landing along the river. ⊠ *15 mi from New Orleans at end of Williams Blvd., off I–10, Kenner* ☎ *504/468–7231* ⊕ *www.rivertownkenner.org* 🎟 *Combined ticket for all museums $15* ⊘ *Tues.–Sat. 9–5.*

MARDI GRAS & JAZZ FEST

2

SHED YOUR INHIBITIONS
and join the revelry downtown ⇨*p.73*

CATCH AN ARMLOAD OF THROWS
from the floats of Bacchus ⇨*p.76*

GET UP EARLY
for a Zulu coconut ⇨*p.76*

AWAKEN YOUR SPIRITUAL SIDE
with the sounds from the Gospel tent ⇨*p.79*

COOL OFF WITH A MANGO ICE
before going to the next stage ⇨*p.81*

By Baty Landis   New Orleans's taste for celebration has been around for as long as the city itself. Travel diaries from the early 18th and 19th centuries record awe and occasional impatience with the never-ending celebrating through the streets of the old French Quarter. During the early 19th century, annual parades were held to honor firefighters, to mark the birthdays of presidents and governors, and on the occasion of births, deaths, and every event in between. Some have their theories: it's the port, the sub-sea-level elevation, or the mosquitoes that give them the fever. New Orleanians don't look for explanations or justifications—they just roll with the party.

MARDI GRAS

What could persuade a prominent New Orleans businessman to wear a pageboy wig, gold crown, jeweled tunic, and white tights in public—and consider it the honor of a lifetime? Or cause people to ask with interest, "Who found the baby in the king cake?" Or prompt little old ladies to jostle strangers and shout the phrase New Orleanians learn at Mama's knee—"Throw me something, Mister!" Come to New Orleans during Mardi Gras and find out.

Don't be smug: if you visit, you'll catch the fervor. After a few moments of astonished gaping, you'll yell for throws, too, draping layers of beads around your neck, sipping from a plastic cup as you prance along the street, bebopping with the marching bands, and having a grand old time.

Mardi Gras (French for "Fat Tuesday") is the final day of Carnival, an entire Christian holiday season that begins on the Twelfth Night of Christmas and comes crashing to a halt on Ash Wednesday, the first day of Lent. Though Mardi Gras is technically merely one day within the season, the term is used interchangeably with Carnival, especially as the season builds toward the big day. As sometimes befalls the Christmas holiday, the religious associations of Carnival serve mainly as a pretext for weeks of indulgence. Also, like Christmas, Carnival claims elaborately developed traditions of food, drink, and music, as well as a blend of public celebration (the parades) and more exclusive festivities, which take the form of elaborate private balls.

On Mardi Gras day, the entire city dons costumes, face paint, and masks, and takes to the streets for the final bash-of-a-celebration before Lent. It's an official city holiday, with just about everyone but the police and bartenders taking the day off. People roam the streets, drinking Bloody Marys for breakfast and switching to beer in the afternoon, and admiring one another's finery. Ragtag bands ramble about with horns and drums, Mardi Gras anthems pour from boom boxes, and king cakes (ring-shape cakes topped with purple, green, and gold sugar) color the streets. Some dozen parades roll through the city's streets along various routes, with large floats carrying riders who throw plastic beads and trinkets to onlookers. They call it America's largest street party, and that seems about right.

History

No one is absolutely sure how Mardi Gras celebrations started. The history of early Louisiana Carnival celebrations isn't really documented until the 1800s, when private balls were held by the descendants of French and Spanish settlers. There were also raucous street processions, where young men wore masks and costumes and sometimes dumped flour on passersby. Then on February 24, 1857, Mardi Gras changed.

At 9 PM, 60 or so men dressed like demons paraded through the streets with two floats in a torch-lighted cavalcade. The group called itself the Mistick Krewe of Comus, after the god of revelry. The krewe was started by men from both New Orleans and Mobile, Alabama, where Mardi Gras parades had begun a few years earlier. Wanting to observe the holiday more fully, these men formed a secret society and sent 3,000 invitations to a ball held at New Orleans's Gaiety Theater. They had begun a tradition. As time passed (with lapses for the Civil War), invitations to the Comus ball became so coveted that one year the krewe captain advertised a $2,000 reward for two missing invitations. Comus crowned Robert E. Lee's daughter, Mildred Lee, its first queen in 1884. Though Comus no longer parades, the krewe still holds its annual ball, one of the city's most exclusive.

Through the years, other groups of men organized Carnival krewes, each with its own distinctive character. In 1872, 40 businessmen founded Rex and sponsored a daytime parade for the Mardi Gras visit of His Imperial Highness the Grand Duke Alexis of Russia. They created a banner of green for faith, gold for power, and purple for justice—these remain the official Carnival colors. The first Rex parade was thrown together quickly with borrowed costumes, and there was no ball. The first reception was not until the next year, when a queen was chosen on the spot at a public ball. Eventually invitations and formal dress became required. Rex still parades on Mardi Gras morning, featuring some of the loveliest floats of Mardi Gras, and holds its lavish ball Mardi Gras night. Rex and his queen are considered the monarchs of the entire Carnival celebration. Their identities are kept secret until Mardi Gras morning, when their pictures claim the front page of the newspaper.

For many decades, krewes were strictly segregated by race; even Jews and Italians were banned from guest lists of the exclusive older balls (known as the old-line krewes). So other segments of society started clubs of their own. A black butler and dance instructor from Chicago started the Illinois Club in 1895. Though this club split into two krewes—the Original Illinois Club and the Young Men's Illinois Club—the debutantes who serve on the courts still perform the founder's dance, the Chicago Glide, in parallel galas. The Illinois clubs don't sponsor parades, but the Zulu Social Aide and Pleasure Club, organized in 1909 by working-class black men, does. The Zulu parade precedes Rex down St. Charles Avenue on Mardi Gras day. Zulu was one of the first krewes to integrate, and today members span the racial and economic spectrums.

After the Depression and World War II, Carnival krewes started popping up everywhere. Some were for doctors, others for businessmen, some for residents of certain neighborhoods, for women, for military men, or for gay men. The gay balls are splendid extravaganzas, with court members dressed in drag and bearing enormous, fantastical headdresses.

Parade standards changed in 1969, when a group of businessmen looking to entertain tourists the Sunday before Mardi Gras founded the Krewe of Bacchus, named after the god of wine. The sassy group stunned the city by setting new rules and strutting out with a stupendous show that dwarfed the old-line parades. The Bacchus floats (designed by Blaine Kern, who creates many of the Carnival parades) were bigger than any seen before, and the king was Danny Kaye, not a homegrown humanitarian but a famous entertainer. The party following the parade was in the old Rivergate Convention Center, not in the Municipal Auditorium or a hotel ballroom. There was no queen and no court, and the party was called a rendezvous, not a ball. All guests could dance, not just members and their wives as was the custom in old-line balls, where nonmembers merely watched the proceedings. The floats rode right into the Rivergate, and you didn't have to be socially prominent—or even white—to join. The crowds have loved Bacchus from day one, and guessing which celebrities will follow the likes of Ron Howard, Nicholas Cage, and Drew Carey as monarch has become equally as popular as wondering about the identity of Rex. The arrival of Bacchus ushered in an era of new krewes with open memberships, and today many of the parades are held by these young groups.

Making the Most of Mardi Gras

Navigating the mammoth crowds and scope of Carnival can be a daunting task, and even careful plans may be disrupted by surprises. This said, there are ways to prepare for the action. Meet the first challenge by finding a place to stay early in the game; make reservations a year ahead if possible. Once you're here, you'll have to decide what kind of Mardi Gras you want to have: family-style or raucous, mainstream or obscure, nighttime or daytime, or a combination. In any case, be sure to establish firm meeting spots and times with your group; confirm home addresses and exchange spare keys. The crowds make it nearly impossible to stick together with more than one other person.

Where to watch parades is an important decision. **Uptown** is the family zone, which is not to say it is not crowded and frenzied. Most activity, though, is focused around the parades; outside parade hours, the streets revert to relative normalcy. The crowds along the Uptown portion of the parade routes are thinner and more docile than those downtown. Particularly good places to catch the parades include the vicinity of the Columns Hotel (3811 St. Charles Ave., between Peniston and Gen. Taylor Sts.), which charges a small entry fee for access to its bar and bathrooms. The expansive front porch provides a good vantage point for those who don't need to catch any more beads. The corner of Napoleon and St. Charles avenues is a crowded but exciting place to watch, as the floats and bands turn onto the St. Charles Avenue. The

Garden District, particularly around Third and Fourth streets, is reasonably family-friendly. Between Jackson Avenue and Lee Circle is a more crowded and energetic (sometimes rowdy) place to watch, and a number of bars and stores on this strip can keep you lubricated and fed. Beyond the parade route, the uptown and Garden District bars see some increased traffic during Mardi Gras season, but nothing compared with the downtown craziness.

The final weekend before Mardi Gras finds locals at annual parties: anyone who lives along a parade route is expected to hold one. Those who don't live or know someone along St. Charles Avenue create their own little home bases on the neutral ground (median). Small children are placed up high in ladder seats, sofas and chairs and sometimes scaffolding line the route, and the uptown neutral ground becomes a nearly unnavigable mass of mini-territories. On Mardi Gras day, costuming begins very early on St. Charles Avenue, and the street is fairly crowded by 8 AM. If you plan to spend time uptown, it is worth getting up and out early to share in the excitement of anticipation. Various independent walking clubs and makeshift bands stroll by, and Rex finally arrives around 10:30, once Zulu has made its turn onto St. Charles at Jackson Avenue.

Most visitors find themselves **downtown** during Mardi Gras, for better or worse. A week or so before Mardi Gras, things heat up along Bourbon Street and throughout the French Quarter. By Mardi Gras weekend the crowds are so thick it is difficult to walk down Bourbon. Drinking, exchanging beads, and exhibitionism are the primary activities along Bourbon, where lines form to enter the bars and drink prices go through the roof. The side streets offer some degree of refuge while still sustaining a high party pitch: one hub of activity is along Decatur Street between Bienville Street and Jackson Square. Most parades roll down Canal Street at some point, and the crowds shift over accordingly to bounce to the marching bands and catch some beads before ducking back into the bars or the street scene. Unlike uptown, where parades are the focal point, downtown the parades seem merely a blip on the screen of general frenzy. And while the Monday before Mardi Gras provides a calm before the storm uptown, as locals make final costume preparations and rest up for the big day, the revelers in the French Quarter
★ are oblivious to any such caution. In fact, **Lundi Gras,** or the Monday before Mardi Gras, has become a major event downtown, especially at Spanish Plaza by the Riverwalk. Zulu, then Rex (Mardi Gras monarchs are commonly referred to simply by the name of their krewe) arrive by boat along the Mississippi and formally greet one another and their subjects at the Spanish Plaza dock. A large stage at Spanish Plaza hosts live music throughout the day. Fat Tuesday itself brings a frenzied climax to the streets of the French Quarter.

In deference to the religious pretext for this holiday, Mardi Gras "ends" with the arrival of Ash Wednesday and the Lenten season. At midnight on Tuesday night, downtown streets are cleared, and policemen in cars and on horses cruise through the French Quarter blaring from their loudspeakers "Mardi Gras is over. Go home."

Parades

Carnival parades begin in earnest two weekends before Mardi Gras, with parades day and night on weekends and every evening during the week. Figuring out which parades roll where and when is crucial. Useful publications with parade listings include Arthur Hardy's *Mardi Gras Guide* and the daily *Times-Picayune*, which publishes a Carnival guide some weeks before Mardi Gras and, in addition, includes a map of each day's parades in that morning's edition. The weekly *Gambit*, which appears in shops and coffeehouses each Sunday, also provides ongoing reports and guidance.

Mardi Gras parades are not the spectator activities that the term "parade" often signifies. The give-and-take between the riders on the floats and parade goers is what defines these events, and you cannot fully experience a parade by watching passively. The communication medium here is the "throws," or gifts the riders throw or hand to spectators. The most common throws are plastic beads, the most elaborate of which are worn like trophies by proud receivers. The beads used to be made of glass, often in Czechoslovakia; a strand of these old beads is now a collector's item. Glass beads reappeared in the Krewe d'Etat parade in 2002 and instantly became one of the prized throws of Mardi Gras. Other favorites include doubloons, or oversize aluminum coins, first introduced by Rex as His Majesty's official currency; plastic cups with the date and theme of the parade; medallion beads with the individual krewe's insignia; and stuffed animals.

Almost all krewes select a different theme each year for their parade. Themes range from the whimsical to the hard-edged political, though always with a tendency toward irreverence. The politically incorrect is part and parcel of the subversiveness that characterizes Carnival, and stabs at government officials, racist or sexist jokes, and the glorification of gluttony are only a few of the offenses that New Orleanians of all colors and backgrounds giggle at gleefully during Mardi Gras. The throws from a given float or parade will sometimes reflect that year's theme, one reason why locals dive for doubloons and plastic cups imprinted with the date and logo.

Between the floats, marching bands play pop and military tunes. Some of these bands represent branches of the military or civic groups from New Orleans or beyond, but most are high-school bands from New Orleans, and they are excellent. The undisputed king among the bands belongs to St. Augustine Senior High, or the Purple Knights. Other stars include the McDonough 35 and Kennedy high-school bands.

The floats and bands make up the bulk of the parades, with the odd walking group or convertible car tossed in here and there. During night parades, an extra ingredient is the flambeaux, torch-bearing dancers who historically lit the way for the parades. These days they provide little more than nostalgia and some fancy stepping to the bands, but they still earn tips along the route for their efforts.

Though parades used to roll through the French Quarter, these days the most popular ones start uptown at Napoleon Avenue, continuing down

St. Charles Avenue to Canal Street, and following Canal to their finish. Though it's chaotic all along the route, Uptown and the Garden District (along St. Charles before Jackson Avenue) tend to be more family-oriented. Heading downtown, parade goers become more numerous: Lee Circle is particularly lively. The real action, though, is along Canal Street itself, where raucous downtowners and drunken tourists converge. Many of the marching bands save their best energy for the turn onto Canal, where the riders generously unload their throws.

Many parades diverge from this route, and parades in the suburbs of Metairie, Kenner, Gretna, St. Bernard Parish, and Covington now keep many families in their own neighborhoods even on Mardi Gras day. In the weeks before Mardi Gras, two quirky parades run through the Quarter. Saturday night two weeks before Mardi Gras brings the **Krewe du Vieux** to Royal Street. Nearly every brass band in town participates, and the small floats are decorated along satirical, often off-color themes. One week later, on the Sunday afternoon one week before Mardi Gras, the **Krewe of Barkus** rolls along a winding route through the Quarter in the vicinity of St. Ann Street, featuring elaborately costumed canines and their proud owners, often in coordinated attire.

ESSENTIAL
PARADES
Though changes sometimes occur, the following parades are staples of Mardi Gras weekend. All follow a standard route down Napoleon Avenue, usually from the direction of the river, to St. Charles Avenue and then Canal, unless otherwise noted.

Friday. The Friday night before Fat Tuesday marks the beginning of the final push to Mardi Gras. **Hermes,** one of the oldest parading krewes, rolls first, followed by **Krewe d'Etat,** a relatively young krewe formed by local business leaders with a taste for satire. The Krewe d'Etat is by definition politically subversive, and the cleverly decorated floats are designed by Henri Schindler, the Mardi Gras master whose only other parade is Rex. In both cases, he designs for the old-style wagon float, as opposed to the more common truck flats. The Krewe d'Etat has a Dictator in place of the usual King and a Revolution instead of a ball (the sort of revolution that is by invitation only). The krewe prides itself on new and imaginative throws, such as a small stuffed jester that changes outfits annually and, when squeezed, drops such pearls of wisdom as "Live to ride—ride to live!," "Hail to the Dictator!," and "Krewe d'Etat rules!"

Saturday. The Saturday before Fat Tuesday notably spotlights the largest women's krewe, **Iris,** which was formed in 1922 and began parading in 1959. Ordinarily pristine members of uptown garden clubs let loose from behind their long masks and white gloves, flirting with the men along the route and tossing flowers to young hunks. Following Iris is **Tucks,** a young, fun parade founded some 35 years ago by Loyola students who would tour through a few uptown streets on the way to their favorite bar, Friar Tucks. The theme is always tongue-in-cheek, and the throws are beautifully coordinated with the decor of the individual floats. A Friar Tuck doll is a must-catch from this parade.

Following Tucks, a several-hour break occurs before **Endymion,** one of the blockbuster parades of the season. Endymion's extravagant floats cannot fit down most of St. Charles Avenue; it rolls instead down Howard Avenue before turning onto the Central Business District (CBD) portion of St. Charles and then Canal Street. It is notorious for delays; in spite of an afternoon starting time, it regularly reaches Canal Street late in the evening. For this reason, and because many of the riders are more interested in viewing breasts than in throwing beads, this parade is a difficult one to attend with children. Endymion finishes by rolling straight into the Superdome for the Extravaganza, a party attended by upwards of 14,000 people.

Sunday. Thoth is a fun daytime parade with a heartwarming peculiarity: it has designed an anomalous route that passes numerous nursing homes and hospitals, including Children's Hospital, at Tchoupitoulas and Henry Clay Avenue, by Audubon Park. The only Mardi Gras parade to follow Magazine Street, it eventually turns onto Napoleon Avenue and rejoins the usual St. Charles–Canal route. The other daytime Sunday parades are **Okeanus** and **Mid-City,** named for the neighborhood it originally rolled through.

One of the great Mardi Gras parades, **Bacchus** takes the St. Charles–Canal route Sunday night. The floats are spectacular, including some regular favorites like the endless Bacchagator and the mammoth King Kong, and some new floats each year. The Budweiser Clydesdales are another crowd-pleaser. The monarch is always a major celebrity. The marching bands are at their horn-swinging best for Bacchus, and the throws pour plentifully from the floats.

Monday. There are no day parades Monday, but Monday night brings one of the oldest krewes and one of the youngest end to end. **Proteus,** formed in 1882, pays tribute to the sea god with beautiful floats in the old wagon style. **Orpheus,** meanwhile, always has the latest in parade technology, such as confetti blowers and automatic plastic cup dispensers. The krewe is Harry Connick Jr.'s project, and the charming crooner's own float is one of the highlights.

MARDI GRAS DAY On Mardi Gras day it seems that every street in the city sees a piece of a procession at one point or another. One of the following krewes is sure to meet your styles and tastes.

St. Charles–Canal parades. Some parade goers simply will not be satisfied returning home without a **Zulu** coconut. If you are one of these people, get up early on Mardi Gras morning to catch the oldest African-American parade, and stand at least as far downtown as Jackson Avenue, where the parade turns onto St. Charles Avenue. If you are not prepared, the black-face riders, some of them in mock African dress, can seem in shockingly bad taste, but these parodies of minstrelsy are the long-standing traditions of the krewe. Zulu rolls down Jackson Avenue, turning onto St. Charles ahead of Rex, and reaching Canal Street around 11 AM, though in keeping with their mischievous customs, this timing can vary dramatically. **Rex,** traditionally regarded as king of Carnival, greets his subjects following Zulu. His floats are intricate, old-fashioned affairs, one of the visual high points of Mardi Gras day. Behind Rex are the truck parades: over 200 flatbed trucks, each rented

Fodor'sChoice
★

and decorated by an independent group, carrying more than 7,000 riders in all. The trucks roll one after another for hours, without bands or walking groups between them.

Walking Clubs and the Mardi Gras Indians. Along with Zulu, Rex, and the truck parades—all of which obediently follow planned and policed routes—Mardi Gras day also brings the haphazard wanderings of the Mardi Gras Indians and the walking clubs. The walking clubs zigzag all over town, stopping in bars and swapping paper flowers and beads for kisses.

A couple of walking clubs have settled into semi-regular routes. The **St. Ann** parade is named after the main gay strip of the French Quarter, where the parade winds up. It begins in the Bywater District and works its way through the Faubourg Marigny District before entering the Quarter. This is your best chance to see the Mardi Gras strutting of the city's most flamboyant queens. The provocatively named **Julu** was, in fact, originally a Jewish group that followed Zulu playing klezmer music. Julu has a large following and parades through Mid-City and Tremé. The founders of Julu include some of New Orleans's best young musicians, and joyous music is still a major part of the event. The Julu crowd takes its costumes very seriously, and the Frenchmen Street scene following the parade is one of the most colorful in town.

Predating most of the major parades, the **Mardi Gras Indians** hold their own rituals in the backstreets on Mardi Gras morning. The Indians are members of African-American organizations who dress in intricately beaded costumes that often take all year to create (the traditional Indians do not wear the same suit two years in a row). The Indians parade through backstreets, chanting songs from the Mardi Gras Indian repertory: some songs are common to all tribes, while some are associated with a specific tribe. Historically, the parading of the Indians through the backstreets of town would lead to physical confrontations and sometimes injuries when one tribe encountered another. Today the confrontations are more ceremonial, but the pridefulness behind the chanting and marching endures, creating a mystical and spiritual backdrop to the parades along the major streets.

The Indian tribes fall into two major categories: uptown and downtown. To seek out the uptown tribes on Mardi Gras morning, venture into the streets across St. Charles Avenue from the Garden District, between Jackson and Washington avenues. The downtown tribes generally revolve around Tremé. To find them, head away from the French Quarter on Ursulines Street.

Mardi Gras Safety

Whether you choose to watch the parades or to give yourself over to the madness of the mass party on Bourbon Street and throughout the Quarter, use common sense, dress comfortably, and leave your valuables safely locked up at home or in safe-deposit boxes at your hotel. Be aware of pickpockets. Don't carry excessive amounts of cash and don't wear jewelry that could tempt the wrong person.

Travel with one or more people rather than alone if possible, and set a permanent meeting spot where your family or group will convene at pre-set times throughout the day.

Though New Orleans is generally lax about rules, the police increase surveillance during the chaotic Carnival season. It is legal to carry alcoholic beverages (but not glass bottles) in the streets, but excessive public drunkenness might draw the attention of the cops. Do not throw anything at the floats or bands of parades, a ticketable and truly hazardous act. On the other hand, throwing change to the flambeaux, or torch carriers, who historically light the way for night parades, is customary.

Finally, although caution is essential, have confidence in the city's 1,700 police officers who patrol the parade routes, ably handling minor glitches as well as major crises.

WOMEN AT MARDI GRAS
A word of warning to women is unfortunately necessary here. During Mardi Gras many men from all over the country and all over the world descend on New Orleans in groups. Packs of guys together with a lot of alcohol can sometimes spell trouble. A common demand women will hear is "Show your tits!" More women than you would imagine flash as barter for good beads; if you feel tempted, be aware that the personal videos shot on Bourbon Street often wind up on cable shows like "Girls Gone Wild!" And if you are groped or feel threatened in any way, be assured that a police officer will probably be in your sight range.

Children & Mardi Gras

In many respects Mardi Gras seems designed for kids. Floats, parades, whimsical gifts, costumes, street vendors with tasty snacks and exciting toys mark the season and revelry carries the day. The daytime parades are most suitable for family-rated fun. If you want to bring children to the evening parades, the Garden District around Third Street is a good option, though no spot is immune from the raucous and the bawdy.

SAFETY
Children are especially vulnerable during Mardi Gras and must be carefully watched. Each year accidents occur when children (or adults) venture too near the wheels of floats. If you have kids with you, pick a spot some way back from the rolling parade. Keep a trained eye on little hands and running feet.

JAZZ & HERITAGE FESTIVAL

Jazz Fest is, in itself, reason enough for a trip to New Orleans. Each year during the last weekend in April and the first weekend in May, just as the summer heat is threatening to set in, the New Orleans Jazz and Heritage Festival roars through town, bursting with more music, food, and fun than any single person could possibly take in. The festival exuberantly exceeds the boundaries of its name, focusing on all aspects of Louisiana music and culture and staging national and international performers as well as local ones. In addition to jazz, you can hear blues, rhythm and blues, Cajun, zydeco, gospel, pop, rock, Latin, and other types of music from around the world.

History

The festival was founded in 1970 by George Wein, who is also responsible for the Newport Jazz Festival. Once he had set his heart on producing a festival in New Orleans, Wein found some young local jazz enthusiasts to do the booking for the small event, originally held in Beauregard Square (now Armstrong Park). Early performers included the Wild Magnolias Mardi Gras Indians, Professor Longhair, Mahalia Jackson, and Duke Ellington. The big names just kept coming as the Fest grew year after year: Fats Domino, Junior Wells, Buddy Guy, Charles Mingus, Ella Fitzgerald, Dr. John, Aaron Neville, Bonnie Raitt, Santana, and Ray Charles have all joined the lesser-known local and regional artists who make up the bulk of the festival. Jazz Fest has now grown into a giant, drawing some half-million people a year and showcasing some 6,000 performers, cooks, and artisans. Regulars make the annual pilgrimage from spots all over the country, and sometimes the world, to sit in the middle of a field with thousands of others, listening to good music and indulging in Creole and Cajun food. Even rain can't sour this crowd: they tramp gleefully through the track, digging their toes into the mud and listening to the same good music.

What Goes On

The festival is divided into two parts: its heart and soul is the Heritage Fair, held at the New Orleans Fair Grounds Race Track, in Mid-City, from 11 AM to 7 PM Friday through Sunday of the first weekend, Thursday through Sunday of the second weekend. Here 12 music stages, a variety of smaller performance and discussion spaces, arts, crafts, food, and endless fun unfolds. When the Fair Grounds close at 7 PM, the other part of Jazz Fest takes over: the evening concerts. These are held in locations throughout town, and ticket prices vary widely ($30–$50 for most), depending on the venue and performer.

Music & Heritage

The Fair Grounds' grandstand and grassy infield together hold 12 stages, each of which sees six or seven different performers a day. Each stage has a special bent: **Congo Square** hosts African and African diaspora music, the **Fais-do-do Stage** has Cajun and zydeco music. The **Heritage Stage** favors traditional New Orleans jazz (affectionately known as "Trad" locally), and the larger **Jazz Tent** showcases nationally recognized practitioners of all kinds of jazz, from swing to avant-garde. The **Gospel Tent** is always lively, with large choruses and smaller groups alike commonly rousing the crowd to its feet. Other specialty stages include the **Blues Tent** and the **Native American Stage.** The **Lagniappe Stage,** outside the grandstand among the horse stalls, hosts a wide range of music and is rarely crowded. Big-name local acts like the Neville Brothers and Dr. John, as well as national stars like Dave Matthews and Ziggy Marley, grace the large stages at either end of the racetrack.

Fodor's Choice
★
★

You will definitely want to carry a music schedule with you, whether purchased in the official Jazz Fest program or torn out of a local publication. Yet the trick here is not to get too hung up on seeing any one

THE SECOND LINE

ONE OF THE GREAT JOYS OF THE JAZZ FEST *is the odd parade that occasionally takes over the pedestrian paths, bursting through the center of the fairgrounds with an explosion of color, sun-brellas, horns, feathers, and fancy footwork. This apparently chaotic event is called a second line.*

The second line is a type of parade historically associated with jazz funerals; the term "second line" is often thought originally to have referred to the secondary group of participants in such a parade, behind the band and the family. "Second line"is also used to refer to the distinctive dance moves that can be glimpsed during New Orleans street parades of all sorts.

During the early 20th century, the New Orleans second line served an important community function. At that time, African-Americans were not allowed to buy insurance, so they formed mutual aid

societies—called Social Aide and Pleasure Clubs—to help members through tough times. When a member's house burned down, or when someone died and their family lacked the funds for a proper funeral, the club would step in to help. Live bands and second-lining become integral parts of the fund-raising efforts. Combined with the city's long-standing penchant for a parade, these activities led to the current "second line" brass-band parade tradition.

Though the second-line tradition waned during the mid-20th century, today it is back with a vengeance. In addition to Zulu's Mardi Gras morning bonanza down St. Charles Avenue, a brass-band-led "second-line" can be found each Sunday from October to March in an inner city neighborhood of New Orleans. But it's the rough-rolling second lines that splash through the Fair Grounds a few times a day during JazzFest that are at the heart of what the festival is really about.

performance. Favorite Fest memories inevitably recall the little-known Cajun group you happened upon while on your way to the mango ice stand or the folk-instrument demonstration encountered while ducking into the grandstand to escape a rain shower. The Heritage Stage hosts some of the most intimate, spontaneous shows at the Fest, and the Gospel Tent becomes an instant favorite with anyone who passes through.

Longtime Fest goers learn to love the **grandstand**. Exhibits of artistic, historical, and culinary interest fill halls and walls; panel discussions take up issues surrounding New Orleans music and culture; and interviews of musicians, artists, and writers are conducted on the indoor Heritage Stage. In the grandstand you might find Mardi Gras Indians sewing elaborately beaded costumes, craftspeople carving pirogues, or chefs giving cooking demonstrations—and samples. For those who are unromanced by portable toilets, bathrooms with indoor plumbing are found on all floors of the grandstand (hint: the higher you go, the shorter the lines). And it's all air-conditioned.

If you still have the energy, by night you can catch full concerts by groups you may have shortchanged during the day. Occasionally, evening concerts feature musicians who are performing at night only. Full sched-

ules and ticket information are available on the Jazz Fest's Web site
(⊕ www.nojazzfest.com).

Food

Jazz Fest's allurements don't stop with the music. Restaurants from all
over Louisiana vie for space in the food stalls, where you can find spicy
Cajun sausage, boiled crawfish, jambalaya, gumbo, and every variety
of po'boy (including alligator), for starters. Come hungry. The cuisine
is all local or regional and all delicious. Portions usually come in two
sizes: choosing the small means you'll have room to taste more good-
ies as the day wears on. Stars include the crawfish bread (bread stuffed
with crawfish, cheese, and seasonings), Crawfish Monica (a pasta cream
dish with crawfish), and soft-shell-crab po'boys. The soft-shell-crawfish
po'boy is a relative splurge, but the portion is large and it is a wonderful novelty. A dish of boiled crawfish can keep you busy through an entire set of music and is a local specialty. The mango ice is a staple for
many, and proceeds benefit the local jazz and heritage radio station. If
you've never had a New Orleans–style snowball, you won't want to miss
the shaved-iced concoctions. A little less sweet and incredibly refresh-
ing is the Strawberry Lemonade. Note that outside food and beverages
are not allowed onto the festival grounds, though bottled water is an
exception. Beer is available from a number of tents around the grounds,
but hard liquor is not served or allowed at the festival.

Shopping

The competition for a crafts booth is nearly as fierce as that for food
stalls. Unlike the cooks, however, the artists represented at Jazz Fest hail
from not only Louisiana but from all over the United States. Craft areas
include Contemporary Crafts, near the Gospel Tent, which sells wares
from nationwide artists and artisans; the Louisiana Marketplace, near
the center of the infield, which showcases folk art from the city and the
region; and a Native American Village, which spotlights performances
and crafts related to Native American culture. Surrounding the Congo
Square stage are stands with African and African-influenced artifacts,
clothing, and accessories. You may be able to bargain at the stands, particularly toward the end of the weekend. Many of the artists have a spot
for only one of the two weekends.

More shopping is scattered through the grandstand, in association with
various local art and cultural displays. A Virgin Megastore outpost
near the grandstand sells CDs by musicians playing at the festival as well
as other New Orleans and Louisiana music.

Festival Basics

Planning

For optimum enjoyment of the food and crafts booths, arrive early, before noon. You can easily access all the food stands, which are crowded
the rest of the day before tapering off after 6 PM. Also, the crowds at
the stages are smaller earlier in the day—and at Jazz Fest, a bigger-name
act does not always mean a richer musical experience.

The traditional place to arrange a rendezvous is at the flagpole in the center of the Fair Grounds, easily visible from any point at the Fest thanks to the lines of small, colorful flags leading up to it. Though convenient, on the busiest days this spot can become too crowded to navigate, and some may prefer to find meeting spots within the air-conditioned grandstand. And when the infield becomes too crowded to navigate comfortably, consider walking along the dirt racetrack itself, which circles beyond the stages. A 15-minute tour around the track provides a quick digest of all the music happening at one time, and you can duck back onto the infield whenever something strikes your fancy. Whatever strategy you adopt, Jazz Fest is one place to rein in the ambition. The sun, heat, swirling crowds, and overwhelming selection of snacks, music, and crafts can create a controlled chaos, and heat exhaustion is a danger. Pace yourself at a relaxed tempo and enjoy.

You can purchase a full program once you arrive at the festival, which includes full schedules and maps, as well as feature pieces. Locals usually simply tear each day's schedule and a map of the Fair Grounds from the *Gambit* weekly or *OffBeat* monthly magazine, both available free in local coffee shops and clubs. The daily *Times-Picayune* also publishes maps and schedules, in its Friday "Lagniappe" section. For advance listings of artists to be featured and other information about the Jazz Fest, you can contact the **New Orleans Jazz & Heritage Foundation** (☎ 504/410–4100 ⊕ www.nojazzfest.com), which sponsors the festival.

What to Wear & Bring

Clothing should be minimal, or light and breezy; it can be blazingly hot at the sun-drenched Fair Grounds. If it rains, all you need is a baseball cap and a light windbreaker or poncho; rain protection can also be as basic as a 30-gallon trash bag. Sunglasses are a must; so is sunscreen. Couture this is not: faded shirts and shorts are the official Jazz Fest habit. Choose sneakers or comfy walking shoes with socks. Remember, this is a racetrack; as diligently as they may nurture the grass, by the end of Jazz Fest it always gives way to dust, mud, and straw. You may bring tarps or blankets into the festival, but no stakes or chairs. At the biggest stages, families and groups of friends stake out territory with various ground covers. If you don't mind the unavoidable tiptoeing over and around your space that the day will bring, this is an excellent way to create a home base for your group.

Children at Jazz Fest

Consider taking the kids to Jazz Fest on one day; leave them at home the next. An area just inside the infield from the grandstand is devoted to children, with music, crafts, and storytelling geared toward kids. A bulletin board in the same area posts schedules and general advice for negotiating the festival with children; nearby, it is possible to "register" your children and create identification tags for them to wear at the festival. The lawn in this kids' area is generally less populated than elsewhere on the Fair Grounds, making it easier to keep an eye on children as they run about. The Kids' Tent, meanwhile, provides shade with your music. The grandstand is another great place for a cool-off, and the generally relaxed atmosphere creates a kid-friendly zone.

Safety

The Jazz Fest itself is completely safe, but be warned that the surrounding neighborhood is somewhat depressed, and petty crime does occur during this time. If you stay at the festival until the bitter end, when it starts to grow dark, be aware of your surroundings as you exit and do not roam the area unless you are familiar with it.

Mardi Gras & Jazz Fest A to Z

To research prices, get advice from other travelers, and book travel arrangements, visit www.fodors.com.

BIKE TRAVEL

Renting bicycles (and locks) is a good way to sidestep the heavy street traffic and parking difficulties that Mardi Gras and Jazz Fest bring. New Orleans is small and flat, and the bike ride from the Garden District to the French Quarter takes about 15 minutes.

If you're biking to Jazz Fest, just follow Esplanade Avenue away from the river, and veer right onto Bayou Road (where everyone else is headed) just before Broad Street. There are supervised bike lots near each festival entrance, though you must bring your own lock.

BUS TRAVEL

Festival shuttles serve major hotels, spots downtown, and City Park. The Regional Transit Authority runs city buses that can also get you there for $1.25. The Jazz Fest Express shuttle service runs a continuous loop between the Fair Grounds and three downtown locations: the Sheraton Hotel, the Wyndham-Canal Place, and Harrah's New Orleans casino. The shuttle runs at least every 30 minutes and costs $10 round-trip. New Orleans Tours also operates a shuttle, with wheelchair accessibility. Stops include City Park, Harrah's New Orleans casino, and several downtown hotels.

Festival shuttles ☎504/529-0500 or 800/366-8882 ⊕www.bigeasytravel.com/jazzfest. html. **New Orleans Tours** ☎ 504/212-5900 ⊕ www.notours.com. **Regional Transit Authority** ☎ 504/248-3900, 504/242-2600 automated information ⊕ www.norta.com.

CAR TRAVEL

PARKING Parking is at a premium during Mardi Gras and Jazz Fest seasons. It's best to use your hotel's facilities, even if it means extra walking to the parade route. During the final weekend of Carnival the French Quarter is closed to automobile traffic; scope out a lot or a spot in the CBD. It is also impossible to cross the parade route at any point in a car, and many bus routes are disrupted. If possible, leave the car behind and take a taxi, the streetcar, a bike, or walk.

At Jazz Fest, parking at the Fair Grounds is extremely limited, and it is best to find another way to get here, if possible. If you must drive, you will have to come early for the privilege of paying for a spot at the Fair Grounds; otherwise, join the rest of the caravan making ever-wider circles beyond the Fest in search of street parking, which is free.

DISABILITIES & ACCESSIBILITY

Because Mardi Gras is a street party, accessibility is open. You'll need to map out accessible restrooms ahead of time.

At Jazz Fest, the festival does its best to assist visitors with disabilities, from providing wheelchairs and special viewing locations and convenient restrooms to doing snack runs to a favorite food booth. However, this is a huge event held mainly on a dirt-and-grass field, and disabled visitors must be ready for a challenge. Service information for people with disabilities is available at the Access Center just inside the grandstand. People with mobility limitations should use the Gentilly Boulevard Vehicular Gate for accessible parking or the Gentilly Boulevard Pedestrian Gate when arriving or leaving by taxi. Wheelchair-accessible shuttle-bus service is available at New Orleans Tours' designated pickup and drop-off points. All grandstand stages have reserved wheelchair spaces and accessible restrooms. Access assistance is available at food booths. TTY (Text Telephone) stations are erected by Fair Central and in the grandstand.

🖫 **Advocacy Center for the Elderly and Disabled** ✉ 225 Baronne St., Suite 2112, 70112 ☎ 504/522-2337 [also TTY], 800/960-7705 [also TTY]. **Jazz Fest Access Center** ☎ 504/522-4786. **New Orleans Tours** ☎ 504/212-5900 ⊕ www.notours.com.

EMERGENCY

At Jazz Fest, a first-aid station inside the track in front of the grandstand, as well as two outposts in the infield, stock bandages, salves, and other basic medical needs. In case of problems more serious than a sunburn or a scrape, full medical facilities are available.

LODGING

Mardi Gras and Jazz Fest draw millions of people from the world over. Make room reservations as soon as possible—a year in advance is not too early. Space can become available off and on as reservations are released leading up to the event. A hotel may have no rooms available one day but 10 the next. Keep trying. Minimum-stay requirements are often in effect at area hotels. Consider bed-and-breakfasts uptown or on Esplanade Avenue. To book a packaged tour, contact Destination Management.

🖫 **Destination Management Inc.** ☎ 504/592-0557 ⊕ www.bigeasytravel.com/jazzfest.html.

RESTROOMS

The city sets up several hundred portable restrooms during Mardi Gras. Many downtown hotels, bars, and restaurants allow only guests to use their public restrooms. Plan ahead. When you do find yourself patronizing a bar or restaurant, take advantage of the restrooms.

At Jazz Fest, the best bathroom spots are on the upper floors of the grandstand. This is well worth the walk; the bathrooms are air-conditioned and clean, and you can wash your hands. Otherwise, use the portable toilets right inside the gate, even if you don't think you need to. They're among the few with no lines, especially important if you're with kids.

STREETCARS

During Mardi Gras, the streetcar does not run along the parade route during parades and for some time before and after. If you are staying uptown, you can take the streetcar as far as Napoleon Avenue, then walk to your preferred parade spot.

TAXIS

Cabs cruise the French Quarter and CBD but rarely beyond. Reliable companies with 24-hour service are United Cabs and Yellow-Checker Cabs. The metered fare is $2.50 at the flag drop, $1.60 per mile, and $1 for each additional passenger. However, cabbies generally turn off the meter during special events, in which case you should arrange the fare before heading off.

United Cabs ☎ 504/522-9771. **Yellow-Checker Cabs** ☎ 504/943-2411.

VISITOR INFORMATION

New Orleans Convention and Visitors Bureau ⊠ 1520 Sugar Bowl Dr., CBD, 70112 ☎ 504/566-5011 or 800/672-6124 🖷 504/566-5021 ⊕ www.visitneworleans.info. **New Orleans Welcome Center** ⊠ 529 St. Ann St., on Jackson Sq., French Quarter, 70116 ☎ 504/568-5661.

WHERE TO EAT

3

Updated By
Sara Roahen

A DISTINCTIVE COOKING STYLE is as deeply embedded in New Orleans's psyche as are its distinctive architecture and music. Each reflects in its own way an exuberance of spirit that has made the city a favorite destination of world travelers. Classifying the city's traditional cooking styles can be frustrating, however. The two major divisions of the cuisine—the urban Creole and the more rustic Acadian (or "Cajun")—often merge in a single dish. Mainstream South Louisiana cooking is fraught with a network of subcuisines drawn from a polyglot of cultures.

Today's menus reflect nearly 300 years of ethnic overlap. The major influences came from France (both before and after the Revolution of 1789), Africa, Spain, the region's Native Americans, the Caribbean, and, later, southern Italy, Germany, and the former Yugoslavia. In the 1980s, Asian chefs joined the culinary melting pot with brand-new treatments of seafood drawn from Louisiana's bountiful coastal wetlands and the Gulf of Mexico.

Despite the increasingly blurred lines separating all these styles, Creole and Cajun, the two mother cuisines, have some distinguishing characteristics. Creole cooking carries an urban gloss, whether it's a proletarian dish of semiliquid red beans atop steaming white rice or a supremely elegant sauce of wine and cream on delicate-flesh fish.

Cajun food, on the other hand, is decidedly more rough hewn and rural. The first waves of Acadian settlers found their way to the Louisiana bayous and marshes in the last quarter of the 18th century. Most had already been farmers and fishermen in Canada and France. Lard was the tie that bound much of the Cajuns' early cooking. For the more sophisticated Creole cooks, it was butter and cream.

To present-day New Orleanians, much of the so-called Cajun food popularized in the 1980s is as exotic as it is to New Yorkers or San Franciscans. One reason is that traditional Cajun gastronomy does not rely heavily on jalapeño peppers, cream sauces, and pasta. Another is that the rest of America discovered chef Paul Prudhomme's blackened fish before Louisiana did. The result is that the number of highly visible New Orleans restaurants serving food that even approaches the lusty spirit of Acadian cooking does not exceed five or six.

The freewheeling menus (as well as the decor and prices) at such legendary places as Commander's Palace, K-Paul's Louisiana Kitchen, Brigtsen's, and Emeril's cover a range of Creole-Acadian influences. Other dining spots in the city—such as Bayona, Gautreau's, and Peristyle—depend more on contemporary tastes and techniques. Their menus are more likely to list lighter, eclectic dishes.

Restaurants serving virtually every variation on the city's culinary style—from po'boys and red beans and rice to old-line dishes lavished with butter or cream—fill the French Quarter. But most ethnic restaurants, from Italian to Vietnamese, are more likely to be found in other parts of New Orleans and its environs.

French Quarter

African

$ ✕ **Bennachin.** New Orleans's Creole cuisine borrows ingredients and techniques from the African diaspora, but Bennachin, which highlights the cooking of Gambia and Cameroon, is one of the city's few truly African restaurants. Beef stews are superb here, specifically one with a tart, gingery, ground melon-seed sauce. All stews come with rice or mashed yams, which you traditionally eat with your hands. Vegetarians have options, including black-eyed-pea fritters, and spicy sautéed spinach served with plantains and coconut rice. Exposed brick walls and African wall hangings surround about a dozen tables and a small open kitchen. It's usually overcrowded but fun. ✉ *1212 Royal St., French Quarter* ☎ *504/ 522–1230* ⚐ *Reservations not accepted* ▤ *AE, D, MC, V* ⛻ *BYOB.*

American

¢–$$ ✕ **Port of Call.** People wait for an hour-plus outside Port of Call every night, in the heavy heat of July and the downpours of September, for fist-thick burgers made from freshly ground beef, grilled to order and served with baked potatoes that are always perfectly fluffy. For the definitive experience, drink a Monsoon while you wait (Port of Call's mind-bending take on the Hurricane), and order your potato "loaded" (with mushrooms, cheddar cheese, sour cream, butter, chives, and bacon bits). Decent pizzas and fine steaks are also available. The dark, smoky barroom isn't suitable for small children. ✉ *838 Esplanade Ave., French Quarter* ☎ *504/523–0120* ⚐ *Reservations not accepted* ▤ *AE, MC, V.*

Cafés & Coffeehouses

★ ¢ ✕ **Café du Monde.** For most visitors, no trip to New Orleans would be complete without a cup of chicory-laced café au lait and a few sugar-dusted beignets in this venerable Creole institution. The tables are jammed at almost any hour with locals and tourists feasting on the views of Jackson Square. The magical time to go is just before dawn, when the bustle subsides and you can almost hear the birds in the crepe myrtles across the way. Four satellite locations (the New Orleans Centre, Riverwalk Marketplace in the CBD, Lakeside Shopping Center in Metairie, Esplanade Mall in Kenner) are convenient but lack the character of the original. ✉ *800 Decatur St., French Quarter* ☎ *504/525–4544* ▤ *No credit cards.*

Cajun-Inspired

$$–$$$$ ✕ **K-Paul's Louisiana Kitchen.** In this comfortable French Quarter café of glossy wooden floors and exposed brick, chef Paul Prudhomme started the blackening craze and added "Cajun" to America's culinary vocabulary. Two decades later, thousands still consider a visit to New Orleans partly wasted without a visit to K-Paul's for his inventive gumbos, fried crawfish tails, blackened tuna, roast duck with rice dressing, and sweet-potato–pecan pie. Prices are steep but servings are generous. Although you may make a reservation these days, it's still tradition to queue up along Chartres Street before the doors open for dinner. ✉ *416 Chartres St., French Quarter* ☎ *504/524–7394* ⚐ *Reservations essential* ▤ *AE, D, DC, MC, V* ☉ *Closed Sun. No lunch.*

New Orleans's centuries-old preoccupation with food often appeals more to the palate and the heart than to the eye or the intellect. The most artfully prepared restaurant dish has a short shelf life if the flavor doesn't live up to the presentation. Today, New Orleans's dining culture is infinitely more diverse than in the days when po'boy sandwiches and elegant French-Creole sauces dominated the culinary spotlight. Asian, Latin American, and Mediterranean cuisines coexist with the traditional Creole-Acadian dishes. The restaurants we list are the cream of the crop in each price category. It's difficult to get a bad meal in this town, so read up on your cuisine options and savor every bite.

3

Brunch

Upscale restaurants on the tourist track often serve very reasonable, fixed-price brunch menus, many of them buffet style. A jazz group often supplies live music. Sunday, from late morning to early afternoon, is the prime time for brunch, although a few restaurants serve brunch on other days, too. Among the more reliable spots for these brunches are Commander's Palace, Palace Café, and Mr. B's Bistro, all for the festive atmosphere and food quality; Arnaud's, for the glittery main dining room, and Elizabeth's, for the down-home southern cooking and attitude on Saturday.

Dress

If you're eating in a luxury restaurant or in one of the old-line, conservative Creole places, dress appropriately. If you don't know whether jackets are required or jeans are frowned upon, telephoning to find out is a simple matter. You'll probably be more comfortable, and so will the restaurant's other customers. Also, you may avoid being turned away at the door (though some formal restaurants do keep loaner jackets on hand). Unless otherwise noted, restaurants listed in this book allow casual dress. Reviews mention dress only when men are required to wear a jacket or a jacket and tie.

Mealtimes

White-tablecloth restaurants in New Orleans adhere to traditional service hours—11 or 11:30 AM to about 2 PM for lunch, and about 6 to 10 PM for dinner. Hunger pangs, however, can be assuaged at any hour in the French Quarter, with such fare as hot dogs from a street vendor to breakfast at any hour in a few places. Sunday and Monday are the most frequent closing days for full-service restaurants. A Saturday lunch, even in a popular upscale restaurant, can be tough to find outside the Quarter. Unless otherwise noted, the restaurants listed in this guide are open daily for lunch and dinner.

Reservations

Most restaurants in New Orleans accept reservations, and many of the very popular places become quickly booked, especially on Friday and Saturday nights. Reservations are always a good idea: we mention them only when they're essential or not accepted. The best strategy is to reserve as soon as you decide where and when you'd like to go; several weeks ahead of time is not too far in advance to reserve for trips during Mardi Gras, Jazz Fest, or other special events. Reconfirm as soon as you arrive. If you must cancel, let the reservations desk know immediately.

Tipping The standard for tipping in New Orleans is no different from that in the rest of the country—at least 15% or 20%. Sales taxes for restaurants are 9.5%, which means that doubling the tax is a widespread practice. This applies not only to fine-dining establishments but also casual places with table service. Rarely is the maitre d' tipped, since gratuities are generally pooled among the service staffs. Most menus contain a notice that a service charge is automatically added to the bill for groups of eight or more.

Wine & Spirits Liquor laws in New Orleans are liberal, although the drinking age is 21 in Louisiana. Liquor is available around the clock, and you can carry open alcoholic beverages on the street (in a cup but not in a bottle). It is not, however, permissible to drive under the influence of alcohol, although the suburbs feature drive-through daiquiri shops.

What It Costs The cost of a meal in the city's more upscale restaurants— with their smart decor, expensive ingredients, and carefully selected wines— is about what you'd expect to pay in other U.S. cities. The bargains are found in the more casual full-service restaurants, where a simple lunch or dinner can frequently be had for much less than $25. However, even the more expensive restaurants offer fixed-price menus of three or four courses for substantially less than what an à la carte meal costs, and coffee or tea is usually included. As a rule, serving sizes are more than generous—some would say unmanageable for the average eater—so many diners order two appetizers rather than a starter and a main course, which can make ordering dessert more practical.

If you are watching your budget, be sure to ask the price of daily specials recited by the waiter or captain. The charge for specials at some restaurants is noticeably out of line with the other prices on the menu. Always review your bill. Even on computerized checks, mistakes do occur. No matter whose favor the mistake is in, it is a courtesy to bring it to your server's attention. Also consider the fixed-price, early-evening specials offered at so many mid-range and upscale restaurants. Eating early can cut your bill in half, and the food quality generally doesn't suffer.

Our restaurant reviews indicate what credit cards are accepted (or not) at each establishment, but if you plan to use a credit card it is a good idea to double-check its acceptability when making reservations or before sitting down to eat.

WHAT IT COSTS				
$$$$	**$$$**	**$$**	**$**	**¢**
AT DINNER over $35	$26–$35	$17–$25	$9–$16	under $9

Restaurant prices are for a main course at dinner, excluding sales tax of 9.5%.

KNOW YOUR CUISINE

NEW ORLEANS'S RESTAURANTS that specialize in local cuisines have been grouped into the following four categories:

Cajun-inspired. Kitchens in these restaurants show direct and recognizable influences from the hearty and rustic cuisine of the southwest Louisiana Acadians. Seasonings are often more intense than in Creole cooking, and pork and game are prominent ingredients.

Contemporary Creole. The food usually includes some traditional Creole dishes, but there's more creativity. Local ingredients are used in novel ways, but the basic flavors adhere to the Creole standards of richness and depth. Trout with pecans and bread-pudding soufflé are typical.

Creole with soul. This food reflects both the robust style of southern black cooks and the spicier aspects of early New Orleans cuisine.

Traditional Creole. These restaurants specialize in rather complex dishes that have been familiar to generations of New Orleans restaurant goers. Shrimp rémoulade, gumbo, trout meunière, and bread pudding are some examples.

Caribbean

$$–$$$ ✕ **Dominique's.** Dominique Macquet's island sensibilities bear testament to his upbringing on Mauritius. There's farm-raised conch all over his menu: baby conch ceviche, baby-conch-and-white-bean chowder, and conch with corn-mirliton (a species of delicately flavored squash) risotto. Dominique's food is sometimes overly ambitious, incorporating too many ingredients to appreciate, but in general the chef's light touch keeps even the most complex combinations from careening over the top. The dining room, with its decorative hints at the island theme, is small for a hotel restaurant. The wine list is knowing if overpriced. ✉ *1001 Toulouse St., French Quarter* ☎ *504/586–8000* ▭ *AE, D, DC, MC, V* ✆ *No lunch.*

Contemporary

$$–$$$$ ✕ **Stella.** Your affection for Stella, named for a character in playwright Tennessee Williams's *Streetcar Named Desire,* may depend on your tolerance of oddly matched, sometimes overly luxurious, ingredients and a French-provincial setting several centuries older than that of the contemporary menu. Chef-owner Scott Boswell loves to improvise. One of the safer bets is a starter of gnocchi, often prepared with a cognac-and-soy cream. The signature seared scallops and shrimp with caviar but-

92 <

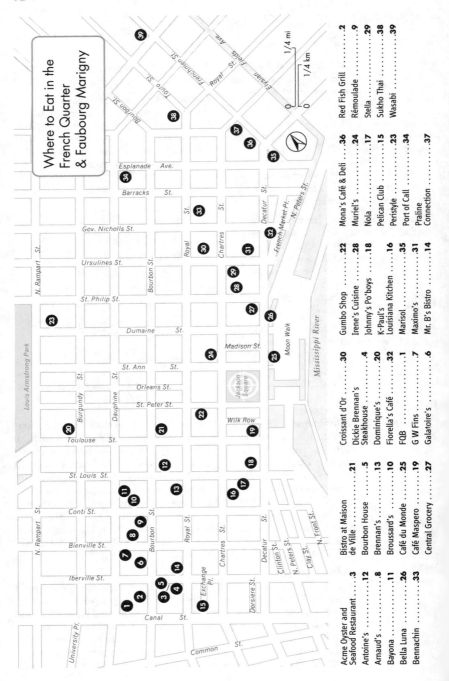

Where to Eat in the French Quarter & Faubourg Marigny

0   1/4 mi
0   1/4 km

Louis Armstrong Park

Mississippi River

Jackson Square

Moon Walk

Wilk Row

Esplanade Ave.

Barracks St.

Gov. Nicholls St.

Ursulines St.

St. Philip St.

Dumaine St.

Madison St.

St. Ann St.

Orleans St.

St. Peter St.

Toulouse St.

St. Louis St.

Conti St.

Bienville St.

Iberville St.

Canal St.

Common St.

N. Rampart St.

Bourbon St.

Royal St.

Chartres St.

Decatur St.

Burgundy St.

Dauphine St.

French Market Pl.

N. Peters St.

Clinton St.

N. Peters St.

Clay St.

N. Front St.

Dorsiere St.

Exchange Pl.

Royal St.

Bourbon St.

Dauphine St.

Burgundy St.

N. Rampart St.

University Pl.

Frenchmen St.

Touro St.

Royal St.

Elysian Fields Ave.

Acme Oyster and
Seafood Restaurant **3**
Antoine's **12**
Arnaud's **8**
Bayona **11**
Bella Luna **26**
Bennachin **33**

Bistro at Maison
de Ville **21**
Bourbon House **5**
Brennan's **13**
Broussard's **10**
Café du Monde **25**
Café Maspero **19**

Croissant d'Or **30**
Dickie Brennan's
Steakhouse **4**
Dominique's **20**
Fiorella's Café **32**
FQB **1**
G W Fins **7**
Galatoire's **27**
Central Grocery **6**

Gumbo Shop **22**
Irene's Cuisine **28**
Johnny's Po'boys **18**
K-Paul's
Louisiana Kitchen **16**
Marisol **35**
Maximo's **31**
Mr. B's Bistro **14**

Mona's Café & Deli . . . **36**
Muriel's **24**
Nola **17**
Pelican Club **15**
Peristyle **23**
Port of Call **34**
Praline
Connection **37**

Red Fish Grill **2**
Rémoulade **9**
Stella **29**
Sukho Thai **38**
Wasabi **39**

ter is a wise entrée choice. Regulars won't allow the chef to remove the Bananas Foster–style French toast from his ambitious menu. ✉ *1032 Chartres St., French Quarter* ☎ *504/587–0091* ▭ *AE, D, DC, MC, V* ☉ *Closed Tues. No lunch.*

$$$ ✕ **Bistro at Maison de Ville.** Small-scale chic is the cachet of this spot, a few steps from the bawdiness of Bourbon Street. Nobody comes in for limb-stretching, since only inches separate the tables, with those along the full-length banquette close enough to become, in effect, a table for 20. But lustrous mahogany and soft light from elegant wall lamps work their magic. From the tiny kitchen come stylish, flavorful creations reflecting a modern approach to Creole and American cooking. The mussels and hand-cut french fries are worth a lunch trip. Wines are perfectly paired and served, and the Belgian general manager always keeps a supply of quality Belgian beers on hand. ✉ *733 Toulouse St., French Quarter* ☎ *504/528–9206* ⟳ *Reservations essential* ▭ *AE, D, DC, MC, V* ☉ *No lunch Sun.*

$$–$$$ ✕ **Bella Luna.** If luxurious surroundings and a knockout view of the Mississippi River are high on your list of priorities, this classically elegant restaurant in the French Market complex should fill the bill. Handsome French-style windows line one wall in the plush main dining room, providing views of the riverbank and the ships and excursion boats gliding by. The kitchen takes an eclectic approach, although its strengths center on meat. Veal schnitzel with spaetzle is a dependable stalwart, as are lamb and beef preparations. The staff is accustomed to special-occasion dinners and will accommodate reasonable requests, including those involving diamond rings. ✉ *French Market near Decatur and Dumaine Sts., French Quarter* ☎ *504/529–1583* ⟳ *Reservations essential* ▭ *AE, D, DC, MC, V* ☉ *No lunch.*

$$–$$$ ✕ **Pelican Club.** Sassy New York flourishes permeate the menu of this smartly decorated but eminently comfortable place in the heart of the French Quarter. Still, evidence of chef Richard Hughes's Louisiana origins also keeps popping up. In three handsome dining rooms he turns out a stew of shellfish inspired by both San Francisco's cioppino and Louisiana's bouillabaisse. A touch of saffron in his jambalaya of chicken, sausage, and shellfish makes it a cousin of Spain's paella. Closer to home is a stuffed artichoke between whose leaves balance buttery scallops and a white-chocolate bread pudding that'll make your toes curl. ✉ *312 Exchange Pl., French Quarter* ☎ *504/523–1504* ▭ *AE, D, DC, MC, V* ☉ *No lunch.*

$$–$$$
Fodor's Choice ✕ **Peristyle.** Some of the most creative cooking in New Orleans emanates from the kitchen of this smartly turned-out yet very approachable lit-
★ tle restaurant on the French Quarter's edge. Chef Anne Kearney takes a thoroughly modern and personal approach to Continental cooking with a superb roasted-beet-and-horseradish-dressed crabmeat salad, a French onion tart with brined anchovies, and a whole squab filled with a dirty rice dressing. The main dining room is swathed in dusty-rose walls and lined with sleek tufted banquettes. Locals covet Friday lunch reservations. Get one if you can. ✉ *1041 Dumaine St., French Quarter* ☎ *504/ 593–9535* ⟳ *Reservations essential* ▭ *D, DC, MC, V* ☉ *Closed Sun. and Mon. No lunch Tues.–Thurs. or Sat.*

$–$$$ ✕ **Bayona.** "New World" is the label Louisiana native Susan Spicer applies to her cooking style, which results in such signature dishes as pan-sautéed sweetbreads wetted with lemon-caper sauce, and fresh salmon fillets in white-wine sauce with house-made sauerkraut. These and other imaginative dishes are served in an early-19th-century Creole cottage that fairly glows with flower arrangements, elegant photographs, and, in one small dining room, trompe-l'oeil murals suggesting Mediterranean landscapes. Don't skimp on the sweet end, as silken ice creams come in flavors like peppermint, buttermilk, and basil. ⊠ *430 Dauphine St., French Quarter* ☎ *504/525–4455* ⌂ *Reservations essential* ☐ *AE, DC, MC, V* ✹ *Closed Sun. No lunch Sat.*

Contemporary Creole

$$–$$$ ✕ **FQB.** Not only is this informal Ritz-Carlton eatery handy when other restaurants are shuttered (a late-night menu is served until 1 AM), the high quality of the food and surroundings make it worthy of attention any time. Nostalgic prints and photos line the walls of the deep, narrow room, which also functions as a bar and late-night music club. From the kitchen come superbly conceived dishes rooted in Creole tradition. The barbecue shrimp, crabmeat Cobb salad, seared fish, and chicken-andouille gumbo are done with exceptional polish and pizzazz. The place swings during Sunday jazz brunch. ⊠ *Ritz-Carlton New Orleans, 921 Canal St., French Quarter* ☎ *504/524–1331* ☐ *AE, D, DC, MC, V.*

★ **$$–$$$** ✕ **Mr. B's Bistro.** The energy never seems to subside in this handsome restaurant, with servers darting between the wood-and-glass screens that reduce the vastness of the dining room. The dependable contemporary Creole menu centers on meats and seafood from a grill fueled with aromatic woods. Pasta dishes, especially the pasta jambalaya with andouille sausage and shrimp, are fresh and creative. The traditional-style bread pudding with Irish-whiskey sauce is excellent, too. Lunchtime finds most of the tables taken up by locals, who like the countrified chicken-andouille gumbo and the distinctly local version of barbecued shrimp. ⊠ *201 Royal St., French Quarter* ☎ *504/523–2078* ☐ *AE, D, DC, MC, V.*

$$–$$$ ✕ **Nola.** Fans of chef Emeril Lagasse who can't get a table at Emeril's in the Warehouse District have this sassy and vibrant French Quarter restaurant as an alternative. Lagasse has not lowered his sights with Nola's menu, as lusty and rich as any in town. The appetizers are as freewheeling as Lagasse's television personality, with Vietnamese stuffed chicken wings listed beside steak tartare. A main-course redfish is swathed in a horseradish-citrus crust before it's plank-roasted in a wood oven. Duck arrives glistening with a whisky-caramel glaze. The combinations seem endless. For dessert, try the coconut-cream or apple-buttermilk pie. ⊠ *534 St. Louis St., French Quarter* ☎ *504/522–6652* ⌂ *Reservations essential* ☐ *AE, D, DC, MC, V* ✹ *No lunch Sun.*

$–$$$ ✕ **Bourbon House.** A yearling perched on one of the French Quarter's busiest corners, this is the Brennan family's biggest and flashiest restaurant yet, and it's a solid hit with seafood aficionados. A chilled seafood platter heaping with combinations of lobster, oysters, caviar, shrimp, mussels, crab, and squid glistens beneath the golden glow of bulbous hanging lamps. Injecting energy into the old warhorses of New Orleans's Creole repertoire is a tightrope walk. Bourbon House nimbly pulls it off with a crab shell filled with luscious seasoned stuffing, and baked oysters Bienville with a jolt of extra pepper. The jumping oyster bar turns out sterling raw ones. ⊠ *144 Bourbon St., French Quarter* ☎ *504/522–0111* ▭ *AE, D, DC, MC, V.*

$–$$$ ╳ **Muriel's.** Among Jackson Square's myriad dining spots, Muriel's is easily the most ambitious, in both its atmosphere and menus. In the large downstairs rooms the city's colorful past is evoked with quaint prints and architectural relics, while diners in comfortable chairs indulge in hearty updated renderings of old Creole favorites. Chef Erik Veney wins tummies over with such combinations as seared foie gras with pear marmalade, and crepes of crawfish and goat cheese. Other dishes stick closer to local tradition, employing sweet potatoes, pecans, Creole tomatoes, mirlitons, and Gulf fish. Occasionally, the faint sounds of freelance jazz from musicians on the Square waft inside. ⊠ *801 Chartres St., French Quarter* ☎ *504/568–1885* ▭ *AE, DC, MC, V.*

Dessert

¢ ╳ **Croissant d'Or.** Locals compete with visitors for a table in this colorful, pristine pastry shop, which serves excellent and authentic French croissants, pies, tarts, and custards, as well as an imaginative selection of soups, salads, and sandwiches. Wash them down with real French breakfast coffee, cappuccino, or espresso. Hours are 7 AM to 4:30 PM daily. ⊠ *617 Ursulines St., French Quarter* ☎ *504/524–4663* ▭ *AE, MC, V* ☻ *Closed the wk after July 4.*

Italian

$–$$$ ╳ **Maximo's.** This place jumps: it also serves Italian fare that's several cuts above the local norm. But don't look for extra space in the deep, narrow room. One haven is a cozy booth along the left wall, an expanse of exposed brick hung with photographs of jazz musicians. A great way to begin is with mussels steeped in a garlicky wine broth. Big nuggets of "fire-roasted" fish and shrimp are marvels of judicious seasoning. Garlic, pepper, and herbs invigorate the natural juices of a veal T-bone. The cellar holds the city's best selection of Italian wines, many modestly priced. ⊠ *1117 Decatur St., French Quarter* ☎ *504/586–8883* ▭ *AE, D, DC, MC, V* ☻ *No lunch.*

★ $–$$ ╳ **Irene's Cuisine.** Its walls are festooned with enough snapshots, garlic braids, and crockery for at least two more restaurants. But this just adds to the charm of this cozy Italian-Creole eatery. From Irene DiPietro's kitchen come succulent roasted chicken brushed with olive oil, rosemary, and garlic; tubes of manicotti bulging with ground veal; and fresh shrimp, aggressively seasoned and grilled before joining linguine glistening with herbed olive oil. The wait can stretch to the 90-minute mark during peak dinner hours, which is just enough time for a bottle of wine, or two, in the convivial little piano bar. ⊠ *539 St. Philip St., French Quarter* ☎ *504/529–8811* ⌕ *Reservations not accepted* ▭ *AE, MC, V* ☻ *No lunch.*

Po'boys & Other Sandwiches

¢–$ ╳ **Café Maspero.** A half-hour wait in line—usually outside the door—is the norm for a sample of Café Maspero's two-fisted hot and cold sandwiches. The pastrami and corned beef are on the greasy side, and the half-pound hamburger (with cheese or chili or both) is long on bulk and short on taste. But low prices and big portions keep 'em coming. Arched doors and windows give the vast brick dining room a little character. Service is perfunctory. ⊠ *601 Decatur St., French Quarter* ☎ *504/523–6250* ⚗ *Reservations not accepted* ▭ *No credit cards.*

★ ¢–$ ✕ **Central Grocery.** This old-fashioned Italian grocery store produces authentic muffulettas, one of the gastronomic gifts of the city's Italian immigrants. Good enough to challenge the po'boy as the local sandwich champs, they're made by filling round loaves of seeded bread with ham, salami, mozzarella, and a salad of marinated green olives. Each sandwich, about 10 inches in diameter, is sold in wholes and halves. You can eat your muffuletta at a counter, but some prefer to take theirs out to a bench on Jackson Square or the Moon Walk along the Mississippi riverfront. The Grocery closes at 5:30 PM. ⊠ *923 Decatur St., French Quarter* ☎ *504/523–1620* ▭ *D, MC, V.*

¢–$ ✕ **Fiorella's Café.** Steps away from the hubbub of the French Quarter's flea market is this casual and friendly bar and eatery specializing in classic po'boys, New Orleans–style plate lunches, and some of the best fried chicken in town. Red beans and rice show up on Monday, meat loaf takes the spotlight on Tuesday, and Thursday is the day for butter beans; hearty breakfasts are an everyday feature. The spaces are tight and rather dark, but prices are easy to swallow. ⊠ *45 French Market Pl. (another entrance at 1136 Decatur St.), French Quarter* ☎ *504/528–9566* ▭ *AE, D, MC, V.*

¢–$ ✕ **Johnny's Po'boys.** Strangely enough, good po'boys are hard to find in the French Quarter. Johnny's compensates for the scarcity with a cornucopia of them, even though the quality is anything but consistent. Inside the soft-crust French bread come the classic fillings, including lean boiled ham, well-done roast beef in a garlicky gravy, and crisply fried oysters or shrimp. The chili may not cut it in San Antonio, but the red beans and rice are respectable. The surroundings are rudimentary. Open until 4 PM. ⊠ *511 St. Louis St., French Quarter* ☎ *504/524–8129* ▭ *No credit cards* ◷ *No dinner.*

Seafood

★ $$–$$$ ✕ **G W Fins.** Seafood is the quarry of many a New Orleans visitor, and G W Fins meets the demand with variety and quality, ranging from gumbos to Australian spanner crabs. A bounty of fish species from around the world is among the menu's lures. The menu changes daily, but typical dishes have included a luscious riff on bouillabaisse, sea bass in a hot-and-sour shrimp stock, and impossibly light lobster dumplings. Try the baked-to-order, deep-dish apple pie. The large dining room's attractive modern decor and spaciousness, and the enthusiastic service, make this a relaxing refuge from the French Quarter's crowds. ⊠ *808 Bienville St., French Quarter* ☎ *504/581–3467* ▭ *AE, D, DC, MC, V* ◷ *No lunch.*

♻ $$–$$$ ✕ **Red Fish Grill.** A high energy level and a riotous color scheme put this big bouncy place right in tune with Bourbon Street's festive atmosphere. Casual is the byword in the central dining space, edged on three sides by banquettes, smaller rooms, and a huge oyster bar, all festooned with images reflecting the menu's focus on seafood. The kitchen's handiwork includes hefty po'boys, a seafood gumbo with alligator sausage, a good selection of grilled fish with buttery sauces, and grilled oysters with lemon and garlic. The signature dessert is a variation on the Bananas Foster theme. ⊠ *115 Bourbon St., French Quarter* ☎ *504/598–1200* 🖃 *AE, D, MC, V.*

Fodor'sChoice ★
⟳ ¢–$$ ✕**Acme Oyster and Seafood Restaurant.** A rough-edge classic in every way, this no-nonsense eatery at the entrance to the French Quarter is a prime source for cool and salty raw oysters on the half shell; shrimp, oyster, and roast-beef po'boys; and state-of-the-art red beans and rice. Table service, once confined to the main dining room out front, is now provided in the rear room as well. Expect rather lengthy lines at the marble-top oyster bar. Crowds lighten in the late afternoon. ⊠ *724 Iberville St., French Quarter* ☎ *504/522–5973* ⟚ *Reservations not accepted* 🖃 *AE, D, DC, MC, V.*

Steak

$$–$$$ ✕**Dickie Brennan's Steakhouse.** "Straightforward steaks with a New Orleans touch" is the axiom at this clubby and luxurious addition to the city's red-meat specialists, the creation of a younger member of the Brennan family of restaurateurs. In spaces lined with dark-cherry walls and a drugstore-tile floor, diners dig into classic cuts of top-quality beef, veal, and lamb. The standard beefsteak treatment is a light seasoning and a brush of butter. Among the several other options are a garlic rub and any of five buttery sauces. The menu doesn't lack for typical New Orleans seafood and desserts, among them a fine shrimp rémoulade and bread pudding. ⊠ *716 Iberville St., French Quarter* ☎ *504/522–2467* 🖃 *AE, DC, MC, V* ☺ *No lunch weekends.*

Traditional Creole

$$$–$$$$ ✕**Brennan's.** Lavish breakfasts of elaborate poached-egg dishes are what first put Brennan's on the map. They're still a big draw from morning to night on the two floors of luxuriously appointed dining rooms in a gorgeous 19th-century building. The best seats include views of the lush courtyard and fountain. Eye-opening cocktails flow freely, followed by the poached eggs sandwiched between such things as hollandaise, creamed spinach, artichoke bottoms, and Canadian bacon. Headliners at lunch or dinner include textbook versions of oysters Rockefeller and seafood gumbo, and Bananas Foster, which was created here. The wine list is a stunner in quantity and quality. ⊠ *417 Royal St., French Quarter* ☎ *504/525–9711* ⟚ *Reservations essential* 🖃 *AE, D, DC, MC, V.*

$$–$$$$ ✕**Arnaud's.** This grande dame of classic Creole restaurants still sparkles. In the main dining room, ornate etched glass reflects light from the charming old chandeliers while the late founder, Arnaud Cazenave, gazes from an oil portrait. The overflow spills into a labyrinth of plush banquet rooms and bars. The ambitious menu includes classic dishes as well as more contemporary ones. Always reliable are cold shrimp Arnaud, in a superb rémoulade, and creamy oyster stew, as well as the fish in crawfish sauce, beef Wellington, and fine crème brûlée. Jackets are requested in the main dining room. ⊠ *813 Bienville St., French Quarter* ☎ *504/523–5433* ⟚ *Reservations essential* 🖃 *AE, D, DC, MC, V* ☺ *No lunch Sat.*

$$–$$$$ ✕**Broussard's.** No French Quarter restaurant surpasses Broussard's for old-fashioned spectacle, a glittery mix of elaborate wall coverings, chan-

deliers, and polished woods, with a manicured courtyard to boot. The German chef-owner has cooked in New Orleans longer than he lived in his homeland, and his menu contains respectable renditions of the fancier Creole standbys further upgraded with Continental touches. Fine entrées include a veal chop moistened with two sauces and a bouillabaisse of Gulf oysters and shrimp, among other fish and shellfish. Dessert crepes swaddling cream cheese and pecans are flamed table-side with strawberry liqueur. ⊠ *819 Conti St., French Quarter* ☎ *504/581–3866* 🖃 *AE, D, DC, MC, V* ⊘ *No lunch.*

$–$$$$ ✕ **Antoine's.** If Antoine's wasn't already a deity, Frances Parkinson Keyes immortalized the restaurant with her 1948 novel *Dinner at Antoine's.* Though some people believe that Antoine's heyday passed before the turn of the 20th century, others wouldn't leave New Orleans without at least one order of oysters Rockefeller, a dish invented here. Other notables on the bilingual menu include *pommes de terre soufflées* (fried potato puffs), pompano *en papillote* (baked in parchment paper), and baked Alaska. Regular customers tend to receive royal treatment from their favorite servers. Tourists generally sit in the front room, but walking through the grand labyrinth is a must. ⊠ *713 St. Louis St., French Quarter* ☎ *504/581–4422* ⌒ *Reservations essential* 🏛 *Jacket required* 🖃 *AE, DC, MC, V* ⊘ *Closed Sun.*

$–$$$ ✕ **Galatoire's.** Galatoire's has always epitomized the old-style French-
Fodor's Choice Creole bistro. Many of the recipes date back to 1905. Fried oysters and
★ bacon en brochette are worth every calorie, and the brick-red rémoulade sauce sets a high standard. Other winners include veal chops in béarnaise sauce, and seafood-stuffed eggplant. The setting downstairs is a single, narrow dining room lit with glistening brass chandeliers; bentwood chairs at the white-cloth tables add to its timelessness. However, the din of the restaurant's regulars often fills the downstairs room, sometimes inhibiting conversation. Reservations are accepted for the upstairs dining rooms only. ⊠ *209 Bourbon St., French Quarter* ☎ *504/ 525–2021* 🏛 *Jacket required* 🖃 *AE, DC, MC, V* ⊘ *Closed Mon.*

¢–$$ ✕ **Rémoulade.** Operated by the owners of the posh Arnaud's, Rémoulade is more laid-back and much less pricey. It serves the same Caesar salad and pecan pie, as well as a few of the starters: shrimp Arnaud in rémoulade sauce, oysters stewed in cream, turtle soup, and shrimp bisque. The marble-counter oyster bar and a mahogany cocktail bar date from the 1870s; a dozen oysters shucked here, paired with a cold beer, easily turns into two dozen, maybe even three. Tile floors, mirrors, a pressed-tin ceiling, and brass lights create an environment made for such New Orleans staples as barbecue shrimp and blackened catfish. It's open every day until around midnight. ⊠ *309 Bourbon St., French Quarter* ☎ *504/523– 0377* 🖃 *AE, D, DC, MC, V.*

¢–$ ✕ **Gumbo Shop.** Even with a thoroughly modern glass door at the rear entrance, this place evokes a sense of old New Orleans. The menu amounts to a roster of relics: jambalaya, shrimp Creole and rémoulade, red beans, bread pudding, and seafood and chicken-and-sausage gumbos heavily flavored with tradition. This may be the only restaurant in the city with a vegetarian gumbo on the daily roster. The patina on the ancient painting covering one wall seems to deepen by the week, and the

WHERE TO REFUEL

FOR THOSE TIMES WHEN ALL YOU WANT IS A QUICK BITE, consider these local chains.

La Madeleine French Bakery: These sunny Gallic eateries, spread throughout Orleans Parish and the suburbs, are part European café and part all-American cafeteria; the main draw is quick soups and salads.

La Boulangerie: French brothers are responsible for the rustic breads, butter-laden croissants, and crisp cheeseless pizzas at three La Boulangerie outposts; with café seating and coffee drinks, the CBD location is a popular daytime hangout.

Lee's Hamburgers: Onions embedded into the freshly ground beef give these cooked-to-order burgers their character. If Lee's fried patties were any thinner, they'd have holes.

PJ's Coffee & Tea Co.: Certain natives feel a strong allegiance to this locally owned Starbucks alternative; the granitas are especially worth hunting down.

Popeye's: Restaurant mogul Al Copeland tapped deep into the New Orleanian belly when he and his people developed recipes for the spicy fried chicken, red beans and rice, and flaky biscuits sold at these fast-food places.

Rue de la Course: Though none matches the consummate coffeehouse vibe of the original Magazine Street location (dubbed "Big Rue"), the various Rue branches sell respectable coffees, teas, sandwiches, and pastries; the chai milkshake is mind-bendingly creamy and good.

---

red-and-white-check tablecloths and bentwood chairs are taking on the aspect of museum pieces. But in all probability that is what accounts for the long lines that form here. ⊠ *630 St. Peter St., French Quarter* ☎ *504/ 525–1486* ⌂ *Reservations not accepted* ☰ *AE, D, DC, MC, V.*

Faubourg Marigny

Contemporary

$$–$$$ ✕ **Marisol.** A shaded garden and frequently superb food are among the assets of this bright attractive restaurant near the Mississippi River. A bold floral design animates the soft gold of the dining room's walls. Owner-chef Peter Vazquez is a self-taught cook whose whole roasted fish is sprinkled with sea salt and roasted to maximum moistness. Thai-style soup of crab and coconut is a marvelous marriage of elegance and fire. Desserts are often strikingly original, as in goat cheese with rose petal syrup, and hot chocolate cake with pistachio ice cream. Wines pair nicely with the food. Saturday and Sunday bring jazz brunches. ⊠ *437 Esplanade Ave., Faubourg Marigny* ☎ *504/943–1912* ☰ *AE, DC, MC, V* ☻ *Closed Mon. and Tues.*

Creole with Soul

¢–$$ ✕ **Praline Connection.** Down-home cooking in the southern-Creole style is the forte of this rather quirky restaurant a couple of blocks from the French Quarter. The fried or stewed chicken, smothered pork chops, fried chicken livers, and collard greens are definitively done, and the soulful filé gumbo, crowder peas with okra, and sweet-potato pie are among the best in town. To all this add moderate prices, a congenial staff, and a neat-as-a-pin dining room, and the sum is a fine place to spend an hour or two. The adjacent sweetshop holds such delights as sweet-potato cookies and Creole pralines. ⊠ *542 Frenchmen St., Faubourg Marigny* ☎ *504/943–3934* ⌧ *Reservations not accepted* ▭ *AE, DC, D, MC, V.*

Japanese

$–$$ ✕ **Wasabi.** If it weren't for the smidgen of a sign jutting from the side of Wasabi's windowless building, you'd never guess at the bright, clean goings-on inside. The restaurant splits into two rooms; you'll wait in the neighborhoody bar area if the dining space is crowded, as it usually is. The fish and rice seem freshest when chef-proprietor Phat Vinh is running the sushi bar; otherwise, a Japanese kitchen turns out succulent beef dishes and great udon noodle soups. The wasabi honey shrimp entrée pairs three unlikely ingredients, but enough people approve that it has become a signature. Open until 2 AM Friday and Saturday. ⊠ *900 Frenchmen St., Faubourg Marigny* ☎ *504/943–9433* ⌧ *Reservations not accepted* ▭ *AE, D, DC, MC, V* ☉ *No lunch weekends.*

Middle Eastern

¢–$ ✕ **Mona's Café & Deli.** The modest and spotless spaces at Mona's are not the most colorful in town. Only the labels on the adjacent deli shelves break the monotony of the room's pale woods. But inside this rather bare and simple spot you'll find some of the best, basic eastern-Mediterranean cooking. Cut open a ball of crunchy fried kibbe and the reward is superbly seasoned beef and lamb. Tabouleh, with lots of parsley and mint flecks, is more than just seasoned bulgur wheat. The gyro sandwiches are meaty, and the falafel ones are flavorful, too. The laid-back service is friendly and efficient. ⊠ *504 Frenchmen St., Faubourg Marigny* ☎ *504/949–4115* ▭ *AE, D, MC, V.*

Thai

$–$$ ✕ **Sukho Thai.** Certainly the most prolific Thai restaurant in the area, Sukho Thai fits snugly into its arty neighborhood with servers wearing all black, an art gallery approach to decorating and brightly colored dishes. Both dry and wet curries are so vibrant that the curry pastes seem made to order. The whole steamed fish brushed with spicy chili sauce gains a citrusy perfume from lemongrass and kaffir lime leaf. Creative house-made desserts take the form of barely sweetened coconut custard and lotus dumplings swimming in ginger broth. Honey-sweetened ginger tea and lime juice compensate for the lack of a liquor license. ⊠ *1913 Royal St., Faubourg Marigny* ☎ *504/948–9309* ▭ *AE, MC, V* ⌖ *BYOB* ☉ *Closed Mon. No lunch.*

CBD & Warehouse District

Cajun-Inspired

$–$$$ ✕ **Bon Ton Café.** The Bon Ton's opening in 1953 marked the first appearance of a significant Cajun restaurant in New Orleans. Its crawfish dishes, gumbo, jambalaya, and oyster omelet have retained their strong following in the decades since. The bustle in the excellently maintained dining room reaches a peak at lunchtime on weekdays, when businesspeople from nearby offices come in droves for the baked eggplant with shrimp, the fried catfish, the turtle soup, and a warm, sugary bread pudding. The veteran waitresses are knowledgeable and fleet-footed. ✉ *401 Magazine St., CBD* ☎ *504/524–3386* 🚊 *AE, DC, MC, V* ☻ *Closed weekends.*

Contemporary

$$$–$$$$ ✕ **New Orleans Grill.** The British furnishings span several centuries in these dazzling dining spaces, with body-hugging chairs and canvases depicting aspects of upper-class England. Chef Jonathan Wright's equally dazzling menus change frequently and are filled with appropriately exotic and sumptuous ingredients; for example: jumbo lump-crab cannelloni with lemongrass, fricassee of frog legs with Jerusalem artichoke velouté, fillet of striped bass with vanilla emulsion and red wine-licorice sauce. The perfect overture would be a little ramekin of Beluga caviar, and the perfect ending a bite-size lavender marshmallow. The wine cellar, with its sterling collection of vintage Bordeaux reds, remains awesome. ✉ *Windsor Court Hotel, 2nd level, 300 Gravier St., CBD* ☎ *504/522–1992* ⚘ *Reservations essential* 🏛 *Jacket required* 🚊 *AE, D, DC, MC, V.*

$$–$$$ ✕ **August.** If the Gilded Age is long gone, someone forgot to tell the folks
Fodor'sChoice at August, whose main dining room shimmers with masses of chande-
★ lier prisms, thick brocade fabrics, and glossy woods. The formalities are toned down considerably in the service, however, and chef John Besh's dazzling, modern technique informs every plate. The prime beef and lamb dishes could hardly be improved, tiny soft-shell crabs crackle with sea flavors, and lumps of back-fin crabmeat and pillows of springy gnocchi glisten in truffle oil. The sommelier is ready to confer with you on the hefty, but surprisingly affordable, wine list. ✉ *301 Tchoupitoulas St., CBD* ☎ *504/299–9777* 🚊 *AE, DC, MC, V* ☻ *Closed Sun. No lunch Sat.*

$$–$$$ ✕ **Cuvée.** With a name that refers to a blend of wines, this restaurant
Fodor'sChoice divides its inspirations between France's Champagne region and South
★ Louisiana. The menu rests on a firm French foundation, but the flavors are often distinctively New Orleans. Talented chef Robert Iacovone sometimes seems unstoppable, like when he fills crepes with rabbit confit, and when he drizzles char-grilled Plaquemines Parish oysters with white truffle oil. Main courses are equally gutsy, as is the wine list, which is overpriced in parts but full of interesting bottles. All are decanted in a soaring space defined by exposed brick and gilt-framed paintings in several styles. ✉ *322 Magazine St., CBD* ☎ *504/587–9001* ⚘ *Reservations essential* 🚊 *AE, DC, MC, V* ☻ *Closed Sun. No lunch Sat.*

$$–$$$ ✕ **Lee Circle.** The owners of Clancy's and Le Parvenu (⇨ Uptown and Outside City Limits) have joined forces to create this spartan but sass-

FOOD GLOSSARY

The following terms appear frequently in this section:

Andouille (pronounced ahn-dooey). A mildly spiced Acadian sausage of lean pork, it often flavors gumbos, red beans and rice, and jambalayas.

Barbecue shrimp. The shrimp are not barbecued but baked in their shells in a blend of olive oil, butter, or margarine and usually seasoned with bay leaf, garlic, and other herbs and spices.

Béarnaise (pronounced bare-nayz). This sauce of egg yolk and butter with shallots, wine, and vinegar is used on meats and fish.

Beignet (pronounced ben-yay). Although a beignet was originally a rectangular puff of fried dough sprinkled with powdered sugar, the term can also refer to fritters or crullers containing fish or seafood.

Bisque. A thick, heartily seasoned soup, bisque is most often made with crawfish, crab, or shrimp. Cream appears in the French versions.

Bouillabaisse (pronounced booey-yah-base). A Creole bouillabaisse is a stew of various fish and shellfish in a broth seasoned with saffron and often more assertive spices.

Boulette (pronounced boo-let). This is minced, chopped, or pureed meat or fish shaped into balls and fried.

Bread pudding. In the traditional version, stale French bread is soaked in a custard mix, combined with raisins and baked, then served with a hot sugary sauce flavored with whiskey or rum.

Café au lait. This hot drink is a blend, often half and half, of strong coffee and scalded milk.

Café brûlot (pronounced broo-loh). Cinnamon, lemon, clove, orange, and sugar are steeped with strong coffee, then flambéed with brandy and served in special pedestaled cups.

Chicory coffee. The ground and roasted root of a European variety of chicory is added to ground coffee in varying proportions. Originally used for reasons of economy, coffee with chicory is now favored by many New Orleanians. It lends an added bitterness to the taste.

Crème brûlée (pronounced broo-lay). Literally, this means "burned cream." It's a custard with a crust of oven-browned sugar.

Dirty rice. In this cousin of jambalaya, bits of meat, such as giblets or sausage, and seasonings are added to white rice before cooking.

Dressed. A po'boy "dressed" contains lettuce, tomato, and mayonnaise or mustard.

Étouffée (pronounced ay-too-fay). Literally, "smothered," the term is used most often for a thick stew of crawfish tails cooked in a roux-based liquid with crawfish, fat, garlic, and green seasonings.

Gumbo. From an African word for okra, it can refer to any number of stewlike soups made with seafood or meat and flavored with okra or ground sassafras (filé powder) and myriad other seasonings. Frequent main ingredients are combinations of shrimp, oysters, crab, chicken, andouille, duck, and turkey. A definitive gumbo is served over white rice.

Jambalaya (pronounced jam-buh-lie-uh). Rice is the indispensable ingredient in this relative of Spain's paella. The rice is cooked with a mix of diced meat and seafood in tomato and other seasonings. Shrimp and ham make frequent appearances in it, as do sausage, green pepper, and celery.

Meunière (pronounced muhn-yehr). This method of preparing fish or soft-shell crab entails dusting it with seasoned flour, sautéing it in brown butter, and using the butter with lemon juice as a sauce. Some restaurants add a dash of Worcestershire sauce.

Mirliton (pronounced merl-i-tawn). A pale green member of the squash family, a mirliton is usually identified as a vegetable pear. The standard preparation is to scrape the pulp from halved mirlitons, fill them with shrimp and seasoned bread crumbs, and bake them.

Muffuletta. The city's southern Italian grocers created this round-loaf sandwich traditionally filled with ham, salami, mozzarella, and a layer of chopped, marinated green olives. Muffulettas are sold whole and in halves or quarters.

Oysters Bienville (pronounced byen-veel). In this dish, oysters are lightly baked in their shells under a cream sauce flavored with bits of shrimp, mushroom, and green seasonings. Some chefs also use garlic or mustard.

Oysters en brochette (pronounced awn-bro-shet). Whole oysters and bits of bacon are dusted with seasoned flour, skewered, and deep-fried. Traditionally, they're served on toast with lemon and brown butter.

Oysters Rockefeller. This dish, baked oysters on the half shell in a sauce of pureed aromatic greens laced with anise liqueur, was created at Antoine's, which keeps its recipe a secret. Most other restaurants make do with spinach.

Panéed veal (pronounced pan-aid). Breaded veal cutlets are sautéed in butter.

Po'boy. A hefty sandwich, the po'boy is made with the local French bread and any number of fillings: roast beef, fried shrimp, oysters, ham, meatballs in tomato sauce, and cheese are common. A po'boy "dressed" contains lettuce, tomato, and mayonnaise or mustard.

Praline (pronounced prah-leen). A sweet patty-shape confection made of pecans, brown sugar, butter and vanilla.

Ravigote (pronounced rah-vee-gote). In Creole usage, this is a piquant mayonnaise, usually with capers, used to moisten blue crabmeat.

Rémoulade (pronounced ray-moo-lahd). The classic Creole rémoulade is a brick-red whipped mixture of olive oil with mustard, scallions, cayenne, lemon, paprika, and parsley. It's served on cold peeled shrimp or lumps of back-fin crabmeat.

Souffléed potatoes. These thin, hollow puffs of deep-fried potato are produced by two fryings at different temperatures.

Tasso (pronounced tah-so). Acadian cooks developed this lean, intensely seasoned ham. It's used sparingly to flavor sauces and gumbos.

ily decorated restaurant that creates innovative food without sacrificing familiar New Orleans flavors. House-made Worcestershire sauce invigorates everything from grilled shrimp set over grits to a meunière sauce spooned over fish. Two signatures—fried oysters with Brie and lemon icebox pie—are locals' bait. Everyone should try them. The wine list is exceptionally composed. Just two blocks from Le Chat Noir, this makes a convenient pre- or post-theater destination. ⊠ *Hotel Le Cirque, 3 Lee Circle, Warehouse District* ☎ *504/962–0915* ⌁ *Reservations essential* ▤ *AE, D, DC, MC, V* ⊗ *No lunch weekends.*

$–$$ ✗ **Cobalt.** The avant-garde decor pervading the two oddly shaped dining rooms in the Hotel Monaco may not be to everybody's taste, especially when placed against Cobalt's rather retro menu. But chef Brack May's culinary innovations rarely get goofy. In fact, at lunch he draws on a simple all-American diner sensibility, preparing slightly upscale versions of blue-plate specials. Evenings bring a more sophisticated menu. The long, languorous bar is a favorite of the young and hip; the short bar menu includes a burger for stevedore appetites, made from freshly ground beef and sharp white cheddar. Service is a bit self-conscious, but the job gets done. ⊠ *333 St. Charles Ave., CBD* ☎ *504/565–5595* ▤ *AE, D, DC, MC, V* ⊗ *No lunch Sat. or Sun. No dinner Mon.*

$–$$
Fodor'sChoice
★
✗ **Herbsaint.** Upscale food and downscale prices are among Herbsaint's assets. Chef Donald Link turns out food that sparkles with robust flavors and top-grade ingredients. "Small plates" and side dishes such as charcuterie, a knock-'em-dead shrimp bisque, gumbos, and cheese- and nut-studded salads are mainstays. More substantial appetites are courted with duck and dirty rice, beef short ribs, and pork belly. For dessert, the chocolate beignets filled with molten chocolate are deserving of love poems. The plates provide most of the color in the often noisy rooms whose walls are painted the green color of a sweet pea. The wine list is expertly compiled and reasonably priced. ⊠ *701 St. Charles Ave., CBD* ☎ *504/524–4114* ⌁ *Reservations essential* ▤ *AE, D, DC, MC, V* ⊗ *Closed Sun. No lunch Sat.*

★ **$–$$** ✗ **Rio Mar.** Chef Adolfo Garcia's largely seafood menu reflects his decidedly Spanish style. Each of the seven ceviches has its own distinct marinade and combination of superfresh seafood. For entrées, try the stewlike *zarzuela* of seafood, with chunks of fin- and shellfish in a peppery red broth, or shrimp piled onto a sauce gently flavored with garlic. Leading the dessert pack is the *tres leches,* a light cake layered with a three-milk custard. The dining room's low ceiling and tiled floor don't make for great acoustics, but the gold-hue walls with their rustic iron ornamentation would not be misplaced in Barcelona. ⊠ *800 S. Peters St., Warehouse District* ☎ *504/525–3474* ▤ *AE, D, DC, MC, V* ⊗ *Closed Sun. No lunch Sat.*

Contemporary Creole

$$–$$$$ ✗ **Emeril's.** Celebrity chef Emeril Lagasse's big and bouncy flagship restaurant is always jammed. A wood ceiling in an oversize basket-weave pattern muffles much of the clatter and chatter. In a far corner, the food bar framed by a dramatic collection of glass-encased spices and legumes seats nine guests who desire special attention from the chef de cuisine. The ambitious menu gives equal emphasis to Creole and modern Amer-

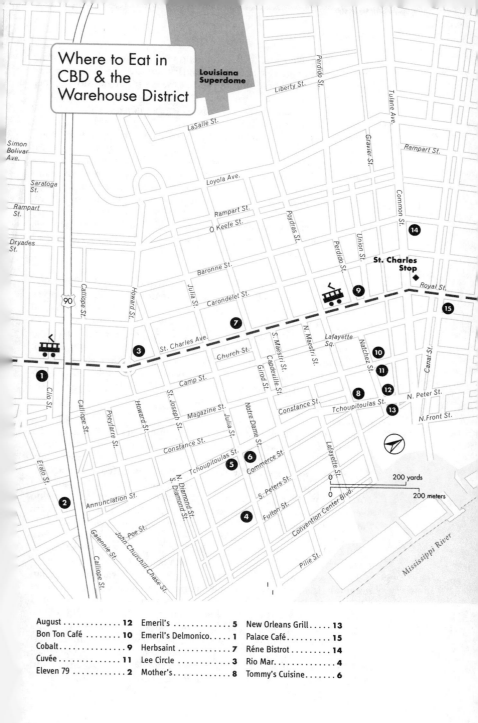

Where to Eat in CBD & the Warehouse District

Louisiana Superdome

ican cooking. Desserts, such as the renowned banana cream pie, verge on the gargantuan. Service is meticulously organized, and the wine list's depth and range should pop the eye of the most persnickety imbiber. ✉ *800 Tchoupitoulas St., Warehouse District* ☎ *504/528–9393* ⩍ *Reservations essential* 🖃 *AE, D, DC, MC, V* ☯ *No lunch weekends.*

$$ ✕ **Palace Café.** Crafted from what used to be New Orleans's oldest music store, this Brennan family stalwart is a convivial spot to try some of the more imaginative contemporary Creole dishes, such as crabmeat cheesecake, stuffed rabbit, and seafood pastas. Desserts, especially the white-chocolate bread pudding and the house-made ice creams, are luscious. Drugstore-tile floors, stained-cherry booths, and soothing beige walls set the mood. The wraparound mezzanine is lined with a large, brightly colored wall painting populated by the city's famous musicians. The kitchen staff continues to prepare a limited bar menu between lunch and dinner services. ✉ *605 Canal St., CBD* ☎ *504/523–1661* ⩍ *Reservations essential* 🖃 *AE, D, DC, MC, V.*

French

$–$$ ✕ **René Bistrot.** The terms on the seasonal menu deliver this unmistakable message: René Bajeux's aim is to re-create the cuisine of his youth in France. His success rate is high, especially with such gems as roasted oysters, sautéed sweetbreads, and garlicky snails with pesto crumbs. The rotisserie turns out roasted ducks and chickens, the latter of which Bajeux prepares with pearl onions and thyme jus, just like his French grandmother once did. The modern dining room, with dashes of color interrupting the expanse of beige, is comfy-cozy, and table service is excellently organized. ✉ *817 Common St. CBD* ☎ *504/412–2580* 🖃 *AE, D, DC, MC, V.*

Italian

$$–$$$ ✕ **Eleven 79.** Although the Italian underpinnings of chef Anthony DiPiazza's cooking are everywhere, a Creole sensibility often emerges here in the dark, elbow-to-elbow confines of this rousingly energetic establishment on the edge of the CBD. Beautifully sautéed veal (piccata, saltimbocca, marsala, etc.) hogs the menu spotlight, along with about a dozen pastas. "Shrimp scampi" is the label on a medium-size ramekin overflowing with a garlic-riddled brown sauce. Other crowd-pleasers are the chicken Milanese, filet mignon, and breaded oysters with a white rémoulade sauce. The crowd in the adjoining bar adds to the festiveness. ✉ *1179 Annunciation St., CBD* ☎ *504/299–1179* ⩍ *Reservations essential* 🖃 *AE, D, DC, MC, V* ☯ *Closed Sun. No lunch Mon.–Sat.*

$–$$ ✕ **Tommy's Cuisine.** With an owner who partnered in the Creole-Italian restaurant Irene's Cuisine (French Quarter) from its opening, plus a chef who cooked at Galatoire's for 35 years, Tommy's Cuisine was bound to win over New Orleanian bellies when it opened in late 2003. You might consider bringing a flashlight for reading the menu in Tommy's two dark, clubby, tightly packed rooms, for you wouldn't want to overlook the panéed oysters; the lamb chops blanketed with béarnaise sauce; or the roasted half chicken saturated with the flavors of rosemary and garlic. ✉ *746 Tchoupitoulas St., Warehouse District* ☎ *504/581–1103* ⩍ *Reservations essential* 🖃 *AE, D, MC, V* ☯ *No lunch.*

Po'boys & Other Sandwiches

¢–$$ ✕ **Mother's.** Tourists line up for down-home eats at this island of blue-collar sincerity amid downtown's glittery hotels. Mother's dispenses delicious baked ham and roast-beef po'boys (ask for "debris" on the beef sandwich and the bread will be slathered with meat juices and shreds of meat), home-style biscuits and jambalaya, and a very good chicken gumbo in a couple of bare-bones dining rooms. Breakfast eggs and coffee are sometimes cold, but that doesn't seem to repel the hordes fighting for seats at peak mealtimes. Service is cafeteria style, with a counter or two augmenting the tables. ⊠ *401 Poydras St., CBD* ☎ *504/523–9656* ⌂ *Reservations not accepted* ⊟ *AE, MC, V.*

Traditional Creole

$$–$$$$ ✕ **Emeril's Delmonico.** Chef Emeril Lagasse bought the traditional, unpretentious, century-old Delmonico and converted it to a large, extravagantly appointed restaurant with the most ambitious revamping of classic Creole dishes in town. The high-ceiling dining spaces are swathed in upholstered walls and superthick window fabrics. Oysters baked on the half shell in various sauces are a reliable option. So are New Orleans–style barbecue shrimp, crawfish in puff pastry, and sautéed fish meunière. Prime dry-aged steaks with traditional sauces have emerged as a specialty in recent years. Plush and polish are the bywords here, and the service can be exemplary. ⊠ *1300 St. Charles Ave., CBD* ☎ *504/525–4937* ⌂ *Reservations essential* ⊟ *AE, D, DC, MC, V* ☽ *No lunch Sat.*

Garden District/Uptown

American

☾ ¢–$ ✕ **Camellia Grill.** Every diner should be as classy as Camellia Grill, a one-of-a-kind eatery that deserves its following. Locals vie until the early-morning hours for one of the 29 stools at the gleaming counter, each place supplied with a large, fresh linen napkin. The hamburger—4 ounces of excellent beef on a fresh bun with any number of embellishments—is one of the best in town. Other blue-ribbon dishes are the chili, the pecan and meringue pies, and the omelets. Everything's made on the premises and served by bow-tied, white-waistcoated waiters with the fastest feet in the business. ⊠ *626 S. Carrollton Ave., Uptown* ☎ *504/866–9573* ⊟ *No credit cards.*

Cafés & Coffeehouses

¢ ✕ **Rue de la Course.** The charm of this coffeehouse on a corner of Magazine Street (supplemented by less charismatic spin-offs elsewhere in town) lies as much in its lived-in look as in its caffe latte, sturdy espresso, and other coffees flavored with vanilla, hazelnuts, or chocolate almond. No gimmickry intrudes on the atmosphere at the "Big Rue," which combines the calm of a library with the spontaneity of an old-fashioned general store (one wall is lined with bins of coffee beans). You can sip an Italian soda or nibble at a sandwich at tables outside and watch uptown life unfold. It closes at midnight. ⊠ *3128 Magazine St., Garden District* ☎ *504/899–0242* ⌂ *Reservations not accepted* ⊟ *No credit cards.*

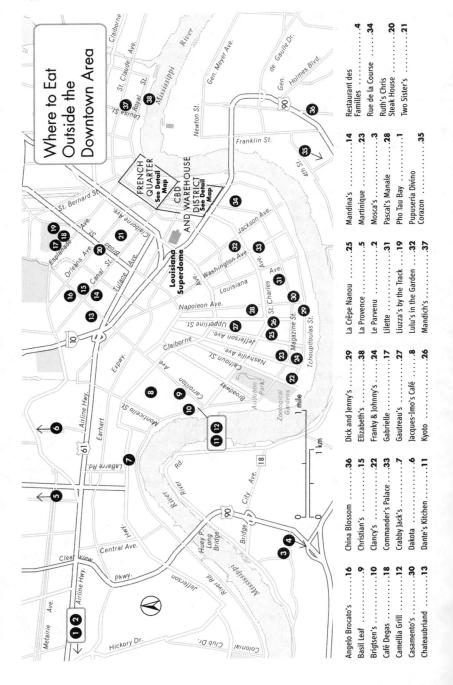

Where to Eat Outside the Downtown Area

Cajun/Creole

$–$$ ✕ **Jacques-Imo's Cafe.** Oak Street might look like any other sleepy urban
Fodor'sChoice thoroughfare by day, but once the sun sets the half-block stretch con-
★ taining Jacques-Imo's Cafe feels like the center of the universe. Prepare
to wait up to two hours in the crowded bar for a table in the boisterous, swamp-theme dining rooms. Fortunately the bartenders are skilled,
and the modest-looking but innovative food is worth it. Deep-fried
roast-beef po'boys, alligator sausage cheesecake, Cajun bouillabaisse,
and panéed duck with sweet-potato sauce are among the excellent only-
at-Jacques-Imo's specialties. Reservations accepted for parties of five or
more. ⊠ *8324 Oak St., Uptown* ☎ *504/861–0886* ▤ *AE, D, DC,
MC, V* ⊘ *Closed Sun. No lunch.*

Caribbean

$$ ✕ **Martinique.** The French Caribbean meets New Orleans in this mod-
est yet charming dining room and its tropical courtyard in a quiet unas-
suming block of upper Magazine Street. A change of ownership early
in 2004 brought with it larger bathrooms and wall sconces from Italy,
but executive chef Kevin Reese remains to carry on the tradition of
Caribbean-theme food. The dishes—many suffused with delicate herbal
and spicy flavors—range from brothy caramelized onion soup cradling
a delicate poached egg to a flatiron steak with beefy mushroom gravy.
Good, too, is the seasonal *blaff*, a Martiniquaise bouillabaisse that's per-
fect for a cool evening. ⊠ *5908 Magazine St., Uptown* ☎ *504/891–8495*
⌁ *Reservations essential* ▤ *AE, MC, V* ⊘ *No lunch.*

Contemporary

$$–$$$ ✕ **Gautreau's.** Modest in size but ambitious in its cooking, this haven
Fodor'sChoice of sophistication is half hidden in a quiet, leafy residential neighborhood.
★ Don't look for a sign outside; there is none. The ever-changing menu
usually includes fine crab cakes, succulent duck confit, sea scallops, and
filet mignon in robust sauces. For dessert, try the superb crème brûlée
or the caramelized banana split. The 40-seat downstairs dining room,
once a neighborhood drugstore, is encased in lustrous oxblood enamel.
Along one wall extends the old pharmacy's original polished wood cab-
inets, now filled with liquors and glassware. ⊠ *1728 Soniat St., Uptown*
☎ *504/899–7397* ⌁ *Reservations essential* ▤ *D, DC, MC, V* ⊘ *Closed
Sun. No lunch.*

★ **$$** ✕ **Lilette.** Proprietor-chef John Harris uses New Orleans culinary traditions as a springboard to Lilette's inspired dishes. Look for such palate
pleasers as *boudin noir* (blood sausage) with cornichon, raw oysters from
all coasts, Gulf fish crusted in crisp potato slices, and hangar steak with
marrow demi-glace. For dessert go for the quenelles of goat cheese and
crème fraîche. The thoughtful wine list is boutique oriented, and the unique
cocktail selection holds even more surprises. Framed mirrors hang along
the maroon walls of the intimate front dining room–cum–bar. A few more
tables fill out a second room and patio. ⊠ *3637 Magazine St., Uptown*
☎ *504/895–1636* ⌁ *Reservations essential* ▤ *AE, D, DC, MC, V*
⊘ *Closed Sun. and Mon.*

$–$$ ✕ **Dante's Kitchen.** Housed in a spacious, oddly configured old cottage
in Riverbend, Dante's Kitchen is a bit out of the mainstream, especially
in this sauce-obsessed town. Chef Emmanuel Loubier, a nine-year vet-

eran of Commander's Palace, prepares seasonal menus for those with a sense of adventure. Fish is wrapped in falafel, a duck confit turnover is brushed with blackberry sauce, and grilled redfish is paired with a pecan-and-green-bean salad. A borscht containing roasted duck can be both satisfying and therapeutic on a hot New Orleans evening. Desserts, such as the sweet-potato and white chocolate pie, are often homey and hearty. ⊠ *736 Dante St., Uptown* ☎ *504/861–3121* ⊟ *AE, D, DC, MC, V.*

★ $–$$ ╳ **Lulu's in the Garden.** You could shop at the farmers' market and cook dinner, or you could eat at Lulu's in the Garden. The menu always includes at least half a dozen well-dressed salads involving ingredients such as beets, nutty sprouts, obscure mushrooms, and fried chicken. Lulu's signature antipasto platter is a collection of seasonal roasted vegetables. Main courses and desserts incorporate similarly farm-fresh ingredients, though this isn't a health-food restaurant—the french fries are tops. Shiny wooden floors, bread baked in terra-cotta flowerpots, and large portraits of European pastries create a quaint environment in which to enjoy such thoughtful food. ⊠ *2203 St. Charles Ave., Garden District* ☎ *504/586–9956* ⊟ *AE, D, MC, V* ☉ *Closed Mon. No lunch Sat. No dinner Tues.*

Contemporary Creole

$$$–$$$$ ╳ **Commander's Palace.** No restaurant captures New Orleans's gastro-
FodorśChoice nomic heritage and celebratory spirit as well as this one. The upstairs
★ Garden Room's glass walls have marvelous views of the giant oak trees on the patio below, and other rooms promote conviviality with their bright pastels. The menu's classics include foie-gras-and-rabbit pie; a spicy and meaty turtle soup; terrific grilled veal chops with grits; and a wonderful sautéed Gulf fish coated with crunchy pecans. Among the addictive desserts is the bread-pudding soufflé. Weekend brunches are less ambitious but also less costly. Jackets are preferred at dinner. ⊠ *1403 Washington Ave., Garden District* ☎ *504/899–8221* ⌖ *Reservations essential* ⊟ *AE, D, DC, MC, V.*

★ $$–$$$ ╳ **Brigtsen's.** Chef Frank Brigtsen's fusion of Creole refinement and Acadian earthiness reflects his years as a protégé of Paul Prudhomme. His dishes add up to some of the best South Louisiana cooking you'll find anywhere. Everything is fresh and filled with deep and complex tastes. The cream-of-oysters-Rockefeller soup is a revelation. Rabbit and chicken dishes, usually presented in rich sauces and gravies, are full of robust flavor. The roux-based gumbos are thick and intense, and the warm bread pudding is worth every calorie. Trompe-l'oeil murals add whimsy to the intimate spaces of this turn-of-the-20th-century frame cottage. ⊠ *723 Dante St., Uptown* ☎ *504/861–7610* ⌖ *Reservations essential* ⊟ *AE, DC, MC, V* ☉ *Closed Sun. and Mon.*

$–$$ ╳ **Clancy's.** Understatement defines the mood at Clancy's. The decor is neutral, with gray walls and a few ceiling fans above bentwood chairs and white linen cloths. The small bar is usually filled with regulars who know one another. Most of the dishes are imaginative treatments of New Orleans favorites. Some specialties, like the fresh sautéed fish in cream sauce flavored with crawfish stock and herbs, are exceptional. Other signs of an inventive chef are the expertly fried oysters matched with warm Brie; the grilled chicken breast in lime butter; and a peppermint ice-cream pie. On more festive nights you may yearn for earplugs. ⊠ *6100 Annunciation St., Uptown* ☎ *504/895–1111* ⌂ *Reservations essential* ☰ *AE, MC, V* ☉ *Closed Sun. No lunch Mon. and Sat.*

★ **$–$$** ✕ **Dick and Jenny's.** Stints at Commander's Palace and Gautreau's have given chef Richard Benz a talent for coming up with innovative dishes that meld logically with familiar combinations of typical New Orleans ingredients. At his and wife Jenny's breezily casual restaurant he produces food that should satisfy both local purists and adventurers. Fried oysters are superfresh and perfectly cooked. The meaty, judiciously seasoned crab cakes arrive atop fried green-tomato slices and a fiery red-pepper sauce. Beef tournedos are lavished with foie gras, port wine, and balsamic vinegar. Helping to enliven the dining room and bar are canvases done by the chef himself. ⊠ *4501 Tchoupitoulas St., Uptown* ☎ *504/ 894–9880* ⌂ *Reservations not accepted* ☰ *AE, DC, MC, V* ☉ *Closed Sun. and Mon. No lunch.*

French

$–$$ ✕ **La Crêpe Nanou.** French chic for the budget-minded is the style in this welcoming little bistro, where, during peak hours, you may have a half-hour wait for a table. Left Bank Paris is evoked with woven café chairs out on the sidewalk and awnings that resemble métro-station architecture. The Gallic focus is summed up by the filet mignon with one of several classic French sauces. Other reliable standbys are the pâté maison, hearty lentil soup, and lavish dessert crepes. Spaces are a little tight in the oddly configured dining areas, but the whimsical paintings and profuse greenery lighten the spirits. ⊠ *1410 Robert St., Uptown* ☎ *504/ 899–2670* ⌂ *Reservations not accepted* ☰ *MC, V* ☉ *No lunch.*

Italian

$–$$ ✕ **Pascal's Manale.** Few restaurants are as closely identified with one dish as this one is with barbecue shrimp. The original version, introduced a half century ago, remains, with jumbo shrimp, still in the shell, cooked in a buttery pool zapped with just the right amount of spice and pepper. The rest of the menu, mostly seafood and Italian-style creations, is uneven. Turtle soup, fried eggplant, and raw oysters are good ways to start. Sautéed veal with shrimp, chicken bordelaise, and seafood with pasta are other reliable choices. The restaurant's popularity with out-of-towners usually means a wait for a table, even if it's reserved. ⊠ *1838 Napoleon Ave., Uptown* ☎ *504/895–4877* ⌂ *Reservations essential* ☰ *AE, MC, V* ☉ *No lunch weekends.*

Japanese

¢–$$ ✕ **Kyoto.** Part of a three-block commercial pocket of residential uptown, Kyoto is as much a neighborhood restaurant as it is a destination for fresh fish and slightly Americanized sushi preparations. Behind the sushi bar in the front room, a female chef oversees the creation of off-menu rolls (the Steve Roll contains tuna, snow crab, salmon, and avocado); the tuna *tataki*, perhaps Kyoto's most frequently ordered item, is a masterpiece of ruby-red tuna, avocado, and a soy sauce tarted up with lime juice. Full of wooden tables and, often, college students, the two dining rooms are bright and relaxed. ⊠ *4920 Prytania St., Uptown* ☎ *504/ 891–3644* ☰ *AE, D, MC, V* ☉ *Closed Sun.*

Seafood

★ ¢-$$ ✗ **Casamento's.** Encased in gleaming white ceramic tiles, Casamento's has been a haven for uptown seafood lovers since 1919. Family members still staff the long, marble raw-oyster bar up front and the immaculate kitchen out back. Between them is a small dining room with a similarly diminutive menu. The specialties are oysters lightly poached in seasoned milk, and fried shrimp, trout, and oysters, impeccably fresh and greaseless. They're served with fried potatoes and a good selection of domestic beers. Even the houseplants have a just-polished look. ✉ *4330 Magazine St., Uptown* ☎ *504/895-9761* ⚓ *Reservations not accepted* ⊟ *No credit cards* ⊙ *Closed Mon. and early June–late Aug.*

¢-$ ✗ **Franky & Johnny's.** Seekers of the quintessential New Orleans neighborhood restaurant need look no further. Team pennants, posters, and football jerseys vie for space on the paneled walls of the low-ceiling bar and dining room while a jukebox blares beneath them. From the kitchen's steaming cauldrons come freshly boiled shrimp, crabs, and crawfish, piled high and ready to be washed down with ice-cold beer. On the day's po'boy roster might be fried crawfish tails or oysters, meatballs in tomato sauce, or roast beef with gravy. Table service is rudimentary. ✉ *321 Arabella St., Uptown* ☎ *504/899-9146* ⚓ *Reservations not accepted* ⊟ *D, MC, V.*

Thai

$-$$ ✗ **Basil Leaf.** Familiar Thai standbys—spring rolls, pad thai, chicken-and-coconut soup, and the like—get a new lease on life in the kitchen of owner-chef Siam Tiparwat. These expertly done traditional dishes are backed up by a slew of thoroughly original creations in the crisp, simple dining room, enlivened with a mural depicting a Buddhist temple. Gently flavored green and red Thai curries, especially those with chicken or shrimp, are prepared with the instinctual talent of a Thai native, as are the firm yet tender dumplings filled with bits of scallop. The restaurant opens weekdays at 2:30 PM and remains open through dinner. ✉ *1438 S. Carrollton Ave., Uptown* ☎ *504/862-9001* ⊟ *AE, D, MC, V* ⊙ *No lunch.*

Mid-City

Cajun/Creole

¢-$ ✗ **Liuzza's by the Track.** Fried oyster po'boys drenched in garlic butter, milky bowls of sweet corn and crawfish bisque, and grilled Reuben sandwiches with succulent corned beef are among the reasons you might decide to tolerate the poor ventilation in this barroom near the racetrack and Jazz Fest grounds. The seafood gumbo is always different and always good—thin in body but heavy in spice. The pièce de résistance here is a barbecue shrimp po'boy, for which the shrimp aren't barbecued at all but rather cooked in a bracing lemon-pepper butter with enough garlic to cure a cold. ✉ *1518 N. Lopez St., Mid-City* ☎ *504/943-8667* ⊟ *AE, D, DC, MC, V* ⊙ *Closed Sun.*

FodorsChoice ★

Contemporary Creole

★ $-$$$ ✗ **Gabrielle.** Bright and energetic and about five minutes by taxi from the French Quarter, Gabrielle is a hit thanks to chef Greg Sonnier's marvelous interpretations of earthy, spicy south Louisiana dishes. Some tables have little elbow room, but a small add-on room has its own homey atmosphere, complete with lace curtains and framed still-life prints. Regulars come for the spicy rabbit and veal sausages, buttery oysters gratinéed with artichoke and Parmesan, a slew of excellent gumbos and étouffées, and fresh-fruit cobblers and shortcakes. Servings are generous and sauces are rich, so you may want to skip lunch before dining here. ⊠ *3201 Esplanade Ave., Mid-City* ☎ *504/948–6233* ♿ *Reservations essential* ▤ *AE, D, DC, MC, V* ⊘ *Closed Sun. and Mon. No lunch Sat.–Thurs.*

Creole with Soul

¢–$ ✕ **Two Sister's.** The bona fide Creole soul experience awaits at this family-owned eatery. Think fried chicken with macaroni and cheese; shrimp-and-okra stew; and deep, dark, oily kitchen-sink gumbo. Chitterlings, smothered rabbit, and stewed hen also roll out of the kitchen in record time, as steam tables keep most of the prepared food warm during the hectic lunch rushes. If you dine you're likely to overhear musicians recapping the previous evening's jazz performance. With its vinyl-topped tables and television, the dining room is far from spotless but the epitome of homey. The kitchen closes at 5:30 PM. ⊠ *223 N. Derbigny St., Mid-City* ☎ *504/524–0056* ▤ *No credit cards* ⊘ *Closed Sun.*

Dessert

★ ¢–$ ✕ **Angelo Brocato's.** Traditional Sicilian fruit sherbets, ice creams, pastries, and candies are the attractions of this quaint little sweetshop that harks back to the time when the French Quarter was peopled mostly by Italian immigrants. The shop has since moved to the Mid-City area, but the cannoli and the lemon and strawberry ices haven't lost their status as local favorites. It closes at 10 PM weekdays, 10:30 PM weekends. ⊠ *214 N. Carrollton Ave., Mid-City* ☎ *504/488–1465* ▤ *D, MC, V.*

French

$$–$$$ ✕ **Chateaubriand.** Normally, the only French element in a steak house is the fried potatoes. But this restaurant breaks the mold and puts its own Gallic spin on the all-American genre. The enormous cut of beef that doubles as the restaurant's namesake is served for two, and it can be either exemplary or disappointing. Other steaks, especially the rib eye, are more reliable. For even better odds on a good dinner, head for the elegant but earthy French soups, the fish dishes, or the grilled duck breast. Dessert means a rather predictable, but competently done, roster of such standbys as crème brûlée, bavarois custard, and lemon crepes. ⊠ *310 N. Carrollton Ave., Mid-City* ☎ *504/207–0016* ▤ *AE, D, DC, MC, V.*

$–$$ ✕ **Café Degas.** Dining at Café Degas is like dining at a sidewalk café in Paris, even though the restaurant is completely covered. There's a tree growing through the center of the dining room, and the clear plastic "wall" abutting the sidewalk along Esplanade Avenue is removable. The fare here—pâté boards, onion soup, steamed mussels, duck in orange sauce, steaks, dessert crepes—is a mixture of French bistro cooking and what you might find at a countryside inn. Employees, some of them French-speaking, are matter-of-fact in a relaxing European way. ⊠ *3127 Esplanade Ave., Mid-City* ☎ *504/945–5635* ▤ *AE, D, DC, MC, V* ⊘ *No lunch Mon.*

Seafood

¢–$ ✕ **Mandina's.** The interior of this white-clapboard corner building is a study in 1940s nostalgia, with its functional bar facing a roomful of laminated tables. Regulars—a cross section of the population—endure a 15-minute wait for a table under an old newspaper clipping or the latest artwork from a brewery. The shrimp rémoulade and old-fashioned gumbo are the logical appetizers. Broiled trout and shrimp, wading in seasoned butter, are tasty, as are the fried oysters and shrimp, the seafood or Italian-sausage po'boys, and the sweetbread pudding. Service is swift and genteel. ⊠ *3800 Canal St., Mid-City* ☎ *504/482–9179* ⌕ *Reservations not accepted* ⊟ *No credit cards.*

Steak

$$–$$$$ ✕ **Ruth's Chris Steak House.** Ruth's Chris is sacred to New Orleans steak lovers. The all-American menu fairly drips with butter, and the main draw is aged U.S. prime beef in he-man portions, charbroiled and served atop a sizzling, seasoned butter sauce. The hefty filet mignon is often taller than it is wide, and a monstrous porterhouse serves several. If the salads lack sparkle, the copious potato dishes are usually first-rate. Lighter entrées (chicken breast, veal, seafood) mollify the health-conscious. The plush but unfussy dining rooms of the flagship Mid-City restaurant are lined in pale-wood paneling and understated landscape paintings. Politicians, both actual and aspiring, are everywhere. ⊠ *711 N. Broad St., Mid-City* ☎ *504/486–0810* ⌕ *Reservations essential* ⊟ *AE, D, DC, MC, V* ☉ *No lunch Sat.*

Traditional Creole

$$–$$$ ✕ **Christian's.** A small church in a residential neighborhood has been turned into a front-rank purveyor of Creole cuisine with numerous French flourishes. On banquettes under stained-glass windows, regulars devour crunchy, smoked soft-shell crab laced with butter, veal in cream with port and morel mushrooms, a Creole-style bouillabaisse, and pork tenderloin with a corn-bread stuffing with bits of andouille sausage and artichoke. The superb recipe for skewered fried oysters with bacon comes from Galatoire's (⇨ French Quarter), and the two restaurants, founded by members of the same family, share other dishes as well. ⊠ *3835 Iberville St., Mid-City* ☎ *504/482–4924* ⌕ *Reservations essential* ⊟ *AE, D, MC, V* ☉ *Closed Sun. and Mon. No lunch weekends.*

Ninth Ward

Southern

¢–$ ✕ **Elizabeth's.** "Real food, done real good" is the motto at Elizabeth's, a real down-home southern joint where the vinyl print tablecloths look just like grandma's, and where breakfast is the most important meal of the day. The breakfast po'boy is a working man's egg-and-sausage sandwich, and the bottomless cups contain darkly bitter coffee and chicory. Owner Heidi Elizabeth Trull outdoes herself for Saturday brunches with breakfast casseroles, stuffed French toast, shrimp and grits, and enough house-made desserts to start a bakery. The staff is spunky, including Trull who emerges from the kitchen to refill coffees, clear plates, and taste her customers' food. ⊠ *601 Gallier St., Bywater* ☎ *504/944–*

9272 ⌖ *Reservations not accepted* ▭ *MC, V* ⊘ *Closed Sun. and Mon. No dinner.*

Traditional Creole

★ **$$–$$$** ╳ **Mandich's.** This many-faceted favorite of locals resists categorizing. It occupies a neat but unremarkable building in a blue-collar neighborhood. The decor—a mix of bright yellow paint, captain's chairs, and wood veneer—won't win prizes. The food ranges from straightforward, home-style dishes to ambitious trout and shellfish dishes. Fried oysters are swathed in a finely balanced butter sauce with garlic and parsley. Shrimp and andouille sausages trade flavors on the grill. The trout Mandich (breaded, broiled, and served with a butter, wine, and Worcestershire sauce) has become a classic of the genre, and more garlic boosts slices of buttery roasted potatoes. ⊠ *3200 St. Claude Ave., 9th Ward* ☎ *504/947–9553* ⌖ *Reservations essential* ▭ *MC, V* ⊘ *Closed Sun. and Mon. No lunch Sat. No dinner Tues.–Thurs.*

Outside City Limits

Cajun/Creole

¢–$ ╳ **Crabby Jack's.** Panéed rabbit po'boys, creative fresh fish specials, and frying impresario Austin Leslie's fried chicken draw legions of urban New Orleanians out to Jefferson. Operated by Jack Leonardi, the swashbuckling chef-proprietor of Jacques-Imo's Cafe (⇨ Uptown), Crabby Jack's is a low-rent boxy joint; it's not exactly comfortable, but since the food is too good to wait, most people eat here. Smoky red beans, muffulettas, and jambalaya are all first rate and cheap, though the creative fresh-fish specials provide a more definitive experience. This is also the site of a seafood wholesaler, and the seasonal boiled seafood couldn't get any fresher. ⊠ *428 Jefferson Hwy., Jefferson* ☎ *504/833–2722* ▭ *AE, MC, V* ⊘ *Closed Sun. No dinner.*

Chinese

☾ **$–$$** ╳ **China Blossom.** The regional Chinese cooking is exemplary in this tidy restaurant across the Mississippi River from the center of town. Uncompromising freshness and imagination mark every aspect of the food, whether the style is Cantonese, Szechuan, or elegant Hong Kong. These qualities are found not only in a whole, butterflied, fried trout and crawfish in spicy lobster sauce but also in such commonplace dishes as egg rolls, lemon chicken, moo shu pork, and wonton soup. A few ornamental objects of lacquer, gilt, and mother-of-pearl adorn the white-and-rust walls of the several dining rooms, and service is by a crisply efficient, affable staff. ⊠ *1801 Stumpf Blvd., at Wright Ave., in Stumpf Blvd. Shopping Center, Gretna* ☎ *504/361–4598* ▭ *AE, D, MC, V* ⊘ *Closed Sun. and Mon.*

Contemporary Creole

$$–$$$ ╳ **Dakota.** Warm colors, lustrous woods, and floral accents set the scene at Dakota. Owner-chef Kim Kringlie's inspirations may be multicultural, but his seasonal menus are solidly grounded in south Louisiana. A crackly soft-shell crab might be stuffed with a variety of expertly seasoned shellfish. Pork tenderloin is smoked and glazed with cane syrup

before it's brushed with a bourbon-barbecue butter. Soft-fleshed tilapia in a crust of Japanese flour and Parmesan is garnished with crabmeat and mushrooms. The many comforts of the dining spaces include outstanding table service. ⊠ *629 U.S. 190, Covington* ☎ *985/892–3712* ▤ *AE, DC, MC, V* ☺ *Closed Sun. No lunch Sat.*

French

$–$$$$ ✕ **Le Parvenu.** Inside a cozy little cottage, Le Parvenu's homey mood is reinforced by pastel-hue dining rooms lined with flouncy drapery and unobtrusive prints. "Classic" is the word that comes to mind time and again with owner-chef Dennis Hutley's French-Creole menus. Breaded lobster tails join lumps of first-quality crabmeat, crawfish, and shrimp in a sauce tinged with cognac. The sweet edge of a plum sauce moderates the earthy flavor of a rack of pink and juicy lamb chops. Cream soups are a specialty, and the best may be a bisque of mirliton (a species of delicately flavored squash) dotted with bits of shrimp and crab. ⊠ *509 Williams Blvd., Kenner* ☎ *504/471–0534* ▤ *AE, DC, MC, V* ☺ *Closed Mon. No dinner Sun.*

$$–$$$ ✕ **La Provence.** It's almost an hour's drive from central New Orleans, but the glorious French-provincial food and relaxing atmosphere of this exceptional restaurant are well worth the trip. Owner-chef Chris Kerageorgiu's elegant yet earthy cooking is consistently satisfying. Roasted duck with garlic warms the soul, and a thick and hearty quail gumbo with rice and andouille sausage is a revelation. Separating the two dining rooms, hung with pleasant Provençal landscape paintings, is a hearth that welcomes you on damp winter days. In warmer seasons, the tree-shaded deck is almost as congenial. ⊠ *U.S. 190, 7 mi from the Lake Pontchartrain Causeway, Lacombe* ☎ *985/626–7662* ⌂ *Reservations essential* ▤ *AE, MC, V* ☺ *Closed Mon. and Tues. No lunch Wed.–Sat.*

Italian

★ **$–$$$**   ✕ **Mosca's.** You may find the decor here either charmingly unpretentious or primitive. The food—combining Louisiana ingredients and Italian ingenuity—is good enough to lure city folk to isolation about a half hour from the city. Baked oysters with bread crumbs, olive oil, garlic, and herbs approach the summit of Italian-Creole cuisine. The Italian shrimp are cooked in an herbed mix of olive oil and spices, the roasted chicken with rosemary is luscious, and the house-made Italian sausage is full of peppery goodness. Getting a table usually means waiting at the bar. The restaurant is difficult to spot, so call for directions. Reservations are not accepted for Saturday. ⊠ *4137 U.S. Hwy. W, Avondale* ☎ *504/436–9942* ▤ *No credit cards* ☺ *Closed Sun. and Mon. No lunch.*

Latin American

♺ ¢   ✕ **Pupuseria Divino Corazon.** What's a pupuseria? Why, a place that serves *pupusas,* of course. And Gloria Salmeron is an expert when it comes to making pupusas, the soft little pork-and-cheese pies from her native El Salvador. They, and everything else—like the sweet-corn tamales, quesadillas, and fried plantains—are filled with a fresh heartiness not easy to find in Latin American restaurants. Mexican dishes, especially the nachos chihuahuas, are almost as good. A large picture of the Sacred Heart of Jesus (the restaurant's namesake) dominates the beautifully tended dining room. This restaurant is quick to get to via the river bridge. ⊠ *2300 Belle Chasse Hwy., Gretna* ☎ *504/368–5724* ⚹ *Reservations not accepted* ⊟ *MC, V* ⊗ *Closed Sun.*

Steak

$$–$$$$ ✕ **Ruth's Chris Steak House.** Ruth's Chris is sacred to New Orleans steak lovers. The all-American menu fairly drips with butter, and the main draw is aged U.S. prime beef in he-man portions, charbroiled and served atop a sizzling, seasoned butter sauce. The hefty filet mignon is often taller than it is wide, and a monstrous porterhouse serves several. If the salads lack sparkle, the copious potato dishes are usually first-rate. Lighter entrées (chicken breast, veal, seafood) mollify the health-conscious. ⊠ *3633 Veterans Blvd., Metairie* ☎ *504/888–3600* ⚹ *Reservations essential* ⊟ *AE, D, DC, MC, V* ⊗ *No lunch Sat.*

Traditional Creole

☾ **$–$$** ✕ **Restaurant des Familles.** No time for a trip to Cajun country? This restaurant about a half-hour's drive from central New Orleans is the next best thing, although you'd better ask for directions when reserving. Just a few yards from the vast windows are the slow-moving waters of Bayou des Familles, providing a primeval tableau. Dramatically illuminated at night, the huge, Acadian-style raised cottage has a kitchen that produces familiar, and very edible, seafood in the Creole style—shrimp rémoulade, crawfish étouffée, turtle soup, redfish meunière, and fried oysters and bacon en brochette. The oyster-and-artichoke soup is one of the best around. ⊠ *Rte. 3134, north of the intersection with Rte. 45, Crown Point* ☎ *504/689–7834* ⚹ *Reservations essential* ⊟ *AE, D, MC, V.*

Vietnamese

¢ ✕ **Pho Tau Bay.** The suburbs contain a proliferation of *pho* (Vietnamese beef noodle soup) houses, as well as more ambitious restaurants such this tidy location of the local Pho Tau Bay chain. Two blocks from Metairie's Lakeside Mall, this eatery serves excellent Vietnamese sausage sandwiches on French bread with cilantro, fresh green chili, and cucumbers; tightly wrapped spring rolls; deep bowls of pho; vermicelli noodle salads brightened with mint; and the high-octane Vietnamese drip coffee made with sweetened condensed milk. The English-speaking staff is happy to educate first timers. ⊠ *3116 N. Arnoult Rd., Metairie* ☎ *504/ 780–1063* ⚹ *Reservations not accepted* ⊟ *AE, D, MC, V* ⊗ *Closed Sun.*

WHERE TO STAY

4

Updated by
Paul A.
Greenberg

DECIDING WHERE TO STAY in New Orleans has everything to do with what you want from your visit. For those who wish to soak up the local color and experience the city's rich culture, a French Quarter hotel or bed-and-breakfast is your best choice. Others who want a quieter, more serene experience in close proximity to major attractions will find comfortable properties Uptown, in the Garden District, and in surrounding areas like the Faubourg Marigny. Business travelers will find the elegant, well-appointed Central Business District hotels convenient, comfortable, and designed with business in mind. Ask about in-room high-speed Internet access and in-hotel wireless service.

Others will appreciate the contemporary chic ambience of historic warehouses and commercial buildings refashioned into elegant hotels in the Warehouse District. These massive spaces and exposed brick walls add distinctive atmosphere to both moderately priced and upscale hotels.

New Orleans honors its European heritage with facilities and services tailored for international travelers, and it attracts families with its increasingly diverse collection of tourist attractions. By design, many hotels are within walking distance of such area attractions as the Aquarium of the Americas, the Entergy IMAX Theater, Riverwalk shopping complex, and Harrah's New Orleans casino. New Orleans, much like New York, is a "walking city." If you are visiting for the first time, try to book one of the hotels that is centrally located and within walking distance of major attractions. Lodging descriptions in this chapter frequently indicate centrally located properties.

More than ever, New Orleans finds itself high on the list of honeymoon destinations. Most major hotels have special package rates for newlywed couples, and distinctively created suites. Check the hotel's Web site for detailed descriptions or call local reservation services for lists of facilities that meet your price and location needs. Be aware that many hotels run Internet-only specials, and you may find price breaks by hotel shopping online.

With respect to physically challenged travelers, all large hotels are in compliance with the Americans with Disabilities Act. Some guesthouses and bed-and-breakfast inns in 19th-century structures are not yet fully equipped for people with disabilities. Hotels are not required by the ADA to equip every room for physically challenged guests, so ask specific questions related to your individual needs.

If you visit the city more than once, try to create a different lodging experience each time. For your first visit, try a large, bustling, downtown hotel; for your next visit, perhaps a romantic getaway in an outlying guesthouse, where old-world charm and atmosphere are so proudly preserved. All have a limited number of rooms, so it is advisable to make reservations as much as a year ahead of time.

French Quarter/Faubourg Marigny

If New Orleans is the heart of Louisiana, the 96-square-block French Quarter is its soul. Although much of the Quarter is commercially oriented to tourism, elegant but comfortable hotels and B&Bs or guest-houses are tucked away in remote residential pockets, and a number of grand imposing lodgings are placed throughout. If you're staying in a busy part of the Quarter, you may want to request a room away from the side of the building that faces the street. In larger hotels be sure to ask for a room with a balcony or view. If you plan to do a lot of walking while in New Orleans, try to stay in a hotel in a high-traffic area. Exercise caution and avoid secluded streets and areas.

Hotels

$$$$　▣ **New Orleans Marriott Hotel.** The Marriott has a fabulous view of the Quarter, the CBD, and the river. It's an easy walk from Riverwalk, the Canal Place mall, and the Convention Center. The rooms are comfortable, the service is friendly, and nightly jazz enlivens the lobby and the Riverview Restaurant, which just happens to have one of the best views of New Orleans anywhere in the city, and possibly the best buffet Sunday brunch in the city. The newly constructed Canal Street streetcar line makes transportation access to most parts of the city convenient. ⊠ *555 Canal St., French Quarter, 70130* ☎ *504/581–1000 or 800/228–9290* 🖨 *504/523–6755* ⊕ *www.marriott.com* ⟳ *1,290 rooms, 54 suites* ♨ *3 restaurants, pool, health club, sauna, bar, lobby lounge, business services, meeting room, parking (fee)* ▤ *AE, D, DC, MC, V.*

$$$$　▣ **Ritz-Carlton New Orleans.** The Ritz-Carlton Hotel Company has converted the historic Maison Blanche department-store building into a luxurious hotel reminiscent of old New Orleans. Rooms have local antiques, oversize marble bathrooms, and plush linens. Club Floor has 57 rooms, including eight suites with concierge and private lounge. The hotel, within walking distance of most attractions and minutes from the Convention Center, borders the French Quarter and faces the CBD. The lobby, adorned in fine art and furnishings, opens onto a luxurious courtyard. The renovated Victor's restaurant on the third floor exceeds conventional expectations for a hotel dining room. Live jazz is piped in from the adjacent lobby lounge. ⊠ *921 Canal St., French Quarter, 70112* ☎ *504/524–1331* 🖨 *504/524–7675* ⊕ *www.ritzcarlton.com* ⟳ *452 rooms, 36 suites* ♨ *2 restaurants, hair salon, spa, 3 bars, parking (fee)* ▤ *AE, D, DC, MC, V.*

$$$$　▣ **Wyndham New Orleans at Canal Place.** The Wyndham was designed with views in mind. The huge, rose, Carrara-marble lobby, with European antiques, jardinieres, and grand piano, is on the 11th floor of the Canal Place shopping mall; tea is served daily in the lobby or the River 127 Restaurant, which has one of the few upscale no-smoking bars in the city. Two-story arched windows overlook the great bend in the Mississippi River and the French Quarter. Rooms have marble foyers and marble baths. Perks on the two executive floors include complimentary Continental breakfast and afternoon hors d'oeuvres. The Aquarium, the Canal Street ferry, Riverwalk, and Harrah's New Orleans casino are nearby. ⊠ *100 Iberville St., French Quarter, 70130* ☎ *504/566–7006 or 800/996–3426* 🖨 *504/553–5120* ⊕ *www.wyndham.com* ⟳ *438 rooms, 41 suites* ♨ *Restaurant, room service, minibars, pool, bar, lobby lounge* ▤ *AE, D, DC, MC, V.*

4

Recent additions to the local hotel inventory have raised the bar on the quality of accommodations in New Orleans. Even century-old hotels such as the Monteleone have renovated guest rooms to compete with newer hotels. Properties are assigned price categories based on a range from least expensive standard double rooms at high season (excluding holidays) to most expensive. We list all facilities available, but we do not specify whether they cost extra. When making accommodation inquiries, always ask what is included and what extra costs you may incur.

Services

Most hotels have private baths, central heating, air-conditioning and private phones. More and more major hotels have added data ports and phones with voice mail; some have wireless Internet service. Most major hotels also have video or high-speed checkout capability and can arrange babysitting. Smaller bed-and-breakfasts and hotels may not have all of these amenities, so ask before you book your room.

Some major hotels have pools and some do not. The crown jewel of downtown, the Ritz-Carlton, does not have a pool. Those that do not have pools have working agreements with nearby health clubs or other facilities to allow guests to use club facilities for a nominal fee. Others, such as the Wyndham New Orleans at Canal Place have rooftop pools with stellar city views.

Driving in New Orleans is sometimes a slow effort, but not impossible. Most hotels have parking available, but it will run you up to $20 a day. Valet parking is usually available at the major hotels. If you park on the street, keep in mind that the meter maids are relentless and ticketing is imminent for illegally parked vehicles. You can save time and headaches by taking cabs from one part of the city to another.

New Orleans is a major destination city for conventions, and family vacationers share almost everything with business travelers. This generally works out well, with the exception of high-traffic periods such as lunchtime in downtown restaurants near the Convention Center. Convention attendees on a tight meeting schedule must vie with families enjoying leisurely visits to local eateries.

Families are well accommodated in area hotels, including such amenities as rollaway beds and fold-out couches. It is best to determine your family's specific needs and ask your reservations agent pertinent questions before booking.

Reservations

High and low seasons are not as easily distinguished as they may be in other cities. Book your room as far in advance as possible; a major credit card is usually needed to guarantee your reservation.

What It Costs

With downtown and French Quarter square footage coming at a hefty premium, some accommodations provide more space for more money; others make up for their compact accommodations with seductive amenities. Hotels such as the downtown W and the International House have followed the East Coast trend of small but fashionable rooms. The trade-off is that you get glassed-in showers for two, upscale toiletries, top-of-the-line sheets and bedding, and every electronic gadget you could want. Rates between these hotel types and larger luxury properties such as the Windsor Court are competitive.

The lodgings we list are the most desirable in each price category, but these rates are subject to updating and change. If you have a favorite facility, stay current on its pricing. Use the Internet to shop around for rooms before booking. Many major hotels occasionally offer Internet special rates.

WHAT IT COSTS				
	$$$$	$$$	$$	$	¢
FOR 2 PEOPLE	over $275	$200–$275	$150–$200	$100–$149	under $100

Prices are for two people in a standard double room in high season, excluding 13% city and state taxes.

$$$–$$$$ ⊡ **Omni Royal Orleans Hotel.** This elegant white-marble hotel built in 1960
Fodor'sChoice is a replica of the grand St. Louis Hotel of the 1800s. Sconce-enhanced
★ columns, gilt mirrors, fan windows, and three magnificent chandeliers re-create the atmosphere of old New Orleans. Rooms, although beginning to show signs of their age, are well appointed with marble baths and marble-top dressers and tables; some have balconies. The old New Orleans map that covers one wall of the lounge will fascinate anyone interested in history. On the lobby level the Rib Room has been one of the city's culinary showpieces for 40 years. The rooftop pool has the best overhead view of the French Quarter in the city. ⊠ *621 St. Louis St., French Quarter, 70140* ☎ *504/529–5333 or 800/843–6664* ⊟ *504/529–7089* ⊕ *www.omnihotels.com* ⊷ *346 rooms, 16 suites* ⚘ *Restaurant, pool, gym, hair salon, 3 lounges, business services, meeting room, parking (fee)* ⊟ *AE, D, DC, MC, V.*

$$$–$$$$ ⊡ **Ramada Plaza Inn on Bourbon Street.** This hotel on the site of New Orleans's original French opera house is not one of the city's most elegant lodgings, but it is well kept, with colorful rooms. Guest rooms facing the courtyard are quieter, but the 32 rooms with Bourbon Street balconies are coveted during Mardi Gras. The hotel is on one of the busiest blocks of Bourbon Street, so be prepared for clamoring activity 24 hours a day outside and in. ⊠ *541 Bourbon St., French Quarter, 70130* ☎ *504/524–7611 or 800/535–7891* ⊟ *504/524–8273* ⊕ *www. innonbourbon.com* ⊷ *186 rooms, 2 suites* ⚘ *In-room data ports, pool, parking (fee)* ⊟ *AE, DC, MC, V.*

$$$–$$$$ ⊡ **Royal Sonesta Hotel.** Step from the revelry of Bourbon Street into the marble elegance of this renowned hotel's lobby, where lush plants enhance a cool, serene atmosphere. Most guest rooms are of average size, furnished with light-color reproduction antiques; many have French doors that open onto balconies or patios. Rooms facing Bourbon Street are noisy, but most rooms are sufficiently soundproof. One restaurant, Begué's, is a local gem. The charming Desire Oyster Bar on the lobby level faces Bourbon Street and serves local seafood delicacies. ⊠ *300*

Bourbon St., French Quarter, 70140 ☎ *504/586–0300 or 800/766–3782* 🖷 *504/586–0335* ⊕ *www.royalsonestano.com* ⤢ *500 rooms, 32 suites* ⚱ *2 restaurants, minibars, pool, gym, bar, nightclub, concierge floor, business services, parking (fee)* ▭ *AE, D, DC, MC, V.*

$$$–$$$$ 🖽 **W Hotel New Orleans French Quarter.** Close to Jackson Square, Bourbon Street, and Canal Street, this sleekly renovated modern hotel has one of the best locations in the Quarter. Most rooms are in the main building, and many have balconies that overlook either the courtyard or Chartres Street. Some have French doors that open directly onto a sundeck. Two of the four carriage-house suites share a cheery sundeck; others overlook a courtyard. The hotel is adjacent to Bacco, a contemporary Italian eatery operated by restaurateur Ralph Brennan. The hotel also provides a "Whatever, whenever" policy—24-hour concierges will find you those barbecued ribs you crave at 3 AM, a deep-tissue massage on command, or even a last-minute gown for a Mardi Gras ball. ☒ *316 Chartres St., French Quarter, 70130* ☎ *504/581–1200 or 800/448–4927* 🖷 *504/523–2910* ⊕ *www.whotels.com* ⤢ *98 rooms, 4 suites* ⚱ *Restaurant, pool, bar, meeting room, parking (fee)* ▭ *AE, D, DC, MC, V.*

$$–$$$$ 🖽 **Chateau Sonesta.** John Kennedy Toole's comic masterpiece, *A Confederacy of Dunces,* begins under the clock of D. H. Holmes department store on Canal Street, now a well-maintained upscale hotel. In Toole's honor, the clock and a statue of the novel's hero, Ignatius J. Reilly, remain. Rooms at the hotel are large, with high ceilings and neutral decor; some have columns and beams, remnants of the original building. Balcony rooms overlook Bourbon Street or Dauphine Street or one of two interior courtyards. Three suites with whirlpool baths surround an atrium. The hotel dining room, Le Chatelaine is open only for breakfast. Ralph Brennan's Red Fish Grill is next to the hotel. ☒ *800 Iberville St., French Quarter, 70112* ☎ *504/586–0800 or 800/766–3782* 🖷 *504/586–1987* ⊕ *www.chateausonesta.com* ⤢ *251 rooms, 11 suites* ⚱ *Restaurant, room service, in-room data ports, minibars, pool, gym, bar, meeting room, parking (fee)* ▭ *AE, D, DC, MC, V.*

★ $$–$$$$ 🖽 **Holiday Inn–Chateau Le Moyne.** This quiet hotel one block off Bourbon Street exudes old-world atmosphere. Eight suites are in Creole cottages off a tropical courtyard; all rooms are furnished with antiques and reproductions and have coffeemakers, hair dryers, and irons and ironing boards. ☒ *301 Dauphine St., French Quarter, 70112* ☎ *504/581–1303 or 800/465–4329* 🖷 *504/523–5709* ⊕ *www.holiday-inn.com* ⤢ *160 rooms, 11 suites* ⚱ *Restaurant, pool, lounge, parking (fee)* ▭ *AE, D, DC, MC, V.*

$$–$$$$ 🖽 **Monteleone Hotel.** The grande dame of French Quarter hotels, with
Fodor's Choice its ornate baroque facade, liveried doormen, and shimmering lobby
★ chandeliers, was built in 1886 and has recently undergone a renovation. The Quarter's oldest hotel now has all room types available with the same luxurious appointments as its brand-new competitors. Rooms are extra large and luxurious, with rich fabrics and a mix of four-poster beds, brass beds, and beds with traditional headboards. Junior suites are spacious, and sumptuous VIP suites come with extra pampering. The slowly revolving Carousel Revolving Bar (⇨ Nightlife) in the lobby is a local landmark. Chef Randy Buck prepares superb food in the Hunt Room

Where to Stay in
Downtown
New Orleans

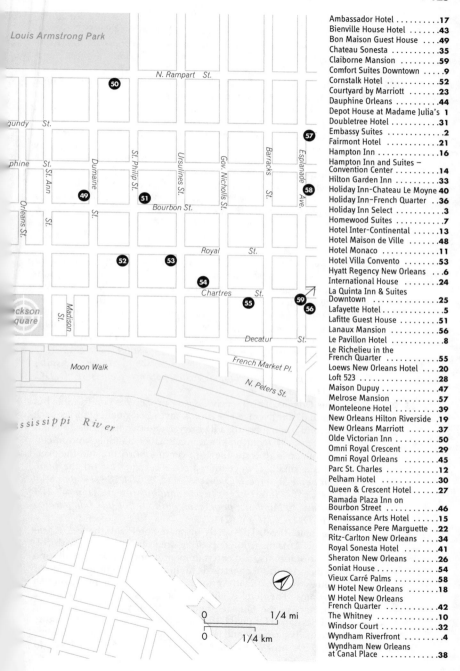

Grill, one of the city's best-kept culinary secrets. ✉ *214 Royal St., French Quarter, 70130* ☎ *504/523–3341 or 800/535–9595* 🖷 *504/528–1019* ⊕ *www.hotelmonteleone.com* ⇨ *598 rooms, 28 suites* ♿ *3 restaurants, pool, gym, bar, concierge, Internet, business services, meeting room* 🖃 *AE, D, DC, MC, V.*

$$$
Fodor'sChoice
★
🖭 **Hotel Maison de Ville.** This small romantic hotel lies in seclusion amid the hustle and bustle of the French Quarter. Tapestry-covered chairs, a gas fire burning in the sitting room, and antiques-furnished rooms all contribute to a 19th-century atmosphere. Some rooms are in former slave quarters in the courtyard; others are on the upper floors of the main house. Breakfast is served with a rose on a silver tray, and port and sherry are available in the afternoon. Other meals can be taken at the intimate adjacent Bistro, a tiny local culinary gem that has one of the best wine selections in the city. (⇨ Dining, French Quarter). Those who seek a special hideaway will love the hotel's Audubon Cottages. ✉ *727 Toulouse St., French Quarter, 70130* ☎ *504/561–5858 or 800/634–1600* 🖷 *504/528–9939* ⊕ *www.maisondeville.com* ⇨ *14 rooms, 2 suites, 7 cottages* ♿ *Restaurant, minibars, pool, parking (fee); no kids under 12* 🖃 *AE, D, DC, MC, V* ⦿ *CP.*

$$$
🖭 **Maison Dupuy.** Seven restored 19th-century town houses surround one of the Quarter's prettiest courtyards, anchored by a spectacular fountain. Most rooms are on the large side, and some have balconies. Chef Dominique Macquet is the guiding force at Dominique, the hotel's stellar restaurant, which specializes in Louisiana and Caribbean cuisine. The adjacent Dominique's Lounge attracts late-night revelers. The hotel is two blocks from Bourbon Street and the heart of the Quarter. ✉ *1001 Toulouse St., French Quarter, 70112* ☎ *504/586–8000 or 800/535–9177* 🖷 *504/525–5334* ⊕ *www.maisondupuy.com* ⇨ *187 rooms, 13 suites* ♿ *Restaurant, pool, health club, nightclub, parking (fee)* 🖃 *AE, D, DC, MC, V* ⦿ *CP.*

$$–$$$
🖭 **Dauphine Orleans.** This French Quarter property is comfortable but not exceptional. The average-size rooms have good-quality fabrics; each has an iron and ironing board, a hair dryer, and two bathrobes. Rooms and suites are in the main building, in a smaller building, and in cottages. The lounge is an erstwhile 19th-century bordello, and the exercise room is a small, 19th-century Creole cottage just off the pool. ✉ *415 Dauphine St., French Quarter, 70112* ☎ *504/586–1800 or 800/521–7111* 🖷 *504/586–1409* ⊕ *www.dauphineorleans.com* ⇨ *104 rooms, 7 suites* ♿ *Minibars, pool, gym, outdoor hot tub, bar, parking (fee)* 🖃 *AE, D, DC, MC, V* ⦿ *CP.*

$–$$$
🖭 **Bienville House Hotel.** This small, intimate hotel with the feel of gracious old New Orleans is in an exciting area of the Quarter with colorful shops, restaurants, and entertainment venues. Here you will find one of the most beautiful courtyards in the city and some lovely rooms with balconies overlooking it. Antiques and reproduction pieces furnish the guest rooms. The hotel is within walking distance of some of the best restaurants in the Quarter, and has its own lobby-level dining room, the Louisiana Heritage Cafe and School of Cooking. The beauty of this hotel is its intimacy and access to most major attractions in the area. ✉ *320 Decatur St., French Quarter, 70130* ☎ *504/529–2345*

🛏 *504/525–6079* ⊕ *www.bienvillehouse.com* 🛏 *80 rooms, 3 suites* ⚱ *Restaurant, pool, bar, dry cleaning, laundry service, meeting room, parking (fee)* ▭ *AE, D, MC, V* ⦿ *BP.*

$–$$ ⊞ **Holiday Inn–French Quarter.** Close to Canal Street, this modern hotel is a good home base for walking into the heart of the French Quarter or the CBD or for boarding the St. Charles Avenue streetcar line. The hotel's restaurant is a T. G. I. Friday's. ⊠ *124 Royal St., French Quarter, 70130* ☎ *504/529–7211 or 800/447–2830* 🛏 *504/566–1127* ⊕ *www.bristolhotels.com* 🛏 *374 rooms* ⚱ *Restaurant, indoor pool, gym, parking (fee)* ▭ *AE, D, DC, MC, V.*

¢–$$ ⊞ **Cornstalk Hotel.** This early-19th-century Victorian mansion is within walking distance of the best restaurants in the Quarter, antiques shops, and boutiques. Surrounded by a 130-year-old "cornstalk" cast-iron fence, it is one of the distinctive small inns in the French Quarter. Elegant chandeliers greet you in the grand entrance-hall lobby. The rooms, with high vaulted ceilings and stunning antique furniture, provide quiet comfort with understated elegance. Breakfast on the balcony as horse-drawn carriages clip-clop by is one of the great local experiences. Literature buffs might be interested to know that Harriet Beecher Stowe found her inspiration for *Uncle Tom's Cabin* here. ⊠ *915 Royal St., French Quarter, 70116* ☎ *504/523–1515* 🛏 *504/522–5558* 🛏 *14 rooms* ▭ *AE, MC, V.*

★ **¢–$$** ⊞ **Le Richelieu in the French Quarter.** Close to the Old Ursuline Convent and the French Market, Le Richelieu combines the friendly personal charm of a small hotel with luxe touches (upscale toiletries, hair dryers)—at a moderate rate. Some rooms have mirrored walls and large walk-in closets, and all have brass ceiling fans, irons, and ironing boards. Balcony rooms have the same rates as standard rooms. An intimate bar and café is off the courtyard, with tables on the terrace by the pool. Many regular customers would never stay anywhere else. ⊠ *1234 Chartres St., French Quarter, 70116* ☎ *504/529–2492 or 800/535–9653* 🛏 *504/524–8179* ⊕ *www.lerichelieuhotel.com* 🛏 *69 rooms, 17 suites* ⚱ *Café, some kitchenettes, some refrigerators, pool, bar, concierge, free parking* ▭ *AE, D, DC, MC, V.*

Guesthouses & Bed-and-Breakfasts

★ **$$$–$$$$** ⊞ **Melrose Mansion.** Down pillows and fine milled soaps; full breakfast served poolside, in a formal dining room, or in your room; and rooms filled with 19th-century Louisiana antiques are among the attractions of this handsome 1884 Victorian mansion. Rooms and suites are spacious, with high ceilings and polished hardwood floors. Cocktails are served each evening in the formal drawing room. Baths are sumptuous affairs; those in suites have hot tubs. All but one of the rooms have a wet bar, and one has a private patio. ⊠ *937 Esplanade Ave., French Quarter, 70116* ☎ *504/944–2255* 🛏 *504/945–1794* ⊕ *www.melrosegroup. com* 🛏 *8 rooms, 4 suites* ⚱ *Pool* ▭ *AE, D, MC, V* ⦿ *BP.*

$$$–$$$$ ⊞ **Soniat House.** This singularly handsome property comprises three meticFodor'sChoice ulously restored town houses built in the 1830s. Polished hardwood floors,
★ Oriental rugs, and American and European antiques are complemented by contemporary artwork. Amenities include Crabtree & Evelyn toiletries, goose-down pillows, and Egyptian cotton sheets. Some rooms and suites

have hot tubs. Exotic plants fill two secluded courtyards, where after-noon cocktails and a breakfast ($11 extra) of homemade biscuits and strawberry jam, fresh-squeezed orange juice, and café au lait can be taken, weather permitting. You'll never forget these biscuits. An on-site antiques shop carries exquisite European furnishings. Many regular New Orleans visitors consider this the city's finest hotel. ⊠ *1133 Chartres St., French Quarter, 70116* ☎ *504/522–0570 or 800/544–8808* 🖷 *504/522–7208* ⊕ *www.soniathouse.com* ⏎ *20 rooms, 13 suites* ⌕ *Concierge, business services, parking (fee)* ⊟ *AE, MC, V.*

$$–$$$$ 🏨 **Vieux Carré Palms.** In a residential neighborhood on the edge of the French Quarter, this elegantly furnished, spacious bed-and-breakfast provides a private, intimate setting and quick access to French Quarter attractions. Fine champagne greets you on your arrival. The smell of fresh French pastries fills the hallways every morning. Rooms are spacious, well appointed, and homey; some face tree-lined Esplanade Avenue. This charmer is definitely one of New Orleans's best-kept secrets—one of the most comfortable inns in the city—and your hosts are as gracious as they come. This inn is for travelers who want privacy, upscale home-style comfort, and easy access to the French Quarter and downtown attractions. ⊠ *723 Esplanade Ave., French Quarter, 70116* ☎ *504/949–2572 or 800/523–9091* 🖷 *504/949–2572* ⏎ *4 suites* ⊟ *MC, V.*

★ $–$$$$ 🏨 **Claiborne Mansion.** Enormous rooms with high ceilings, canopy or four-poster beds, polished hardwood floors, and rich fabrics embellish this handsome 1859 mansion in Faubourg Marigny, on the fringe of the French Quarter. The house overlooks Washington Square Park and has a lush, dramatically lighted rear courtyard and pool. Although spacious and elegant, the house is charming and intimate. Celebrities regularly book it for the privacy, but families appreciate its suites with separate bedrooms. This place is a true local gem. ⊠ *2111 Dauphine St., Faubourg Marigny, 70116* ☎ *504/949–7327* 🖷 *504/949–0388* ⊕ *www.claibornemansion. com* ⏎ *2 rooms, 5 suites* ⌕ *In-room VCRs, pool* ⊟ *AE, MC, V* ⦿ *BP.*

$$–$$$ 🏨 **Lafitte Guest House.** A four-story 1849 French-style manor house, the Lafitte is meticulously restored, with rooms decorated with period furnishings. Room 40 takes up the entire fourth floor and overlooks French Quarter rooftops, and Room 5, the loft apartment, overlooks the beautiful courtyard. Breakfast can be brought to your room, served in the Victorian parlor, or enjoyed in the courtyard, and the owner serves wine and hors d'oeuvres each evening. ⊠ *1003 Bourbon St., French Quarter, 70116* ☎ *504/581–2678 or 800/331–7971* 🖷 *504/581–2677* ⊕ *www.lafitteguesthouse.com* ⏎ *14 rooms, 2 suites* ⌕ *Cable TV, concierge; no smoking* ⊟ *AE, D, DC, MC, V* ⦿ *CP.*

$$–$$$ 🏨 **Lanaux Mansion.** This Italianate mansion dates from 1879 and has 14-foot ceilings upstairs and down, as well as some of the original wall-paper, cornices, ceiling medallions, and mantels. The Lanaux Suite in the main house and the cottage in the rear courtyard are Victorian, with such touches as displays of antique clothing. The house includes the original library, with shelves full of books, and a kitchen with a big open fireplace. Each suite has a refrigerator, microwave, coffeemaker, and fixings for a Continental breakfast. All accommodations have phones with voice mail, irons and ironing boards, and hair dryers. ⊠ *547 Esplanade*

Ave., French Quarter, 70116 ☎ *504/488–4640 or 800/729–4640* 🖷 *504/ 488–4639* 📠 *3 suites, 1 cottage* ▤ *No credit cards* ⭕| *CP.*

$–$$$ 🖼 **Hotel Villa Convento.** The Campo family provides round-the-clock service in this four-story 1848 Creole town house. Although it's just blocks from the Quarter's tourist attractions, shopping, and great restaurants, this guesthouse is on a surprisingly quaint, quiet street, close to the Old Ursuline Convent. Each morning you can have croissants and fresh-brewed coffee on the lush patio. Furnished with reproductions of antiques, rooms vary in price; some have balconies, chandeliers, or ceiling fans. ✉*616 Ursulines St., French Quarter, 70116* ☎ *504/522–1793* 🖷 *504/524– 1902* ⊕*www.villaconvento.com* 📠*25 rooms* ▤*AE, D, DC, MC, V* ⭕|*CP.*

$–$$$ 🖼 **Olde Victorian Inn and Spa.** Gracious hospitality and Victorian elegance define this bed-and-breakfast at the edge of the Quarter on historic Rampart Street. High ceilings, lace, and floor-to-ceiling windows evoke its 19th-century past. Guests often vie for the Chantilly Room, an authentically detailed Victorian accommodation with a private balcony that overlooks Louis Armstrong Park. All rooms have private baths; some have balconies. You'll wake to the aroma of baked goods prepared on premises before the breakfast hour. Miss Celie's Day Spa provides full spa services, which you can have administered outdoors in the lush, covered courtyard. Ask about the chef's tasting menu, prepared by the owners three times a week. ✉ *914 Rampart St., French Quarter, 70116* ☎ *504/522–2446 or 800/725–2446* 🖷 *504/897–0248* ⊕ *www.oldevictorianinn.com* 📠 *6 rooms* ▤ *AE, MC, V.*

¢–$$ 🖼 **Bon Maison Guest House.** Quaint accommodations lie within the gates of this 1840 town house on the quiet end of Bourbon Street. Rooms in the former slave quarters, off the lush brick patio with tropical plants, are pleasantly furnished and have ceiling fans. Two large suites with kitchenettes are in the main house. There's no elevator—so be prepared for lots of stair climbing to upper floors. ✉ *835 Bourbon St., French Quarter, 70116* ☎🖷 *504/561–8498* ⊕ *www.bonmaison.com* 📠 *3 rooms, 2 suites* ▤ *MC, V.*

CBD & Warehouse District

The CBD and Warehouse District, also referred to as the "Arts District" because of the proliferation of great galleries, is perfect for those who prefer accommodations in luxurious high-rise hotels or in one of the city's ever-increasing collection of smaller boutique hotels. All the hotels listed are within walking distance of the French Quarter, and shuttles, taxis, buses, and the St. Charles Avenue streetcar are readily available. Most hotels are within walking distance of two of the city's primary attractions, the Ogden Museum of Southern Art and the National D-Day Museum. If you're walking in the CBD and Warehouse District after dark, it's wise to stay on populated main streets. In the larger hotels, always ask for seasonal or package-rate availability. If you are traveling as part of a convention, ask for the convention rate.

Hotels

$$$$ 🖼 **Loews New Orleans Hotel.** A refashioned bank building in the heart of downtown is now home to this plush 21st-century hotel. Its West In-

CloseUp

LODGING ALTERNATIVES

Apartment Rentals

If you want a home base that's roomy enough for a family and comes with cooking facilities, consider a furnished rental. These can save you money, especially if you're traveling with a group. Home-exchange directories sometimes list rentals as well as exchanges.

The following agency handles furnished apartments: **Hideaways International** (✉ 767 Islington St., Portsmouth, NH 03801 ☎ 603/430–4433 or 800/843–4433 📠 603/430–4444 ⊕ www. hideaways.com) has an annual membership $145.

Bed & Breakfasts

Bed-and-breakfasts provide an intimate alternative to hotels and motels, and New Orleans has many charming accommodations of this kind. Bed & Breakfast, Inc.—Reservations Service represents a variety of accommodations in all areas of New Orleans. New Orleans Bed & Breakfast and Accommodations represents properties citywide, including private homes, apartments, and condos.

Bed & Breakfast, Inc.—Reservations Service (✉ 1021 Moss St., Box 52257, 70152 ☎ 504/488–4640 or 800/729–4640 📠 504/488–4639 ⊕ www. historiclodging.com). **New Orleans Bed & Breakfast and Accommodations** (✉ 671 Rosa Ave., Suite 208, Metairie 70005 ☎ 504/838–0071 or 888/240–0070 📠 504/838–0140 ⊕ www. neworleansbandb.com).

Hostels

No matter what your age, you can save on lodging costs by staying at hostels. In some 4,500 locations in more than 70 countries around the world, Hostelling International (HI), the umbrella group for a number of national youth-hostel associations, offers single-sex, dorm-style beds and, at many hostels, rooms for couples and family accommodations. Membership in any HI national hostel association, open to travelers of all ages, allows you to stay in HI-affiliated hostels at member rates; one-year membership is about $28 for adults (C$35 for a two-year minimum membership in Canada, £14 in the U.K., A$52 in Australia, and NZ$40 in New Zealand); hostels charge about $10–$30 per night. Members have priority if the hostel is full; they're also eligible for discounts around the world, even on rail and bus travel in some countries.

Hostelling International—USA (✉ 8401 Colesville Rd., Suite 600, Silver Spring, MD 20910 ☎ 301/495–1240 📠 301/495–6697 ⊕ www.hiusa.org). **Hostelling International—Canada** (✉ 205 Catherine St., Suite 400, Ottawa, Ontario K2P 1C3 ☎ 613/237–7884 or 800/663–5777 📠 613/237–7868 ⊕ www.hihostels.ca). **YHA England and Wales** (✉ Trevelyan House, Dimple Rd., Matlock, Derbyshire DE4 3YH, U.K. ☎ 0870/870–8808, 0870/ 770–8868, 0162/959–2600 📠 0870/770–6127 ⊕ www.yha.org. uk). **YHA Australia** (✉ 422 Kent St., Sydney, NSW 2001 ☎ 02/9261–1111 📠 02/9261–1969 ⊕ www.yha.com.au). **YHA New Zealand** (✉ Level 1, Moorhouse City, 166 Moorhouse Ave., Box 436, Christchurch ☎ 03/379–9970 or 0800/278–299 📠 03/365–4476 ⊕ www.yha. org.nz).

dies–style lobby provides a welcoming atmosphere to arrive in, and the bright spacious rooms are enriched with local artwork and soothing colors. The Cafe Adelaide and the Swizzlestick Lounge, both on the lobby level, are owned and operated by the same family that owns the legendary Commander's Palace Restaurant. The hotel is across the street from Harrah's New Orleans casino and within walking distance of most major downtown attractions. ⊠ *300 Poydras St., CBD, 70130* ☎ *504/595–5310* 🖷 *504/595–5329* ⊕ *www.loewshotels.com* ⇥ *273 rooms, 12 suites ⟡ Café, cable TV, minibars, indoor pool, gym, spa, lounge, dry cleaning, laundry services, concierge, Internet, business services* ⊟ *AE, D, DC, MC, V.*

$$$–$$$$ 🖭 **Hyatt Regency New Orleans.** This luxurious Hyatt has a streamlined lobby with fountains, Oriental rugs, and glittering chandeliers. Go for a corner room, where two walls of windows give great views. Most rooms in the Lanai Building face the pool, and each one has a private patio or balcony. Special rooms for female travelers are larger, close to the elevators, and come with hair dryers, makeup mirrors, irons, and ironing boards. The Regency Club Floor provides upgraded amenities and extra-large guest rooms up to 575 square feet. The revolving Top of the Dome steak house has a great view of the city. A glass atrium connects the hotel with the New Orleans Centre shopping mall and the Superdome. ⊠ *500 Poydras Plaza, CBD, 70113* ☎ *504/561–1234 or 800/233–1234* 🖷 *504/523–0488* ⊕ *www.hyatt.com* ⇥ *1,184 rooms, 100 suites ⟡ 4 restaurants, pool, sports bar, laundry service, parking (fee)* ⊟ *AE, D, DC, MC, V.*

★ **$$$–$$$$** 🖭 **Le Pavillon Hotel.** Magnificent chandeliers adorn the European-style lobby of this historic hotel dating from 1907, and a handsome collection of artwork lines the corridors. Another dramatic feature is the marble railing in the clubby Gallery Lounge, originally from the Grand Hotel in Paris. Guest rooms have high ceilings and identical traditional decor; suites are particularly luxurious. The elegant Crystal Room has a huge salad-and-pasta lunch buffet weekdays. The hotel bar is grand, yet clubby, and one of the most civilized spots in the city for an afternoon cocktail. ⊠ *833 Poydras St., CBD, 70112* ☎ *504/581–3111 or 800/535–9095* 🖷 *504/522–5543* ⊕ *www.lepavillon.com* ⇥ *219 rooms, 7 suites ⟡ Restaurant, pool, gym, hot tub, bar, laundry service, parking (fee), no-smoking floor* ⊟ *AE, D, DC, MC, V.*

$$$–$$$$ 🖭 **Renaissance Arts Hotel.** Art lovers looking to stay close to downtown but not in the CBD should check out this new hotel, in what was once a former furniture warehouse. Local art gallery owner Arthur Rogers hand-selected every piece of art in the hotel and opened a second location of his nationally acclaimed gallery on the lobby level. Rooms are furnished with a minimalist bent, but are quite comfortable, spacious, and well designed. La Cote Brasserie is the hotel's restaurant. ⊠ *700 Tchoupitoulas St., Warehouse District, 70130* ☎ *504/613–2330* 🖷 *504/613–2331* ⊕ *www.marriott.com* ⇥ *208 rooms, 9 suites ⟡ Restaurant, in-room data ports, in-room safes, minibars, cable TV, pool, lounge, concierge, Internet, business services* ⊟ *AE, D, DC, MC, V.*

$$$–$$$$ 🖭 **Renaissance Pere Marquette Hotel.** Inside this historic downtown property rooms are generously sized and surprisingly quiet, even though the hotel sits in the middle of the Central Business District. Ideal for business travelers, the hotel is close to downtown attractions such as Harrah's New Orleans casino and the Aquarium of the Americas. The rooms are a bit stark and the lobby is rather uninviting, but the service makes up for some of the atmospheric deficiencies. The on-site restaurant is Rene Bistrot, one of the hottest dining spots in town. ⊠ *817 Common St., CBD, 70112* ☎ *504/525–1111* 🖷 *504/525–0688* ⊕ *www. renaissancehotels.com* 🛏 *275 rooms, 5 suites* ⚭ *Restaurant, room service, in-room data ports, in-room safes, cable TV with movies, pool, gym, lounge, shop, babysitting, laundry service, concierge, business services* 🚍 *AE, D, DC, MC, V.*

$$$–$$$$ W **Hotel New Orleans.** The sleek, contemporary blend of East Coast sophistication and southern charm will appeal to fans of Ian Schraeger–inspired accommodations. The lobby has a trendy upscale look. Rooms are decorated in red and black, with first-rate amenities such as Aveda bath products and beds with goose-down pillows and comforters; 100 are designated as home-office rooms. The Rande Gerber–designed Whiskey Blue lounge is on the lobby level. ⊠ *333 Poydras St., CBD, 70130* ☎ *504/525–9444 or 800/777–7372* 🖷 *504/586–9928* ⊕ *www. whotels.com* 🛏 *423 rooms, 23 suites* ⚭ *Café, in-room data ports, health club, 3 lounges, Internet, parking (fee)* 🚍 *AE, D, DC, MC, V.*

$$$–$$$$ **Windsor Court Hotel.** Exquisite, gracious, elegant, eminently civi-
FodorśChoice   lized—these words are frequently used to describe Windsor Court, but
★   all fail to capture the wonderful quality of this hotel. From Le Salon's scrumptious afternoon tea, served daily in the lobby, to the unbelievably large rooms, this is one of *the* places to stay in New Orleans. Plush carpeting, canopy and four-poster beds, stocked wet bars, marble vanities, oversize mirrors, and dressing areas are just some of the pampering touches. High-speed Internet access accommodates business travelers, as does a fully equipped business center. The smoke-free Grill Room (⇨ Dining, CBD and Warehouse District) was renovated in 2003 with stunning results, and the Polo Lounge has one of the best martini presentations to be found. The hotel is four blocks from the French Quarter. ⊠ *300 Gravier St., CBD, 70130* ☎ *504/523–6000 or 800/262–2662* 🖷 *504/596–4513* ⊕ *www.windsorcourthotel.com* 🛏 *58 rooms, 266 suites, 2 penthouses* ⚭ *2 restaurants, in-room data ports, pool, health club, hot tub, sauna, steam room, lobby lounge, laundry service, parking (fee)* 🚍 *AE, D, DC, MC, V.*

$$$–$$$$ **Wyndham Riverfront Hotel.** A circular drive with a splashing fountain and greenery sweeps to the entrance of the Wyndham, which occupies a full block across the street from the Convention Center. Four masonry buildings from a former 19th-century rice mill and silo make up the hotel. Light fills the large lobby. Rooms vary in size and shape; those in the former mill are smaller but have higher ceilings, and rooms in the erstwhile silo, called extended kings, are larger. ⊠ *701 Convention Center Blvd., CBD, 70130* ☎ *504/524–8200 or 800/996–3426* 🖷 *504/524–0600* ⊕ *www.wyndham.com* 🛏 *202 rooms, 2 suites* ⚭ *Restaurant, room service, in-room data ports, gym, bar, laundry service, business services, parking (fee), no-smoking rooms* 🚍 *AE, D, DC, MC, V.*

$$–$$$$ 🏨 **Fairmont Hotel.** At this grand hotel built in 1893, the marble floor and

Fodor'sChoice Victorian splendor of the massive busy lobby evoke a more elegant and

★ gracious era. Rooms have special touches such as down pillows, terry robes, upscale toiletries, and bathroom scales; suites have fax machines. The lobby-level Sazerac Grill has an airy cosmopolitan feel. During the holiday season the Fairmont's lobby is completely engulfed in strands of white angel hair. Renovations have kept the Fairmont one of the finest hotels in the South. ✉ *123 Baronne St., CBD, 70140* 🕾 *504/529–7111 or 800/527–4727* 🖷 *504/529–4764* ⊕ *www.fairmontneworleans.com* ⇦ *700 rooms, 85 suites* ↺ *3 restaurants, 2 tennis courts, pool, gym, hair salon, 2 bars, parking (fee)* ⊟ *AE, D, DC, MC, V.*

$$–$$$$ 🏨 **Hotel Inter-Continental.** One of the major convention hotels, the Inter-Continental is a modern rose-granite structure overlooking St. Charles Avenue. Public spaces include a spacious, inviting second-floor lobby and a peaceful sculpture garden. Guest rooms are large and well lighted, with matching quilted spreads and draperies. The VIP level contains some of the city's finest suites. Other special amenities here are TV teleconferencing and complimentary Continental breakfast and afternoon cocktails. The main dining room is the Veranda (⇨ Dining, CBD and Warehouse District), showcasing the well-known culinary skills of Chef Willy Cohn. Pete's Pub, on the lower level, is a local favorite for lunch and happy hour. ✉ *444 St. Charles Ave., CBD, 70130* 🕾 *504/525–5566 or 800/445–6563* 🖷 *504/585–4387* ⊕ *www.intercontinental.com* ⇦ *482 rooms, 20 suites* ↺ *3 restaurants, minibars, pool, gym, pub, dry cleaning, laundry service, parking (fee)* ⊟ *AE, D, DC, MC, V.*

$$–$$$$ 🏨 **Hotel Monaco.** The imaginatively renovated Masonic Temple building now houses this 19-story gem. Pets receive special turndown service with biscuits and Evian water. Rooms are spacious, with pillow-top mattresses, high-quality linens, and soothing textures and colors. Some have even been designed for extra-tall guests, with 9-foot king beds and heightened showerheads. The lobby houses the first-rate Cobalt restaurant. ✉ *333 St. Charles Ave., CBD, 70130* 🕾 *504/561–0010 or 866/685–8359* 🖷 *504/310–2777* ⊕ *www.monaco-neworleans.com* ⇦ *250 rooms, 22 suites* ↺ *Restaurant, health club, bar, laundry service, concierge, parking (fee), some pets allowed* ⊟ *AE, D, DC, MC, V.*

$$–$$$$ 🏨 **International House.** The lobby of this boutique hotel is an architectural dream, with 23-foot-high ceilings, ornate pilasters, marble floors, and seasonally changing decor. Fine linens and fabrics enhance the guest rooms, which, although small, are attractively decorated in a contemporary New Orleans style, with stereo CD players and black-and-white photographs of jazz greats. Bathrooms, some with glass-enclosed double shower stalls, are sleek and contemporary. The hotel holds Loa, a trendy, see-and-be-seen cocktail spot. ✉ *221 Camp St., CBD, 70130* 🕾 *504/553–9550 or 800/633–5770* 🖷 *504/553–9560* ⊕ *www.ihhotel.com* ⇦ *119 rooms, 3 suites* ↺ *Restaurant, gym, bar, meeting room, parking (fee)* ⊟ *AE, D, MC, V.*

★ $$–$$$$ 🏨 **Lafayette Hotel.** This small brick building has housed the Lafayette ever since it was built in 1916. Handsome millwork, brass fittings, and marble baths adorn the inn throughout. The lobby is tiny but chic, and guest rooms are spacious and sunny. Some rooms have four-poster beds;

all have cushy easy chairs and ottomans. Shelves lined with books are a homey touch. Some rooms on the second floor have floor-length windows opening onto a balcony; a number overlook Lafayette Square. On the lobby level is Rasputin, a Russian restaurant with a vodka bar. ⊠ *600 St. Charles Ave., CBD, 70130* ☎ *504/524–4441 or 800/733–4754* 🖷 *504/523–7327* ⊕ *www.thelafayettehotel.com* ⌨ *24 rooms, 20 suites* ⌂ *Restaurant, minibars, dry cleaning, laundry service, concierge, Internet, parking (fee), no-smoking rooms* ▭ *AE, D, DC, MC, V.*

$$–$$$$ ▣ **Loft 523.** Think Frank Lloyd Wright mixed with a SoHo loft and you'll easily picture this sleek seductive loft hotel. It's so subtle from the outside, you may have trouble finding it among the surrounding buildings. Once inside, the atmosphere is strictly contemporary and chic. Cavernous limestone bathrooms, stone vanity tables, Frette linens, Fortuny lamps, and DVD surround-sound systems make this an adult playground. A personal assistant is assigned to you at check-in for your entire stay. ⊠ *523 Gravier St., CBD, 70130* ☎ *504/200–6523* ⊕ *www.loft523.com* ⌨ *16 rooms* ⌂ *Room service, in-room data ports, cable TV, in-room VCRs, gym, bar, concierge, Internet* ▭ *AE, D, DC, MC, V.*

$$–$$$$ ▣ **New Orleans Hilton Riverside.** This sprawling multilevel complex is smack on the Mississippi with superb river views. Guest rooms have French-provincial furnishings; the 180 rooms that share a concierge have fax machines. On Sunday the hotel's Kabby's Restaurant hosts a jazz brunch. The Riverfront streetcar stops out front. Adjacent to Riverwalk Shopping Center and Aquarium of the Americas, and directly across the street from Harrah's New Orleans casino, the hotel has a resident golf pro and a four-hole putting green. ⊠ *Poydras St. at the Mississippi River, CBD, 70140* ☎ *504/561–0500 or 800/445–8667* 🖷 *504/568–1721* ⊕ *www.hilton.com* ⌨ *1,600 rooms, 67 suites* ⌂ *4 restaurants, putting green, 8 tennis courts, 2 pools, fitness classes, health club, hair salon, outdoor hot tub, massage, sauna, racquetball, squash, 7 lounges, business services, parking (fee), no-smoking floor* ▭ *AE, D, DC, MC, V.*

$$–$$$$ ▣ **Omni Royal Crescent.** Old-fashioned pampering mixes well with state-of-the-art technology in this chic boutique hotel. All guest rooms come with plush robes, slippers, iron and ironing board, and umbrella; some king rooms have hot tubs. Some baths and closets, however, are small. The outdoor rooftop pool and well-equipped fitness center are designed along the lines of a Roman bath. "Get Fit" rooms have a portable treadmill, Get Fit Kit, and healthy snacks in the refreshment center. ⊠ *535 Gravier St., CBD, 70130* ☎ *504/527–0006 or 800/843–6664* 🖷 *504/523–0806* ⊕ *www.omnihotels.com* ⌨ *98 rooms, 7 suites* ⌂ *Restaurant, minibars, pool, health club, sauna, dry cleaning, laundry facilities, concierge, business services, meeting room, parking (fee), some pets allowed, no-smoking rooms* ▭ *AE, D, DC, MC, V.*

$$–$$$$ ▣ **Queen & Crescent Hotel.** Intimate and tasteful, this hotel two blocks outside the French Quarter is a good alternative to the megahotels that surround it. Guest rooms are small but tastefully appointed, and come with in-room coffeemakers, hair dryers, and ironing boards. The hotel is within walking distance of Harrah's New Orleans casino, Riverwalk, and great restaurants. ⊠ *344 Camp St., CBD, 70130* ☎ *504/587–9700 or 800/975–6652* 🖷 *504/587–9701* ⊕ *www.queenandcrescenthotel.*

com ↪ *196 rooms* ⚇ *In-room safes, minibars, gym, meeting room, travel services, parking (fee), no-smoking rooms* ⊟ *AE, D, DC, MC, V.*

$$–$$$$ 🏨 **The Whitney, A Wyndham Historic Hotel.** The historic Whitney Bank Building has been classically restyled into a true European-style hotel. Listed on the National Register of Historic Places, this sumptuously elegant property is in the middle of downtown, with Harrah's New Orleans casino, Riverwalk, and the French Quarter all within walking distance. Rooms include comfy pillow-top mattresses, robes, slippers, upscale toiletries and amenities, and ergonomic chairs. The hotel restaurant, 56 Degrees, serves Asian fusion cuisines. ⊠ *610 Poydras St., CBD, 70130* ☎ *504/581–4222 or 800/996–3426* 🖷 *504/207–0100* ⊕ *www. wyndham.com* ↪ *70 rooms, 23 suites* ⚇ *Restaurant, in-room data ports, gym, bar, Internet, no-smoking rooms* ⊟ *AE, D, MC, V.*

$–$$$$ 🏨 **Comfort Suites Downtown.** A boon for budget travelers, this former office building is four blocks from the French Quarter. It has an uninspiring lobby but large, well-equipped, one-room suites; luxury suites have whirlpool baths. The sauna, hot tub, and free morning paper are pleasant surprises, and the first five local calls are free. ⊠ *346 Baronne St., CBD, 70112* ☎ *504/524–1140 or 800/524–1140* 🖷 *504/523–4444* ⊕ *www.comfortinn.com/hotel/la071* ↪ *102 suites* ⚇ *In-room safes, microwaves, refrigerators, gym, hot tub, sauna, bar, laundry facilities, business services, parking (fee)* ⊟ *AE, D, DC, MC, V* ⊦◎⊣ *CP.*

$$$ 🏨 **Doubletree Hotel.** This chain hotel is close to the river, across the street from Canal Place mall, and a block from the French Quarter. The small comfortable lobby is adorned with flower arrangements and bowls of potpourri, along with the hotel's trademark jar of chocolate-chip cookies. Decor is country French, and rooms have an open airy feeling with pastel draperies and spreads and light-color furniture. Rooms ending in 05 are larger. The staff is exceptionally helpful. ⊠ *300 Canal St., CBD, 70130* ☎ *504/581–1300 or 800/222–8733* 🖷 *504/522–4100* ⊕ *www. doubletreeneworleans.com* ↪ *363 rooms, 15 suites* ⚇ *Restaurant, pool, health club, bar, lounge, laundry service, parking (fee), no-smoking rooms* ⊟ *AE, D, DC, MC, V.*

$$$ 🏨 **Sheraton New Orleans.** The oversize atrium-like lobby of this hotel is usually bustling with conventioneers. A tropical atmosphere permeates the Pelican Bar, which presents jazz nightly and sells a fine assortment of cigars. Café Promenade encircles the second level. Executive rooms come with many special amenities, but even the regular guest rooms are spacious and well appointed. Expect top-quality service. The hotel is across Canal Street from one of the great downtown eateries, the Palace Café (⇨ Dining, CBD and Warehouse District). ⊠ *500 Canal St., CBD, 70130* ☎ *504/525–2500 or 800/253–6156* 🖷 *504/592–5615* ⊕ *www. sheratonneworleans.com* ↪ *1,100 rooms, 72 suites* ⚇ *3 restaurants, pool, health club, bar, lobby lounge, parking (fee), no-smoking rooms* ⊟ *AE, D, DC, MC, V.*

$$–$$$ 🏨 **Courtyard by Marriott.** Occupying a handsomely restyled downtown office building, this Marriott exudes privacy. Rooms have dark woods and pastel prints; the ones with two double beds are largest and have a desk. Balcony rooms overlooking St. Charles Avenue are much in demand during Mardi Gras—this corner of St. Charles is one of the Car-

nival hot spots. The restaurant is open for breakfast only, but the hotel is within walking distance of restaurants and most other attractions. ⊠ *124 St. Charles Ave., CBD, 70130* ☏ *504/581–9005 or 800/321–2211* 🖷 *504/581–6264* ⊕ *www.marriott.com* ➴ *140 rooms* ⚐ *Restaurant, indoor pool, gym, hot tub, parking (fee)* ☰ *AE, D, DC, MC, V.*

$$–$$$ 🖭 **Hampton Inn and Suites–Convention Center.** Two century-old warehouses have been converted into a French colonial–style hotel that is comfortable, architecturally distinctive, and moderately priced. The grand lobby has original hardwood floors and exposed brick walls, and the lobby bar overlooks the pool and the lush garden courtyard. Rooms are large and airy, with four-poster beds and wood floors; many overlook a park. The hotel is on the edge of the Warehouse District, directly across the street from the convention center. ⊠ *1201 Convention Center Blvd., Warehouse District, 70130* ☏ *504/566–9990 or 800/292–0653* 🖷 *504/566–9997* ⊕ *www.hamptoninn.com* ➴ *288 rooms* ⚐ *Pool, gym, bar, business services, parking (fee)* ☰ *AE, D, DC, MC, V* ⏀ *CP.*

$$–$$$ 🖭 **Hilton Garden Inn New Orleans Downtown.** The proximity to major attractions makes this hotel a popular draw for those who enjoy walking. Rooms are cheerfully appointed, and the private courtyard is one of the most charming in the area. Other comforts include a hot tub with a breathtaking view of the city skyline. ⊠ *1001 S. Peters St., Warehouse District, 70130* ☏ *504/525–0044* 🖷 *504/525–0035* ⊕ *www. hiltongardeninn.com* ➴ *284 rooms* ⚐ *In-room data ports, microwave, refrigerator, room TVs with movies and video games, pool, gym, lounge, concierge, Internet, business services* ☰ *AE, D, DC, MC, V.*

$$–$$$ 🖭 **Homewood Suites by Hilton.** One of the city's newest lodging entrants is also one of the most central and spacious. Contemporary furnishings mix easily with traditional New Orleans ambience. High ceilings, big windows, and a kid-friendly atmosphere make this all-suites hotel a local treasure. Complimentary breakfast is served every morning; the manager's reception in the evening has light snacks and beverages. ⊠ *901 Poydras St., CBD, 70112* ☏ *504/581–5599* 🖷 *504/581–9133* ⊕ *www. homewoodsuites.com* ➴ *166 suites* ⚐ *In-room data ports, kitchens, microwaves, refrigerators, 2 pools (1 indoor), exercise equipment, gym, hot tub, baby-sitting, Internet* ☰ *AE, D, DC, MC, V.*

$–$$$ 🖭 **Embassy Suites.** If your primary target is the Convention Center or the contemporary art galleries and the museum collection of the Warehouse District, this is a great choice. The balconied high-rise sits right on Gallery Row. All suites have a bedroom and separate parlor (with a TV in each room and three phones) and coffeemaker; most have balconies. Room service is available from the Sugar House restaurant. The Lofts at Embassy Suites is in a separate building just around the corner, and is within walking distance of the Morial Convention Center. ⊠ *315 Julia St., CBD, 70130* ☏ *504/525–1993 or 800/362–2779* 🖷 *504/ 525–3437* ⊕ *www.embassyneworleans.com* ➴ *347 suites* ⚐ *Restaurant, in-room data ports, microwaves, refrigerators, wading pool, gym, outdoor hot tub, meeting room* ☰ *AE, D, MC, V* ⏀ *BP.*

¢–$$$ 🖭 **Ambassador Hotel.** Guest rooms at this hotel conveniently bordering the CBD and Warehouse District have real character. Four-poster iron beds, armoires, and local jazz prints are among the furnishings. Exposed brick walls, ceiling fans, and wood floors add to the ambience of the pre–Civil War building. This is a good alternative to huge convention hotels, but it's still just steps from all the major downtown attractions and shopping, as well as the Convention Center. Ambassador is one of the few pet-friendly hotels downtown. ⊠ *535 Tchoupitoulas St., CBD, 70130* ☎ *504/527–5271 or 888/527–5271* 🖷 *504/599–2110* ⊕ *ahno. com* ⟿ *165 rooms* ⚘ *Restaurant, lounge, meeting room, parking (fee), some pets allowed* 🖃 *AE, D, DC, MC, V.*

¢–$$$ 🖾 **Parc St. Charles.** This upscale Best Western property is on one of the Big Easy's best Carnival corners, at the intersection of Poydras Street and St. Charles Avenue. Rooms in the intimate hotel are decorated with contemporary furniture, and large plate-glass windows provide lots of light and wide views of the bustling CBD. Executive-level rooms come with data ports and a fax-scanner-printer. Panasia, serving Thai cuisine, is the hotel's restaurant. ⊠ *500 St. Charles Ave., CBD, 70130* ☎ *504/ 522–9000 or 888/211–3447* 🖷 *888/211–3448* ⊕ *www.parcstcharles. com* ⟿ *120 rooms, 2 suites* ⚘ *Restaurant, some in-room data ports, in-room safes, pool, health club, bar, parking (fee), no-smoking rooms* 🖃 *AE, D, DC, MC, V.*

¢–$$$ 🖾 **Pelham Hotel.** A restored four-story office building houses the chic Pelham, an ideal place for those who want to be in the center of the CBD—near Riverwalk, Harrah's New Orleans casino, and the Convention Center—but who seek a quiet alternative to the bustling convention hotels. The small lobby has a green-marble floor and fresh flowers. Rooms are small; some have four-poster beds and all have marble baths with terry robes and English soaps. Inside rooms, though attractively furnished, have no windows. You can use the fitness center and pool at the nearby Sheraton or at private health clubs. Huey's Diner, on the lobby level, serves comfort food and other diner fare 24 hours. ⊠ *444 Common St., CBD, 70130* ☎ *504/522–4444 or 800/659–5621* 🖷 *504/539–9010* ⊕ *www.thepelhamhotel.com* ⟿ *60 rooms* ⚘ *Restaurant, room service, in-room safes, dry cleaning, laundry service, concierge, parking (fee)* 🖃 *AE, D, DC, MC, V.*

$–$$ 🖾 **Hampton Inn.** This moderately priced facility is among several office buildings that have been converted into hotels. The lobby, with lavish furnishings and decor, is an oasis in the midst of a bustling CBD. Rooms are large and comfortable, and all baths have hair dryers. Among the safety features are key-access elevators. Two blocks from Bourbon Street, the Hampton Inn is surrounded by great restaurants and tourist attractions. ⊠ *226 Carondelet St., CBD, 70130* ☎ *504/529–9990 or 800/426–7866* 🖷 *504/529–9996* ⊕ *www.hamptoninn.com* ⟿ *187 rooms* ⚘ *Coffee shop, gym, concierge, parking (fee)* 🖃 *AE, D, DC, MC, V* 🍽 *CP.*

$–$$ 🖾 **Holiday Inn Select.** This high-end, eight-story Holiday Inn is across the street from the Convention Center. It is built around a three-story atrium and has a handsome lobby with marble floors and wood paneling. All rooms are soundproof and have desks and two phones with voice mail and speed dials. Executive rooms and suites have two phone lines, call waiting, and speakerphones. Other amenities include irons and ironing boards, coffeemakers, and hair dryers. Several noteworthy restaurants, Riverwalk, and Harrah's New Orleans casino are nearby. ⊠ *881 Convention Center Blvd., Warehouse District, 70130* ☎ *504/ 524–1881 or 800/465–4329* 🖷 *504/528–1005* ⊕ *www.basshotels.com/*

holiday-inn 🛏 *168 rooms, 2 suites* ⚿ *Restaurant, in-room data ports, health club, bar, laundry facilities, business services, no-smoking rooms* 🚭 *AE, D, DC, MC, V* ⎮◯⎮ *CP.*

$ ⊞ **La Quinta Inn and Suites Downtown.** Rooms are surprisingly well appointed at this hotel, despite the moderate rates. Every room has an oversize desk, built-in closets, and a large bathroom with bright tile floor. The hotel is within walking distance of downtown and the French Quarter attractions and shopping. The St. Charles Avenue streetcar is one block from the front door. ⊠ *301 Camp St., CBD, 70130* ☎ *504/ 598–9977* 🖷 *504/598–9978* ⊕ *www.laquinta.com* 🛏 *166 rooms, 16 suites* ⚿ *Indoor pool, health club, laundry facilities, meeting rooms* 🚭 *AE, D, DC, MC, V.*

Guesthouses & Bed-and-Breakfasts

¢–$ ⊞ **Depot House at Madame Julia's.** What once was Madame Julia's Boarding House is now a charming, no-frills collection of Creole town houses dating from 1830. Rooms with shared baths and queen-size beds make up this somewhat spartan but clean and well-kept inn. Simple antiques create a warm homey atmosphere. Breakfast is served in the "urban garden" tent. Near major attractions, this bed-and-breakfast is recommended for those on a budget who appreciate authentic local ambience. What it lacks in extras it makes up in convenience and service. ⊠ *748 O'Keefe St., CBD, 70113* ☎ *504/529–2952* 🖷 *504/529–1908* 🛏 *24 rooms without bath* ⚿ *No room phones, no room TVs* 🚭 *AE, MC, V.*

Garden District/Uptown

These areas are ideal for those who prefer accommodations away from downtown. All the following are on or close to fashionable, mansion-lined St. Charles Avenue, where the streetcar runs (24 hours) to the CBD and the French Quarter in a mere 15–20 minutes. The trip can be longer at night owing to less-frequent service; a taxi is a better option if you are out late. Walking in this area after dark is not recommended.

Hotels

$$$ ⊞ **Clarion Grand Boutique Hotel.** You can't miss this high-wattage property on St. Charles Avenue. The decor of the all-suites hotel is considerably tamer than that in the restaurant downstairs; touches of marble, glass, brass, and wrought iron make it a perfect choice for a romantic weekend getaway. Some suites have in-room hot tubs. Room service is available from Copeland's Cheesecake Bistro downstairs. You can work off some of that contemporary Creole cuisine at a nearby fitness facility. ⊠ *2001 St. Charles Ave., Garden District, 70130* ☎ *504/558–9966 or 800/976–1755* 🖷 *504/522–8044* ⊕ *www.nolahotels.com/grandboutique* 🛏 *44 suites* ⚿ *Restaurant, in-room data ports, refrigerators, meeting room, parking (fee)* 🚭 *AE, D, DC, MC, V.*

★ $$$ ⊞ **Pontchartrain Hotel.** Maintaining the grand tradition is the hallmark of this elegant, European-style hotel, which has reigned on St. Charles Avenue since 1927. Accommodations range from lavish sun-filled suites to small pension-type rooms with showers only (no bathtubs). The Pontchartrain has been the honeymoon hotel for couples like Prince Aly Kahn and Rita Hayworth; suite names will tell you who else has passed

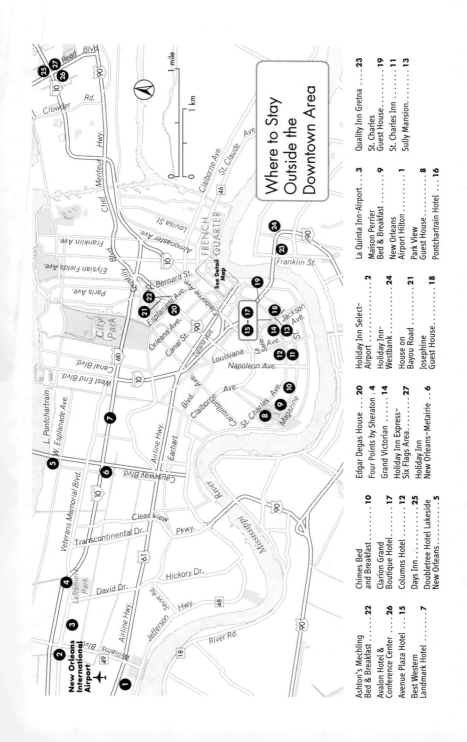

Where to Stay Outside the Downtown Area

Ashton's Mechling
Bed & Breakfast **22**
Avalon Hotel &
Conference Center **26**
Avenue Plaza Hotel ... **15**
Best Western
Landmark Hotel **7**

Chimes Bed
and Breakfast **10**
Clarion Grand
Boutique Hotel....... **17**
Columns Hotel **12**
Days Inn **25**
Doubletree Hotel Lakeside
New Orleans **5**

Edgar Degas House ... **20**
Four Points by Sheraton . **4**
Grand Victorian **14**
Holiday Inn Express–
Six Flags Area........ **27**
Holiday Inn
New Orleans–Metairie . **6**

Holiday Inn Select–
Airport **2**
Holiday Inn–
Westbank **24**
House on
Bayou Road **21**
Josephine
Guest House.......... **18**

La Quinta Inn–Airport ... **3**
Maison Perrier
Bed & Breakfast **9**
New Orleans
Airport Hilton........ **1**
Park View
Guest House.......... **8**
Pontchartrain Hotel ... **16**

Quality Inn Gretna **23**
St. Charles
Guest House.......... **19**
St. Charles Inn **11**
Sully Mansion........ **13**

through. Nowadays, though, more businesspeople than celebrities stay here. ✉ *2031 St. Charles Ave., Garden District, 70140* ☎ *504/524–0581 or 800/777–6193* 🖷 *504/524–7828* ⊕ *www.pontchartrainhotel.com* 🛏 *99 rooms, 19 suites* ♨ *2 restaurants, piano bar, concierge, parking (fee)* ▤ *AE, D, DC, MC, V.*

$–$$ 🏠 **Avenue Plaza Hotel.** The spartan lobby belies the amenities found here. Public areas include a romantic lounge with dark-wood panels from a French chalet. The spacious rooms have generous dressing areas; decor is either traditional or art deco—both are equally appealing. The health club has a Turkish steam bath, Swiss showers, and a Scandinavian sauna, which you can use for $5 per day. The pool is in a pleasant courtyard setting, and a sundeck and hot tub are on the roof. ✉ *2111 St. Charles Ave., Garden District, 70130* ☎ *504/566–1212 or 800/535–9575* 🖷 *504/525–6899* ⊕ *www.avenueplazahotel.com* 🛏 *256 suites* ♨ *Restaurant, kitchenettes, refrigerators, pool, health club, hair salon, hot tub, sauna, bar, parking (fee)* ▤ *AE, D, DC, MC, V.*

$–$$ 🏠 **Columns Hotel.** This impressive, white-columned 1883 Victorian-style hotel is listed on the National Register of Historic Places. The wide veranda, set with cloth-covered tables for outdoor dining or cocktails, is very inviting, as are the two period-furnished parlors. Dark and intimate, the lounge is a favorite with locals and has excellent live progressive jazz on Tuesday and Thursday. There's also a Sunday jazz brunch. One of the most impressive staircases you will ever climb leads to large, somewhat sparsely furnished, rooms. ✉ *3811 St. Charles Ave., Uptown, 70115* ☎ *504/899–9308 or 800/445–9308* 🖷 *504/899–8170* ⊕ *www.thecolumns.com* 🛏 *20 rooms* ♨ *Dining room, bar; no room TVs* ▤ *AE, MC, V* ⦿ *CP.*

¢ 🏠 **St. Charles Inn.** The canopied entrance to this small uptown hotel is almost hidden from view, squeezed as it is between a restaurant and a café. The inn has good-size modern rooms, each with a dressing area and cable TV. Rooms in the front with a St. Charles Avenue view are best unless streetcar noise bothers you. Continental breakfast and a newspaper are brought to your room each morning. The staff is friendly and accommodating. A great advantage of staying at this hotel is the spate of great new restaurants that have all opened within quick walking distance. ✉ *3636 St. Charles Ave., Garden District, 70115* ☎ *504/899–8888 or 800/489–9908* 🖷 *504/899–8892* 🛏 *40 rooms* ♨ *Free parking* ▤ *AE, D, DC, MC, V* ⦿ *CP.*

Guesthouses & Bed-and-Breakfasts

$$–$$$$ 🏠 **Grand Victorian Bed & Breakfast.** Just a block and a half from Commander's Palace, the Grand Victorian more than lives up to its lofty name. Each lavishly appointed room evokes old Louisiana with period pieces and distinctive private baths. The Greenwood Suite includes a hot tub, stained-glass windows, and a private balcony that extends across the front of the house and overlooks historic St. Charles Avenue. A common balcony on the second floor, shaded by aged oak trees, stands atop a traditional New Orleans garden. A Continental breakfast is served in either the dining room or the porte cochere balcony. ✉ *2727 St. Charles Ave., Garden District, 70130* ☎ *504/895–1104 or 800/977–0008* 🖷 *504/896–8688* ⊕ *www.gvbb.com* 🛏 *8 rooms* ♨ *Dining room, in-room data ports* ▤ *AE, D, MC, V.*

$$–$$$ ▣**Maison Perrier Bed & Breakfast.** This 1890s Victorian mansion reportedly housed a gentlemen's club, and rooms have been named after the ladies of the evening who entertained there. Rooms are spacious and comfortable with high ceilings and exceptionally large, well-appointed private baths. Some even have hot tubs. An authentic voodoo high priestess who knows her way around praline French toast and Belgian waffles prepares breakfast. In the afternoon, wine and cheese are served in the charming front parlor. Ask about seasonal and festival package rates. ⊠ *4117 Perrier St., Uptown, 70115* ☎ *504/897–1807 or 888/610–1807* 🖷 *504/ 897–1399* ⊕ *www.maisonperrier.com* ⤴ *7 rooms* ♢ *In-room data ports* ⊟ *AE, D, MC, V.*

$–$$$ ▣ **Sully Mansion.** New Orleans architect Thomas Sully built this handsome, rambling, Queen Anne–style house more than a century ago. In the foyer, where a grand piano sits, light filters through stunning, pastel-color stained-glass windows that are original to the house. The public rooms have high ceilings, oil paintings, fireplaces, tall windows with swagged floor-length drapes, and Victorian hand-me-downs. Neighbor to other grand mansions, the house is on a tree-lined street and is a block from the St. Charles Avenue streetcar. ⊠ *2631 Prytania St., Garden District, 70130* ☎ *504/891–0457* 🖷 *504/899–7237* ⊕ *www.sullymansion. com* ⤴ *5 rooms, 2 suites* ⊟ *AE, D, MC, V* ⦙◎⦙ *CP.*

$–$$
Fodor'sChoice
★
▣ **Chimes Bed and Breakfast.** Jill and Charles Abbyad's charming uptown residence has rooms in the main house and a converted carriage house with hardwood or slate floors. The Abbyads maintain a homey environment with all the conveniences found in large hotels: hair dryers, irons, stereos, coffeemakers, and private entrances. Continental breakfast is served in the airy dining room; afterward you can relax in the butterfly garden in the courtyard. English, French, Arabic, and Spanish are spoken in the house, and children are welcome. ⊠ *1146 Constantinople St., Uptown, 70115* ☎ *504/488–4640 or 800/729–4640* 🖷 *504/488–4639* ⤴ *5 rooms* ♢ *Cable TV, some pets allowed; no smoking* ⊟ *No credit cards* ⦙◎⦙ *CP.*

$–$$ ▣ **Josephine Guest House.** This restored Italianate mansion, one block from St. Charles Avenue, was built in 1870. European antiques fill the rooms, and Oriental rugs cover gleaming hardwood floors. Four rooms and a parlor are in the main house; two smaller but still spacious rooms are in the *garçonnier*. The bathrooms are oversize and plush. A Creole breakfast complete with homemade biscuits can be brought to your room or taken on the secluded patio. ⊠ *1450 Josephine St., Garden District, 70130* ☎ *504/524–6361 or 800/779–6361* 🖷 *504/523–6484* ⊕ *www. resobase.com/destinations/new-orleans/josephine* ⤴ *6 rooms* ⊟ *AE, D, DC, MC, V* ⦙◎⦙ *CP.*

¢–$ ▣ **Park View Guest House.** Adjacent to beautiful Audubon Park, this Victorian guesthouse has graced St. Charles Avenue as an uptown landmark since 1884. Rooms on the east side have great views of the park. The general rule here is that you get either antiques or a view: brass beds and ceiling fans are found in the "view" rooms. There is a lounge with TV and fireplace and a bay-window dining room where breakfast is served. ⊠ *7004 St. Charles Ave., Uptown, 70118* ☎ *504/861–7564* 🖷 *504/861–1225* ⊕ *www.parkviewguesthouse.com* ⤴ *22 rooms, 16 with bath* ⊟ *AE, D, MC, V* ⦙◎⦙ *CP.*

¢–$ ▣ **St. Charles Guest House.** Simple and affordable, this European-style pension is in four buildings one block from St. Charles Avenue. Rooms in the A and B buildings are larger; the small "backpacker" rooms share a bath. A pleasant surprise is the large swimming pool with deck. Proprietors Dennis and Joanne Hilton will occasionally delight you with an impromptu crawfish boil or an introduction to New Orleans's red beans and rice. ⊠ *1748 Prytania St., Garden District, 70130* ☎ *504/ 523–6556* 🖷 *504/522–6340* ⊕ *www.stcharlesguesthouse.com* ⇨ *30 rooms, 24 with bath* ⚴ *Pool; no a/c in some rooms* ▤ *AE, MC, V* ⦿ *CP.*

Mid-City

Guesthouses

★ $$–$$$$ ▣ **House on Bayou Road.** This circa-1798 West Indies–style Creole plantation home, set on 2 acres of lawns and gardens, has rooms filled with Louisiana antiques, including handsome four-poster featherbeds. Accommodations are in the main house as well as in detached cottages. The grand suite in the private cottage has a skylight over the bed, bookshelves, and a whirlpool bath. A favorite of celebrities, this inn has hosted Dan Aykroyd, Alfre Woodard, Fran Drescher, and Brad Pitt. A cooking school is conducted on the premises. The house is in a remote setting, and walking in the area is not encouraged. ⊠ *2275 Bayou Rd., Bayou St. John, 70119* ☎ *504/945–0992, 504/949–7711, or 800/882–2968* 🖷 *504/945–0993* ⊕ *www.houseonbayouroad.com* ⇨ *8 rooms, 1 cottage* ⚴ *Pool* ▤ *AE, DC* ⦿ *BP.*

★ $–$$$ ▣ **Edgar Degas House.** The French impressionist lived here from 1872 to 1873. This historic home, built in 1852, retains its original floor plan and colors. Second-floor rooms are spacious, and have chandeliers that hang from 14-foot ceilings; one has a whirlpool bath; another a balcony. Although adorned with Degas's works, the third-floor garret rooms are small and have no windows. Parlors on the first floor display reproductions of the artist's works. You can have breakfast in a small private rear courtyard. ⊠ *2306 Esplanade Ave., Mid-City, 70119* ☎ *504/821–5009 or 800/755–6730* 🖷 *504/821–0870* ⊕ *www.degashouse.com* ⇨ *9 rooms* ▤ *AE, MC, V* ⦿ *CP.*

¢–$$ ▣ **Ashton's Mechling Bed & Breakfast.** Few details have been missed in re-creating this sumptuous 1861 mansion. Eight distinctively appointed guest rooms have a range of beds, including iron, Shaker, and four-poster. The full breakfast includes such treats as *pain perdu* (French toast), eggs Benedict, and eggs and crab cakes. Fresh baked goods and snacks are constantly replenished in the house. The common parlor has a selection of great books, and the backyard is intimate and quiet. The B&B is nine blocks from the French Quarter. Owners Patrick and Karma Ashton provide full concierge services. ⊠ *2023 Esplanade Ave., Mid-City, 70116* ☎ *504/942–7048 or 800/725–4131* 🖷 *504/947–9382* ⊕ *www.ashtonsbb. com* ⇨ *8 rooms* ▤ *AE, MC, V* ⦿ *BP.*

Kenner/Airport

Hotels

★ $$ ▣ **New Orleans Airport Hilton.** Directly across from the New Orleans International Airport is this unexpectedly elegant hotel. The decor throughout is superb, with muted pastel colors that coordinate well with the soft-pink Caribbean-style exterior. The handwoven area rugs are from England. ✉ *901 Airline Hwy., Kenner 70062* 🕾 *504/469–5000 or 800/872–5914* 🖷 *504/466–5473* ⊕ *www.neworleans.hilton.com* ⊃ *317 rooms, 2 suites* ⚫ *Restaurant, putting green, tennis court, pool, gym, bar, business services, airport shuttle, parking (fee)* ▭ *AE, D, DC, MC, V.*

$–$$ ▦ **Holiday Inn Select–Airport.** Many of the rooms here face the dome-covered pool area. It's convenient to I–10 and close to Rivertown, U.S.A., and the Treasure Chest riverboat casino. All rooms have hair dryers, irons, and ironing boards. ✉ *2929 Williams Blvd., Kenner 70062* 🕾 *504/467–5611 or 800/887–7371* 🖷 *504/469–4915* ⊕ *www.holiday-inn.com* ⊃ *303 rooms, 1 suite* ⚫ *Restaurant, pool, gym, hot tub, bar, meeting room, airport shuttle, free parking* ▭ *AE, D, DC, MC, V.*

¢–$ ▦ **La Quinta Inn–Airport.** This hotel with a southwestern motif offers free local phone calls and allows children under 18 to stay free in their parents' room. The Esplanade Mall, Treasure Chest casino (accessible by casino-run shuttle), and Rivertown, U.S.A., are nearby. ✉ *2610 Williams Blvd., Kenner 70062* 🕾 *504/466–1401 or 800/531–5900* 🖷 *504/466–0319* ⊕ *www.laquinta.com* ⊃ *190 rooms 6 suites* ⚫ *In-room data ports, pool, gym, meeting room, airport shuttle, free parking, no-smoking rooms* ▭ *AE, D, DC, MC, V* ⦿ *CP.*

Metairie

Hotels

★ $$–$$$ ▦ **Doubletree Hotel Lakeside New Orleans.** This upscale hotel with plenty of amenities is part of a glass office complex that towers beside Lake Pontchartrain. The art deco–style lobby has marble mirrors and brass touches. Upon arrival you receive the chain's de rigueur chocolate-chip cookies. A shuttle takes you to the French Quarter at a minimal charge. ✉ *3838 N. Causeway Blvd., Metairie 70002* 🕾 *504/836–5253 or 800/222–8733* 🖷 *504/836–5262* ⊕ *www.doubletreelakeside.com* ⊃ *198 rooms, 12 suites* ⚫ *Restaurant, 2 tennis courts, health club, hair salon, bar, meeting room, airport shuttle, no-smoking rooms* ▭ *AE, D, DC, MC, V.*

¢–$ ▦ **Best Western Landmark Hotel.** This 17-story, centrally located hotel has oversize rooms, a top-floor restaurant with a view of the city, and two corporate-level executive floors with special amenities. Be sure to ask about special-event package rates. ✉ *2601 Severn Ave., Metairie 70002* 🕾 *504/888–9500* 🖷 *504/889–5792* ⊕ *www.nolahotels.com/landmarkbw/index.html* ⊃ *342 rooms* ⚫ *Cable TV, pool, lounge, free parking* ▭ *D, DC, MC, V.*

¢–$ ▦ **Four Points by Sheraton.** This hotel is convenient to I–10; it's also across the street from Lafrenière Park, which has barbecue areas, a walking track, sports fields, and duck-filled lagoons. Spacious rooms are decorated with a southern flair. ✉ *6401 Veterans Blvd., Metairie 70003* 🕾 *504/885–5700 or 800/465–4329* 🖷 *504/454–8294* ⊕ *www.starwood.com* ⊃ *220 rooms, 3 suites* ⚫ *Restaurant, pool, hot tub, bar, airport shuttle, free parking* ▭ *AE, D, DC, MC, V.*

¢–$ ▦ **Holiday Inn New Orleans–Metairie.** This hotel has easy access to I–10 and a free shuttle to the Lakeside Shopping Mall. Rooms are clean and the service is friendly. ⊠ *3400 I–10 Service Rd., Metairie 70001* ☏ *504/833–8201 or 800/522–6963* 🖷 *504/838–6829* ⊕ *www.holiday-inn.com* ⟲ *193 rooms* ⟳ *Restaurant, pool, bar, free parking* ▭ *AE, D, DC, MC, V.*

Westbank

Hotels

¢–$ ⊞ **Holiday Inn—Westbank.** Don't get confused—the address here is exactly the same as at the Quality Inn Gretna, but this hotel is a few blocks farther along the expressway, on the opposite side of the expressway when coming off the Crescent City Connection Bridge. Golfers stay here during tournaments at the nearby English Turn Golf and Country Club. ⊠ *100 Westbank Expressway, Gretna 70053* ☏ *504/366–2361 or 800/ 465–4329* 🖷 *504/362–5814* ⊕ *www.holiday-inn.com* ⟲ *311 rooms, 6 suites* ⟳ *Restaurant, pool, bar, free parking* ▭ *AE, D, DC, MC, V.*

¢–$ ⊞ **Quality Inn Gretna.** This hotel is just across the Crescent City Connection and near the Oakwood Shopping Mall. In the Skybox Lounge you can treat yourself to a panoramic view of New Orleans and the Mississippi River. Rooms are average but clean. ⊠ *100 Westbank Expressway, Gretna 70053* ☏ *504/366–8531 or 800/635–7787* 🖷 *504/ 362–9502* ⟲ *168 rooms* ⟳ *Restaurant, pool, bar, free parking* ▭ *AE, D, DC, MC, V.*

New Orleans East

Hotels

¢–$ ⊞ **Avalon Hotel and Conference Center.** This impressive property provides easy access to I–10, downtown New Orleans, and Six Flags New Orleans theme park. It's family-friendly and a nice value. ⊠ *10010 I–10 Service Rd., New Orleans East, 70127* ☏ *504/378–7000* 🖷 *504/378– 7800* ⊕ *www.avalonneworleans.com* ⟲ *174 rooms* ⟳ *Restaurant, pool, Internet, free parking* ▭ *D, DC, MC, V.*

¢–$ ⊞ **Days Inn.** Clean, pleasant, and functional, this is a good alternative for those on a budget who want to be in reasonable driving distance of the city. It's convenient to shopping centers and Six Flags New Orleans theme park. ⊠ *5801 Read Blvd., New Orleans East, 70127* ☏ *504/241– 2500 or 800/331–6935* 🖷 *504/245–8340* ⊕ *www.daysinn.com* ⟲ *143 rooms* ⟳ *Pool, business services, free parking, no-smoking rooms* ▭ *AE, D, MC, V.*

¢   ⊞ **Holiday Inn Express–Six Flags Area.** This hotel is convenient if you're planning to visit Six Flags New Orleans theme park. It has reasonable rates and free Continental breakfast, and it is 25 minutes from downtown New Orleans. This spot is ideal for families with small children. ⊠ *10020 I–10 Service Rd., New Orleans East, 70127* ☏ *504/244–9115 or 800/465–4329* 🖷 *504/244–9150* ⊕ *www.expressneworleans.com* ⟲ *140 rooms, 2 suites* ⟳ *In-room data ports, microwaves, refrigerators, pool, health club, no-smoking rooms* ▭ *AE, D, MC, V.*

NIGHTLIFE &
THE ARTS

5

IMBIBE WITH THE LOCALS
at Lafitte's Blacksmith Shop ⇨*p.152*

UP YOUR STYLE QUOTIENT
along the copper bar at Loa ⇨*p.154*

CHILL OUT TO THE TRAD-JAZZ SOUNDS
at Preservation Hall ⇨*p.161*

GET DOWN-HOME AND FUNKY
at the Maple Leaf ⇨*p.163*

FEEL THE VIBES
of the city's R&B Queen
at Lion's Den ⇨*p.164*

NIGHTLIFE

Updated by
Baty Landis

NO AMERICAN CITY PLACES SUCH A PREMIUM ON PLEASURE as New Orleans. From the well-appointed lounges of swank hotels to raucous French Quarter bars and sweaty dance halls to funky dives and rocking clubs in far-flung neighborhoods, this city is serious about frivolity.

During Mardi Gras, Jazz Fest, and special events such as the Sugar Bowl, human traffic is tight in the French Quarter. On more relaxed weekends and during the week, club-hopping on the old rues can be as charming as tapas-tasting in Madrid, although the trashy and tacky vibe along Bourbon Street can drag the ambience down. Not that you must stay in the Quarter to have fun. Bar culture, with or without live music, is taken seriously here, and anywhere you go in the city you're sure to find a wine bar, pub, or dive—subdued or lively, vacant or crowded, romantic or raunchy—to suit your tastes. Uptown, most bars are frequented by students from Tulane and Loyola universities. A sizable gay and lesbian community claims favorite haunts throughout town.

In the city that cradled jazz and helped birth the blues, it should be no surprise that music thrives in rhythmic abundance in the streets, clubs, cafés, and concert halls. Even if you never take in live music at home, it's worth venturing out when you visit New Orleans. Music—not limited to jazz—is a rich tradition here, and the city seems to brim with natural talent. Louis Armstrong, Louis Prima, Harry Connick Jr., and Dr. John all played in the small, cramped clubs of New Orleans before hitting it big. Members of the Marsalis and Neville families are popular regulars on the entertainment scene. The clubs are intimate, the music mighty, so be sure to step out—don't miss an unusually accessible sound and rhythm treat.

Nightlife Around Town

Bars tend to open in the early afternoon and stay open well into the morning hours; live music, though, follows a more restrained schedule. Some jazz spots and clubs in the French Quarter stage evening sets around 6 PM or 9 PM; at a few clubs, such as the Palm Court, the bands actually finish by 11 PM. But this is the exception: for the most part, gigs begin between 10 and 11 PM, and locals rarely emerge for an evening out before 10. Keep in mind that the lack of a legal closing time means that shows advertised for 11 may not start until after midnight.

The **French Quarter** and the **Faubourg Marigny** are the easiest places to hear music. Dozens of quality bands play nightly within walking distance of one another, and the myriad dining options make it convenient to spend a whole evening here. Frenchmen Street in the Marigny is currently the hottest music strip in town: at the time of writing, seven clubs within a two-block stretch host live music most nights. If you can't choose, the curb outside Café Brasil is a good place to perch, perhaps taking in a show through Brasil's windows and listening for the scoop on which bands are hot that night. In this area, hanging out on the street can be as much fun as entering a club: the sidewalks and street are often crowded with revelers with "go cups" enjoying the sounds from a club, watching street performers, or taking a breather between sets. Most clubs along this strip charge a $5–$7 cover or none at all, although Café Brasil sometimes hosts larger ensembles for $10 and Snug Harbor, the premiere modern jazz venue in town, can be pricier still.

Uptown is just as rich in clubs, although they are far less concentrated, tucked instead down various residential and commercial streets. A minor hub has formed around the Riverbend area, far uptown where the streetcar turns from St. Charles Avenue onto Carrollton Avenue. Cooter Brown's, right at the levee, is a good pre- or post-show stop for imported beers and local grub, served all night. Some blocks away, near Carrollton and Oak Street, the Maple Leaf hosts live music any night of the week. Around the corner you will find Carrollton Station, also with live bands, although walking the few short blocks is not a good idea. A last resort for many night owls, Snake and Jake's crouches inconspicuously on a residential street across Carrollton Avenue. Although driving the two minutes from one spot to the next might seem silly, it is not safe to walk. It's best to call for a taxi after dark.

The **Warehouse District** harbors a number of good bars and clubs, most of them favoring the industrial feel that the neighborhood's heritage suggests. The enormous New Orleans Convention Center runs along the edge of this district, and at regular intervals the food and drink purveyors nearby fill with dazed conventioneers. As the Warehouse District blends with the **Central Business District (CBD)**, establishments become more upscale and polished.

Perhaps the edgiest local scene is in the **Bywater** District, home to many low-key bars, straight, gay, and mixed. The corner of Royal and Franklin streets forms something of a hub, with a spattering of bars catering to a varied crowd. Farther downtown you can be sure to find one of the hippest events of the week when Kermit Ruffins plays Vaughan's every Thursday. Along St. Claude, a handful of idiosyncratic venues beckons the adventurous, though extreme caution is essential—it's best to take a cab when venturing here.

In **Mid-City,** the neighborhood surrounding City Park, the bars are populated almost entirely by regulars from the neighborhood; live music is less common here, but not unheard of. Also nestled here are cozy neighborhood bistros that turn out superb dishes. A strong lesbian community lives here and frequents the bars, restaurants, and cafés. A taxi is again recommended to get to this area of town.

Music is one of New Orleans's richest resources and biggest drawing cards, with a selection of venues as broad as the types of music you'll find inside them. Many establishments listed in this chapter as simply bars or lounges nonetheless host some live music—sometimes it's almost hard to get away from it. If you have never visited the city before, you should consider the following standouts, which are described in more detail later in the chapter. Famous institutions such as **Preservation Hall** and the **Palm Court Jazz Café** carry the torch of traditional jazz. Next door to Preservation Hall is the internationally known watering hole **Pat O'Brien's,** where the atmosphere is loud and lively until very late.

The modern brass-band renaissance continues to evolve at **Donna's Bar & Grill** and in smoky little "kitty" clubs in Tremé. Snug Harbor hosts more formal jazz performances, both local and national. Across the street, the Spotted Cat cedes the mike to two bands per night. The lineup at **Tipitina's** varies nightly, from rhythm and blues to rock, jazz, and funk, with Cajun dancing on Sunday evening. Swinging singles and happy couples alike dance to toe-tapping Cajun music and its black counterpart, zydeco, seven nights a week at **Mulate's** and **Michaul's**, and frequently at the **Maple Leaf** and the **Mid-City Bowling Lanes** (known informally as the Rock 'n' Bowl). New Orleans rhythm and blues—which shook the world during the 1950s and '60s thanks to Fats Domino and the Meters—still flourishes at such atmospheric corner bars as R&B great Irma Thomas's **Lion's Den** and at **Tipitina's.**

Bright Lights, Big Easy

One legacy of New Orleans's Caribbean cultural climate that comes as a pleasant shock to many visitors is the city's tolerant attitude toward alcohol. Most bars stay open as long as a crowd is on hand: with 24-hour liquor licenses, closing time is strictly voluntary. Revelers can leave a bar and take their drinks along. Whiskey, beer, or wine can be purchased anywhere, anytime, at such unlikely outlets as gas stations or drive-through daiquiri depots.

Many bars advertise the Hurricane—a rum-and-fruit concoction that is the signature drink at **Pat O'Brien's,** which is the best place to order one. Less Hawaiian Punch-y than the Hurricane is the light-pink Monsoon, a specialty at **Snug Harbor.**

Perhaps the most famous local drink is the Sazerac, brewed of bourbon and bitters, with a coating of ersatz absinthe. The **Sazerac Bar** in the Fairmont Hotel does a stellar job with its namesake.

Practical Matters

In neighborhood clubs hosting music or just serving drinks, it's best to bring cash. Some take plastic but others do not. This is a pay-as-you-go kind of town.

Dress codes are as rare as snow in New Orleans, although a few restaurants insist that men wear sport coats. On any given night in the French Quarter, and especially during the Carnival season, you'll see everything from tuxedos and ball gowns to T-shirts and torn jeans.

Many bars on Bourbon Street entice visitors by presenting live bands and/or strip shows with no cover charge. They make their money by imposing a two-drink minimum, with draft beer or soft drinks—served in small glasses—costing $5 to $8 apiece. Prices range from $4 to $8 a drink in hotel lounges and get cheaper as you move farther away from downtown or the Quarter. Music clubs generally charge a flat cover between $5 and $30, with the high-end prices usually reserved for national touring artists. A single admission covers all sets for the evening at a given club.

A **music calendar** is broadcast daily on WWOZ, 90.7 FM, the community radio station devoted to New Orleans music, at the top of each odd hour. For detailed and up-to-date listings, consult the Friday "Lagniappe" entertainment supplement of the *Times-Picayune* or *Gambit,* the alternative weekly that appears on Sunday and is carried free in many bars, cafés, and stores. The *TP*'s daily listing also covers many clubs. The monthly *OffBeat* magazine has in-depth music coverage and listings and is available at many hotels, stores, and restaurants; by the end of the month, though, listings in *OffBeat* become less reliable. Many clubs also post entertainment calendars on their Web sites. Never be shy about calling clubs to ask what kind of music a given group plays. It's a good idea to call before going anywhere, since hours may vary from day to day.

Bars & Lounges

French Quarter

★ **Arnaud's Cigar Bar.** Sophistication awaits in the form of rich cigars and fine liquor served up in posh surroundings where no detail goes unobserved—even the air quality is filtered and refined. After a round or two, venture upstairs to the bizarre one-room Germaine Wells Mardi Gras Museum, showcase for many ball gowns worn by the Arnaud's relative, the queen of various Carnival balls. ⊠ *813 Bienville St., French Quarter* ☎ *504/523–5433.*

Bombay Club. Those partial to the cocktail, be it shaken or stirred, will appreciate the extensive selection of vodkas, single-malt scotches, ports, and cognacs here—the martinis approach high art. The plush, paneled interior creates a comfort zone for anyone nostalgic for the glory days of the British Empire. This bar in the Prince Conti Hotel hosts soft live music nightly. ⊠ *830 Conti St., French Quarter* ☎ *504/586–0972.*

Carousel Revolving Bar. A veritable institution, this piano bar in the Monteleone Hotel has a revolving carousel that serves as a centerpiece, with the bar stools revolving around the service area. The weak of stomach can opt for stationary seating beyond the carousel. On nights when the pianist is on duty, be prepared to join in the sing-alongs. ⊠ *214 Royal St., French Quarter* ☎ *504/523–3341.*

Cat's Meow. Karaoke rules in this boisterous club. If you can check your inhibitions at the door, the sing-along chaos can be thoroughly cathartic. Songbirds of all ages flock here; even Louisiana girl Britney Spears has tested her chops at the Cat's Meow—in less-famous days, of course. ⊠ *701 Bourbon St., French Quarter* ☎ *504/523–1157.*

Chart Room. Tourists join old-school locals from the Quarter and beyond in this dingy but lovable little bar not far from Canal Street. You'll get a better value on your drinks here than many places in the Quarter. ⊠ *300 Chartres St., French Quarter* ☎ *504/522–1708.*

Coop's Place. Casual drinking and supping, Louisiana style, is the order of the day at Coop's. The po'boys and gumbo, available into the wee hours, are some of the best found in the Quarter; a selection of 20 bottled beers and 6 on draft complement whatever you're having. A crankin' jukebox and popular pool table round out the laid-back bar experience. The bars along this strip of Decatur—the 1100 and 1200 blocks—sees a steady stream of regulars from the neighborhood and the service industry. ⊠ *1109 Decatur St., French Quarter* ☎ *504/525–9053.*

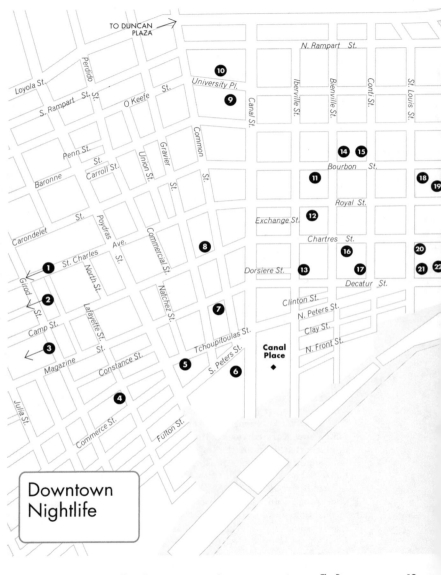

Downtown Nightlife

Crescent City Brewhouse. This convivial brewpub is known for its extensive menu of micro- and specialty brews; Abita Amber is a local favorite, but be sure to ask your server what's good—many of the selections are brewed on the premises. Live local music is a dinnertime staple here. The river view from the second-floor balcony is worth a stop. ✉ *527 Decatur St., French Quarter* ☎ *504/522–0571.*

The Dungeon. This aptly named, rather creepy bar caters to those who like to admire skulls and chains under the influence. It is a cult destination and frequently plays host to the rich and famous. Open nightly starting at midnight. ✉ *738 Toulouse St., French Quarter* ☎ *504/523–5530.*

Old Absinthe House. This popular watering hole draws mainly out-of-towners from afternoon to late at night. The decor consists of hundreds of business cards pinned to one wall, money papered on another, and absinthe jugs hanging from the ceiling. It is a refreshingly low-key diversion from the rest of Bourbon Street. ✉ *240 Bourbon St., French Quarter* ☎ *504/523–3181.*

Kerry Irish Pub. One of a number of pleasant Irish-influenced bars along this strip of Decatur Street, Kerry's is a small, friendly wisp of a pub. They have no-cover live music most nights, and Guinness on draft. ✉ *331 Decatur St., French Quarter* ☎ *504/527–5954.*

Fodor'sChoice **Lafitte's Blacksmith Shop.** Very popular with locals, Lafitte's is an atmospheric bar in a rustic 18th-century cottage. Regulars often sing along around the pianist, but the small outdoor patio is also appealing. You won't feel like you're on Bourbon Street here. ✉ *941 Bourbon St., French Quarter* ☎ *504/522–9397.*

Molly's at the Market. Molly's is a downtown staple. A friendly, rather brightly lit bar, it attracts literary types during the afternoon and evening and service industry folks later on. This is where the bartenders from other downtown spots wind up after their shifts. ✉ *1107 Decatur St., French Quarter* ☎ *504/525–5169.*

★ **Napoleon House Bar and Cafe.** This vintage watering hole has long been popular with writers, artists, and various other free spirits; locals who wouldn't be caught dead on Bourbon Street come here often. It is a living shrine to the New Orleans school of decor: faded grandeur. Murmuring ceiling fans, diffused light, and a tiny patio create a timeless escapist mood. The house specialty is a Pimm's Cup cocktail; a menu including sandwiches, soups, salads, and cheese boards is also available. This is the perfect place for late-afternoon people-watching, an evening nightcap, or the beginning of an up-until-dawn bender. ✉ *500 Chartres St., French Quarter* ☎ *504/524–9752.*

O'Flaherty's Irish Channel Pub. Here's the spot if you find yourself hankering for a Guinness or a single-malt in a jovial pub setting. Proprietor Danny O'Flaherty often regales his guests with Irish fiddling, and Saturday nights bring Irish dance classes. Local folk musicians set up here many other nights of the week. For a more peaceful evening, opt for the smaller barroom to your right as you walk into the central courtyard. ✉ *508 Toulouse St., French Quarter* ☎ *504/529–1317.*

Orleans Grapevine Wine Bar and Bistro. Pressed-tin ceilings and a player piano distinguish this subtly sophisticated wine bar within earshot of Bourbon Street but worlds away. An extensive wine list includes many choice selections by the glass, and if you need a snack, a select but complete French-inspired menu provides a nice alternative to a rich Creole meal. ⊠ *720 Orleans Ave., French Quarter* ☎ *504/523–1930*.

Pat O'Brien's. One of the biggest tourist spots in town is also the home of the oversize alcoholic beverage known as the Hurricane. Many people like to take their glass home as a souvenir; be aware that the deposit charged at the time of purchase should be refunded if you opt not to take the souvenir glass with you when you leave. Actually five bars in one, Pat O's claims to sell more liquor than any other establishment in the world. The bar on the left through the entrance is popular with Quarterites, the patio in the rear draws the young (and young at heart) in temperate months, and the piano bar on the right side of the brick corridor packs in raucous celebrants year-round. ⊠ *718 St. Peter St., French Quarter* ☎ *504/525–4823*.

Faubourg Marigny & Bywater

d.b.a. A little slice of New York City comes courtesy of this southern branch of New York's East Village hot spot. The polished look of the two rooms sits a bit uneasily among the rough-and-ready feel more typical of New Orleans bars, but the fine Scotch selection, among a plethora of other liquors, is unparalleled. Modern jazz or folk bands play in the back corner. ⊠ *616 Frenchmen St., Faubourg Marigny* ☎ *504/942–3731*.

Markey's Bar. It's true—Irish bars really are everywhere. In the center of the determinedly ungentrified Bywater District, this friendly bar serves as a beacon to transplants and longtime locals alike. Guinness on tap is $3, and pool is free. Arrive prepared to make new friends. ⊠ *640 Louisa St., at Royal St., Bywater* ☎ *504/943–0785*.

Mimi's. Marigny and Bywater residents have rushed gratefully to Mimi's, the district's first trendy nightspot. Overlooking the intersection of Franklin and Royal streets, this pleasant spot occupies the renovated frame of a commercial structure that has weathered more than a century and now rests at the hub of the new downtown. It's a bit overdetermined to be a New Orleans natural, but Mimi's fits the bill for anyone wishing to explore new territory. ⊠ *2601 Royal St., Faubourg Marigny* ☎ *504/942–0690*.

R Bar. A jukebox full of rock anchors this eclectic bar, the better half of a "bed-and-beverage" operation. In addition to the wayward locals who drift here late at night to play games of pool and twirl atop leopard-print bar stools in plus-size shades, lesbians have found a haven in the vinyl booths. ⊠ *1431 Royal St., Faubourg Marigny* ☎ *504/948–7499*.

Saturn Bar. A hideaway for those tired of scenes, this very un-bar bar and junque shop sits in überhipness on the edge of the Bywater District. ⊠ *3067 St. Claude Ave., Faubourg Marigny* ☎ *504/949–7532*.

CBD & Warehouse District

Bridge Lounge. A broad, industrial-style space is dressed up with subtle modern touches—spot lighting along the bar, dog portraits on the back wall—in this satellite of the Warehouse District bar scene. Actually within the Lower Garden District, the Bridge Lounge is emblematic of the Warehouse District's continuing expansion. ⊠ *1201 Magazine St., Warehouse District* ☎ *504/299–1888*.

Club 360°. At the tip-top of the World Trade Center building on the river, this dance club has fabulous views to accompany the pounding beats. It's a late-night spot, with customers regularly driving in from the suburbs for a night of abandon. A changing lineup of DJs keeps the partyers happy. ☒ *2 Canal St., CBD* ☏ *504/595–8900.*

Corporation Bar & Grill. Conventioneers looking for an escape flock to the lunch specials served in this simple barroom and return a few hours later for happy hour. Just a block from the Convention Center, both the bar and the regular clientele have been here since long before the Warehouse District was hip. ☒ *931 S. Peters St., Warehouse District* ☏ *504/ 527–6069.*

Ernst Cafe. Ernst has been operating as a bar since the first years of the 20th century, and the classic interior and upstairs balcony provide a welcome respite to conventioneers, lawyers from nearby firms, and service-industry folks finishing shifts at surrounding hotels. ☒ *600 S. Peters St., Warehouse District* ☏ *504/525–8544.*

Fairmont Hotel. The hotel has three distinctive lounges worth a stop. Fairmont Court has varied music on Friday and Saturday nights. Down the hall from the Fairmont Court is the smaller, more elegant Sazerac Bar— with its renowned art-deco mural by painter Paul Ninas. Next door, the hotel's Sazerac Restaurant presents elegant piano music nightly. This is a good stop before or after a classical concert in the Orpheum Theater across the street. ☒ *123 Baronne St., CBD* ☏ *504/529–7111.*

★ **Loa.** Just off the lobby of the fashionable International House hotel, this equally fashionable bar exudes a sense of urban cool unusual in laid-back New Orleans. Though it is upscale, Loa is also friendly, and even those in jeans will find a comfortable perch along the copper bar or at one of the low, candlelit tables beside picture windows looking onto the streets of the CBD. Drinks are expensive, but you pay for the stylish vibe. ☒ *221 Camp St., CBD* ☏ *504/200–6514.*

Ugly Dog Saloon. An expansive barroom with big-screen sports, video games, and two pool tables, the Ugly Dog also happens to serve some of the best barbecue in town. Lunchtime brings conventioneers, while dinner and late-night dining are the province of locals. Exceptionally friendly bartenders welcome one and all. ☒ *401 Andrew Higgins Dr., Warehouse District* ☏ *504/569–8459.*

Vic's Kangaroo Café. The Australian-born owner brings Down Under food to the Warehouse District. Vic's is a relaxed place with a dartboard, a good selection of beers, and dozens of picture books on Australia. ☒ *636 Tchoupitoulas St., Warehouse District* ☏ *504/524–4329.*

Whiskey Blue. Like its chic New York City counterpart, this whiskey bar in the W Hotel New Orleans in the CBD upholds the tradition of cool sophistication—expensive icy drinks and sleek beauties who glide in and out. ☒ *333 Poydras St., CBD* ☏ *504/525–9444.*

Uptown

Bruno's. The quintessential college bar beckons, just four blocks from the Tulane campus. Here find pool, darts, video poker, pennants on the walls, and sports on the tube. A regular crowd of business types congregates here after work; the college kids take over around 10 PM. ☒ *7601 Maple St., Uptown* ☏ *504/861–7615.*

The Bulldog. The dawg has 50 different draft beers as well as an extensive bottled selection on a trendy strip of Magazine Street. This is a favorite haunt for Gen X, but other age groups are warmly welcomed—particularly if they are trivia buffs. A local group of trivia contestants often battles in informal competition. ⊠ *3236 Magazine St., Garden District* ☎ *504/891–1516.*

Fodor'sChoice **Columns Hotel.** An evening cocktail on the expansive front porch of the ★ Columns, shaded by centuries-old oak trees, is one of the more romantic New Orleans experiences. The Victorian Lounge, with period decor and plenty of decaying elegance, draws a white-collar crowd of all ages. On a given night you might catch a top local jazz combo or flamenco dancers. ⊠ *3811 St. Charles Ave., Uptown* ☎ *504/899–9308.*

Cooter Brown's. Popular with the Tulane crowd, this rambling tavern at the levee serves the best bar food in town. An exhaustive list of imported beers, oysters on the half shell, and gooshy cheese fries are staples. The St. Charles Avenue streetcar drops you 20 paces from the front door. ⊠ *509 S. Carrollton Ave., Uptown* ☎ *504/866–9104.*

F&M Patio Bar. For some people, an all-nighter in New Orleans isn't complete until they've danced on top of the pool table at this perpetually open hangout. There's a loud jukebox, a popular photo booth, and a late-night kitchen (it gets going around 8 and keeps serving until early in the morning). The tropical patio can actually be peaceful at times. You'll need a car or a taxi to get here. ⊠ *4841 Tchoupitoulas St., Uptown* ☎ *504/895–6784.*

Fat Harry's. A long tradition of late-night underage drinking prevails at this comfortable bar. If you prefer to avoid the scene, come at dusk and enjoy excellent margaritas at the St. Charles Avenue–front outdoor tables to the accompaniment of streetcars rumbling by. ⊠ *4330 St. Charles Ave., Uptown* ☎ *504/895–9582.*

The Kingpin. Devoted regulars line the bar in this small, red-tone watering hole and make googly eyes at the lookers mixing the drinks. The only shuffleboard table in town and an intimate back room are highlights, along with regular Elvis parties marking important dates in the life of the King. ⊠ *1307 Lyons St., Uptown* ☎ *504/891–2373.*

Mayfair Lounge. Little more than an extended corridor with a pool table around the bend, the Mayfair is nonetheless a comfort zone for many locals looking for a casual drink. In addition to pool, you'll find those other bar essentials—video poker and an excellent jukebox—and that's about all. Ring the doorbell for admittance. ⊠ *1505 Amelia St., Uptown* ☎ *504/581–3777.*

St. Joe's. Instantly intimate, this wood-paneled hideaway hums with locals. Dry martinis are a favorite libation here; pool tables in back attract a dedicated crew. ⊠ *5535 Magazine St., Uptown* ☎ *504/899–3744.*

Snake and Jake's. A last resort for many night owls, this dim box of a place, identified by the year-round Christmas lights, is by exhaustion's necessity subdued. Don't arrive before 2 AM. ⊠ *7612 Oak St., Uptown* ☎ *504/861–2802.*

Mid-City & Beyond

Finn McCool's. Tucked back in Mid-City is this neighborhood Irish bar, complete with pool table and your favorite stout. They're not used to

CloseUp

LATE-NIGHT EATS

EATING IS AN ART in New Orleans—but at 3 AM, it is perhaps not a high-brow art. In a city of 24-hour liquor licenses and clubs that stay open till the last customer leaves, plenty of entrepreneurs are willing to feed you at any hour, but more likely with hamburgers and cheese fries than with étouffée and shrimp creole. Here are enough reliable spots to cover the various nightlife areas, and a few that are worth a drive across town.

Avenue Pub. Known for its eccentric clientele, the Avenue Pub nonetheless has a couple of cozy, hideaway booths. More importantly, they turn out great specialty burgers off the grill, served 24 hours. Got the munchies bad? Try the Dagwood or the ABC. ⊠ 1732 St. Charles Ave., Lower Garden District ☎ 504/586–9243.

Café du Monde. At the end of some nights, only a mouthful of sugary fried dough will do. Café du Monde is ready with beignets and coffee or hot chocolate. They pride themselves on never, ever closing. ⊠ 800 Decatur St., French Quarter ☎ 504/525–4544.

Camellia Grill. No longer open the fabled hours of yore, the old-time diner Camellia Grill nonetheless serves up great hangover or pre-hangover grub until at least 1 AM (3 AM on weekends). The Freeze—something between a milkshake and a smoothie—is a classic. ⊠ 626 S. Carrollton Ave., Uptown ☎ 504/866–9573.

Clover Grill. Join devoted Quarterites and the remains of danced-out queens from St. Ann Street for waffles and cheeseburgers, all grilled under abandoned hubcaps right before your eyes, 24 hours a day. ⊠ 900 Bourbon St., French Quarter ☎ 504/598–1010.

Cooter Brown's. Here you'll find the best cheese fries in town, along with oysters on the half shell and superior po-boys, till at least 2 AM (later on weekends). The beer selection, by the way, is unsurpassed. ⊠ 509 S. Carrollton Ave., Uptown ☎ 504/866–9104.

F&M Patio Bar. It ain't pretty, but if you can weave your way through the swaying last-ditch partyers, F&M's has one of the most treasured late-night kitchens in town. Overflowing cheese fries are the staple here. ⊠ 4841 Tchoupitoulas St., Uptown ☎ 504/895–6784.

Huey's 24/7 Diner. Almost upscale but not quite, Huey's is just a slightly prettified diner that keeps the promise of its name. Location in the CBD near many downtown hotels increases its appeal, though, and the breakfast items are quite good. ⊠ 200 Magazine St., CBD ☎ 504/539–9010.

La Peniche. A short stroll from the music clubs of Frenchmen Street, La Peniche is the post-party kitchen of choice among musicians and various hipsters. Pancakes, omelettes, and burgers, along with local specialties like red beans and rice, are served 24 hours. They're closed Tuesday night through Thursday morning. ⊠ 1940 Dauphine St., Faubourg Marigny ☎ 504/943–1460.

tourists, but all are welcome at this unusually affable spot. ✉ *3701 Banks St., Mid-City* ☎ *504/486–9080.*

Pal's. Small, blue, and out-of-the-way, Pal's is a surprisingly hip little hideaway for locals in the Bayou St. John area. It sits just two blocks from the bayou, but don't walk it; the neighborhood is not the safest. ✉ *949 N. Rendon St., Bayou St. John* ☎ *504/488–7257.*

Tyler's Jazz Club and Beer Garden. Neither a jazz club nor a beer garden, Tyler's is nonetheless an inviting, capacious bar near Bayou St. John. A long, neon-punctuated bar and two pool tables vie for attention, and small tables provide a comfortable setting for enjoying the po'boys and other local specialties that issue from the kitchen. The drink specials are dangerously cheap, and the kitchen stays open until 6 AM. ✉ *3841 Orleans Ave., Bayou St. John* ☎ *504/482–7207.*

Coffeehouses

Neutral Ground Coffee House. This 1960s-style coffeehouse attracts an artsy crowd, including adventurous local high schoolers who want to hear live music but can't get into the bars yet. Sofas, chessboards, laid-back counter service, and a bulletin board encourage an intimacy unmatched in most other cafés. On Sunday night there's an open mike for any aspiring musician. On other nights, a string of singer-songwriters and contemporary or traditional folk artists performs. It's a 20-minute cab ride from downtown and is open every night from 7 PM until 1 AM. ✉ *5110 Danneel St., Uptown* ☎ *504/891–3381.*

P. J.'s Coffee & Tea Cafes. This chain of coffeehouses has locations throughout New Orleans; the original is on Magazine Street, uptown. Though the decor favors a country-bumpkin shade of pink, the coffee is excellent, and the cold-brewed iced coffee—a New Orleans specialty—is the best in the city. Most locations are open until 11 PM. ✉ *7624 Maple St., Uptown* ☎ *504/866–7031* ✉ *5432 Magazine St., Uptown* ☎ *504/895–2190* ✉ *945 Magazine St., Warehouse District* ☎ *504/525–0522.*

Royal Blend. In the French Quarter, with a beautiful outdoor patio, this spot serves rich coffees, desserts, and muffins from early in the morning until 8 PM, 11 PM on weekends. ✉ *623 Royal St., French Quarter* ☎ *504/523–2716.*

Rue de la Course. Pressed tin, polished wood, and green-frosted lamp shades create the comfortable, slightly worn look of 19th-century Europe. This is what a coffeehouse should be: smart and un-yuppified, with plenty of hot java choices and cool sounds. ✉ *1500 Magazine St., Lower Garden District* ☎ *504/529–1455* ✉ *3128 Magazine St., Garden District* ☎ *504/899–0242* ✉ *219 N. Peters St., French Quarter* ☎ *504/523–0206* ✉ *1140 S. Carrollton Ave., Uptown* ☎ *504/861–4343.*

True Brew Café/True Brew Theater. This airy spot serves coffee, pastries, salads, sandwiches, and cocktails from 6:30 AM on weekdays, 7:30 AM on weekends. Weekends and some weeknights bring local slapstick theater, stand-up comedy, and cabaret. ✉ *200 Julia St., Warehouse District* ☎ *504/524–8441.*

Gambling

Admission to all the casinos is free, but you must be 21 or older to enter. Harrah's New Orleans is the only land-based casino and is by far the largest and nicest, even though it's basically a sea of slot machines with a few tables thrown in. The other casinos are all on boats, which remain dockside. The casinos are all open 24 hours daily.

Bally's Casino Lakeshore Resort. Docked on the south shore of Lake Pontchartrain, 15 minutes from downtown, *Bally's Casino* has 30,000 square feet of gaming on two levels; a 250-seat buffet; 46 gaming tables; and 1,213 slot machines. ⊠ *1 Stars and Stripes Blvd., New Orleans East* ☎ *504/248–3200 or 800/572–2559* ⊕ *www.ballysno.com.*

Boomtown Belle Casino. On the west bank of the Mississippi River, the *Boomtown Belle* is docked at the Harvey Canal, 10 mi from New Orleans. The vessel has 30,000 square feet of gaming space and accommodates 1,600 passengers. Besides the 1,100 slots and 46 gaming tables, the casino has a café, arcade, and lounge. ⊠ *4132 Peters Rd., Harvey* ☎ *504/366–7711* ⊕ *www.boomtowneworleans.com.*

Harrah's New Orleans. Commanding the foot of Canal Street, this beaux-arts-style casino is the largest such facility in the South. Its 100,000 square feet hold 2,900 slots and 120 gaming tables. Valet parking is available. ⊠ *4 Canal St., CBD* ☎ *504/533–6000 or 800/427–7247* ⊕ *www.harrahs.com.*

Treasure Chest Casino. Seven minutes from the airport on Lake Pontchartrain, the *Treasure Chest* has 900 slot machines, 50 gaming tables, and the area's largest poker room. There's a no-smoking gaming area. The kitchen serves Louisiana specialties; a free shuttle operates to and from nearby hotels. ⊠ *5050 Williams Blvd., Kenner* ☎ *504/443–8000 or 800/298–0711* ⊕ *www.treasurechestcasino.com.*

Gay Bars & Nightclubs

New Orleans has a sizable gay and lesbian community. The rowdier gay bars are on and around St. Ann Street, in the French Quarter; the Faubourg Marigny and Bywater are also gay hubs, but establishments in these neighborhoods are more subtle. A vibrant scene for black men of various orientations (drag is prevalent) is along North Rampart Street, between Ursulines and St. Peter streets. Many lesbians live in the Mid-City area, but there is no single concentration of bars. As is often the case, far more establishments are available to gays than to lesbians. Although the list below only touches the surface of the gay scene, it includes nearly all specifically lesbian spots at the time of writing.

The inside scoop on local goings-on appears in *Ambush* and *Southern Voice,* local biweekly newspapers that provide lists of current events in addition to news and reviews. A slick glossy called *Eclipse* contains nightlife coverage. A good daytime hangout for scouting the latest trends in the lesbian community is **C. C.'s Coffee House** (⊠ 2800 Esplanade Ave., Mid-City ☎ 504/482–9865). The **Faubourg Marigny Bookstore** (⊠ 600 Frenchmen St., Faubourg Marigny ☎ 504/945–1103) carries all local gay and lesbian publications. The **Lesbian and Gay Community**

Center of New Orleans (✉ 2114 Decatur St., Faubourg Marigny ☎ 504/945–1103 ⊕ www.lgccno.net) is a good source of current tips on bars and activities. The center also hosts a Friday-night movie series; check the Web site for current schedules.

Bars

Bourbon Pub. This 24-hour video bar with a mostly young male clientele has been popular for two decades. ✉ *801 Bourbon St., French Quarter* ☎ *504/529–2107.*

Café Lafitte in Exile. Gay men have been gathering for ages at this large and lively 24-hour bar, best known for its balcony overlooking Bourbon Street. ✉ *901 Bourbon St., French Quarter* ☎ *504/522–8397.*

Chet's Place. A soft-spoken bunch of gay men religiously makes this low-profile piano bar a destination on the Bywater rounds. When the delicate fingers of the pianist are not in action, unpardonably bad piped music prevails—*Auld Lang Syne,* for example, played out of season. ✉ *706 Franklin Ave., Bywater* ☎ *504/948–4200.*

Country Club New Orleans. Much more than a bar, this 19th-century mansion opens up the backyard in summer to expose a large, clothing-optional pool, dozens of lounge chairs, and a poolside cabana bar. Reasonable summer memberships are available; the single-day rate is $8 and includes use of the showers and weight room. All are welcome, but be warned (or promised) that bare male flesh of all ages prevails. Inside, an all-season bar (no cover) has a half dozen or so luxuriously appointed sitting rooms. Thursday night is game night. ✉ *634 Louisa St., Bywater* ☎ *504/945–0742.*

Cowpokes. This mixed-gender gay scene exudes all the enthusiasm of Quarter spots without the overcrowding. Friday and Saturday nights are devoted to country dancing, while Wednesday nights bring karaoke. ✉ *2240 St. Claude Ave., Faubourg Marigny* ☎ *504/947–0505.*

Friendly Bar. True to its name, this convivial spot coddles gays and lesbians alike around a spacious bar just a few blocks from the French Quarter. ✉ *2301 Chartres St., Faubourg Marigny* ☎ *504/943–8929.*

Matrixxx. Though the name and the proprietors keep changing, this location has housed gay bars of various stripes for several years. Matrixxx prefers the title "queer bar," to include the broadest possible spectrum of gender identities. The Sunday tea dance (which actually begins at 12:01 Saturday night, with a brunch break at 11 AM) is a rarity in New Orleans. ✉ *940 Elysian Fields Ave., Faubourg Marigny* ☎ *504/944–4888.*

Rawhide. As the name indicates, this is a rowdy—and sexually charged—leather-and-Levi's bar. It's two blocks from Bourbon Street and is open around the clock. ✉ *740 Burgundy St., French Quarter* ☎ *504/525–8106.*

Sanctuary. This is a laid-back lesbian bar next to the Galleria mall at Causeway and I–10. ✉ *2301 Causeway Blvd., Metairie* ☎ *504/834–7979.*

Wit's Inn. Lesbians have laid claim to the Thursday Ladies' Night at this down-to-earth, rather brightly lit bar right in the center of Mid-City. ✉ *141 N. Carrollton Ave., Mid-City* ☎ *504/486–1600.*

Dance Bars

Big Daddy's. This Bywater staple has a lively dance scene every Friday night, with Candy at the turntable and Billy capturing all the attention on the dance floor. ✉ *2513 Royal St., Bywater* ☎ *504/948–6288.*

Oz. This dance-and-cruise bar is one of the Quarter's most popular spots for young gay men and their admirers of any gender—24 hours a day. ✉ *800 Bourbon St., French Quarter* ☎ *504/593–9491.*

Parade Disco. This glitzy, high-energy disco above Bourbon Pub draws a young crowd of men (mostly gay) and some women. Mixes of classic, pop, and techno disco create a dance-lover's delight. ✉ *801 Bourbon St., above Bourbon Pub, French Quarter* ☎ *504/529–2107.*

Music Venues

For a city of only 473,000 (the metro area is 1,263,000), New Orleans has a vast selection of live music. To list every club and bar would be a massive undertaking: the clubs selected here host good bands on a regular basis, usually most nights of the week. Venues come and go in the precarious music business, so check the city's various publications to keep up-to-date.

The heaviest concentration of live music is in the French Quarter and Faubourg Marigny, and high standards of musicianship prevail despite the sometimes tawdry atmosphere. Most people discover the Quarter's hot spots as they explore the district on foot. Some of the descriptions in this section of neighborhood clubs outside the Quarter and downtown are a bit longer, as these places are generally less familiar to out-of-towners.

Show times can vary greatly. French Quarter clubs hosting traditional jazz get rolling early in the evening, usually by 8 PM; several present music in the afternoons as well, especially on weekends. The first set at most neighborhood clubs begins after 10 PM; unless a club has late-night music on a regular basis, the last set usually ends by 2 AM. Call ahead to double-check times and ask for directions if you need them. Remember that in a city with no closing time there is also no compulsion to start punctually, no matter what you are told over the phone.

French Quarter

Chris Owens Club. A famous French Quarter figure, the reluctantly aging Chris Owens is still an energetic female dancer and entertainer with a slightly risqué act. The late Al Hirt often played here. ✉ *500 Bourbon St., French Quarter* ☎ *504/523–6400.*

★ **Donna's Bar & Grill.** Donna's is a great place to hear traditional jazz, R&B, and the city's young brass bands in an informal neighborhood setting. On Monday night many of the city's top musicians stop by after their regular gigs to sit in for the diverse sets of drummer Bob French; free red beans and rice are served. ✉ *800 N. Rampart St., French Quarter* ☎ *504/596–6914.*

Funky Butt at Congo Square. Named after jazz pioneer Buddy Bolden's signature tune and housed in art-deco splendor, this club is a top spot for contemporary jazz. Local talent and local connoisseurs are both found in plentiful supply here; Jason Marsalis, of the local musical dynasty, often plays here. ✉ *714 N. Rampart St., French Quarter* ☎ *504/558–0872.*

House of Blues. Despite its name, blues is a relatively small component in the booking policy, which also embraces rock, jazz, country, soul, funk, world music, and more, performed by everyone from local artists to international touring acts. A gospel brunch is a rousing Sunday staple. The adjoining restaurant has an eclectic menu, including vegetarian dishes and classic southern cuisine, served in ample portions at reasonable prices. The **Parish**, a smaller, more intimate offshoot upstairs from the main house, sometimes hosts local groups. ⊠ *225 Decatur St., French Quarter* ☎ *504/529-2583 concert line.*

Margaritaville Café. Yes, it's named after *that* song. Jimmy Buffett's devoted fans, called "parrotheads," flock to this shrine to the singer-songwriter-author that has live music by local and regional blues, rock, and zydeco performers afternoon and night. Menu items such as the "Cheeseburger in Paradise" derive from Buffett songs, and several varieties of the salt-rimmed signature drink are served. Decor consists mainly of Buffett photos, and the man himself does appear occasionally. ⊠ *1104 Decatur St., French Quarter* ☎ *504/592-2565.*

O'Flaherty's Irish Channel Pub. In this casual setting, proprietor Danny O'Flaherty often regales his guests with Irish fiddling, and Saturday nights bring Irish dance classes. Other nights host top-notch visiting artists playing Irish, Scottish, and other folk music. ⊠ *508 Toulouse St., French Quarter* ☎ *504/529-1317.*

Palm Court Jazz Café. Banjo player Danny Barker immortalized this restaurant in his song "Palm Court Strut." The best of traditional New Orleans jazz is presented in a classy setting with tile floors, exposed brick walls, and a handsome mahogany bar. There are decent creature comforts here; regional cuisine is served, and you can sit at the bar and rub elbows with local musicians. A wide selection of records, tapes, and CDs is on sale. ⊠ *1204 Decatur St., French Quarter* ☎ *504/525-0200.*

★ **Preservation Hall.** The jazz tradition that flowered in the 1920s is enshrined in this cultural landmark by a cadre of distinguished New Orleans musicians, most of whom were schooled by an ever-dwindling group of elder statesmen who actually played with Louis Armstrong et al. There is limited seating on benches—many patrons end up squatting on the floor or standing in back—and no beverages are served or allowed. Nonetheless, the legions of satisfied customers regard an evening here as an essential New Orleans experience. ⊠ *726 St. Peter St., French Quarter* ☎ *504/522-2841 or 504/523-8939.*

off the beaten path

ERNIE K-DOE'S MOTHER-IN-LAW LOUNGE – Ernie K-Doe, rhythm-and-blues legend and one of the city's most eccentric personalities, died in 2001 to much ado. K-Doe's wife, the charming Miss Antoinette, is a celebrity in her own right. She presides over this eclectic, living-room-style bar, which regularly fills with jovial groups of her friends. Memorabilia from Ernie K-Doe's career comprises the chief decor. The bar is in Tremé, a neighborhood adjacent to the French Quarter. The area is not safe for walking, but taxis from the Quarter are quick and inexpensive. ⊠ *1500 N. Claiborne Ave., Tremé* ☎ *504/947-1078.*

OLD POINT BAR – You can take the ferry or drive to this Algiers Point tavern that sometimes hosts live music. The bar feels like an old roadhouse, as it sits opposite the levee, where croaking frogs easily outnumber passing vehicles. A checkered floor, plywood stage, long comfy bar, and pool table in the back draw a casual crowd of locals. Modern jazz/funk is typical here, although as always you should consult *Gambit* or call for the current lineup before heading out. ⊠ *545 Patterson St., Algiers Point* ☎ *504/364–0950.*

Faubourg Marigny & Bywater

Café Brasil. For many years, Café Brasil has been entrenched at the central Marigny corner of Frenchmen and Chartres streets. Music, poetry readings, dance benefits, art shows—Brasil has seen it all, and when a popular local band is playing, it still throbs. Modern jazz and experimental theater draw smaller crowds of serious listeners who sit at comfortably spaced tables. ⊠ *2100 Chartres St., Faubourg Marigny* ☎ *504/949–0851.*

Checkpoint Charlie's. This bustling corner bar draws young locals who shoot pool and listen to blues and rock, whether live or from the jukebox—24 hours a day, 7 days a week. There's also a paperback library and a fully functioning Laundromat. ⊠ *501 Esplanade Ave., Faubourg Marigny* ☎ *504/949–7012.*

Dragon's Den. This most bohemian of music cafés, above a Thai restaurant, provides pillows on the floor and hosts live music most every night. ⊠ *435 Esplanade Ave., Faubourg Marigny* ☎ *504/949–1750.*

★ **Snug Harbor.** This intimate club just outside the Quarter is one of the city's best rooms for soaking up modern jazz, blues, and R&B. It is the home base of such esteemed talent as vocalist Charmaine Neville and pianist-patriarch Ellis Marsalis (father of Wynton and Branford). The dining room serves good local food but is best known in town for its burgers. Budget-conscious types can listen to the band through speakers in the bar without paying the rather high cover charge. ⊠ *626 Frenchmen St., Faubourg Marigny* ☎ *504/949–0696.*

Spotted Cat. One of the more pleasant places to hear music in town is on the rattan furniture in the window front of this comfortable little bar. Two bands play per night, and the vibe ranges from contemplative jazz to sweaty salsa. ⊠ *623 Frenchmen St., Faubourg Marigny* ☎ *504/943–3887.*

Vaughan's. This neighborhood joint lights up on Thursday for Kermit Ruffins's jazz sets. The neighborhood is not the safest, so a taxi is a necessity. ⊠ *800 Lesseps St., at Dauphine St., Bywater* ☎ *504/947–5562.*

CBD & Warehouse District

★ **Circle Bar.** A collection of meandering spaces lands you in the tiny living room at this intimate club on Lee Circle, where jazz, blues, funk, and experimental groups play just about every night. Regular customers, though, are just as happy to hover around the bar. ⊠ *1032 St. Charles Ave., Warehouse District* ☎ *504/588–2616.*

Howlin' Wolf. A former grain-and-cotton warehouse holds a capacious club that's popular with locals. A grab bag of alternative rock, hip-hop, Latin music, and progressive country fills the schedule. Visiting musicians often hang out and may sit in. ⊠ *828 S. Peters St., Warehouse District* ☎ *504/529–5844.*

★ **Mermaid Lounge.** This funky little box of a bar under the overpass to the Mississippi River Bridge presents a wide variety of acts, including local rock, funk, brass bands, and classic country. It is not easy to find the place: take Tchoupitoulas Street away from the French Quarter; as you approach the overpass, jag right onto Annunciation and turn right on John Churchill Chase. The club is a block ahead on the left. ⊠ *1102 Constance St., Warehouse District* ☏ *504/524–4747.*

Michaul's Live Cajun Music Restaurant. Spacious and homey, Michaul's has a huge dance floor on which patient teachers give free Cajun dance lessons until around 11 PM nightly except Sunday, mostly to visitors, though locals check it out from time to time. The Cajun food is authentic if not inventive. ⊠ *840 St. Charles Ave., Warehouse District* ☏ *504/522–5517.*

Mulate's. Across the street from the Convention Center, this large restaurant seats 400, and the dance floor quickly fills with couples twirling and two-stepping to authentic Cajun bands from the countryside. Regulars love to drag first-timers to the floor for impromptu lessons. The home-style Cajun cuisine is quite good, and the bands play until 10:30 or 11 PM. ⊠ *201 Julia St., Warehouse District* ☏ *504/522–1492.*

Uptown

Carrollton Station. Small and cozy, this club showcases up-and-coming blues acts and local singer-songwriters. You can take the St. Charles Avenue streetcar here. ⊠ *8140 Willow St., Uptown* ☏ *504/861–9718.*

Dos Jefes Uptown Cigar Bar. This intimate uptown establishment smokes with a menu that includes more than 40 premium cigars, single-malt Scotches, brandies, whiskeys, ports, and wine by the glass. There's live music—usually jazz—nightly. A cab or a car will get you here. ⊠ *5535 Tchoupitoulas St., Uptown* ☏ *504/891–8500.*

Le Bon Temps Roulé. Amble way up Magazine Street (a cab or car is probably best) and you can enjoy this little jewel of a casual bar and music spot. Rock, blues, jazz, or funk bands play every night in a back room. Locals favor Le Bon Temps not only for its music but also for its pool tables. ⊠ *4801 Magazine St., Uptown* ☏ *504/895–8117.*

FodorśChoice **Maple Leaf.** An absolute institution, the Maple Leaf presses middle-
★ school science teachers together with the latest crop from Tulane University and everyone in between. Down-home and funky, with pressed-tin walls and overworked ceiling fans, this atmospheric place hosts blues, zydeco, R&B, and more. The Rebirth Brass Band has held court here every Tuesday night for the past 15 years; the gig is an essential part of many locals' social routines. There's a romantic tropical patio out back, and the sidewalk out front is often filled with locals in the know. Poetry readings are held on Sunday at 3 PM. Although the club is only a few blocks from the Oak and Carrollton streetcar stop, it's best to take a cab. ⊠ *8316 Oak St., Uptown* ☏ *504/866–9359.*

★ **Tipitina's.** The original Tip's was founded in the mid-1970s as the home base for Professor Longhair, the pioneering rhythm-and-blues pianist and singer who died in 1980; the club takes its name from one of his most popular songs. A bust of "Fess" stands prominently near the front door; first-timers should place their hand upon his bald head upon entering in a one-time homage. As the multitude of concert posters on the walls indicates, Tip's hosts a wide variety of local and global acts. For about a decade Bruce Daigrepont has played a weekly Cajun dance on Sunday, 5 PM–9 PM; free red beans and rice are served. ⊠ *501 Napoleon Ave., Uptown* ☏ *504/895–8477.*

Mid-City

Lion's Den. This is a place to drift away from the mainstream and immerse yourself in an authentic New Orleans atmosphere, particularly if Miss Irma Thomas, an inspiration to the early Rolling Stones, is here. When she's not on tour, and particularly during the Carnival season, the city's undisputed R&B queen sometimes performs at her own club. Call first to see what's on and take a cab here. Music usually starts at 10 PM. ⊠ *2655 Gravier St., Mid-City* ☎ *504/821–3745.*

★ **Mid-City Bowling Lanes Rock 'n' Bowl.** The phrase "Only in New Orleans . . ." applies to this combination bowling alley and music club in Mid-City. Dancers may spill over into the lanes when a favorite band such as zydeco legend Boozoo Chavis takes the stage. Blues, R&B, rock, swing, and Cajun music are all presented. Thursday is zydeco night, bringing the best musicians in from rural Louisiana. Be sure to ask club owner John Blancher for a dance lesson. ⊠ *4133 S. Carrollton Ave., Mid-City* ☎ *504/482–3133.*

Rollin' on the River

The audience for these themed cruises is 99% visitors, including busloads of tour groups. The food is merely adequate, but the city is so rich with high-quality musicians that you can count on taking in some very good music along with the scenery. Both companies listed here depart from Woldenberg Riverfront Park, along the French Quarter.

Creole Queen Paddle Wheeler. Among the various cruises on the Big Muddy is a "Dinner on the River & All That Jazz" outing. Boarding and a Creole buffet begin at 7 PM; cruises are from 8 to 10. Traditional New Orleans jazz by veteran players accompanies the journey. ⊠ *Poydras St. Wharf at Riverwalk, French Quarter* ☎ *504/529–4567 or 800/ 445–4109* ⊕ *www.neworleanspaddlewheels.com* ⊙ *Departures daily.*
Steamboat Natchez. The city's only authentic steamboat stern-wheeler hosts an evening excursion with traditional jazz by the Dukes of Dixieland and a Cajun-Creole buffet. Boarding is at 6 PM; the cruise is from 7 to 9. ⊠ *Toulouse St. Wharf behind Jackson Brewery, French Quarter* ☎ *504/586–8777 or 800/233–2628* ⊕ *www.steamboatnatchez.com* ⊙ *Departures daily; Fri. and Sat. only Thanksgiving–Mardi Gras.*

THE ARTS

The performing arts are alive and well in New Orleans. A number of small theater and dance companies present an impressive variety of regional-level fare. In addition, local colleges and universities such as Tulane, Loyola, Dillard, Xavier, and the University of New Orleans have sizable fine-arts departments. Many performances are of outstanding caliber. The New Orleans Center for Creative Arts (NOCCA) hosts topnotch performances of dance, music, and theater on its modern Bywater campus. For current listings, consult the daily calendar in the *Times-Picayune* and its "Lagniappe" Friday entertainment section. *Where* and *Gambit* are free publications (distributed in hotels and other public places) that also have up-to-date entertainment news.

Ticket prices for theater and for concerts vary widely, from $10 for performances at smaller venues to $70 for top acts at major halls. You can purchase tickets from box offices. **Ticketmaster** (☎ 504/522–5555) sells tickets for performances at many venues.

Classical Music

New Orleans has a rich history of classical music. Philharmonic orchestral and chamber groups thrived during the 19th century, giving rise to many performers and composers, including the famed classical composer Louis Moreau Gottschalk. As jazz achieved society status during the 20th century, classical music took a backseat; however, many professional and amateur players ensure the scene stays active.

Louisiana Philharmonic Orchestra. Always good and sometimes excellent, the orchestra performs a wide range of classical works in the **Orpheum Theater** (✉ 129 University Pl., CBD) and has a **Casual Classics Series** (✉ 4545 Williams Blvd., Kenner) at the Pontchartrain Center. Guest conductors and artists are often top-notch. The flexible programming includes children's concerts and free concerts in parks around the city; ticket prices for regular concerts are $13–$65. ✉ *305 Baronne St., Suite 600, CBD* ☎ *504/523–6530* ⊕ *www.lpomusic.com.*

Friends of Music. This organization brings superior performers from all over the world to Tulane University's **Dixon Hall** (✉ Tulane University, Willow Street entrance Uptown ☎ 504/865–5267). Concerts take place approximately once a month, and tickets usually cost $10–$20. ☎ *504/895–0690* ⊕ *www.friendsofmusic.org.*

Jefferson Performing Arts Society. A wonderful cultural source, if a bit out of the way, the society stages musicals, ballets, recitals, and operas. ✉ *400 Phlox St., Metairie* ☎ *504/885–2000* ⊕ *www.jpas.org.*

Loyola University. An excellent music department hosts regular performances, including Wednesday concerts at noon and the occasional opera. ✉ *6363 St. Charles Ave., Uptown* ☎ *504/865–3037* ⊕ *www.loyno.edu.*

FodorśChoice
★   **New Orleans Center for Creative Arts (NOCCA).** The marvelous high-school music program at NOCCA sponsors guest performances in addition to first-rate student concerts on its modern campus in the Faubourg Marigny/Bywater District. The guests are often world-class artists. ✉ *2800 Chartres St., Bywater* ☎ *504/940–2787* ⊕ *www.nocca.com.*

Trinity Artist Series. Gratifying concerts of all types—solo, choral, orchestral, and chamber—fill the vaulted interior of Trinity Episcopal Church most Sunday evenings. The artists are usually local or regional, though the occasional star does pass through. Admission is free, and a relaxed, enjoyable evening is assured. ✉ *1329 Jackson Ave., Garden District* ☎ *504/522–0276* ⊕ *www.trinityc.net/trinity_artist_series.htm.*

Dance

Jefferson Ballet Theatre. This children's ballet company stages regular performances at various theaters, including an annual rendition of *The Nutcracker.* ✉ *3621 Florida Ave., Lakefront* ☎ *504/468–1231.*

New Orleans Ballet Association. The only major professional dance troupe in the city presents classical and modern ballet in the Mahalia Jackson

Theater of the Performing Arts from September through May. ⊠ *Theater, Armstrong Park at Basin St., Tremé* ☎ *504/565–7470, 504/522–0996 ballet association* ⊕ *www.nobadance.com.*

Film

The film scene is pretty bleak in New Orleans, although a determined clique of film buffs and filmmakers remains persistently optimistic about a blossoming just around the corner. It is true that the New Orleans Film Festival has been gaining momentum of late, claiming most of the downtown attention for two weeks each October. The selections listed below screen a variety of nonmainstream films. First-run Hollywood movies appear, among other theaters, at the modern, multiplex **Palace Theaters** (⊠ 1200 Elmwood Park Blvd., Jefferson Parish ☎ 504/734–2020).

Canal Place Cinemas. Art films and less well-known works, along with first-run films, are screened at this small cinema in the fashionable mall. ⊠ *Canal Place, 333 Canal St., French Quarter* ☎ *504/581–5400.*

Film Buffs Institute. This Loyola University program screens independent, old-time, and foreign films during the school year. ⊠ *Loyola University, 6363 St. Charles Ave., Uptown* ☎ *504/865–2152.*

New Orleans Film Festival. The New Orleans Film and Video Society presents this two-week festival in early October, bringing in top international films and visits from directors and screenwriters. ☎ *504/523–3818* ⊕ *www.neworleansfilmfest.com.*

Zeitgeist. This alternative arts center screens some of the most outstanding independent, experimental, and foreign films in release. Zeitgeist also stages theater and visual art in its large, open space. A cab is advisable. ⊠ *1724 Oretha Castle Haley Blvd., Lower Garden District* ☎ *504/525–2767* ⊕ *www.zeitgeistinc.org.*

Music Venues

Free year-round musical events are held in the city's parks and universities. Louisiana also has a glorious tradition of festivals of all types, including music. New Orleans is no exception, the most famous examples being Mardi Gras and Jazz Fest ⇨ Chapter 2). The French Quarter Festival, in early April, is a relative newcomer, but already very successful. The festival fills Woldenberg Riverfront park with music, food, and crafts. So when you're scanning the events calendar, check out the festivals.

The city has several major concert facilities. **Kiefer UNO Lakefront Arena** (⊠6801 Franklin Ave., Lakefront ☎504/280–7222 ⊕www.saengertheatre. com), of the University of New Orleans, is a great venue for major rock concerts.

The **Mahalia Jackson Theater of the Performing Arts** (⊠ 801 N. Rampart St., in Armstrong Park, Tremé ☎ 504/565–7470) is home to the city's opera company and also hosts the occasional symphonic concert. The **New Orleans Arena** (⊠ 1501 Girod St., CBD ☎ 504/587–3800 ⊕ www. neworleansarena.com) is the venue of choice for hip-hop and pop stars. The **Saenger Performing Arts Center** (⊠ 143 N. Rampart St., Tremé ☎ 504/524–2490) stages a Best of Broadway series as well as national headliners.

Opera

New Orleanians have had a long love affair with opera. The first grand opera staged in North America was performed here, and during the mid-19th century New Orleans had three full-time opera companies, including one specifically for Creoles of color. New Orleans was always part of the "European" tour for an ambitious production, and it was here that the great European divas wanted absolutely to be heard in the United States. But those days came to an end with Reconstruction, and ever since the French Opera House burned down in 1919 the city has not had an aria arena per se. Still, through the 20th century the city continued to produce famous singers, including Norman Treigle, Phyllis Treigle, Ruth Falcon, and Jeanne-Michelle Charbonnet.

Jefferson Performing Arts Society. This vibrant regional cultural center produces a couple of operas each year, usually in English translation. ✉ *400 Phlox St., Metairie* ☎ *504/885–2000* ⊕ *www.jpas.org.*

New Orleans Opera Association. The October–March season generally showcases four operas; performances are held at the Mahalia Jackson Theater of the Performing Arts. ✉ *Theater, 801 N. Rampart St., in Armstrong Park, Tremé* ☎ *504/565–7470, 504/529–2278 association* ⊕ *www.neworleansopera.org.*

Theater

Anthony Bean Community Theater. This active community theater also houses an acting school, providing young local actors with a ready audience. Productions include musical dramatizations of musicians' biographies, as well as straight dramas in small but careful productions. Some casts include local bigwigs. ✉ *1333 S. Carrollton Ave., Uptown* ☎ *504/862–7529* ⊕ *www.anthonybeantheater.com.*

★ **Contemporary Arts Center.** The center has two theaters that stage experimental works, productions by local playwrights, musical performances, and multimedia events. ✉ *900 Camp St., Warehouse District* ☎ *504/528–3800* ⊕ *www.cacno.org.*

Junebug Productions. One of the region's most accomplished African-American theater companies presents outstanding, progressive-minded productions at venues around the Crescent City and nationwide. Call to find out what's currently on the boards. ☎ *504/524–8257.*

Le Chat Noir. Come to the cabaret for a scintillating mix of comedy revues, chanteuses, theater, tango, piano trills, and pop standards. In the heart of the arts district, this cat is sleek, elegant, and eclectic, with plenty of warm wood and cool tile, all polished to the highest gloss. The patrons, whether in their twenties or fifties, are appropriately urbane. ✉ *715 St. Charles Ave., Warehouse District* ☎ *504/581–5812* ⊕ *www. cabaretlechatnoir.com.*

★ **Le Petit Théâtre.** The oldest continuously running community theater in the United States occupies a historic building in the French Quarter and puts on quality plays year-round. It has a children's corner in addition to its usual fare of classics, musicals, and dramas, often on local themes. Events in the Tennessee Williams Festival take place here in March. ✉ *616 St. Peter St., French Quarter* ☎ *504/522–2081* ⊕ *www.lepetittheatre.com.*

NORD Theater. A division of the New Orleans Recreation Department presents works by local playwrights at Gallier Hall. ⊠ *545 St. Charles Ave., enter on Lafayette St., CBD* ☎ *504/565–7860.*

Rivertown Repertory Theatre. This community theater stages contemporary musicals, comedy, and drama several times a year. ⊠ *325 Minor St., Kenner* ☎ *504/468–7221.*

Saenger Performing Arts Center. A splendidly restored theater built in 1927, the Saenger showcases national and international talent. Broadway revivals and road shows come here, and pop and rock performers also often take the stage. ⊠ *143 N. Rampart St., Tremé* ☎ *504/524–2490* ⊕ *www.saengertheatre.com.*

Southern Repertory Theater. This is an established venue for local and regional experimental theater. The company also presents regional classics, such as works by Tennessee Williams. ⊠ *Canal Place, 3rd level, 333 Canal St., French Quarter* ☎ *504/522–6545* ⊕ *www.southernrep.com.*

Stage to Stage Inc. Call this company for the schedule of **Summer Stages Children's Theater,** which presents kid- and family-oriented productions around the city. ⊠ *225 Baronne St., CBD* ☎ *504/598–3800.*

Tulane University. Best known for its summer bills of fare, the university has several theater groups that stage top-notch productions. **Summer Lyric Theatre** (☎ *504/865–5269*) produces three crowd-pleasing musicals every summer, while Tulane's **Summer Shakespeare Festival** (☎ *504/ 865–5105*) interprets the Bard in imaginative, high-quality productions. ⊠ *Tulane University Campus, Uptown* ⊕ *www2.tulane.edu.*

SHOPPING

6

Updated by
Sharon
Donovan

THE FUN OF SHOPPING IN NEW ORLEANS is in the many regional items available throughout the city, in the smallest shops or the biggest department stores. Plan on taking home samples of the city's flavors: pralines (pecan candies), seafood (packaged to go), Louisiana red beans and rice, coffee (pure or with chicory), and Creole and Cajun spices (cayenne pepper, chili, and garlic). Packaged mixes make the to-go route quite simple for such local favorites as jambalaya, gumbo, beignets, and the sweet red local cocktail called the Hurricane.

Art is in the eye of the beholder—and the festivalgoer—thanks to colorful posters celebrating Mardi Gras, the New Orleans Jazz & Heritage Festival, and the Crescent City Classic, among dozens of events which prompt such artistic focus. Many of the annual issues quickly become collector's items. Ceramic or feather masks can serve as attire during Mardi Gras and as attractive wall hangings during the rest of the year. Mardi Gras costumes, beads, and doubloons make wonderful gifts, too. Posters, photographs, and paintings on canvas and slate capture scenes in New Orleans. Jewelry, antiques, ceramics, carved wooden toys, kites, and wreaths of dried flowers are often handmade and make lovely gifts and souvenirs.

The vast array of sounds of New Orleans are available in music stores and in a variety of live-music venues (such as Preservation Hall). A wide spectrum, including Dixieland jazz, contemporary jazz, swinging Cajun and zydeco, and the wallop and wail of rhythm and blues wafts down city streets and permeates neighborhoods.

All major and independent bookstores carry books about the city. Local history, photography, and cookbooks, as well as guides to special-interest sightseeing, and books that specialize in local cultural and ethnic history are especially popular. At the handful of independently operated bookshops, perseverance yields a treasure of local literature and lore, as the inventory spans old photographs, posters, and postcards.

Many clothing shops sell wearables popular in the semitropical heat: Panama hats, lacy lingerie, and the ubiquitous T-shirt and sports clothes. Designer fashions are available in such national department stores as Macy's and Saks Fifth Avenue, and delightful vintage clothing is sold in several shops.

Shopping guides in most of the tourist magazines available in hotel rooms and lobbies keep track of the latest comings and goings of shops. The Welcome Center of the New Orleans Metropolitan Convention and Visitors Bureau on the St. Ann Street side of Jackson Square also has pamphlets on shopping.

For information on store hours, *see* Business Hours *in* Smart Travel Tips A to Z. If you're visiting from outside the United States, *see* Taxes *in* Smart Travel Tips A to Z for information about a sales-tax rebate.

SHOPPING NEIGHBORHOODS

The main shopping areas in the city are the French Quarter, with its narrow streets lined with specialty, gift, and antiques shops and art galleries;

BLITZ TOURS

Study your map and then plunge into one of the following shopping itineraries arranged by special interest.

Mardi Gras Shopping Blitz

New Orleans during Mardi Gras is not for the faint of heart. If you think you're bashful, spend some evenings at a couple of parades and you'll be out bagging beads with the rest of 'em, hollering and scrambling. Carnival is a time for letting down your hair and just generally getting down. Way down. No, you don't have to make a complete fool of yourself, but hey! Everybody else does. Having now made the decision to get into the swing of things, you'll want to choose your costume and mask. In the French Quarter, a good starting place is the **Community Flea Market,** where face-painters are ready to make your fantasies come true and some costume possibilities are easy to spot. From there, walk over to Royal Street to check out the wigs and way-out makeup at **Fifi Mahony's.** Another helpful stop is the **Little Shop of Fantasy,** where masks, boas, tiaras, and other accessories are in good supply. There are masks and more masks farther up Royal Street, at **Rumors.** If you've decided to costume in vintage clothing, or maybe lingerie passing for a bit of clothing, take the Magazine Street bus and browse through the threads at **House of Lounge** and **Funky Monkey.** Just remember, the Lord of Misrule reigns during Mardi Gras, so suit up, step out, and have a ball.

Crescent City to Go!

Face it: there's no way you're going to make it to all of those famous New Orleans restaurants. But you can take a taste of the city home with you, boxed though it may be. It's almost unheard of for anyone to leave town without at least one box of sweet-sweet pralines. Locals and tourists alike turn up at all hours for café au lait and sugary beignets at **Café du Monde,** which sells Creole coffee and boxed beignet mix. It will ship anywhere in the country, so you can try your hand at making these hole-less doughnuts. For authentic pralines and samples of other local candy making, head to one of the two **Laura's Candies** to study the options there. Wander away from the Quarter and try your luck at **Riverwalk Marketplace,** which is loaded with candy shops. **Creole Delicacies & Cookin' Cajun** will supply you with cooking lessons and just about all the ingredients you need to re-create those dishes back home. And if you can't quite duplicate the taste of red beans and rice, crawfish étouffée, jambalaya, beignets, and pralines, you'll just have to return to the Crescent City— like everybody else.

the Central Business District (CBD), which has department stores and clothing, specialty, and jewelry shops; the Warehouse District, popular for Julia Street's contemporary-arts galleries; Magazine Street, known for its antiques shops and galleries; and the Riverbend/Maple Street area uptown, with its neighborhood and specialty shops.

French Quarter

In these blocks lined with narrow storefronts, the shopping experience is as much a treasure hunt as a well-scripted scenario. Don't rush: a bistro or café is nearby for a rest stop.

Jax Brewery (⊠ 600 Decatur St., French Quarter ☎ 504/566–7245 ⊕ www.jacksonbrewery.com), a onetime beer factory, operates three connected indoor malls that house a mix of local shops and national chains. The Brewhouse, on Decatur Street across from Jackson Square, occupies a historic building in which Jax beer was once brewed. A Virgin Megastore loaded with books and music occupies considerable square footage in the Brewhouse. Adjacent to the Brewhouse, and connected by indoor and outdoor walkways, is the Millhouse.

Antiques

The French Quarter is well known for its fine antiques shops, located mainly on Royal and Chartres streets. The **Royal Street Guild** (☎ 504/524–1260 ⊕ www.royalstreetguild.com), a merchants' association, distributes informative brochures in shops and hotels. Local art and antiques shopping consultant **Macon Riddle** (☎ 504/899–3027 ⊕ www.neworleansantiquing.com) conducts half- and full-day shopping expeditions by appointment.

Annette's of Rue Royal (⊠ 304 Royal St., French Quarter ☎ 504/525–4445) is a delightful little shop stocked with paintings, porcelain, crystal, and estate jewelry, with a special touch of 1850s- and 1860s-style chests and pedestals.

Brass Monkey (⊠ 235 Royal St., French Quarter ☎ 504/561–0688 ⊕ www.thebrassmoney.com) is a tiny storefront with a treasure chest of Limoges boxes, English Staffordshire porcelains, Venetian glass, and antique walking sticks.

Dixon & Harris (⊠ 237 Royal St., French Quarter ☎ 504/524–0282 ⊕ www.dixon-antiques.net) shows off its extensive array of French and English furniture, 19th-century bronze sculptures, imported clocks, chandeliers, paintings, and estate jewelry in an opulent gallery. Check the online catalog for discounts.

French Antique Shop (⊠ 225 Royal St., French Quarter ☎ 504/524–9861 ⊕ www.gofrenchantiques.com) displays a large selection of European chandeliers and furniture, sconces, mirrors, porcelain objects, and hand-carved marble mantels.

Keil's Antiques (⊠ 325 Royal St., French Quarter ☎ 504/522–4552 ⊕ www.keilsantiques.com) fills three floors with 18th- and 19th-century crystal chandeliers, furniture, estate jewelry, and art.

Lucullus (⊠ 610 Chartres St., French Quarter ☎ 504/528–9620) carries a stylish collection of culinary antiques, including 18th- and 19th-century walnut French farm tables, English bone china, and charming oddities such as sterling-silver asparagus eaters.

M. S. Rau, Inc. (✉ 630 Royal St., French Quarter ☎ 504/523–5660 or 800/544–9440 ⊕ www.rauantiques.com) is a tremendous source for French, English, and American antique furniture, as well as American cut glass, porcelain, Georgian silver tea urns and flatware, and estate jewelry.

Mirror Mirror (✉ 933 Royal St., French Quarter ☎ 504/566–1990 ⊕ www.mirrorx2.com), aptly named, gleams with mirrors from the 18th century to the early 20th century, from European, Georgian, Victorian, Louis Philippe, and art deco and art nouveau.

Moss Antiques (✉ 411 Royal St., French Quarter ☎ 504/522–3981) has a large selection of walking sticks and antique and estate jewels, as well as fine French and English furnishings, paintings, a whimsical oyster plate collection, and silver vases, tea caddies, and desert services.

Rothschild's Antiques (✉ 241 and 321 Royal St., French Quarter ☎ 504/523–5816 ⊕ www.rothschildsantiques.com) carries English and French furniture, and an extensive selection of silver, jewelry, mantels, and clocks from the 18th through the 20th century.

Royal Antiques (✉ 307–309 Royal St., French Quarter ☎ 504/524–7033 ⊕ www.royalantiques.com) specializes in French and English 18th- and 19th-century furnishings, including traditional and provincial furniture, bronze and iron sconces, and chandeliers,

Soniat House Antiques Galleries (✉ 1130, 1138, and 1139 Chartres St., French Quarter ☎ 504/522–0570 ⊕ www.soniatanituqes.com), run by the owner of the Soniat House hotel (➪ Lodging, French Quarter), sells mostly 18th- and 19th-century French, Italian, and Swedish furniture and decorative accessories.

Waldhorn & Adler (✉ 343 Royal St., French Quarter ☎ 504/581–6379 ⊕ www.waldhornadlers.com) is New Orleans's oldest antiques store, established in 1881. Among its most noteworthy pieces are period antique French and English furniture, estate jewelry, and watches from such manufacturers as Rolex, Patek Philippe, and Cartier.

★ **Whisnant Galleries** (✉ 222 Chartres St., French Quarter ☎ 504/524–9766 ⊕ www.whisnantantiques.com) is a magic castle of wonders, from such antique weaponry as 16th- to 19th-century swords and daggers to 18th- to 19th-century American firearms and African and Asian mask sculptures.

Art & Crafts Galleries

Bergen Putman Gallery (✉ 730 Royal St., French Quarter ☎ 504/523–7882 or 800/621–6179 ⊕ www.bergenputnamgallery.com) showcases more than 10,000 prints, including limited editions and original prints of Jazz Fest and Mardi Gras, as well as posters and prints by local artists.

Casell Gallery (✉ 818 Royal St., French Quarter ☎ 504/524–0671 ⊕ www.casellgallery.com) specializes in etchings, posters, prints of New Orleans artists, and original pastels by Joachim Casell whose images range from swampscapes and seascapes to New Orleans street scenes.

The Crabnet (✉ 925 Decatur St., French Quarter ☎ 504/522–3478 ⊕ www.thecrabnet.com) has a large collection of duck carvings, handcrafted fishing lures, wildlife prints, and decorative waterfowl carvings.

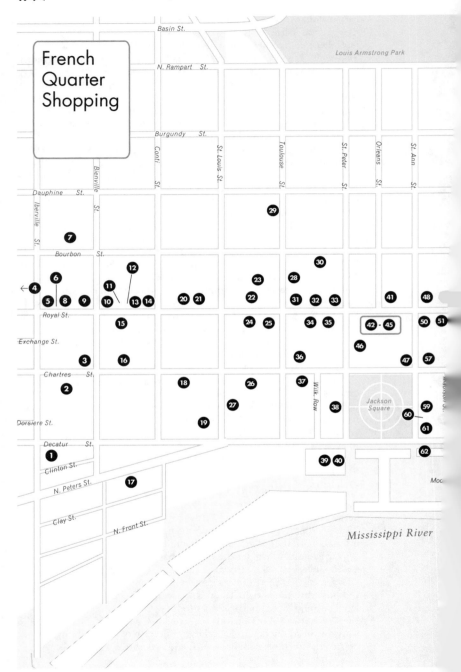

French
Quarter
Shopping

Louis Armstrong Park

Mississippi River

N. Rampart St.

1/4 mi

0

0

1/2 km

Burgundy St.

St. Philip St.

Ursulines St.

Gov. Nichols St.

Dauphine St.

Bourbon St.

53 54 55

Royal St.

56

56

73

Chartres St.

56

7

68

72

70 71

Decatur St.

French Market Pl.

75 →

74 →

76 →

N. Peters S

Crescent Gallery (⊠ 628 Toulouse St., French Quarter ☎ 504/525–5255 ⊕ www.crescentgallery.net) deals exclusively in native New Orleans artist Rolland Golden's abstract realist images of regional rural landscapes in watercolor, acrylic, and oil.

Elliott Gallery (⊠ 540 Royal St., French Quarter ☎ 504/523–3554 ⊕ www.elliottgallery.com), a long-established gallery, is devoted to contemporary artists, including Theo Tobiasse, Max Papart, Nissan Engel, James Coignard, David Schneuer, and Garrick Yrondi.

Fodor'sChoice **A Gallery for Fine Photography** (⊠ 241 Chartres St., French Quarter
★ ☎ 504/568–1313 ⊕ www.agallery.com) sells vintage, modern, and fine-art photography. In addition to pioneers such as E. J. Bellocq, Ansel Adams, and Julia Margaret Cameron, the store also has works by such contemporary masters as Annie Liebovitz, Walker Evans, and Helmut Newton.

Gallery Rinard (⊠ 738 Royal St., French Quarter ☎ 504/522–6536 ⊕ www.galleryrinard.com) is like walking onto the set of *Willy Wonka and the Chocolate Factory,* where felines and canines rule. Matt Rinard's paintings of sly animals and Georg Williams's endearing portraits of dogs and cats share space with artists who have similar humorous views of the animal kingdom's antics.

Hanson Gallery (⊠ 229 Royal St., French Quarter ☎ 504/524–8211 ⊕ www.hansongallery-nola.com) showcases paintings, sculpture, and fine-art prints from such contemporary artists as Leroy Neiman (think sports celebrities Muhammad Ali and Shaquille O'Neal in bold primary colorful strokes) and Peter Max (think of iconic images of American flags and angels).

Kurt E. Schon, Ltd. (⊠ 510 and 523 St. Louis St., French Quarter ☎ 504/524–5462 ⊕ www.kurteschonltd.com) is a high-end gallery specializing in 18th- and 19th-century European paintings. The showrooms are spacious and hushed, attended by a staff extremely well schooled in art history.

La Belle Galerie & the Black Art Collection (⊠ 309 Chartres St., French Quarter ☎ 504/529–3080 ⊕ www.labellegalerie.com) focuses on black music, history, and contemporary life and culture through posters, limited-edition graphics, vintage images, paintings, and sculpture.

Michalopoulos (⊠ 617 Bienville St., French Quarter ☎ 504/558–0505 ⊕ www.michalopoulos.com) showcases New Orleans architecture and street scenes, French country landscapes captured in oil paintings, and serigraphs of James Michalopoulos.

Rodrigue Studios (⊠ 721 Royal St., French Quarter ☎ 504/581–4244 ⊕ www.georgerodrique.com) is home base for the work of Cajun artist George Rodrigue and his famous "blue dog" series, his interpretive Cajun culture images of folklife and folk characters in paintings and serigraphs.

Southern Expressions (⊠ 521 St. Ann St., Jackson Sq., French Quarter ☎ 504/525–4530) leans toward comfort art of soothing subjects and colors. Among the dozen regional painters represented are Tommy McAfee's romantic French Quarter street and architectural scenes and John Akers's precise wildlife and landscapes paintings.

Vintage 429 (⊠ 429 Royal St., French Quarter ☎ 504/529–2288 ⊕ www.vintage429.com) houses a collection of autographed memorabilia, including a B. B. King guitar, Elvis albums, Muhammad Ali boxing trunks and gloves, and first editions of such books as Harper Lee's *To Kill a Mockingbird*.

Books

With all the creativity oozing out of New Orleans, it shouldn't be too surprising that the French Quarter has been home, or at least a temporary retreat, for dozens of nationally recognized authors. Given this literary heritage, bookstores thrive, with a penchant for providing local authors a leg up on shelf-space exposure. Cookbooks and local history books are available in gift shops throughout the Quarter. Fun for any collector are the various musty used-book shops you'll find scattered throughout the neighborhood.

Fodor'sChoice ★ **Faulkner House Books** (✉ 624 Pirate's Alley, French Quarter ☎ 504/524-2940 ⊕ www.faulknerhousebooks.usa), in the house where William Faulkner lived and wrote in the 1920s, is stocked with rare and out-of-print books by southern authors. The shop hosts the annual Words & Music Festival, which salutes Faulkner and new southern writers and musicians.

Librairie Book Shop (✉ 823 Chartres St., French Quarter ☎ 504/525-4837) has the Quarter's largest selection of local lore in books, old posters, and postcards.

Clothing & Accessories

The prevailing fashion sense in New Orleans is a curious mix of sassy and sexy, spiked with a hefty dose of vintage. New is never necessarily better. The most sought-after pieces may be a contemporary style, but its character lies in the antique lace around the collar or a fur pelt from an antiquated wrap now used to accent the cuff.

Body Hangings (✉ 835 Decatur St., French Quarter ☎ 504/524-9856 ⊕ www.bodyhandings.com) is the place to go for that hard-to-find cape, cloak, or shawl. This shop holds a trove of these handmade articles in various of styles, sizes, and fabrics.

Cajun Clothing Co. (✉ Jax Brewery, French Quarter ☎ 504/523-6681 ⊕ www.perlis.com), an outlet of Perlis (⇨ Magazine Street), carries clothing for men, women, and children; its specialty is its crawfish-embroidered shirts and ties.

Fodor'sChoice ★ **Fifi Mahony's** (✉ 934 Royal St., French Quarter ☎ 504/525-4343 ⊕ www.fifi-mahony.com) is drag-queen heaven, with custom wigs, wild accessories, and a fun-loving creative staff.

★ **Fleur de Paris** (✉ 712 Royal St., French Quarter ☎ 504/525-1899) has more than 300 custom-made women's hats fashioned from straw to felt, festooned with a mind-boggling choice of ribbons, flowers, feathers, and veils. The lavish display windows alone are worth a visit to the shop.

The Grace Note (✉ 900 Royal St., French Quarter ☎ 504/522-1513), a must for the eclectic dresser, sells an artistic mix of vintage clothing and hand-sewn contemporary pieces trimmed in vintage laces.

Trashy Diva (✉ 825 Chartres St., French Quarter ☎ 504/581-4555 ⊕ www.trashydiva.com) sells 1920s-1950s vintage-inspired beaded dresses, sexy shawls, lacy corsets, slip dresses, and extravagant hats that are just the tip of this retro-fashion iceberg.

Victoria's Shoes (✉ 532 Chartres St., French Quarter ☎ 504/568–9990) is the footwear emporium of choice among the fashion set. Jimmy Choo, Charles David, and Giuseppe Zanotti are just some of the shoe gods available here.

Violets (✉ 808 Chartres St., French Quarter ☎ 504/569–0088) is bound to steal your heart with an incomparable girlie collection of ruffles, lace, bangles, and crystal beads—in the form of dresses, boudoir wear, and jewelry—and plain old-fashioned romance.

Wehmeier's Belt Shop (✉ 719 Toulouse St., French Quarter ☎ 504/525–2758 ⊕ www.wehmeiers.com) displays finely crafted alligator and exotic leather goods, including belts, wallets, handbags, boots, and shoes.

Food & Gift Packages

Food is the lifeblood of the city and one of its most favorite flavored exports. Just about any item you taste test in a restaurant is possible to have packed up and shipped safely home, from confection and vegetable to all the spices in between.

Aunt Sally's Praline Shop (✉ 810 Decatur St., in the French Market, French Quarter ☎ 504/524–3373 ⊕ www.auntsallys.com) will tempt your sweet tooth with a fresh, flavorful array of pralines, from the original confection spike with pecans to newer fabrications of chocolate and triple-chocolate ingredients. Watch the confectioners at work, cooking up the traditional disks, 2½ inches round or the pralinette at half the size. The shop also has a variety of other handmade candies and Louisiana spices and foodstuffs.

Café du Monde (✉ 800 Decatur St., French Quarter ☎ 504/525–4544 ⊕ www.cafedumonde) is a French Quarter landmark, selling café au lait and beignets in its open-air café. You can take home all the Café du Monde products, including coffee, doughnut mix, mugs, cups, and even prints and posters of the place.

Farmers' Market (✉ N. Peters St. in the French Market, French Quarter ☎ 504/522–2621 ⊕ www.frenchmarket.org) is a 24-hour emporium where Louisiana's farmers sell their seasonal produce, including pecans, sugarcane, mirlitons, Creole tomatoes, strawberries, and okra. Garlic wreaths hang from the rafters of the building where the great chefs of New Orleans shop for their kitchens.

Gumbo Ya-Ya (✉ 219 Bourbon St., French Quarter ☎ 504/522–7484 ⊕ www.gumboyaya.com) carries spices, cookbooks, and gift packages.

FodorŝChoice ★ **Laura's Candies** (✉ 938 Royal St. and 331 Chartres St., French Quarter ☎ 504/525-3880 or 800/992–9699 ⊕ www.laurascandies.com) has been turning out mouthwatering pralines and confections since 1913. Their chocolate candies are fabulous, too. One of the signature specialties, Mississippi Mud, is a murky concoction of milk or dark chocolate laced with caramel.

Vieux Carré Wine and Spirits (✉ 422 Chartres St., French Quarter ☎ 504/568–9463) caters to the sophisticated palate with a superb selection of wines, liquors, and one of the city's best selections of beer. The shop has more than 100 brands of domestic and imported beers, some very difficult to find. You can also get a go-cup of wine or stop by for one of the frequent wine tastings.

Jewelry

The best jewels in the French Quarter are going to be relics of one era or another. Shops have mastered the art of the estate pieces and empower clients to transition the jewelry into their own era by customizing to their respective taste.

Currents . . . (⊠ 305 Royal St., French Quarter ☎ 504/522–6099 ⊕ www. currents.com) is a chic store in which Terry and Sylvia Weidert create their own designs in 14- and 18-karat gold and platinum.

Joan Good Antiques (⊠ 809 Royal St., French Quarter ☎ 504/525–1705 or 800/526–5414 ⊕ www.joangood.com) has beautiful garnets, cameos, aquamarines, topaz, and marcasite creations, as well as some antique Japanese pieces, Amari ceramic, and porcelain.

The Quarter Smith (⊠ 535 St. Louis St., French Quarter ☎ 504/524–9731) carries estate jewelry; Ken Bowers will also create a piece of your own design.

Masks

The masks worn at Mardi Gras are popular as gifts, souvenirs, and decorative pieces. Be careful of cheap imitations; the better handcrafted, locally made masks bear the artist's insignia and are more expensive than the mass-produced ones. A ceramic or feather mask may start at around $10, but run as high as $3,500, depending on the materials, artistry, and size.

FodorsChoice **Little Shop of Fantasy** (⊠ 517 St. Louis, French Quarter ☎ 504/529–4243
★ ⊕ www.littleshopoffantasy.com) carries masks from fun dress-up to works of art. It also stocks such whimsical accessories as angel wings, devil horns, tiaras, boas, and fans.

Rumors (⊠ 513 Royal St., French Quarter ☎ 504/525–0292 ⊕ www. rumorsno.com) carries a huge range of art and wearable masks by more than 200 artists, as well as colorful jewelry and voodoo dolls, ranging in height from 2½ inches to 24 inches and accessorized with small charms to ward off evil spirits.

Serendipitous Masks (⊠ 831 Decatur St., French Quarter ☎ 504/522–9158) has an excellent selection of masks—feathered with ostrich, turkey, rooster tail, and peacock plumes—made by artists on the premises.

Yesteryear's (⊠ 626 Bourbon St., French Quarter ☎ 504/523–6603) has elaborate feather masks made by owner Teresa Latshaw. Voodoo dolls and folklore objects are also sold.

Music

You don't get too far into the French Quarter without your fingers or feet unconsciously keeping time with a random melody wafting through the air. The source may spring from an open window, street musicians, or a lone crooner belting out a song from memory. Although you can't really capture these sounds, you can easily tap into other sounds representative of the city in the music stores.

FodorsChoice **Louisiana Music Factory** (⊠ 210 Decatur St., French Quarter ☎ 504/586–
★ 1094 ⊕ www.louisianamusicfactory.com) is the best source for New Orleans and regional music, new and old. In addition to the records, tapes,

CDs, and books, weekly live music sampler sessions infuse this spot with a sense of spontaneity.

Rock and Roll Collectibles (⊠ 1214 Decatur St., French Quarter ☎ 504/561–5683 ⊕ www.rockcollectibles.org) buys, sells, and trades records, tapes, CDs, and videos. Many of the more than 30,000 vinyl records are relics from the 1920s to the 1930s. In addition to rock, Cajun, zydeco, R&B, country, and jazz are also represented.

Tower Records (⊠ 408 N. Peters St., French Quarter ☎ 504/529–4411 ⊕ www.towerrecords.com), a huge branch of the national chain, sells records, CDs, and DVDs. An entire section, called the Louisiana Room, contains a selection of music by 2,000 artists.

Virgin Megastore (⊠ Jackson Brewhouse, 620 Decatur St., French Quarter ☎ 504/671–8100 ⊕ www.virgin.com) has three floors of records, CDs, DVDs, videos, and books, including a large selection of Louisiana music and books.

Novelties & Gifts

No place like the French Quarter provides a novel view of life and its array of shops celebrating it. In each, the ambience alone is worth the price of admission.

Café Havana (⊠ 842 Royal St., French Quarter ☎ 504/569–9006 or 800/860–2988 ⊕ www.cafehavana.com) sells pipes, tobacco, and other accessories and operates a coffee bar.

Coghlan Gallery (⊠ 710 Toulouse St., French Quarter ☎ 504/525–8550), housed in the historic Lion's Court, has a peaceful courtyard with displays of locally crafted fountains, statuary, and other garden accessories.

Community Flea Market (⊠ Governor Nicholls St., in the French Market, French Quarter ☎ 504/596–3420 ⊕ www.frenchmarket.org) is an open-air market with dozens of vendors selling jewelry, clothing, leather goods, art, CDs, and local crafts. Typically, the market is open daily 7 AM–8 PM, but hours can vary, depending on the weather and season.

Crafty Louisianians (⊠ 523 Dumaine St., French Quarter ☎ 504/528–3094) resembles a down-home crafts fair thanks to its variety of work from more than 70 New Orleans and Louisiana artists. The pottery, paintings, woven baskets, and carved ducks and birds are first-rate.

Esoterica Occult Goods (⊠ 541 Dumaine St., French Quarter ☎ 504/581–7711 ⊕ www.onewitch.com) specializes in "Tools of the Occult Arts and Sciences," such as gris-gris, potions, and books on the occult. The shop also gives tarot readings and holds past-life regressions and astrological consultations.

French Market Gift Shop (⊠ 824 Decatur St., French Quarter ☎ 504/522–6004) presents a colorful and appealing display of accents, New Orleans mementos, and Louisiana crafts.

The Idea Factory (⊠ 838 Chartres St., French Quarter ☎ 504/524–5195 ⊕ www.ideafactoryneworleans.com) excels at what they call "wood graphics"—carving your name, company logo, or hobby into a freestanding piece. The store also carries clever wooden toys, hand-carved board games, and puzzle boxes.

Importicos (⊠ 736 Royal St., French Quarter ☎ 504/523–0306 ⊕ www.importicos.com) is a rich source for textiles, folk art, jewelry, clothing, and other wares from all over the world, with particular emphasis on Indonesia, Mexico, and Bali. The Magazine Street site is the "home and garden" store.

Royal Cameo Glass (✉ 636 Royal St., French Quarter ☎ 504/522–7840 ⊕ www.royalcameo.com) speaks to the lover of studio glass. Find Lotton art glass, cameo glass, and an impressive selection of pieces by American studio glass artists.

Santa's Quarters (✉ 1025 Decatur St., French Quarter ☎ 504/581–5820 or 800/262–8717) is crammed with holiday decorations in all price ranges. They're especially good on pieces that weave in New Orleans with Christmas.

Sigle's Historic New Orleans Metal Craft (✉ 935 Royal St., French Quarter ☎ 504/522–7647) sells original cast-iron wall planters, handcrafted since 1938; these are often seen on Quarter balconies and patios.

Perfumes

Lacing your way through the French Quarter's narrow streets, you are likely to catch a whiff of an exotic scent on one corner only to have it replaced with another a block away. Something is always blooming and the resident perfume shops have perfected the bottling of that elusive air quality.

Bourbon French Parfums (✉ 815 Royal St., French Quarter ☎ 504/522–4480 ⊕ www.neworleansperfume.com) has been custom-blending fragrances since 1843. Among its more than 30 signature scents for women is Kus Kus, a soft powdery scent of 84 oils; for men, the Eau de Cologne is a fresh citrus blend of a 200-year-old formula attributed to Napoléon Bonaparte.

FodorśChoice
★ **Hové Parfumeur, Ltd.** (✉ 824 Royal St., French Quarter ☎ 504/525–7827) creates and manufactures fine fragrances for men and women. Oils, soaps, sachets, and potpourri are made to order on the premises. You can cherry-pick from among a number of "house" favorites such as Tea Olive, the essence of the sweet-olive flower that envelopes the city on hot steaming nights, or Vetivert, extracted from the root that grows throughout the city.

Toys

Do not be deceived by the "grown-up" impression that toys are for children only. Shopkeepers are well aware of the playful side of adults and cater to that common denominator in all of us. Whether showcasing primped and pampered dolls or battalions of tiny military soldiers, the toy stores are flights of youthful fantasy for all ages.

Ginja Jar (✉ 611 Royal St., French Quarter ☎ 504/523–7643) has a large collection of porcelain and Madame Alexander dolls, as well as cuddly bears in mohair and fur, and hand-carved walking sticks.

Le Petit Soldier Shop (✉ 528 Royal St., French Quarter ☎ 504/523–7741 ⊕ www.lepetitsoldiershop.com) stocks whole armies, from sword- and spear-wielding ancient Roman and Greek soldiers to Desert Storm troopers with machine guns. Each toy soldier is beautifully crafted and hand-painted.

Little Toy Shoppe (✉ 900 Decatur St., French Quarter ☎ 504/522–6588 ✉ 513 St. Ann St., French Quarter ☎ 504/523–1770) carries Madame Alexander dolls in a dozen different series, as well as miniature die-cast metal cars celebrating the decades of automotive progress from the 1932 Model-T to the 2000 Hummer. **Oh Susannah** (✉ 518 St. Peter St., French Quarter ☎ 504/586–8701) showcases pricey collector's dolls, including those from Annette Hinestedt and Hildegard Gunzel. Dolls of all types are ubiquitous in the French Quarter, but this shop has the edge.

CBD & Warehouse District

Amid the high-tech and boutique hotels that fill the CBD, you'll find tony shopping malls, middle- and high-end chain stores, and the occasional artisan's studio. Nearby, in the heart of the Warehouse District, art and crafts galleries line Julia Street, the premier avenue of the arts for New Orleans, and spill over into the adjoining streets.

Canal Place (✉ 333 Canal St., CBD ☎ 504/522–9200 ⊕ www. theshopsatcanalplace.com), at the river end of Canal Street and the edge of the French Quarter, is a beehive of activity with more than 60 shops that include Saks Fifth Avenue, Gucci, Williams-Sonoma, the Pottery Barn, Banana Republic, Ann Taylor, and Brooks Brothers. **New Orleans Centre** (✉ 1400 Poydras St., CBD ☎ 504/568–0000 ⊕ www.neworleanscentre.com), which adjoins the Superdome and the Hyatt Regency hotel, houses more than 65 shops, including Macy's, Gap, and Lord & Taylor. **Riverwalk Marketplace** (✉ 1 Poydras St., Warehouse District ☎ 504/522–1555 ⊕ www.riverwalkmarketplace.com), along the riverfront, has a ½-mi-long marketplace with 140 local (including Café du Monde) and chain shops and restaurants such as Gap, Banana Republic, and Victoria's Secret.

Art & Crafts Galleries

Galleries are a growth industry in New Orleans, especially in and around the Julia Street corridor. Coordinated art openings are held the first Saturday of each month, with galleries staying open until 9 or 10 PM, most serving wine and cheese. Check out the daily newspaper and other local publications for special events. Brochures with maps of the Warehouse Arts District are available in most hotels and other public spots. Most galleries are open Tuesday–Saturday 10–5, but some are open on Monday as well. It's best to call to confirm a gallery's opening and closing times.

Ariodante (✉ 535 Julia St., Warehouse District ☎ 504/524–3233) has elegant, custom-made display cases in which the gallery sets forth its high-end contemporary crafts. But even the best items—the beautiful glass, for example—are reasonably priced. Almost everything here—bowls, jewelry, vases, and more—is both beautiful and practical. **Arthur Roger Gallery** (✉ 432 Julia St., Warehouse District ☎ 504/522–1999 ⊕ www.artroger.com) represents many fine contemporary Louisiana artists, including Lin Emery, Jacqulyn Bishop, and Willy Birch, and has a national profile as well, with glass artist Dale Chihuly and filmmaker-photographer John Waters. Shows are often provocative and imaginative. **The Contemporary Arts Center** (✉ 900 Camp St., Warehouse District ☎ 504/523–1216 ⊕ www.cacno.org), although not on Julia Street it-

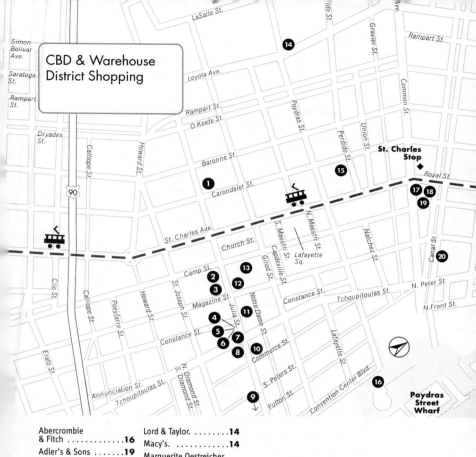

CBD & Warehouse District Shopping

self, is the mother of all Warehouse District galleries, with a spectacular lobby. The CAC is focusing more and more on local and regional artists, while not neglecting national trends. The Cyber Bar & Café here can cure temporary gallery-hopping exhaustion.

George Schmidt Gallery (✉ 626 Julia St., Warehouse District ☎ 504/592–0206 ⊕ www.georgeschmidt.com) is a one-of-a-kind showplace for the works of George Schmidt, who creates shows of "history painting, narrative art, and other reactionary works on canvas and paper." From small-scale monotypes to mural-size depictions of historic moments, his work captivates with the scope of its subjects and its attention to detail.

Heriard-Cimino Gallery (✉ 440 Julia St., Warehouse District ☎ 504/525–7300 ⊕ www.heriard-cimino.com) shows contemporary artists with minimalist sensibilities, including photographers, painters, and sculptors.

Jonathan Ferrara Gallery (✉ 841 Carondelet St., Warehouse District ☎ 504/522–5471 ⊕ www.jonathanferraragallery.com) reflects the owner's open fervent attitude toward art, eagerly seeking out the new and the unexpected. It's one of the few New Orleans galleries that embraces installation art. Opening-night parties are legendary, with music and performance art.

LeMieux Gallery (✉ 332 Julia St., Warehouse District ☎ 504/522–5988 ⊕ www.lemieuxgalleries.com) is distinguished by what its director refers to as "Third-Coast Art," the work of artists along the Gulf Coast from Louisiana to Florida. It displays both fine arts and crafts from these artists and also represents the works of the late Paul Ninas, one of New Orleans's finest abstract artists.

Marguerite Oestreicher Fine Art (✉ 720 Julia St., Warehouse District ☎ 504/581–9253) packs a punch in a small space. The gallery seeks out some of the most interesting painters and sculptors from around the country. The enthusiastic staff assists the owner in assembling contemporary art with a difference: you can always count on being amused or challenged—or both—by what you see on these walls.

New Orleans School of Glassworks and Printmaking Studio (✉ 727 Magazine St., Warehouse District ☎ 504/529–7277 ⊕ www.neworleansglassworks.com) is the South's largest glassblowing and printmaking studio. Here you'll find imaginative glass—both practical and art pieces—as well as metal sculptures. You may have the opportunity to view glassblowers at work.

★ **Steve Martin Studio** (✉ 624 Julia St., Warehouse District ☎ 504/566–1390 ⊕ www.stevemartinstudio.com) showcases the artist-owner's romantic wire sculptures. Among the gallery's other artists, painters Ashley Longshore and John Kaine and sculptor Scott Gentry are important emerging regional artists.

Sylvia Schmidt Gallery (✉ 400 Julia St., Warehouse District ☎ 504/522–2000) represents some of the finest contemporary realist painters of the region and has an inclination for the whimsical, especially in the work of Louisiana artists Robert Warrens and Sibylle Peretti.

Books

Deville Books (✉ 344 Carondelet St., CBD ☎ 504/525–1846) is a charming old-fashioned bookstore with plenty of browsing room, a super-knowledgable staff, and a special expertise in New Orleans and southern literature.

Clothing

Abercrombie & Fitch (⊠ Riverwalk Marketplace, Warehouse District ☎ 504/522–7156 ⊕ www.abercrombie.com) carries sportswear and casual clothes popular with Gen X crowds.

Banana Republic (⊠ Canal Place, CBD ☎ 504/581–2478 ⊕ www.bananarepublic.com) displays stylish, tailored casual wear.

Brooks Brothers (⊠ Canal Place, CBD ☎ 504/522–4200 ⊕ www.brooksbrothers.com) is internationally known for classic tailored clothing for men; you'll find women's wear here, too.

Clarks (⊠ Riverwalk Marketplace, Warehouse District ☎ 504/568–0070 ⊕ www.clarksusa.com) specializes in the comfort-first footwear of the British Clarks line and also carries other easy-on-the-foot brands such as Ecco.

Gap (⊠ Riverwalk Marketplace, Warehouse District ☎ 504/529–4962 ⊕ www.gap.com) and its siblings **GapKids** and **Baby Gap** (⊠ Riverwalk Marketplace, Warehouse District ☎ 504/522–5828) are great places to shop for comfortable, straightforward fashions for infants, children, and young adults.

Meyer the Hatter (⊠ 120 St. Charles Ave., CBD ☎ 504/525–1048 or 800/882–4287 ⊕ www.meyerthehatter.com) is the lollapalooza of hats. Open since 1894, the cluttered, friendly shop is primarily known for men's hats but has a few women's, too. Dress hats are here in profusion along with fun Kangols and tweedy caps.

Rubenstein Brothers (⊠ 102 St. Charles Ave., CBD ☎ 504/581–6666 ⊕ www.rubensteinsfashion.com) is the premier men's clothing store in New Orleans and also has a women's shop. Labels include Brioni, Zegna, Burberry, Prada, Bruno Magli, Valentino, and Missoni.

The Walking Co. (⊠ Riverwalk Marketplace, Warehouse District ☎ 504/522–9255 ⊕ www.walkingco.com) is all about comfortable shoes, preferably with a bit of style. In addition to Birkenstock, Timberland, Mephisto, and other brands, the shop also carries canvas hats, hiking staffs, and folding canes.

Department Stores

Lord & Taylor (⊠ New Orleans Centre, CBD ☎ 504/581–5673) sells designer and casual clothes with a classic look for men, women, and children, and carries other department-store fare.

Macy's (⊠ New Orleans Centre, CBD ☎ 504/592–5985 ⊕ www.macys.com) covers three floors with an emphasis on clothing, accessories, and housewares.

Food

★ **Creole Delicacies & Cookin' Cajun** (⊠ Riverwalk Marketplace, Warehouse District ☎ 504/523–6425 or 800/523–6425 ⊕ www.cookincajun.com) sells New Orleans and Louisiana spices, mixes, cookbooks, and cookware up front and dispenses two-hour cooking classes in the back. A great place for cooks and aspiring cooks.

Godiva Chocolatiers (⊠ Riverwalk Marketplace, Warehouse District ☎ 504/522–1269 ⊕ www.godiva.com) is renowned the world over for its elegantly shaped and packaged chocolates, even if they aren't a local specialty.

Furniture & Home Furnishings

Christopher Maier Studio (✉ 329 Julia St., Warehouse District ☎ 504/586–9079 ⊕ www.christophermaier.com) showcases the work of the distinguished local furniture maker. Maier's sleek modern furniture is inspired by historic, mythological, or regional ideas. Some of his armoires resemble the aboveground tombs in the city's cemeteries. His workshop is on the premises.

Ray Langley Interiors (✉ 434 Julia St., Warehouse District ☎ 504/522–2284) is "Truth or Dare" land. Are you ready for the Madonna lifestyle? Do you want to pretend that you live in one of the trendy South Beach hotels in Miami? Ray Langley can provide you with oversize furniture in outrageous colors, and accessories to boot. You'll probably find it hard to resist.

Gifts

Rapp's Luggage and Gifts (✉ 604 Canal St., CBD ☎ 504/568–1953) is a locally owned variety store specializing in fine leather goods and unusual gift items such as a briefcase that serves as a portable bar.

Riverwalk Marketplace (✉ 1 Poydras St., Warehouse District ☎ 504/522–1555 ⊕ www.riverwalkmarketplace.com) has dozens of specialty shops with dazzling displays of toys, crafts, cards, and curios. Look for **Masks and Make Believe, It's a Dog's World,** and the **New Orleans Cathouse.**

Jewelry

Adler's (✉ 722 Canal St., CBD ☎ 504/523–5292) is a branch of the New Orleans jewelry store noted for watches, engagement rings, wedding presents, and top-of-the-line silver.

Bernard K. Passman Gallery (✉ Riverwalk Marketplace, 1 Poydras St., Warehouse District ☎ 504/525–4581 ⊕ www.passman.com) displays black-coral jewelry crafted by the eponymous artist.

Magazine Street

Magazine Street is one of the oldest and most diverse shopping districts in New Orleans, second only to the French Quarter. Named for the French word for shop—*magasin*—this street runs parallel to St. Charles Avenue (although several blocks are closer to the river) and passes through old established neighborhoods. Along Magazine Street's 6 mi, from Canal Street to Carrollton, you can find dozens of intriguing antiques and jewelry shops, bric-a-brac vendors, vintage and handmade children's clothing stores, and art galleries. The district is primarily known for its antiques, which range from museum-quality European imports to shabby-chic 1950s furniture.

Shops tend to come in clumps along the route, from Felicity Street to Nashville Avenue. The main stretch of shops begins at the intersection of Melpomene and Magazine streets. The No. 11 Magazine Street bus runs there from Canal Street, and the St. Charles streetcar stops within blocks of this shopping district. The best and safest way to shop on Magazine Street is by car; the sections between the cluster of shops can be somewhat unsafe for those not familiar with the area.

Almost all the shops are efficient at shipping and will help arrange to have your purchases sent directly to your home. The **Magazine Street Merchants Association** (☎ 800/387–8924 ⊕ www.magazinestreet.com) publishes a free brochure with maps and store descriptions. You'll find it in most hotels or you can request a brochure from its Web site.

Macon Riddle (☎ 504/899–3027 ⊕ www.neworleansantiquing.com) is a one-woman antiques and collectibles encyclopedia. She shares her expertise in half- or full-day shopping expeditions tailored to clients' needs.

Antiques

Ann Koerner Antiques and Interiors (✉ 4021 Magazine St., Uptown ☎ 504/899–2664) displays a great collection of 19th-century French antiques, including sideboards, chests, and chairs.

Antiques Magazine (✉ 2028 Magazine St., Uptown ☎ 504/522–2043) specializes in lighting, with some fixtures dating from the 1850s. The shop also has rare oyster plates and Victorian furniture.

As You Like It (✉ 3033 Magazine St., Uptown ☎ 504/897–6915 or 800/ 828–2311 ⊕ www.asyoulikeitsilvershop.com) sells a wide selection of discontinued and hard-to-find American sterling-silver tea services, trays, and flatware—including Victorian, art-nouveau, and art-deco pieces.

Bep's Antiques (✉ 2051 Magazine St., Uptown ☎ 504/525–7726 ⊕ www. bepsantiques.com) is a great browsing place for English tables, chairs, and sideboards.

FodorśChoice ★ **Bush Antiques** (✉ 2109–2111 Magazine St., Uptown ☎ 504/581–3518 ⊕ www.bushantiques.com) showcases antique French beds, sleigh beds, day beds, canopy beds, and religious art.

Charbonnet & Charbonnet (✉ 2728 Magazine St., Uptown ☎ 504/ 891–9948 ⊕ www.charbonnetantiques.com), where there is an on-site cabinet workshop, specializes in large mid-19th-century cupboards and chests made from Irish and English pine.

Didier, Inc. (✉ 3439 Magazine St., Uptown ☎ 504/899–7749) sells fine American furniture from the 1800s to the 1850s, as well as paintings and prints.

Dodge Fjeld (✉ 2033 Magazine St., Uptown ☎ 504/581–6930) is the place for vintage clocks. The shop also has a special affinity for antique desks.

Gloria Slater Antiques (✉ 2115 Magazine St., Uptown ☎ 504/561– 5738) carries Italian and French pieces, including armoires, decorative arts, and mirrors. The shop also stocks light fixtures and chandeliers.

Home Hook and Ladder (✉ 4100 Magazine St., Uptown ☎ 504/895–4480 ⊕ www.homehookandladder.com) has two floors of antiques in almost every category, from furniture and garden decorations to art.

Jean Bragg Gallery (✉ 3901 Magazine St., Uptown ☎ 504/895–7375) is the best source in the city for much-sought-after Newcomb pottery and George Ohr pottery.

Jon Antiques (✉ 4605 Magazine St., Uptown ☎ 504/899–4482) carries an outstanding collection of 18th- and 19th-century English and Con-

Magazine
Street
Shopping

Between Gen. Taylor St. and Louisiana Ave.

0   1/4 mi

0   1/2 km

tinental furniture; the shop is an excellent source for ironstone and porcelain, antique boxes, and tea caddies.
Latitudes (✉ 3701 Magazine St., Uptown ☎ 504/895–9880 ⊕ www. latitudesneworleans.com) carries top-quality imported Indonesian, Chinese, and Tibetan furnishings, accessories, and decorative arts.
Royal Crescent Antiques (✉ 4118 Magazine St., Uptown ☎ 504/891–5600) specializes in elegant French and English furniture, furnishings, accents, and gifts.
Stan Levy Imports (✉ 1028 Louisiana Ave., at Magazine St., Uptown ☎ 504/899–6384 ⊕ www.stanlevyimports.com) carries a massive collection of English, French, Italian, and American antiques.
Uptowner Antiques (✉ 3828 Magazine St., Uptown ☎ 504/891–7700) displays high-end French and Italian antiques from the 18th and 19th centuries.
Wirthmore Antiques (✉ 3900 Magazine St., Uptown ☎ 504/899–3811 ✉ 3727 Magazine St., Uptown ☎ 504/269–0660 ⊕ www. wirthmoreantiques.com) is devoted to French-provincial antique furniture and accessories. You'll feel that you've wandered into a 19th-century European village.

Art & Crafts Galleries
Carol Robinson Gallery (✉ 840 Napoleon Ave., at Magazine St., Uptown ☎ 504/895–6130 ⊕ www.carolrobinsongallery.com) exhibits primarily southern painters and sculptors inside a handsome Victorian house.
Cole Pratt Gallery (✉ 3800 Magazine St., Uptown ☎ 504/891–6789 ⊕ www.coleprattgallery.com) displays paintings by regional artists.
Lionel Milton Gallery (✉ 1818 Magazine St., Uptown ☎ 504/522–6966 ⊕ www.lionelmiltongallery.com) is home for the rising young artist made famous on MTV's "Real World." You'll find his vibrant hip-hop art available on canvas, posters, postcards, and prints.
Thomas Mann Gallery I/O (✉ 1804 Magazine St., Uptown ☎ 504/899–9900 ⊕ www.thomasmann.com) showcases the New Orleans artisan's high-tech-meets-romance "jewelry objects" such as necklaces, pins, earrings, rings, and sculpture.
Wyndy Morehead (✉ 3926 Magazine St., Uptown ☎ 504/269–8333) is a modern presence with painters and sculptors who aren't afraid of bold, bright colors. Painters John Torina, Eric Abrect, and James Leonard are among the gallery's best.

Books
Beaucoup Books (✉ 5414 Magazine St., Uptown ☎ 504/895–2663) specializes in fiction and local and regional titles; has a children's room; and hosts author signings and readings.
Garden District Book Shop (✉ 2727 Prytania St., Uptown ☎ 504/895–2266) stocks a selection of regional books and new fiction. Gothic novelist Anne Rice starts all her book tours here. The shop carries autographed copies and limited editions of her work.
Octavia Books (✉ 513 Octavia St., Uptown ☎ 504/899–7323 ⊕ www. octaviabooks.com) is a handsome new bookstore that invites leisurely browsing. You'll find a strong selection of architecture, art, and fiction titles.

Clothing

Funky Monkey (✉ 3127 Magazine St., Uptown ☎ 504/899–5587) mixes vintage clothing with hipster couture. Punk, 1950s, and Hawaiian-shirt trends are all here, along with a young, hip staff.

House of Lounge (✉ 2044 Magazine St., Uptown ☎ 504/671–8300 ⊕ www.houseoflounge.com) is a plush valentine of a shop that abounds in bustiers, slips, panties, hosiery, and gowns. Hard-to-find articles such as Cuban hosiery are often in stock.

Joan Vass (✉ 2917 Magazine St., Uptown ☎ 504/891–4502 or 800/338–4864 ⊕ www.joanvass.com) is the queen of American sportswear, with classic interchangeable pieces made from cotton and other soft knits.

Perlis (✉ 6070 Magazine St., Uptown ☎ 504/895–8661 ⊕ www.perlis. com) is a New Orleans institution for classic men's and women's sportswear. The shop's signature are the popular crawfish-embroidered shirts and ties.

U Topia (✉ 5408 Magazine St., Uptown ☎ 504/899–8488) carries simple unfussy linen tops, slacks, dresses, and skirts from the upscale Flax label. The shop also displays handmade furniture.

Jewelry

Anne Pratt (✉ 3937 Magazine St., Uptown ☎ 504/891–6532) creates interesting Mexican-style jewelry in silver and gold, as well as popular iron furniture.

C. Susman Estate Jewelry (✉ 3933 Magazine St., Uptown ☎ 504/897–9144) carries Magazine Street's best collection of art-nouveau and art-deco estate jewelry; the store also stocks art pottery, art glass, and collectibles.

Katy Beh (✉ 3701 Magazine St., Uptown ☎ 504/896–9600 ⊕ www. katybeh.com) is a favorite address for fashionable uptowners, who delight in the delicately embellished pins, bracelets, earrings, and pendants. Fine featherlight designs are a hallmark of the artisan.

RABH (✉ 3005 Magazine St., Uptown ☎ 504/897–0811 or 800/826–7282) displays pins, necklaces, bracelets, and other jewelry by local artisan Ruby Ann Bertram-Harker, whose designs are inspired by New Orleans culture and architecture.

Music

★ **Jim Russell Records** (✉ 1837 Magazine St., Uptown ☎ 504/522–2602 ⊕ www.jimrussellrecords.com) carries everything from early ragtime to current hip-hop. Although the shop stocks some new recordings, its glory is its endless bins of LPs, 78s, and 45s.

Musica Latina (✉ 4714 Magazine St., Uptown ☎ 504/895–4227) is owned by Honduran-born, New Orleans–raised Yolanda Estrada, whose love for all Latin music is reflected in this funky little shop.

Novelties & Gifts

Aux Belles Choses (✉ 3912 Magazine St., Uptown ☎ 504/891–1009 ⊕ www.abcneworleans.com) is a dreamy little cottage of French and English delights. Richly scented soaps, vintage and new linens, antique enamelware, and collectible plates are among the most popular wares.

Bon Montage (✉ 3719 Magazine St., Uptown ☎ 504/897–6295) carries upscale infant and toddler clothes and china, crystal, silver, porcelain, and decorative arts that make excellent wedding gifts.

Orient Expressed Imports (✉ 3905 Magazine St., Uptown ☎ 504/899–3060 ⊕ www.orientexpressed.com) specializes in blue-and-white imported porcelain, vases, ceramics, and hand-smocked children's clothing.

The Quilt Cottage (✉ 801 Nashville Ave., off Magazine St., Uptown ☎ 504/895–3791) sells quilts, including antiques and contemporary (some on the cutting edge of quilt art), and everything for the quilter, with a wide-ranging fabric selection.

★ **Relics** (✉ 2010 Magazine St., Uptown ☎ 504/524–9190) is famous for its gorgeous pillows handcrafted from vintage fabrics and deconsecrated vestments. The shop also stocks amusing advertising signs, garden decor, jewelry, and offbeat furniture.

Scriptura (✉ 5423 Magazine St., Uptown ☎ 504/897–1555) is a temple to writing, with elegant and unusual stationery, Mont Blanc pens, leather-bound journals, photo albums, and assorted paraphernalia.

Shadyside-Potsalot Pottery (✉ 3823 Magazine St., Uptown ☎ 504/897–1710) is the studio and shop of master potter Charles Bohn. All pieces are made on-site, and include raku, stoneware, and more fanciful work.

★ **Simon of New Orleans** (✉ 2126 Magazine St., Uptown ☎ 504/561–0088) has wildly colorful fantasies painted on found materials by French expatriate chef-turned-artist Simon Hardeveld. The shop also carries rustic antiques.

Two Chicks (✉ 2917 Magazine St., Uptown ☎ 504/896–8855) is the spot to shop for items unusual and witty. You'll find art to display and wear as well as can't-miss accents for the home.

Maple Street/Riverbend

This area exudes an old-fashioned, small-town feeling, where most of the shops are housed in turn-of-the-20th-century cottages. On Maple Street the shops run for six blocks, from Carrollton Avenue to Cherokee Street; in Riverbend, they dot the streets surrounding the shopping center on Carrollton Avenue. To reach both areas from downtown, ride the streetcar until St. Charles Avenue becomes Carrollton Avenue; then get off at the next stop, the corner of Maple Street and Carrollton Avenue.

Art & Crafts Galleries

Nuance/Louisiana Artisans Gallery (✉ 728 Dublin St., Uptown ☎ 504/865–8463 ⊕ www.nuanceglass.com) shows the handblown art glass of owner Arden Stewart and work by a variety of regional jewelry makers, fabric artists, and toy makers.

The **Sun Shop** (✉ 7722 Maple St., Uptown ☎ 504/861–8338) sells pottery, jewelry, Native American masks, and handwoven rugs, blankets, and quilts. For more than 20 years the proprietor has been traveling all over the United States and Central America to select handcrafted works. The shop is closed July and August.

Books

Maple Street Book Shop (✉ 7523 Maple St., Uptown ☎ 504/866–4916 ⊕ www.maplestreetbookshop.com) is a favorite with authors, who drop by to shop and trade literary news. The shop stocks a strong selection of regional books, new fiction, travel, and poetry.

Maple Street Children's Book Shop (✉ 7529 Maple St., Uptown ☎ 504/ 861–2105 ⊕ www.maplestreetbookshop.com), next door to the Maple Street Book Shop, is the best place in town for children's literature.

Clothing

Angelique & Victoria's Shoes (✉ 7725 Maple St., Uptown ☎ 504/866– 1092) is two stores in one, both trendsetters. Angelique's carries hot designers such as Diane Von Furstenberg, Nanette Lepore, and BCBG. Victoria's Shoes are equally rarified, including Jimmy Choo, Chaplier, and Jack Gomme.

C. Collection (✉ 8141 Maple St., Uptown ☎ 504/861–5002) resembles a sorority-house closet, jammed with hip, flirty clothes that make the under-25 heart soar. The XOXO, Espirit, and other similar brands range from casual to date-night dressy.

Encore Shop (✉ 7814 Maple St., Uptown ☎ 504/861–9028) has previously-owned clothes with impressive labels, including Escada and New Orleans designers who specialize in Mardi Gras dresses. It's the fundraising resale shop for the local symphony and is heavy on conservative styles and formal wear. Like those of most volunteer operations, its hours are limited, but it's worth the effort.

Gae-Tana's (✉ 7732 Maple St., Uptown ☎ 504/865–9625) is the favorite of stylish uptown mothers and daughters who love the low-slung hip-hugger jeans, linen tops, dressy skirts, and cool accessories.

Yvonne LaFleur (✉ 8131 Hampson St., Uptown ☎ 504/866–9666 ⊕ www.yvonnelafleur.com) would make Cinderella feel at home with its swirls of silk, ribbon, lace, and flowers. Elaborate ball gowns and wedding dresses hang from the ceiling like chandeliers, and tiaras have their own counter.

Food

La Madeleine Bakery & Cafe (✉ 601 S. Carrollton Ave., Riverbend, Uptown ☎ 504/861–8662 ⊕ www.lamadeleine.com) sells delicious fresh pastries, soups, salads, pastas, quiches, and sandwiches. Dine in the cheery dining room or take along sustenance for later.

P. J.'s Coffee & Tea Co. (✉ 7624 Maple St., Uptown ☎ 504/866–7031 ⊕ www.pjscoffee.com), a local chain, sells imported coffee beans and exotic teas. Pastries can be purchased in the café and enjoyed at umbrella-covered tables on the patio with cups of freshly brewed coffee or tea.

SIDE TRIPS FROM NEW ORLEANS

7

DISCOVER THE OLD SOUTH
on a day trip to Nottoway ⇨*p.203*

WANDER ABOUT THE GARDENS
at Rosedown Plantation ⇨*p.207*

FIND DAFFORD'S MURALS
in downtown Lafayette ⇨*p.213*

GET YOUR CAJUN MOJO WORKIN'
at a Saturday morning jam
at the Savoy Music Center ⇨*p.221*

TRY THE CRAWFISH CORN BREAD
at Café des Amis ⇨*p.222*

Updated by
Baty Landis

ALTHOUGH NEW ORLEANS HAS NEVER BEEN A TYPICAL OLD SOUTH CITY, the word "Dixieland" was coined here in the early 19th century. But you'll have to look way to the west of town to find the antebellum world the term conjures up. Between New Orleans and Baton Rouge, the romantic ruins of plantation homes alternate with the occasional restored manor, often open to visitors. Anyone with an interest in the history of the Old South or a penchant for a picturesque drive along country roads should wheel out to spend at least half a day along the antebellum grand route, the Great River Road.

Other popular day trips include tours of the swamps and bayous that surround New Orleans. *Bayou* comes from a Native American word that means "creek." The brackish, slow-moving waters of south Louisiana were once the highways and byways of the Choctaw, Chickasaw, and Chitimacha. Two centuries ago Jean Lafitte and his freebooters easily hid in murky reaches of swamp, which were covered with thick canopies of subtropical vegetation; pirate gold is said still to be buried here. The state has an alligator population of about 500,000, and most of them laze around in the meandering tributaries and secluded sloughs of south Louisiana. Wild boars, snow-white egrets, bald eagles, and all manner of other exotic creatures inhabit the swamps and marshlands. A variety of tour companies, large and small, take groups to swampy sites a half hour to two hours away from the city center. Everyone is placed onto a boat and guided through the still waters, past ancient gnarled cypresses with gray shawls of Spanish moss. Guides explain the state's flora and fauna and the swamp traditions of the trappers who once settled here. (For swamp tour operators, *see* Sightseeing *in* Smart Travel Tips A to Z.)

South Louisiana, cradle of the Cajun population, is decidedly French in flavor. In small communities along the coast and in the upland prairie, Cajun French is still spoken, although just about everyone also speaks English. After a hard day's work fishing or working crawfish ponds, rural residents of Cajun Country often live up to the motto *Laissez les bon temps rouler!* which means "Let the good times roll!"

If you have time for an overnight trip, you can combine a visit to Cajun Country with a trip along River Road, perhaps even squeezing in a swamp tour on the way. Just head out from New Orleans on I–10, U.S. 61 (Airline Highway), or River Road and stop at the plantations that interest you; then you can continue on to Cajun Country. You will find bed-and-breakfasts throughout the region, as well as chain hotels in the Lafayette and Baton Rouge areas.

About the Restaurants

Part of the considerable charm of the region west of New Orleans is the Cajun food, popularized by Cajun chef Paul Prudhomme, a native of Opelousas. This is jambalaya, crawfish pie, and filé gumbo country, and nowhere else on earth is Cajun food done better than in the region in which it originated. Cajun food is often described as the robust, hot-peppery country kin of Creole cuisine. It is a cuisine built upon economy—heavy on the rice and the sauces, lighter on the meats—and heavily reliant upon African cooking traditions. Indigenous sea creatures

Music

Music beats at the heart of Cajun life. Only the cuisine rivals it as an expression of this unique culture. Nearly everyone plays music at least casually, and such musical dynasties as the Cheniers, Menards, and Delafoses pass skills, techniques, and reputation from generation to generation. Ensembles of fiddles, accordions, and guitars produce eminently danceable folk music, with songs sung in Cajun French. Zydeco music, closely related to Cajun, adds washboard and drums to the mix and has more of a blues-rock feel to it. The songs are both plaintive and exuberant, describing the nature of life on the plains, swamps, and bayous. Although Cajun and zydeco music ring across the radio waves, in homes, and at some restaurants throughout the week, the weekend brings a real outpouring of musical activity. Saturday morning and afternoon are devoted to Cajun music, played in small gatherings and in bars beginning at 8 AM. Zydeco music rocks back-road barns and country clubs on Friday and Saturday nights.

7

Plantation Houses

A drive along the winding River Road provides conflicting images. The sweeping artistry of the grand plantation houses stands in the eerie shadow of massive chemical plants that operate on the Mississippi today, and plantation ruins sometimes appear in the middle of a cow field or alongside a bayou, directly testifying to this clash between old and new. The houses themselves vary greatly, reflecting the area's long history. Some are low-slung, West Indies–style structures that are relatively humble, while others are grandly columned mansions. The interiors are meticulously preserved or restored in some cases, dingy and crumbling in others. Sometimes the less pristine homes can make the fascinating histories related by the docents still more vivid.

turn up in étouffées, bisques, and pies, and on almost every Acadian menu are jambalaya, gumbo, and blackened fish. Alligator meat is a great favorite, as are boudin and andouille sausages. Cajun food is very rich, and portions tend to be ample. Biscuits and grits are breakfast staples, and many an evening meal ends with bread pudding.

Cajun cuisine extends beyond Cajun Country itself, and into many of the restaurants along River Road. North of Baton Rouge, however, in St. Francisville, more typical southern fare prevails. Here you will still find po'boys and sometimes gumbo, but barbecue is more common than boudin. (For explanations of many Cajun foods, *see* Chapter 3.)

About the Hotels

Some of the handsome antebellum mansions along River Road are also B&Bs in which you may roam the high-ceiling rooms before bedding down in a big four-poster or canopied bed. The greatest concentration of accommodations in Cajun Country is in Lafayette, which has an abundance of chain properties. In nearby towns are charming B&Bs, where friendly hosts can give you insider tips about touring the region. St. Francisville is valued as one of the best B&B towns in the South.

WHAT IT COSTS				
	$$$$	$$$	$$	$	¢
RESTAURANTS	over $30	$23–$30	$16–$22	$10–$15	under $10
HOTELS	over $150	$121–$150	$90–$120	$50–$89	under $50

Restaurant prices are for a main course at dinner. Hotel prices are for two people in a standard double room in high season, excluding 8% sales tax.

PLANTATION COUNTRY

The area designated Plantation Country envelopes a cascade of plantations along the Great River Road leading west from New Orleans, plus a reservoir of fine old homes north of Baton Rouge, around the picturesque town of St. Francisville. Louisiana plantation homes range from the grandiose Nottoway on River Road to the humble, lived-in Butler-Greenwood near St. Francisville. Some sit upon an acre or two; others, such as Rosedown, are surrounded by extensive, lush grounds.

The River Road plantations are closely tied to New Orleans culture and society: it was here that many of the city's most prominent families made their fortunes generations ago, and the language and tastes here are historically French. The St. Francisville area, on the other hand, received a heartier injection of British-American colonial culture during the antebellum era, evidenced in the landscaped grounds of homes such as Rosedown and the restrained interior of Oakley House, where John James Audubon lived while in the area.

Baton Rouge, the state capital, provides a midpoint between the River Road plantations and St. Francisville and has some interesting sights of its own. Chain hotels in Baton Rouge provide a convenient base for explorations in both directions, though the bed-and-breakfasts scattered nearer the plantations are considerably more atmospheric.

The Great River Road

The Old South is suspended in an uneasy state of grace along the Great River Road, where the culture that thrived here during the 18th and 19th centuries, both elegant and disturbing, meets the blunt ugliness of the industrial age. Between New Orleans and Baton Rouge, gracious and beautifully restored antebellum plantations built along the Mississippi are filled with period antiques, ghosts of former residents, and tales of Yankee gunboats. Yet industrial plants mar the scenery, and the man-made levee, constructed in the early 20th century in a desperate ploy to keep the mighty Mississippi on a set course, obstructs the river views that plantation residents once enjoyed. Still, you can always park your car and climb up on the levee for a look at Ol' Man River.

Between the Destrehan and San Francisco plantations you will drive through what amounts to a deep bow before the might of the Mississippi: the Bonnie Carre Spillway is a huge swath of land set aside specifically to receive the river's periodic overflow, thus protecting New Orleans, 30 mi downriver.

The Great River Road is also called, variously, Route or LA 44 and 75 on the east bank of the river and Route or LA 18 on the west bank. "LA" and "Route" are interchangeable; we use Route throughout this chapter. Alternatives to the Great River Road are I–10 and U.S. 61; both have signs marking exits for various plantations. All the plantations described are listed on the National Register of Historic Places, and some of them are B&Bs. Plantation touring can take anywhere from an hour to two days, depending upon how many houses you want to see.

Numbers in the margin correspond to points of interest on the Plantation Country map.

Destrehan Plantation

❶ *23 mi west (upriver) of New Orleans.*

The oldest plantation left intact in the lower Mississippi Valley, this simple West Indies–style house, built in 1787 by a free man of color, is typical of the homes built by the earliest planters in the region. The plantation is notable for the hand-hewn cypress timbers that were used in its construction and for the insulation in its walls, made of *bousillage,* a mixture of horsehair and Spanish moss. Some days bring period demonstrations of indigo dying, candle making, or open-hearth cooking; an annual fall festival with music, crafts, and food is held during the second weekend in November. A costumed guide leads you on a 45-minute tour through the house, which is furnished with period antiques and some reproductions. You are free to explore the grounds, including several smaller structures and massive oak trees borne down by their weighty old branches, on your own. ⊠ *13034 River Rd., Destrehan* ☎ *985/764–9315* ⊕ *www.destrehanplantation.org* ✉ *$10* ☉ *Daily 9–4.*

WHERE TO EAT   ✕ **Nelson Seafood.** Join workers from surrounding plants and other lo-
¢–$$ cals at this no-frills luncheonette halfway between Destrehan and San Francisco plantations. As you walk in the door, the various smells hint at what is ahead: the freshest seafood, grilled, fried, and boiled. Oysters on the half shell, crawfish pies, and apple beignets are also on the board. ⊠ *14620 River Rd., New Sarpy* ☎ *985/764–3112* ▤ *MC, V.*

San Francisco Plantation

❷ *18 mi west of Destrehan Plantation, 35 mi west of New Orleans.*

An elaborate steamboat Gothic house completed in 1856, San Francisco presents an intriguing variation on the standard plantation styles, with galleries resembling the decks of a ship. The house was once called St. Frusquin, a name derived from a French slang term, *sans fruscins,* which means "without a penny in my pocket"—the condition its owner, Valsin Marmillion, found himself in after paying exorbitant construction costs. Valsin's father, Edmond Bozonier Marmillion, had begun the project. Upon his father's death, Valsin and his German bride, Louise von Seybold, found themselves with a plantation on their hands. Unable to return to Germany, Louise brought German influence to south Louisiana instead. The result was an opulence rarely encountered in these parts:

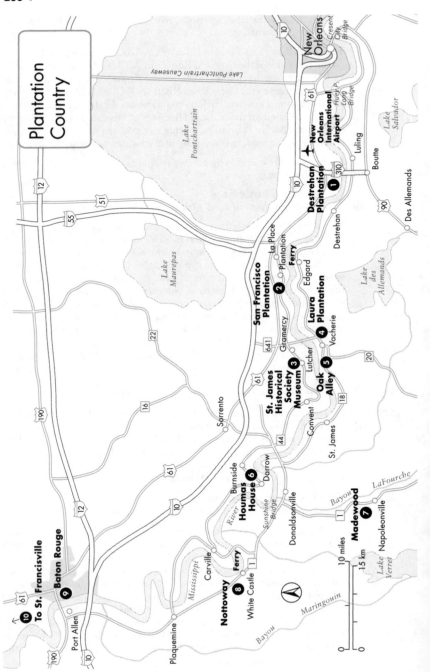

ceilings painted in trompe l'oeil, hand-painted "toilets" with primitive flushing systems, and cypress painstakingly rendered as marble. Tour guides impart the full fascinating story and more on the 45-minute tour through the main house. An authentic one-room schoolhouse and a slave cabin have been installed on the grounds, which you can tour at your leisure. Louisiana novelist Frances Parkinson Keyes used the site as the model for her book *Steamboat Gothic.* ✉ *2646 River Rd., Garyville* ☎ *985/535–2341 or 888/322–1756* ⊕ *www.sanfranciscoplantation. org* ◷ *$10* ☉ *Daily 9:30–5.*

St. James Historical Society Museum

❸ *10 mi west of San Francisco Plantation, 45 mi west of New Orleans.*

From Native American mounds to lumber mills to sugar plantations, the St. James Historical Society presents a colorful overview of the changing face of life on River Road through artifacts, photographs, and a narrated diorama of the area. Here you can learn about the local tobacco trade, trapping culture, and the blacksmith shops that were once a staple of every plantation. Spread through a cottage and a cluster of smaller cypress structures, this thoroughly charming, homegrown museum is also the best place to get information on the St. James Bonfire tradition. Around Christmas, on the weekend before the winter solstice, communities along the river torch large log tepees that they build along the levee while bands play and food is served (⇨ On the Calendar in the front of the book for more information). In St. John, St. Charles, St. James, and Ascension parishes, these bonfires have been a tradition for more than 200 years. ✉ *1988 Jefferson Hwy. (River Rd.), Lutcher* ☎ *225/869–9752* ◷ *Free* ☉ *Mon.–Thurs. 10–3 (dependent upon volunteer availability).*

WHERE TO EAT   ✗ **Nobile's Restaurant.** A restored and rather grand historic building
★ ¢–$$ houses this excellent restaurant in tiny Lutcher, near the St. James Historical Society Museum. Daily lunch specials highlight such southern favorites as smothered pork chops or turkey with corn-bread dressing. Grilled fish, homemade soups, and shrimp and oyster specials are always available. The high-ceilinged dining room draws ladies' lunches and businesspeople, though it is casual enough for families, too. ✉ *2082 W. Main St., Lutcher* ☎ *225/869–8900* ▭ *AE, MC, V.*

Laura Plantation

★❹ *8 mi southeast of St. James Historical Society Museum, 57 mi west of New Orleans.*

Nowhere else on River Road will you get a more intimate, well-documented presentation of Creole plantation life than at Laura Plantation. The narrative of the guides is built on first-person accounts, estate records, and original artifacts from the Locoul family, who built the simple, Creole-style house in 1805. Laura Locoul, granddaughter of the builders, kept a detailed diary of plantation life, family fights, and the horrors of slavery. The information from Laura's diary and the rugged slave cabins out back provide an unvarnished glimpse into the institution of slavery. Senegalese slaves at Laura are believed to have first told folklorist Alcee Fortier the tales of B'rer Rabbit; his friend Joel Chandler Harris used the stories in his Uncle Remus tales. ✉ *2247 River Rd.*

(Rte. 18), Vacherie ☎ *225/265–7690 or 888/799–7690* ⊕ *www. lauraplantation.com* ✉ *$10* ⊙ *Daily 9:30–5 (last tour at 4).*

WHERE TO EAT ✕ **B&C Cajun Deli.** This small shop and deli serves the tastiest seafood
¢–$ gumbo ever ladled into a Styrofoam bowl. Try it with a dash of hot sauce
and a sprinkle of filé, or sample the alligator and garfish po'boys. Finish with a scoop of soft and chewy bread pudding. The deli has fresh
and frozen catfish, crawfish, alligator, and turtle meat harvested from
the nearby swamps. You can buy seafood packed to travel. ✉ *2155 Rte.
18, beside Laura Plantation, Vacherie* ☎ *225/265–8356* ⊟ *AE, D,
MC, V* ⊙ *Closed Sun. No dinner.*

Oak Alley

★ ❺ *3 mi west of Laura Plantation, 60 mi west of New Orleans.*

Built between 1837 and 1839 by Jacques T. Roman, a French-Creole
sugar planter from New Orleans, Oak Alley is the most famous of all
the antebellum homes in Louisiana and an outstanding example of
Greek Revival architecture. The 28 gnarled oak trees that line the drive
and give the columned plantation its name were planted in the early 1700s
by an earlier settler, though the oaks proved more resilient than the
dwelling he must have built here. A guided tour introduces you to the
grand interior of the manor, furnished with period antiques. Be sure to
take in the view from the upper gallery of the house and to spend time
exploring the expansive grounds. A number of late-19th-century cottages behind the main house provide simple overnight accommodations. ✉ *3645 River Rd. (Rte. 18), Vacherie* ☎ *225/265–2151 or 800/
442–5539* ⊕ *www.oakalleyplantation.com* ✉ *$10* ⊙ *Nov.–Feb., daily
9–5; Mar.–Oct., daily 9–5:30.*

Houmas House

❻ *29 mi northwest from San Francisco Plantation, 58 mi west of New
Orleans.*

Houmas House, surrounded by live oaks and expansive lawns, is as pleasantly situated as any home along River Road. The house here is actually two buildings, of quite different styles, joined together. In 1790
Alexander Latil built the smaller rear house in the French–Spanish Creole style that was becoming popular in New Orleans. The Greek Revival mansion was added to the grounds in 1840 by John and Caroline
Preston, who eventually connected the two structures with an arched
carriageway. The structure is beautiful, though a recent renovation has
introduced a veneer that rather jars with the hard-earned patina gracing most of Plantation Country. With time, no doubt, Houmas House
will settle back into its own shoes. ✉ *40136 Rte. 942, ½ mi off Rte.
44, Burnside* ☎ *225/473–7841* ⊕ *www.houmashouse.com* ✉ *$20*
⊙ *Daily 9–5.*

WHERE TO EAT ✕ **The Cabin.** Yellowed newspapers cover the walls, and antique farm
$–$$$ implements dangle here and there in a 150-year-old slave
cabin–cum–restaurant. Crawfish étouffée and other Cajun seafood
dishes are specialties, but you can also choose po'boys, burgers, or
steaks. ✉ *Rtes. 44 and 22, Burnside* ☎ *225/473–3007* ⊟ *AE, D, MC,
V* ⊙ *No dinner Sun. and Mon.*

Madewood

➐ *20 mi south of Houmas House, 74 mi west of New Orleans.*

This galleried, 21-room Greek Revival mansion with its massive white columns was designed by architect Henry Howard and completed in 1854. The house, across the road from Bayou Lafourche, has an enormous freestanding staircase and 25-foot-high ceilings, and is best experienced overnight (⇨ Where to Stay): the B&B experience is magnificent. ⊠ *4250 Rte. 308, 2 mi south of town, Napoleonville* ☎ *504/369–7151 or 800/375–7151* ⊕ *www.madewood.com* ⊠ *$10* ☉ *Daily 10–4.*

WHERE TO STAY

★ $$$$

🏠 **Madewood.** Expect gracious hospitality, lovely antiques, and canopied beds in both the 21-room main house and Charlet House, a smaller structure on the plantation grounds. Guests come here for the social experience as well as the elegant accommodations: a southern dinner is shared in the formal dining room at 7 PM, preceded by a cocktail hour in the sitting room. Reserve far ahead, and expect to make new friends. The cost of a room includes breakfast, dinner, and a tour of the house. ⊠ *4250 Rte. 308, Napoleonville 70390* ☎ *800/375–7151* ⊕ *www. madewood.com* ⇱ *5 rooms, 3 suites* ⊟ *AE, D, MC, V* ⏋◯⏌ *MAP.*

Nottoway

➑ *33 mi northwest of Madewood, 70 mi west of New Orleans.*

Fodor'sChoice

★

The South's largest plantation house, Nottoway, should not be missed. Built in 1859, the mansion is a gem of Italianate and Greek Revival style. With 64 rooms, 22 columns, and 200 windows, this white castle (the town of White Castle was named for it) was the crowning achievement of architect Henry Howard. It was saved from destruction during the Civil War by a Northern officer (a former guest of the owners, Mr. and Mrs. John Randolph). Nottoway has a white ballroom famed in these parts for its crystal chandeliers and hand-carved columns. You can stay here overnight, and a formal restaurant serves three meals daily. ⊠ *30907 Rte. 405, 2 mi north of White Castle* ☎ *225/545–2730* ⊕ *www. nottoway.com* ⊠ *$10* ☉ *Daily 9–5.*

WHERE TO STAY

$$$–$$$$

🏠 **Nottoway.** The largest antebellum plantation in the South, this stunner is fun to wander around at night. You can sit on the upstairs balcony and watch the ships go by on the river. In this antiques-filled B&B, three suites come with a bottle of champagne; if you stay in the other rooms—in the main house, its wings, and surrounding cottages—you receive a complimentary glass of sherry. Mornings begin with a Continental breakfast in bed, followed by a full breakfast on the ground floor. ⊠ *30907 Rte. 405, White Castle 70788* ☎ *225/545–2730 or 866/428– 4748* ⊕ *www.nottoway.com* ⇱ *12 rooms, 3 suites* ⚲ *Restaurant, pool* ⊟ *AE, D, MC, V* ⏋◯⏌ *BP.*

Baton Rouge

➒ *80 mi northwest of New Orleans via I–10.*

Hemmed in as it is by endless industrial plants, Baton Rouge does not look like much from the road. Yet government history enthusiasts, especially those traveling with children, will want to stop here on their way through the south Louisiana countryside. Baton Rouge, the state capitol, has several interesting and readily accessible sights, including the attractive state capitol grounds and an educational planetarium. This is the city from which colorful, cunning Huey P. Long ruled the state; it is also the site of his assassination. Even today, more than half a century after Long's death, legends about the controversial governor and U.S. senator abound.

The parishes to the north of Baton Rouge are quiet and bucolic, with gently rolling hills, high bluffs, and historic districts. John James Audubon lived in West Feliciana Parish in 1821, tutoring local children and painting 80 of his famous bird studies. In both terrain and traits, this region is more akin to North Louisiana than to south Louisiana—which is to say, the area is very southern.

Louisiana Arts & Science Museum. Housed in a 1925 Illinois Central railroad station across from the Old State Capitol, this idiosyncratic but high-quality museum brings together a contemporary art gallery, an Egyptian tomb exhibit, a children's museum and discovery zone, and a state-of-the-art planetarium, which is also kid-friendly. The planetarium presents regular shows, but if you miss one, there is a miniversion in the domed "media globe" outside the theater. Call for specific times. The museum also houses the nation's second-largest collection of sculptures by 20th-century Croatian artist Ivan Mestrovic, many of which adorn the entrance hall. ⊠ *100 S. River Rd.* ☎ *225/344–5272* ⊕ *www. lasm.org* ✍ *$5; additional charge for planetarium shows.* ⊗ *Tues.–Fri. 10–4, Sat. 10–5 (planetarium 10–8), Sun. 1–5.*

Old Arsenal Museum. Only one Revolutionary War battle was fought outside the 13 original colonies, and it was fought on the state capitol grounds. These days the grounds are pleasantly landscaped, but this restored heavy-duty powder magazine, set atop a knoll beneath the towering state capitol, recalls the spot's bellicose history. The museum inside has informational exhibits in powder kegs that open and light up, displays on Louisiana's Native American history, and a giant jigsaw puzzle, which compares the grounds as they appear today with how they appeared in 1865. ⊠ *State capitol grounds* ☎ *225/342–0401* ✍ *$1* ⊗ *Tues.–Sat. 9–4.*

Old State Capitol. When this Gothic/Victorian fantasia was completed in 1850, it was declared by some to be a masterpiece, by others a monstrosity. No one can deny that the restored building is colorful and dramatic. In the entrance hall a stunning purple, gold, and green spiral staircase winds toward a stained-glass atrium. The building now holds the **Louisiana Center for Political and Governmental History**, an education and research facility with audiovisual exhibits. The "assassination room," an exhibit covering Huey Long's final moments, is a major draw. In the House chamber a multimedia show plays every hour beginning at 10:15, with the last show at 4. ⊠ *100 North Blvd., at River Rd.* ☎ *225/342–0500* ✍ *$4* ⊗ *Tues.–Sat. 10–4, Sun. noon–4.*

Rural Life Museum. This 5-acre complex, run by Louisiana State University, is an outdoor teaching and research facility. With three major areas—

the Barn, the Working Plantation, and Folk Architecture—the compound's 20 or so rustic 19th-century structures represent the rural life of early Louisianians. The working plantation's several buildings include a grist-mill, a blacksmith's shop, and several outbuildings. ⊠ *4650 Essen La., off I–10* ☎ *225/765–2437* 🎫 *$7* ☉ *Daily 8:30–5.*

State Capitol Building. Still called the "New State Capitol," this building has housed the offices of the governor and Congress since 1932. It is a testament to the personal influence of legendary governor Huey Long that the funding for this massive building was approved during the Great Depression, and that the building itself was completed in a mere 14 months. You can tour the first floor, richly decked with murals and mosaics, and peer into the halls of the Louisiana legislature. Huey Long's colorful personality eventually caught up with him: he was assassinated in 1935, and the spot where he was shot (near the rear elevators) is marked with a plaque. At 34 stories, this is America's tallest state capitol; an observation deck on the 27th floor affords an expansive view of the Mississippi River, the city, and the industrial outskirts. ⊠ *900 N. 3rd St.* ☎ *225/342–7317* 🎫 *Free* ☉ *Daily 8–4:30 (tower until 4).*

USS Kidd. A Fletcher-class destroyer, the USS *Kidd* is a World War II survivor restored to its V-J Day configuration. A self-guided tour takes in more than 50 inner spaces of this ship and also the separate **Nautical Center** museum. Among the museum's exhibits are articles from the 175 Fletcher-class ships that sailed for the United States, a collection of ship models, and a restored P-40 fighter plane hanging from the ceiling. ⊠ *305 S. River Rd. (Government St. at the levee)* ☎ *225/342–1942* ⊕ *www. usskidd.com* 🎫 *$6* ☉ *Daily 9–5.*

Where to Stay & Eat

★ $$–$$$$ ✕ **Juban's.** An upscale bistro with a lush courtyard and walls adorned with art, Juban's is a family-owned and -operated restaurant not far from LSU campus. Tempting main courses of seafood, beef, and veal dishes, as well as roasted duck, rabbit, and quail, highlight the sophisticated menu. The Hallelujah Crab (soft-shell stuffed with seafood and topped with "creolaise" sauce) is a specialty, and Juban's own mango tea is delicious. The warm bread pudding is something to write home about. ⊠ *3739 Perkins Rd. (Acadiana Shopping Center)* ☎ *225/346–8422* ▣ *AE, D, DC, MC, V* ☉ *Closed Sun. No lunch Mon. and Sat.*

$$–$$$$ ✕ **Mike Anderson's.** This lively seafood spot manages to be a lot of things to a lot of people: first-daters, families, groups of friends, and solo diners all find a warm welcome here. Locals of every stripe praise the seafood here, and it is true that the food is good, fresh, and consistent. But what Mike's does best is atmosphere. In these comfortable, subtly rustic surroundings, it's hard to have a bad dining experience. ⊠ *1031 W. Lee Dr.* ☎ *225/766–7823* ▣ *AE, D, MC, V.*

¢–$$$ ✕ **Ruffino's.** A broad clubby dining room invites long visits over the best Italian cuisine in town. Local ingredients find their way into hearty Italian preparations, such as the marinara baked shrimp and the shrimp scampi. A romantic bar area includes some smoking tables just off the main dining areas. The restaurant is a few minutes east from downtown along I–10. ⊠ *18811 Highland Rd., Exit 166 off I–10* ☎ *225/753–3458* ▤ *AE, D, DC, MC, V* ☺ *No lunch.*

$$–$$$$ 📺 **Embassy Suites.** This centrally located property has two-room suites, with peach-and-green decor, mahogany furniture, and a wet-bar area with microwave, coffeemaker, and mini-refrigerator. A two-hour cocktail happy hour and a full breakfast, cooked to order, are included in the room rate, and the service is quite good across the board. ⊠ *4914 Constitution Ave., 70808* ☎ *225/924–6566 or 800/362–2779* 🖶 *225/ 923–3712* ⊕ *www.embassysuites.com* ⇗ *223 suites ⚭ Restaurant, room service, indoor pool, sauna, steam room, bar, shop, laundry service, airport shuttle* ▤ *AE, D, DC, MC, V* ⦿ *BP.*

$–$$$$ 📺 **Marriott Baton Rouge.** This high-rise hotel has somewhat formal rooms and public spaces with traditional furnishings. The top four floors offer VIP perks such as Continental breakfast and afternoon hors d'oeuvres and cocktails. ⊠ *5500 Hilton Ave., 70808* ☎ *225/924–5000 or 800/228–9290* 🖶 *225/926–8152* ⇗ *300 rooms, 3 suites ⚭ Restaurant, room service, health club, lobby lounge, laundry service, concierge, business services, airport shuttle, no-smoking rooms* ▤ *AE, D, DC, MC, V* ⦿ *CP.*

St. Francisville

❿ *25 mi north of Baton Rouge on U.S. 61.*

A cluster of plantation homes within a half-hour drive, a lovely, walkable historic district, renowned antiques shopping, and a wealth of comfortable B&Bs draw visitors and locals from New Orleans to overnight stays in St. Francisville. The town is a two-hour drive from New Orleans, so it is also possible to make this a day trip.

St. Francisville's historic district, particularly along Royal Street, is dotted with markers identifying basic histories of various structures, most of them dating to the late 18th or early 19th century. The region's Anglo-Protestant edge, in contrast to the staunchly French-Catholic tenor of the River Road plantations, is evidenced by the prominent **Grace Episcopal Church,** sitting proudly atop a hill in the center of town and surrounded on all sides by a peaceful, Spanish moss–shaded cemetery. The smaller (though older) Catholic cemetery is directly across a small fence from the Episcopal complex.

Butler-Greenwood Plantation. This home has been occupied by the same family since its construction in the 1790s, and with much of the same furniture. This renders the house a bit musty and quirky compared to other, more showpiece-oriented plantations in the area, providing an intimate picture of day-to-day living in such a home. Butler-Greenwood is relatively modest in size, and the tour focuses on details such as dress (several items of clothing worn by the family's ancestors are on display) and china (a beautiful set has been in the family for generations). A complete set of coveted rosewood furniture, still with the original upholstery, is of particular interest. ⊠ *8345 U.S. 61* ☎ *225/635–6312* ⊕ *www. butlergreenwood.com* 🎟 *$5* ☺ *Mon.–Sat. 9–5, Sun. 1–5.*

Greenwood Plantation. The original Greenwood Plantation was built in 1830 in imposing Greek Revival style. Sadly, that structure burned in the 1960s, and the current house is largely a restoration. It is quite impressive nonetheless. The surrounding grounds comprise a working plantation that produces hay and pecans, and raises cattle. Fully furnished with some of the original antiques and portraits, the house also has a widow's walk and a 70-foot hall with silver doorknobs and hinges. It has been the location for six movies, including *North and South*. ⊠ *6838 Highland Rd. (Rte. 968), 3 mi. off Rte. 66* ☏ *225/655–4475 or 800/ 259–4475* ⊕ *www.greenwoodplantation.com* ⊠ *$7* ⊙ *Mar.–Oct., daily 9–5; Nov.–Feb., daily 10–4.*

The Myrtles. A 110-foot gallery with Wedgwood-blue cast-iron grillwork makes a lovely setting for the weddings and receptions frequently held at the Myrtles. The house was built around 1796 and has elegant formal parlors with rich molding and faux-marble paneling. The upper floor is a bed-and-breakfast, thus limiting the scope of the daytime guided tour. The house is reputedly haunted, and the fun Friday- and Saturday-night mystery tours are perhaps more of a draw than the daytime tours. The Oxbow Carriage House Restaurant, beside the house, is a fine place for dinner. ⊠ *7747 U.S. 61, about 1 mi north of downtown St. Francisville on U.S. 61* ☏ *225/635–6277 or 800/809–0565* ⊕ *www. myrtlesplantation.com* ⊠ *$8, mystery tours $10* ⊙ *Daily 9–5.*

★ **Rosedown Plantation and Gardens.** The opulent house at Rosedown dates from 1835, is beautifully restored, and nestles in 28 acres of exquisite formal gardens. The original owners, Martha and Daniel Turnbull, spent their honeymoon in Europe, and Mrs. Turnbull fell in love with the formal gardens she saw there. She had the gardens at Rosedown laid out even as the house was under construction, and she spent the rest of her life lovingly maintaining them. The state of Louisiana recently purchased Rosedown, and the beauties of the restored manor, including 90% of the original furniture, can be appreciated during a thorough one-hour tour led by park rangers. Be sure to allow ample time for roaming the grounds after the tour. ⊠ *12501 Rte. 10, off U.S. 61* ☏ *225/635–3332 or 800/376–1867* ⊕ *www.lastateparks.com* ⊠ *$10, $5 grounds only* ⊙ *Daily 9–5.*

off the
beaten
path

LOUISIANA STATE PENITENTIARY AT ANGOLA – The notorious Angola prison is a half-hour drive from St. Francisville, at the dead end of Route 66. Wryly nicknamed "The Farm," Angola was once a working plantation, with prisoners for field hands. The prison has been immortalized in countless songs and several films and documentaries, including *Dead Man Walking* and *Angola Prison Rodeo—the Wildest Show in the South*. A small museum outside the prison's front gate houses a fascinating, eerie, and often moving collection of photographs documenting the people and events that have been a part of Angola. Items such as makeshift prisoner weapons and the electric chair used for executions until 1991 are also on display. ⊠ *Rte. 66* ☏ *225/655–2592* ⊠ *$5* ⊙ *Weekdays 8–4:30, Sat. 9–5, Sun. 1–5.*

OAKLEY HOUSE AND AUDUBON STATE COMMEMORATIVE AREA –
A few miles south of St. Francisville, off U.S. 61, is the 100-acre park

where John James Audubon did a major portion of his *Birds of America* studies. The three-story Oakley Plantation House on the grounds is where Audubon tutored the young Eliza Pirrie, daughter of Mr. and Mrs. James Pirrie, owners of Oakley. The simple, even spartan interior contrasts sharply with the extravagances of the River Road plantations and provides evidence of the Puritan influence in this region. The grounds, too, are reminiscent of the English penchant for a blending of order and wilderness in their gardens. You must follow a short path to reach the house from the parking lot. A state-run museum at the start of the path provides an informative look at plantation life as it was lived in this region 200 years ago. ⊠ *11788 Rte. 956, 2 mi south of St. Francisville off U.S. 61* ☎ *225/635–3739 or 888/677–2838* ⊕ *www.lastateparks.com* ◻ *Park and plantation $2* ⊙ *Daily 9–5.*

Where to Stay & Eat

$–$$$ ╳ **Oxbow Carriage House Restaurant.** A fine dining establishment in the shadow of the Myrtles Plantation, the Oxbow is a boon to overnighters in the St. Francisville area. The dining room is elegant yet intimate, with white tablecloths and earth-tone decor. The cuisine is contemporary, drawing from a wealth of culinary traditions. Reservations are accepted for large parties only; it is best to arrive early to claim a table and your share of specials such as oysters in ginger garlic sauce and lump crabmeat, crawfish, and broccoli au gratin. The menu changes daily, following the seasons and fresh local ingredients. ⊠ *7747 U.S. 61, at the Myrtles Plantation* ☎ *225/635–6276* ▭ *AE, D, DC, MC, V* ⊙ *Closed Mon. No dinner Sun.*

★ ¢–$$ ╳ **Roadside BBQ & Grill.** Looking for southern barbecue? Here it is—ribs, pork, and chicken grilled to perfection. Most astonishing, though, are the sophisticated specials that hit the chalkboard on the weekends, such as crab cakes topped with sautéed shrimp, and rib eye topped with lump crabmeat. Right on U.S. 61, this joint is roadside in both location and connotation, complete with corrugated metal along the walls and dangerous dips in the pine floors. But with due respect to the many fine Cajun and Creole establishments nearby, this is as good a meal as you'll find in these parts. ⊠ *6129 U.S. 61* ☎ *225/635–9696* ▭ *AE, D, DC, MC, V.*

$$–$$$$ ▣ **The Myrtles.** If you don't mind a deep legacy of hauntings, the Myrtles is a pleasant and convenient place to stay, just a few miles beyond the center of St. Francisville. The guest rooms fill the second floor of the plantation house and a couple of outlying buildings. A Continental breakfast is served beside the gift shop; in nice weather, many guests opt for the outdoor tables behind the house. The fine Oxbow Carriage House Restaurant serves excellent lunches and dinners and is another good reason to stay here. ⊠ *7747 U.S. 61, 70775* ☎ *225/635–6277 or 800/809–0565* ⊟ *225/635–5837* ⊕ *www.myrtlesplantation.com* ⬳ *6 rooms, 2 suites* ▭ *AE, D, MC, V* ⦿❙ *CP.*

$–$$$$ ▣ **Barrow House & Printer's Cottage.** Along St. Francisville's historic Royal Street, these two old houses hold some of the most comfortable bed-and-breakfast accommodations in the area, with antique furnishings in most of the rooms. Breakfast is Continental; full breakfast is available for a small surcharge. A cassette walking tour of town is included.

✉ *9779 Royal St., 70775* ☎ *225/635–4791* ⊕ *www.topteninn.com*
🛏 *5 rooms, 3 suites* 🍽 *AE, D, MC, V* ⑪ *CP.*

Plantation Country A to Z

To research prices, get advice from other travelers, and book travel arrangements, visit ⊕ *www.fodors.com*

AIR TRAVEL
Baton Rouge is served by American, Continental, Delta, and Northwest.

AIRPORTS
Baton Rouge Metropolitan Airport is 12 mi north of downtown.
🛈 Airport Information **Baton Rouge Metropolitan Airport** ✉ 9430 Jackie Cochran Dr. ☎ 225/355-0333.

BUS TRAVEL
Greyhound Southeast Lines has frequent daily service from New Orleans to Baton Rouge and surrounding towns.
🛈 Bus Information **Greyhound Southeast Lines** ☎ 800/231-2222 ⊕ www.greyhound.com.

CAR TRAVEL
From New Orleans, the fastest route to the River Road plantations is I–10 west to I–310 to Exit 6, River Road. Driving time to the nearest plantation (Destrehan) is about 20 minutes from the airport. Alternatives to the Great River Road are to continue on either I–10 or U.S. 61 west; both have signs marking exits for various plantations. Route 18 runs along the west bank of the river, Route 44 on the east.

I–10 and U.S. 190 run east–west through Baton Rouge. I–12 heads east, connecting with north–south I–55 and I–59. U.S. 61 leads from New Orleans to Baton Rouge and north. Ferries across the Mississippi cost $1 per car; most bridges are free. Route 1 travels along False River, which is a blue oxbow lake created ages ago when the mischievous, muddy Mississippi changed its course. The route wanders past gracious homes and small lakeside houses.

EMERGENCIES
Dial 911 for assistance. Hospital emergency rooms are open 24 hours a day at Baton Rouge General Medical Center and Our Lady of the Lake Medical Center. Walgreens has a 24-hour pharmacy.
🛈 Hospitals **Baton Rouge General Medical Center** ✉ 3600 Florida Blvd. ☎ 225/387-7000. **Our Lady of the Lake Medical Center** ✉ 5000 Hennessy Blvd. ☎ 225/765-6565.
🛈 24-Hour Pharmacy **Walgreens** ✉ 4747 S. Sherwood Forest Blvd. ☎ 225/292-8975.

VISITOR INFORMATION
🛈 Tourist Information **Baton Rouge Area Convention and Visitors Bureau** ✉ 730 North Blvd., Box 4149, Baton Rouge 70804 ☎ 225/383-1825 or 800/527-6843 ⊕ www.visitbatonrouge.com. **Louisiana Visitor Information Center** ⓓ Louisiana State Capitol Bldg., State Capitol Dr., Box 94291, Baton Rouge 70808-9291 ☎ 225/342-7317 ⊕ www.louisianatravel.com. **West Feliciana Historical Society Information Center** ✉ 364 Ferdinand St., St. Francisville ☎ 225/635-6330.

CAJUN COUNTRY

French Louisiana, lying amid the bayous, rice paddies, and canebrakes to the west of New Orleans, has become famous in the rest of the country for its food (jambalaya and blackened fish) and music (both Cajun and zydeco). The Cajun culture dates from about 1604, when French settlers colonized a region they called l'Acadie in the present-day Canadian provinces of Nova Scotia and New Brunswick. The British seized control of the region in the early 18th century and the French were expelled. Their exile was described by Henry Wadsworth Longfellow in his epic poem "Evangeline." Many Acadians eventually settled in 22 parishes of southwestern Louisiana. Their descendants are called "Cajun," a corruption of "Acadian"; some continue the traditions of the early French settlers, living by fishing and fur trapping.

Cajun culture is decidedly rural, rooted in a spattering of tiny towns and in the swamps and bayous that wind among them. Driving from one village to the next, antiques shoppers and nature lovers alike will find bliss. Live oaks with ragged gray buntings of Spanish moss form canopies over the bottle-green bayous. Country roads follow the contortions of the Teche (pronounced *tesh*), the state's longest bayou, and meander through villages where cypress cabins rise up out of the water on stilts and moored fishing boats and pirogues scarcely bob on the sluggish waters.

Many visitors to this region are surprised to hear the dialect for the first time. Cajun French is an oral tradition in which French vocabulary and approximate grammar encounter the American accent, and it differs significantly from what is spoken in France. English is also spoken throughout Cajun Country, but you will hear Gallic accents and see many signs that read ICI ON PARLE FRANÇAIS (French spoken here).

Numbers in the margin correspond to points of interest on the Cajun Country map.

Lafayette

Lafayette (pronounced lah-fay-*ette*), 128 mi west of New Orleans and the largest city in Cajun Country, is a major center of Cajun life and lore, the "big city" in the middle of the countryside. It's an interesting and enjoyable town, with some worthwhile historical and artistic sights. The simulated Cajun villages at **Vermilionville** and **Acadian Village** provide lively introductions to the traditional Cajun way of life. Excellent restaurants and B&Bs make Lafayette a good jumping-off point for exploring the region.

Numbers in the text correspond to numbers in the margin and on the Lafayette map.

a good walk

The city's downtown (called Lafayette Centre) is an amalgam of Victorian, Acadian, art deco, and modern structures centered on the intersection of Main and Jefferson streets. The district has survived the explosive growth of suburbs on all sides and supports a lively turn-of-the-20th-century commercial section, a museum complex, and a couple of very soulful lunchrooms.

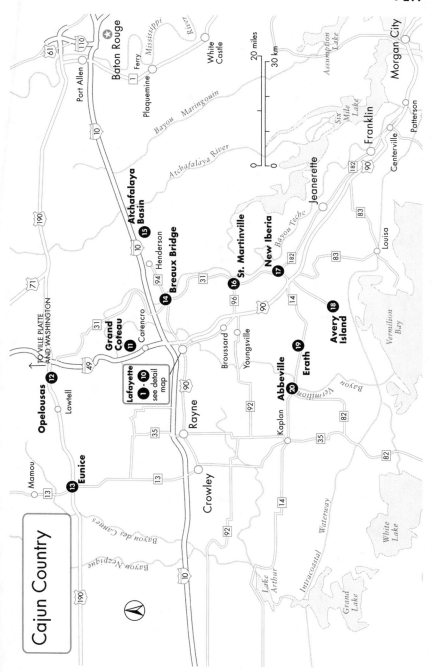

Cajun Country

Baton Rouge
Port Allen
White Castle
Plaquemine
Ferry
Mississippi River
Bayou Maringouin
Atchafalaya River
Atchafalaya Basin **15**
Henderson
Breaux Bridge **14**
St. Martinville **16**
New Iberia **17**
Jeanerette
Franklin
Morgan City
Patterson
Centerville
Louisa
Assumption Lake
Six Mile Lake
Bayou Teche
Grand Coteau **11**
Carencro
Opelousas **12**
Lawtell
Lafayette **1 · 10** see detail map
TO VILLE PLATTE AND WASHINGTON
Broussard
Youngsville
Avery Island **18**
Erath **19**
Abbeville **20**
Vermilion Bay
Bayou Vermilion
Kaplan
Rayne
Crowley
Eunice **13**
Mamou
Bayou des Cannes
Bayou Nezpique
Lake Arthur
Intracoastal Waterway
White Lake
Grand Lake

20 miles
30 km

Park on St. John Street (a quarter buys a full hour of metered street parking) and begin your walk on the northern edge of downtown at **St. John the Evangelist Cathedral ❶ ⌐**. From the steps of the cathedral, head two blocks east on Main Street to the **Lafayette Courthouse ❷**, where the clerk displays a huge collection of historic photographs. Exit the courthouse onto Lafayette Street and walk south two blocks to the **Alexander Mouton House and Lafayette Museum ❸**, with its Acadian and Civil War artifacts. Return to Convent Street and stroll two blocks east to reach Jefferson Street, downtown Lafayette's main commercial thoroughfare. Presiding over this intersection are the deco-style Le Centre Internationale de Lafayette and a glowering statue of native son and Confederate Civil War hero Alfred Mouton.

Turning left, walk along Jefferson Street. On your left in the 700 block will emerge the epic and colorful "Premier, Dernier et Toujours," a massive mural by Louisiana native Robert Dafford. Along Jefferson Street you will pass law offices, shops, and galleries, including the excellent **Jefferson Street Market ❹**. At the corner of Congress Street is the high-quality **Lafayette Natural History Museum and Planetarium ❺**, and a block farther along are two more Robert Dafford murals. Turn right onto Garfield Street, then right again onto Polk Street: here you enter a landscaped zone of the city center that harbors a fun **Children's Museum ❻** and, beyond the museum, pleasant spaces for a post-walk break.

TIMING   To see all the sites downtown, including the museums, allow several hours, including time for breakfast or lunch at one of the eateries on Jefferson Street. If you visit on the weekend, some of the municipal buildings will be closed.

Sights to See

❸ **Alexander Mouton House and Lafayette Museum.** Built in 1800 as the *maison dimanche,* or "Sunday house," of town founder Jean Mouton, this galleried town house with a mid-19th-century addition now preserves local history. The older section is an excellent example of early Acadian architecture and contains artifacts used by settlers. The main museum contains Civil War–era furnishings and memorabilia and a Mardi Gras exhibit. ⊠ *1122 Lafayette St.* ☎ *337/234–2208* ⊡ *$3* ⊙ *Tues.–Sat. 9–4:30, Sun. 1–4.*

☙ ❻ **Children's Museum of Acadiana.** Good on a rainy day or to soak up extra energy in the kids, this museum is basically a large indoor playground, with some educational games and exhibits. ⊠ *201 E. Congress St.* ☎ *337/232–8500* ⊡ *$5* ⊙ *Tues.–Sat. 10–5.*

❹ **Jefferson Street Market.** A collective of artists, artisans, and dealers fills the deep hall of this market. Antiques and mod kitsch, refined gifts and quirky artwork—this market has it all, and all generally of a very high caliber. Changing contemporary art exhibits claim the central gallery space. ⊠ *538 Jefferson St.* ☎ *337/233–2589* ⊙ *Weekdays 10–5, Sat. 10–5:30.*

❷ **Lafayette Courthouse.** The courthouse contains an impressive collection of more than 2,000 historical photographs of life in the Lafayette area. There are images of famous politicians such as Dudley LeBlanc and Huey Long working the stump and scenes from the great flood of 1927.

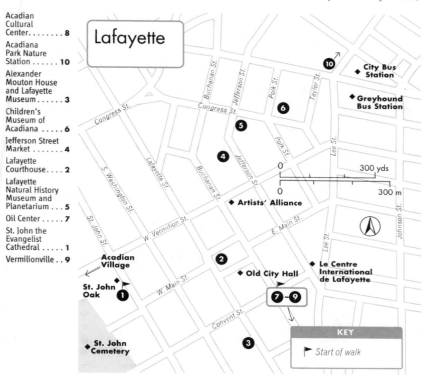

Many of the pictures are displayed on the second floor. ✉ *800 Buchanan St.* ☎ *337/233–0150* ⊙ *Weekdays 8:30–4:30.*

🐾 ❺ **Lafayette Natural History Museum and Planetarium.** Opened in 2003, this sparkling natural-history museum includes rooftop observatories, changing exhibitions, and lots of fun hands-on science for kids. ✉ *433 Jefferson St.* ☎ *337/291–5544* ⊕ *www.lnhm.org* 💲 *$5* ⊙ *Tues. 9 AM–9:30 PM, Wed.–Fri. 1–5, Sat. 10–6, Sun. 1–6.*

Murals. There are several outdoor murals by Robert Dafford in the center of Lafayette Centre. A Cajun accordion is on the side of **Lee Furniture** (✉ 314 Jefferson St.); a Louisiana swamp scene is across from **Dwyer's Café** (✉ 407 Jefferson St.) (⇨ Dining); and splashy cars are on the **Jefferson Tower Building** (✉ 556 Jefferson St.). The microcosm of Lafayette inside the garage at Parc Auto du Centre Ville, at the corner of Polk and Vermilion streets, is the work of local artist Tanya Falgout.

▶ ❶ **St. John the Evangelist Cathedral.** This cathedral, constructed in 1913, is a Romanesque structure with Byzantine touches. Union troops encamped on the grounds during the Civil War. In the cemetery beside the church are aboveground tombs of town founder Jean Mouton, Civil War hero General Alfred Mouton, and Cidalese Arceneaux. Arceneaux is believed to be the daughter of Gabriel, the lost love of Longfellow's Evangeline. Next to the cathedral is the 400-year-old St. John Oak, one of the charter members of the silent but leafy Louisiana Live Oak Society. ✉ *914 St. John St.* ☎ *337/276–4576.*

a good drive

Outside the small downtown area, the only way to see Lafayette is by car. To the east, on the banks of Bayou Vermilion, the Vermilionville theme park and the Acadian Cultural Center provide entertaining presentations on Cajun history and culture. Acadian Village is about 8 mi away and re-creates life in the early 1800s, after the French-Canadians had fled from Nova Scotia to Louisiana.

From I–10, head south on U.S. 167, the main route connecting Lafayette with the village of Abbeville to the south. Turn right onto Johnston Street and continue into the center of town, crossing Jefferson Street and turning left ½ mi later, onto St. Mary Boulevard. Here you will pass through the bustling campus of the University of Southwestern Louisiana. Travel through four lights and turn right on Girard Park Drive (not Girard Park Clearing), which skirts the edge of Girard Park.

Beyond the park, turn left on Auditorium Street, then left again onto Heymann Boulevard to enter the **Oil Center** ❼ ↱, a cluster of single-story 1950s-style offices and shops that was the original home of Louisiana's offshore oil industry.

Turn right on Oil Center Drive, then left on West Pinhook Road. Travel a mile and turn right on the Evangeline Thruway (U.S. 90). Take a left at University Avenue, which will be the first light after crossing Bayou Vermilion. Beyond Lafayette Regional Airport, on the left will be the **Acadian Cultural Center** ❽, a museum with information on all aspects of Cajun culture, and **Vermilionville** ❾, a simulated Acadian village on the banks of Bayou Vermilion.

At the entrance to the Acadian Cultural Center, University Avenue becomes Surrey Street, a winding road that passes through the working-class neighborhoods of north Lafayette. Turn left onto Surrey Street, go 1½ mi, and turn right on Louisiana Avenue. Travel 2 mi on Louisiana Avenue and turn right onto Alexander Street. Less than a mile east of Louisiana Avenue, on the left side, is the heavily forested **Acadiana Park Nature Station** ❿. You will have to park and walk 10 minutes along a path through light woods to reach the station.

TIMING   The drive can be completed in 45 minutes, but allot at least an hour each for Vermilionville, the Acadiana Park Nature Station, and the Acadian Cultural Center, and for strolling the shops of the Oil Center.

Sights To See

❽ **Acadian Cultural Center.** A unit of the Jean Lafitte National Historical Park and Preserve, the center traces the history of the area through numerous audiovisual exhibits of food, music, and folklore. Be sure to watch the introductory film, which is a dramatization of the Acadian exile. Black-and-white clips from the 1929 movie *The Romance of Evangeline* are incorporated in the film; aficionados of early motion pictures will love it. ✉ *501 Fisher Rd.* ☎ *337/232–0789* ✇ *Free* ☉ *Daily 8–5.*

off the
beaten
path

ACADIAN VILLAGE – A re-creation of an early-19th-century bayou settlement, the village is on 10 wooded acres with a meandering bayou crisscrossed by wooden footbridges. Most structures here were constructed during the early 19th century; they were moved here to create this representative "village," though they actually represent a broad range of Acadian architectural styles. Each house is decorated with antique furnishings. The rustic general store, blacksmith shop, and chapel are replicas of 19th-century buildings. ⊠ *200 Greenleaf Dr., south of downtown* ☎ *337/981–2364 or 800/962–9133* ⊕ *www.acadianvillage.org* ✑ *$7* ☉ *Daily 10–5.*

🔟 Acadiana Park Nature Station. Naturalists are on hand in the interpretive center at this three-story cypress structure, which overlooks a 40-acre park. Discovery boxes help children get to know the wildflowers, birds, and other outdoorsy things they'll see on the 3½-mi nature trail. Free guided trail tours take place every Saturday and Sunday at 1 PM. ⊠ *1205 E. Alexander St.* ☎ *337/291–8448* ⊕ *www.naturestation.org* ✑ *Free* ☉ *Weekdays 8–5, weekends 11–3.*

➐ Oil Center. This 16-square-block conglomeration of odd one-story offices and stores was the center of Louisiana's offshore oil industry for three decades. Many companies have moved to Houston or New Orleans and have been replaced by an expanding medical complex, dominated by Lafayette General Hospital. Among the offices are eateries, cigar and wine stores, and upscale shops. The **Lafayette Art Gallery** (⊠412 Travis St. ☎ 337/269–0363 ✑ Free ☉ Tues.–Fri. noon–5) sponsors permanent and temporary exhibits here, in a series of spaces through the Oil Center. ⊠ *Bordered by Girard Park Dr., Oil Center Dr., Heymann Blvd., and Audubon Blvd.*

➒ Vermilionville. Directly behind the Acadian Cultural Center, a living-history village re-creates the early life of the region's Creoles and Cajuns, focusing on the late 1800s to early 1900s. There are exhibits in 22 Acadian-style structures, including a music hall where live Cajun or zydeco music is played every weekend. A large rustic restaurant serves Cajun classics, and cooking demonstrations are held on weekends. ⊠ *300 Fisher Rd., off Surrey St.* ☎ *337/233–4077 or 866/992–2968* ⊕ *www.vermilionville.org* ✑ *$8* ☉ *Tues.–Sun. 10–4.*

Where to Eat

$$–$$$$ ✗ **Café Vermilionville.** This 19th-century inn with crisp white napery and old-brick fireplaces serves French and Cajun fare. Among the specialties are pecan-crusted tilapia and Creole bronzed shrimp. This is a favorite spot for special occasions among Lafayette residents. ⊠ *1304 W. Pinhook Rd.* ☎ *337/237–0100* ⊕ *www.cafev.com* ▤ *AE, D, DC, MC, V* ☉ *Closed Sun. No lunch Sat.*

★ $–$$$$ ✗ **Prejean's.** Oyster shuckers work in a cozy bar at this local favorite in a cypress house with a wide front porch and a 50-foot shrimp boat parked outside. People gather at tables with red-and-white-check cloths to partake of Prejean's seafood platter (gumbo, fried shrimp, oysters, catfish, and seafood-stuffed bell peppers) as well as Cajun rack of elk, American buffalo au poivre, and steak and chicken prepared in various ways.

There's live Cajun music, and usually dancing, nightly. ⊠ *3480 U.S. I–49 N* ☎ *337/896–3247* ⊕ *www.prejeans.com* ▤ *AE, D, DC, MC, V.*

$$–$$$ ✕ **Charley G's.** This chic yet friendly seafood grill is a popular spot for locals seeking a creative and delicious bite. Charley G's is famous for the duck and andouille gumbo, grilled fish, crab cakes, and soft-shell crabs. Desserts are divine. ⊠ *3809 Ambassador Caffery Pkwy.* ☎ *337/ 981–0108* ⊕ *www.charleygs.com* ▤ *AE, DC, MC, V* ⊙ *Closed Sun.*

¢–$ ✕ **Dwyer's Café.** People jam this diner as early as 5 AM for hot biscuits and grits. Dwyer's serves red beans and rice, jambalaya, pot roast, burgers, and omelets, and has been going strong since 1927. ⊠ *323 Jefferson St.* ☎ *337/235–9364* ▤ *AE, MC, V* ⊙ *No dinner.*

¢–$ ✕ **T-Coon's Café.** This lively diner serves hearty (half orders are recommended) Cajun lunches such as smothered rabbit or stuffed pork chops with two vegetables, rice, and gravy. Locals gather in the back room for conversation, jokes, and raucous songs in French. ⊠ *740 Jefferson St.* ☎ *337/232–3803* ▤ *AE, MC, V* ⊙ *Closed weekends. No dinner.*

Where to Stay

$–$$$$ ▦ **Lafayette Hilton & Towers.** Mirrored pillars and medieval tapestries fill the ballroom-size lobby, and guest rooms seem only slightly smaller. Traditional furnishings outfit the standard rooms; rooms on concierge floors come with hot tubs and wet bars. Riverside rooms of this high-rise overlook the Bayou Vermilion, though the hotel is on a heavily commercialized strip. ⊠ *1521 W. Pinhook Rd., 70503* ☎ *337/235–6111 or 800/332–2586* ⊜ *337/237–6313* ⊕ *www.hilton.com* ⟿ *327 rooms* ⌂ *Restaurant, pool, gym, bar, concierge floor, airport shuttle, helipad* ▤ *AE, D, DC, MC, V.*

★ $$–$$$ ▦ **Bois des Chênes Inn.** This B&B is housed in the 19th-century Mouton Plantation. An upstairs suite can accommodate five, and has early Acadian antiques; downstairs, the Louisiana Empire Suite has a queen-size bed, and the Victorian Suite a double bed. Breakfast is prepared by proprietress Marjorie Voorhies, and her husband, Coerte Voorhies, conducts unusually informative boat tours through the surrounding swamps. A complimentary glass of wine and a tour through the home is included in the room rate. ⊠ *338 N. Sterling St., 70501* ☎ *337/233–7816* ⊕ *www.boisdeschenes.com* ⟿ *3 rooms* ▤ *AE, MC, V* ⦿ *BP.*

$$ ▦ **T'Frere's House.** Built in 1880 of native cypress and handmade bricks, "little brother's house" has been a B&B since 1985. About 2 mi south of the Oil Center, the Acadian-style house with Victorian trim is furnished with French and Louisiana antiques. Additional accommodations are in an Acadian-style cottage behind the main house. You are greeted with a complimentary "T'julep" and "Cajun canapés," hors d'oeuvres made with boudin. ⊠ *1905 Verot School Rd., 70508* ☎ *337/984–9347 or 800/984–9347* ⊕ *www.tfreres.com* ⟿ *6 rooms* ▤ *AE, D, MC, V* ⦿ *BP.*

Nightlife & the Arts

NIGHTLIFE Pick up a copy of the *Times of Acadiana* or the trendier *Independent* to find listings for *fais-do-dos*, zydeco dances, and other events. These free weeklies are available in hotels, restaurants, and shops.

CAJUN & ZYDECO MUSIC

IT'S 9 AM on a typical Saturday morning in the Cajun prairie town of Mamou, and Fred's Lounge (⇨ Nightlife and the Arts in Eunice) is already so full that people are spilling out the door. Inside, Cajun singer Donald Thibodeaux gets a nod from the radio announcer, squeezes his accordion, and launches into a bluesy rendition of "Pine Grove Blues." Oblivious to the posted warning, THIS IS NOT A DANCEHALL, the packed bar begins to roil. Fred's Lounge may not be a "formal" dance hall, but plenty of dancing is done here; it gets especially lively during Mamou's Mardi Gras and Fourth of July celebrations. And every Saturday morning for more than 40 years, live Cajun radio shows have been broadcast from the late Fred Tate's lounge. Cajuns who have chank-a-chanked late Friday night pack into Fred's on Saturday morning, waltzing around the ropes and keeping Tante Sue, the feisty bartender, very busy. Things get revved up at 8 AM and keep going till 1 PM, and the show is aired on Ville Platte's KVPI radio (1250 AM).

You needn't be a detective to find indigenous music in south Louisiana. Just spin the radio dial, or roll down your window while driving past an old bar on some country road, and you are likely to hear the wheeze of a Cajun accordion or the scrape of spoons on a zydeco rubboard.

Music has been an integral expression of Cajun culture since early Acadian immigrants unpacked string instruments and gathered in homes for singing and socializing. With the growth of towns, these house parties—called fais-do-dos (pronounced fay-doh-doh, from "go to sleep" in French)—were supplanted by dance halls. Accordions, steel guitars, and drums were added and amplified to be heard over the noise of crowded barrooms. The term fais-do-do comes from words mothers murmured to put their babies to sleep while the fiddlers tuned up before a dance.

Cajun music went through some lean years in the 1940s and '50s when the state attempted to eradicate the use of the Cajun-French language, but today folks of all ages can enjoy Cajun music at street festivals and restaurants such as Randol's, Prejean's, and Mulate's, which serve equal portions of seafood and song. These places not only provide an opportunity for the music and dance tradition to be passed on to a new generation but also serve as magnets for Cajun dance enthusiasts from around the world.

Zydeco, the dance music of rural African-Americans of south Louisiana, is closely related to Cajun music, but with a slightly harder, rock-influenced edge. The best place to find the music is in one of the roadside dance halls where it is played on the weekends. Modern zydeco and Cajun music are both accordion-based, but zydeco tends to be faster and incorporate heavy percussion and electric instruments; electric guitars and washboards (called a frottoir), largely absent from Cajun music, are staples of zydeco. Zydeco bands often play soul- and rhythm and blues–inflected tunes sung in Creole French.

Whatever music you find in Cajun Country, you can expect a warm welcome and a full dance floor. South Louisiana music is dance music, and many visitors are surprised when there is no applause. Appreciation is best shown in lively two-stepping and waltzes. Dance is the universal language of Cajun Country, but don't worry if you're not fluent; there is always someone happy to lead you around the floor and leave you feeling like a local.

Major concerts are held at the **Cajundome** (✉ 444 Cajundome Blvd. ☎ 337/265–2200). The **Heymann Performing Arts Center** (✉ 1373 S. College Rd. ☎ 337/291–5540) hosts concerts and theatrical productions of all types.

On Friday evening from April through June and September through November, **Downtown Alive!** (✉ Jefferson St. at Main St. ☎ 337/291–5566 ⊕ www.downtownalive.org) draws dancing crowds to downtown Lafayette, where bands play on an open-air stage. **El Sid–o's** (✉ 1523 N. St. Antoine ☎ 337/235–0647) is a family-run zydeco club with music on the weekends. Sid Williams manages the club while his brother's band, Nathan and the Zydeco Cha-Chas, performs frequently.

Grant Street Dance Hall (✉ 113 W. Grant St. ☎ 337/237–8513 ⊕ www. grantstreetdancehall.com) is a large venue hosting roots and rock-and-roll music by local and touring bands. **Randol's** (✉ 2320 Kaliste Saloom Rd. ☎ 337/981–7080 or 800/962–2586), a good Cajun restaurant, also has music and dancing nightly.

FESTIVALS   The biggest bash in this neck of the woods is the **Courir de Mardi Gras** (February or March), which showcases colorful parades and King Gabriel and Queen Evangeline. For information, contact the Lafayette Convention and Visitors Commission (☎ 337/232–3808 or 800/346–
★   1958). Lafayette's **Festival International de Louisiane** (✉ Box 4008, 70502 ☎ 337/232–8086), which takes place on the last weekend of April, is a free music festival, rivaling the Jazz Fest in New Orleans, that fills the streets with entertainers, artisans, and chefs from French-speaking nations and communities. The annual **Festival Acadiens** is a huge music-and-food fest in Lafayette, held the third weekend in September. For information, contact the **Lafayette Convention and Visitors Commission** (☎ 337/232–3808 or 800/346–1958).

Shopping

ANTIQUES   A cooperative of vendors sells antiques, as well as works by local artists and craftspeople in **Jefferson Street Market** (✉ 538 Jefferson St. ☎ 337/233–2589 ☉ Mon.–Sat. 10–5). Look for beautiful cypress pieces and handwoven textiles. A good browsing place is the **Lafayette Antiques Market** (✉ 3108 Johnston St. ☎ 337/981–9884), a mecca for collectors of antique armoires, 19th-century porcelain, jewelry, and art. **Ruins & Relics** (✉ 800 Jefferson St. ☎ 337/233–9163) holds 7,000 square feet of antique furniture, art, and accessories, including antique china, porcelain, jewelry, and sterling.

FOOD   The fresh French bread and pastries baked at **Poupart's Bakery** (✉ 1902 Pinhook Rd. ☎ 337/232–7921) rival Paris's best.

Grand Coteau

⓫ *11 mi north of Lafayette.*

Grand Coteau nestles against a sweeping ridge that was a natural levee of the Mississippi River centuries ago. The tiny village (about 10 square blocks) of 1,100 residents may be the most serene place in south Louisiana. More than 70 structures are listed on the National Register of Historic Places, including Creole cottages, early Acadian-style homes, and the grand Academy and Convent of the Sacred Heart. Martin Luther King Drive (Route 93) is the main thoroughfare.

A magnificent avenue of pines and moss-hung oaks leads to the entrance of the **Academy and Convent of the Sacred Heart,** founded in 1821 as the first of the international network of Sacred Heart schools, and the site of the only Vatican-certified miracle to occur in the United States. The miracle occurred when a very ill novitiate at the convent said novenas to John Berchmans, who appeared to her twice. The novitiate, Mary Wilson, was cured, and Berchmans was canonized in 1888. You may enter a shrine on the exact site of the miracle and (by appointment only) tour a museum with artifacts dating from the school's occupation by Union troops during the Civil War. ⊠ *1821 Academy Rd., end of Church St.* ☎ *337/662–5275* ⊕ *www.ashcoteau.org* ⊠ *$5* ⊘ *Weekdays 9–5.*

In one of Grand Coteau's historic cottages, the **Kitchen Shop** specializes in regional cookbooks and cooking supplies, in addition to a wide range of gifts and other merchandise. It also has prints and greeting cards by famed local photographer John Slaughter. In a tearoom, pastry chef Nancy Brewer prepares scones, cookies, and a rich torte she calls *gateau-na-na.* ⊠ *296 Martin Luther King Dr., at Cherry St.* ☎ *337/662–3500* ⊘ *Tues.–Sat. 10–5, Sun. 1–5.*

Where to Eat

$$$–$$$$ ✕ **Catahoula's.** This stylish yet simple restaurant in a renovated former dry-goods store serves ambitious contemporary cuisine prepared with Mediterranean flair, yet with Cajun roots ever in evidence. The menu changes seasonally, ensuring the freshest ingredients and preparations. Depending on the time of year, the menu includes such inventions as firm Gulf shrimp wrapped in a flour tortilla with grilled onions, poblano peppers, and feta cheese, or smoked seafood–stuffed soft-shell crab with strawberry-fig butter. The decor is spare, and highlights artistic representations of the Catahoula Hound, Louisiana's state dog. ⊠ *234 Martin Luther King Dr.* ☎ *337/662–2275 or 888/547–2275* ⊟ *AE, D, MC, V* ⊘ *Closed Mon. No lunch Tues.–Thurs. and Sat. No dinner Sun.*

Opelousas

⑫ *15 mi north of Grand Coteau.*

Opelousas is the third-oldest town in the state—Poste de Opelousas was founded in 1720 by the French as a trading post. It is a sleepy spot with a historic central square, a provincial museum, and several excellent zydeco clubs within spitting distance. At the intersection of I–49 and U.S. 190, look for the **Opelousas Tourist Information Center** (☎ 337/948–6263), where you can get plenty of information; arrange for tours of historic homes; and see memorabilia pertaining to Jim Bowie, the Alamo hero who spent his early years in Opelousas.

Nightlife & the Arts

The roads surrounding Opelousas are *the* place to catch authentic, sweaty zydeco music. Beloved **Richard's Club** (⊠ U.S. 190, Lawtell ☎ 337/543–6596) is a rural, wood-frame zydeco club west of Opelousas

OUT ON THE WATER

LEGEND HAS IT that somewhere in the Atchafalaya swamp lives a catfish more than 6 feet long. Although that "whopper" may or may not be true, what can't be disputed is Louisiana's claim to be a sportsmen's paradise. Ever since chef Paul Prudhomme blackened his first redfish caught in local waters, the secret has been out—there are plenty of fish to be had almost everywhere in Louisiana.

The **Gulf of Mexico** and its brackish-water coastal marsh region have made Louisiana famous for shrimp, blue crab, oysters, and fish. And folks are looking for much more than just oil out at the rigs in the Gulf. Whether you choose to troll around the rigs or to anchor for some casting, you'll find brag-size lemonfish, cobia, snapper, yellowfin tuna, speckled trout, Spanish and king mackerel, sailfish, wahoo, and even pompano. Many of the marinas in Grand Isle, Cocodrie, and Venice offer charter-fishing trips that include all fishing tackle, fuel, soft drinks, ice, and someone to bait your hook during the trip and clean your fish when it's over. Prices range from $200 to $500 a day depending on where you fish and the length of the trip. Trips range from four to eight hours or overnight. If you're not inclined to pay for a charter, there are plenty of piers, wharves, bridges, and jetties like those at Grand Isle State Park to give you easy access to the open water.

If you're lucky enough to be in Louisiana during the last weekend in July, you may want to try your hand at one of the great fishing events in the world, the **Grand Isle Tarpon Rodeo** (☎ 985/787–2997). Every year, records are broken in several categories, including redfish, grouper, shark, flounder, and—of course—tarpon.

If saltwater fishing isn't your thing, don't worry: there's plenty of freshwater to go around. Top spots include the **Atchafalaya Basin,** Louisiana's magnificent 800,000-plus-acre natural swampland with facilities at Lake Fausse Point State park; and **Toledo Bend Reservoir,** a 186,000-acre bass-fishing paradise lined with campgrounds, marinas, and North Toledo Bend State Park. There are numerous oxbow lakes such as **False River,** north of Baton Rouge, and **Lake Bruin,** where you can find scads of bream, goggle-eye, and perch.

Also very popular are the **swamp and gator tours.** Most tour operators offer convenient departure times (usually mid-morning and mid-afternoon) and hotel pickups in New Orleans. Most tour operators use pontoon boats, but—depending on the size of the group—a bass boat might be used. Anticipate from one to two hours on the water and 45 minutes' commute time to and from New Orleans. Prices generally range from $15 to $30 per person. Expect to see coypu or nutria, a member of the rodent family that resembles a beaver in appearance and size; egrets (a white, long-necked heron with flowing feathers); turtles; and the occasional snake. During the warmer months, alligator sightings are commonplace; many of the guides use either chicken or marshmallows to attract them. Plant life includes Spanish moss, cypress, water oaks, and water hyacinths (a member of the lily family). Swamp tours are readily available in New Orleans, Lafayette, and Houma (⇨ Sightseeing Tours in Smart Travel Tips A to Z).

For information on fishing licenses and for maps, contact the **Louisiana Department of Wildlife and Fisheries** (✉ Box 98000, Baton Rouge 70898-9000 ☎ 225/765–2800 ⊕ www.wlf.state.la.us). The New Orleans Convention and Visitors Bureau (⇨ Visitor Information in Smart Travel Tips A to Z) can provide a list of charter fishing companies.

with music most weekends. **Slim's Y-Ki-Ki** (✉ U.S. 182 ☎ 337/942–9980), a rural zydeco club since 1947, has huge industrial fans to cool down the stomping dance crowd that gathers here on Friday and Saturday nights. Plaisance, near Opelousas, holds a **Zydeco Festival** (☎ 337/942–2392) in early fall.

Shopping

For Cajun and zydeco music recordings and related products, **Floyd's Record Shop** (✉ 434 E. Main St., Ville Platte ☎ 337/363–2185 ⊕ www.floydsrecordshop.com) is well worth the drive.

Eunice

⑬ *20 mi southwest of Opelousas.*

As home to some of Cajun music's most prominent proponents and establishments, tiny Eunice lays claim to some heft within the Cajun music world. Saturday is the best time to visit: the day begins with a Cajun music jam at the **Savoy Music Center** and ends with the variety show *Rendez-Vous des Cajuns*, in Eunice's Liberty Theatre. The **Eunice Museum** is in a former railroad depot and contains displays on Cajun culture, including Cajun music and Cajun Mardi Gras. ✉ *220 S. C. C. Duson Dr.* ☎ *337/457–6540* 🎟 *Free* ☉ *Tues.–Sat. 8–noon and 1–5.*

The large **Prairie Acadian Cultural Center,** part of the Jean Lafitte National Historical Park, has well-executed exhibits that trace the history and culture of the Prairie Acadians, whose lore and customs differ from those of the Bayou Acadians around Lafayette. Food, crafts, and music demonstrations are held on Saturday. ✉ *250 W. Park Ave.* ☎ *337/262–2862* 🎟 *Free* ☉ *Tues.–Fri. 8–5, Sat. 8–6.*

Fodor'sChoice ★ The **Savoy Music Center and Accordion Factory** includes a music store and, in back, a Cajun accordion workshop. Proprietor Marc Savoy's factory turns out about five accordions a month for people around the world. On Saturday morning, accordion players and other instrumentalists tune up during jam sessions in the shop. Musicians from all over the area drop in. ✉ *U.S. 190, 3 mi east of town* ☎ *337/457–9563* 🎟 *Free* ☉ *Tues.–Fri. 9–noon and 1:30–5, Sat. 9–noon.*

The area surrounding Eunice is the major stomping ground for an annual event, **Courir de Mardi Gras,** which takes place on Mardi Gras Day. Costumed horseback riders dash through the countryside, stopping at farmhouses along the way to shout, "*Voulez-vous recevoir cette bande de Mardi Gras* (Do you wish to receive the Mardi Gras band)?" The answer is always yes, and the group enlarges and continues, gathering food for the street festivals that wind things up. For information, contact the Lafayette Convention and Visitors Bureau.

Nightlife & the Arts

★ **Fred's Lounge** hops on Saturday from about 8 AM until 1 PM when the Cajun band strikes up and dancers take to the tiny dance floor. A regular radio broadcast captures the event. Drive north from Eunice on Route 13 to Mamou, a town so small you can drive around it in five minutes. ✉ *420 6th St., Mamou* ☎ *337/468–5411* 🎟 *Free.*

In addition to showcasing the best Cajun and zydeco bands, **Rendez-Vous des Cajuns,** a two-hour variety program, presents local comedians and storytellers and even a "Living Recipe Corner." The show, mostly in French, has been dubbed the Cajun Grand Ole Opry; it's broadcast every Saturday on local radio and TV from a 1924 movie house. ✉ *Liberty Center for the Performing Arts, 200 Park Ave., at 2nd St.* ☎ *337/457–7389* *$5.*

Breaux Bridge

★ 14 *10 mi northeast of Lafayette, 20 mi southeast of Grand Coteau.*

A dyed-in-the-wool Cajun town, Breaux Bridge is known as the Crawfish Capital of the World. During the first full weekend in May, the Crawfish Festival draws more than 100,000 visitors to this little village on Bayou Teche. Once a wild place, old Breaux Bridge has attracted a small arts community that includes renowned Louisiana photographer Debbie Fleming Caffery and has traded its honky-tonks for B&Bs, antiques shops, and restaurants.

This town of 8,000 has a Main Street (Route 31) occupied largely by antiques shops. You can pick up a city map and information at the **Chamber of Commerce** (✉ 314 E. Bridge St. ☎ 337/332–5406 🌐 www.breauxbridgelive.com), at the foot of the bridge that gives Breaux Bridge its name, about ½ mi south of I–10.

Where to Stay & Eat

★ $$–$$$$ ✕ **Café des Amis.** The culinary heart and soul of downtown Breaux Bridge rests in this renovated old store just a block from Bayou Teche. In warm weather the doors are flung open and locals and visitors gather to enjoy hospitality that is second only to the food. Sample the ambience over cocktails or coffee at the bar, or take a table and try the extraordinary turtle soup or the crawfish corn bread. Three icebox pies are served daily. Breakfast here should be savored, from the fresh-squeezed orange juice to the *oreille de cochon* (pastry-wrapped boudin), *couche-couche* (couscous-based cereal), and black java. Saturday mornings bring the popular Zydeco Breakfast, featuring a live band and dancing. ✉ *140 E. Bridge St.* ☎ *337/332–5273* ▭ *AE, D, MC, V* ⊙ *Closed Mon. and Tues. No dinner Sun.*

$–$$$ ✕ **Mulate's.** A roadhouse with flashing yellow lights outside and red-and-white-check plastic tablecloths inside, Mulate's is a Cajun eatery, a dance hall (live Cajun music every night), and a family gathering place that has been featured on many national TV programs. A dressed-down crowd digs into stuffed crabs and the Super Seafood Platter. ✉ *325 Mills Ave. (Rte. 94)* ☎ *337/332–4648 or 800/422–2586* ▭ *AE, MC, V.*

$$–$$$ Fodor'sChoice ★ **Maison des Amis.** The owners of Café des Amis renovated this 19th-century house on the bank of Bayou Teche with comfort and relaxation in mind. Each room has a private entrance and a queen-size bed covered with luxurious linens and pillows. A pier and gazebo are perfect for watching moonlight over the bayou. The complimentary Cajun breakfast at Café des Amis is not to be missed. ✉ *140 Bridge St., 70517* ☎ *337/509–3399* 🌐 *www.cafedesamis.com* *3 rooms, 1 suite* ▭ *AE, D, MC, V* *BP.*

Nightlife

La Poussière (✉ 1212 Grand Point Rd. ☎ 337/332–1721) is an ancient Cajun honky-tonk where local favorite Walter Mouton plays every Saturday. They also have live music on Sunday.

Atchafalaya Basin

⓯ *5 mi northeast of Breaux Bridge, 12 mi east of Lafayette.*

The Atchafalaya Basin is an eerily beautiful 800,000-acre wilderness swamp, characteristic of south Louisiana's exotic wetlands. Boating enthusiasts, bird-watchers, photographers, and nature lovers are drawn by vast expanses of still water, cypresses standing knee-deep in water and dripping with Spanish moss, and blue herons taking flight. The basin is best viewed from one of the tour boats that ply its waters, but it is possible to explore around its edges on the 7 mi of Henderson's Levee Road (also known as Route 5; I–10, Exit 115), which provides several opportunities to cross the levee and access swamp tours, bars, and restaurants on the other side.

Pontoon boats at **McGee's Landing** take passengers daily for 1½-hour tours of the Atchafalaya Basin. McGee's is a 25-minute drive east of Lafayette. Tour times are contingent upon the presence of at least four passengers. ✉ *Levee Rd. (from I–10, Exit 115 at Henderson; 1 block south of the highway turn left on Rte. 352 and follow it 7 mi east over Bayou Amy; turn right atop the levee onto Levee Rd.), Henderson* ☎ *337/228–2384* 🎫 *Tour $12* ☉ *Tours daily at 10, 1, and 3.*

Angelle's Whiskey River Landing (✉ 1¾ mi south of Rte. 352, on the Levee Rd. on the left) is the departure point for **Angelle's Swamp Tours** (☎ 337/228–8567 ⊕ www.angelleswhiskeyriver.com) and the site of the lively **Angelle's Atchafalaya Basin Bar** (☎ 337/228–8567). On Sunday afternoon, when the last tour boat comes in, Cajun bands play in a dance hall right over the water for the traditional Sunday fais-do-do. The music usually starts around 4 PM and attracts a crowd of fishermen, locals, and visitors. Beer and burgers are served.

St. Martinville

⓰ *15 mi south of Breaux Bridge.*

St. Martinville, along winding Bayou Teche, is the heart of Evangeline country. It was founded in 1761 and became a refuge for royalists who escaped the guillotine during the French Revolution. Known as Petit Paris, this little town was once the scene of lavish balls and operas. It's a worthwhile stop, but neighboring towns are better for dining and nightlife.

Longfellow's poem about the star-crossed lovers Evangeline and Gabriel is based on a true story. According to the oft-told tale, the real-life lovers, Emmeline Labiche and Louis Arceneaux, met for the last time under the **Evangeline Oak** (✉ Evangeline Blvd. at Bayou Teche). Louis arrived in St. Martinville, a major debarkation port for the refugees, but it was many years before Emmeline came. Legend has it that the two saw each other by chance just as she stepped ashore. He turned deadly pale with shock and told her that, having despaired of ever seeing her again, he was betrothed to another. *The Romance of Evangeline* was filmed in St. Martinville in 1929. The privately owned movie was never distributed, but clips from it are incorporated in the film presentation at the Jean Lafitte National Historical Park Acadian Cultural Center (⇨ Acadian Cultural Center *in* Lafayette). Its star, Dolores Del Rio, posed for the bronze statue of Evangeline that the cast and crew donated to St. Martinville; it is in the cemetery behind the church of St. Martin de Tours, near the final resting place of Emmeline Labiche.

Shaded by giant live oaks draped with Spanish moss, the 157-acre **Longfellow-Evangeline State Commemorative Area** has picnic tables and pavilions, a boat launch, and early Acadian structures. A small museum traces the history of the Acadians. The Evangeline legend claims that Louis Arceneaux, on whom Gabriel was based, lived in the **Acadian House** on the park's grounds, but there is no evidence that he did. The house was built in the mid-18th century of handmade bricks, and it contains Louisiana antiques. ⊠ *1200 N. Main St. (Rte. 31), ½ mi north of St. Martinville* ☎ *337/394–3754 or 888/677–2900* ☜ *$2* ☉ *Daily 9–5.*

The **Petit Paris Museum** on the church (St. Martin de Tours) square contains historical records, Carnival costumes, a video history of Mardi Gras, and a chariot exhibit. The chariots are from an annual one-of-a-kind event, the Chariot Parade—a colorful procession of wagons, made by children, that depict anything from a streetcar to a castle. The children and their fanciful chariots circle the church square beginning at dusk on the third Sunday of August. ⊠ *103 S. Main St.* ☎ *337/394–7334* ☜ *$1* ☉ *Daily 9:30–4:30.*

St. Martin de Tours (⊠ 123 S. Main St. ☎ 337/394–4203) is the mother church of the Acadians and one of the country's oldest Catholic churches; the 1836 building was erected on the site of an earlier church. Inside is a replica of the Lourdes grotto and a baptismal font said to have been a gift from Louis XVI. Emmeline Labiche is buried in the small cemetery behind the church.

Where to Stay

$–$$$ ⛳ **Old Castillo Bed & Breakfast.** In the late 19th century the Castillo Hotel, a two-story redbrick building next to the Evangeline Oak and Bayou Teche, was an inn for steamboat passengers and a gathering place for French royalists. Rooms are large and have hardwood floors, early-Louisiana antiques, and decorative touches such as marble tabletops, cheval mirrors, and pitchers and washbowls. ⊠ *220 Evangeline Blvd., 70582* ☎ *337/394–4010 or 800/621–3017* ☒ *337/394–7983* ☞ *5 rooms* ☐ *AE, D, MC, V* ⦿ *BP.*

New Iberia

★ ⑰ *14 mi south of St. Martinville.*

New Iberia is known as the Queen City of the Teche because of its proximity to the bayou and its high profile in the sugar industry. Spanish settlers founded the town in 1779, naming it after the Iberian Peninsula. The grand homes of sugarcane planters dominate the residential section of Main Street. Park downtown or stay in one of the classy B&Bs here and you can easily walk to the bayou, restaurants, and attractions in the historic business district. Downtown stretches eight blocks east and west on Main Street (Route 182) from the intersection of Center Street (Route 14). Shadows-on-the-Teche is at this intersection and is a good place to park.

The **Conrad Rice Mill** is the country's oldest rice mill still in operation, dating from 1912, and it produces a distinctive wild pecan rice. Tours are conducted on the hour between 10 AM and 3 PM. ☒ *307 Ann St.* ☎*337/367–6163 or 800/551–3245* ⊕*www.conradricemill.com* ☜*$3.25* ⊙ *Mon.–Sat. 9–5.*

★ **Shadows-on-the-Teche,** one of the South's best-known plantation homes, was built on the bank of the bayou for wealthy sugar planter David Weeks in 1834. Surrounded by 2 acres of lush gardens and moss-draped oaks, the two-story rose-hue house has white columns, exterior staircases sheltered in cabinets (cabinet-like enclosures), and a pitched roof pierced by dormer windows. Shadows, a museum property of the National Trust for Historic Preservation, is authentically restored and furnished. The lively tour includes historical tidbits gleaned from 40 trunkfuls of documents related to the home, discovered during the 1990s. ☒ *317 E. Main St.* ☎ *337/369–6446* ⊕ *www.shadowsontheteche.org* ☜ *$7* ⊙ *Daily 9–4:30.*

The tour boats at **Airboats Inc.** (☒ 11 mi northeast of New Iberia, Loreauville ☎ 337/229–4457 ☜ $20) will take you across miles of lotus-covered water to a majestic stand of 200-year-old cypresses before they skid into shallow alligator ponds. Powered by an airplane propeller attached to a car engine, airboats are faster and louder than any other tour craft and can run on very shallow water. Tours are by appointment.

Where to Stay & Eat

¢–$$ ✕ **Lagniappe Too.** Lighter fare than you'd expect in Cajun Country is served at this casual café just a block from Shadows-on-the-Teche. The owners' paintings and oversize stuffed dolls add personal touches. Fresh and spicy green salads as well as marinated chicken salad dotted with pecans and olives are great starters. Sandwiches are carefully prepared; for something richer, try the steaks and the bread pudding. ☒ *204 E. Main St.* ☎ *337/365–9419* ☐ *AE, D, DC, MC, V* ⊙ *Closed Sun. No lunch Sat. No dinner Mon.–Thurs.*

$$–$$$ ✕▥ **leRosier.** The elegant leRosier is a 19th-century house across from Shadows-on-the-Teche plantation. Guest rooms have private entrances and are in an original outbuilding. Although rooms are small and have few windows, each has a king bed; two have hot tubs. ☒ *314 E. Main St. 70560* ☎ *337/367–5306 or 888/804–7673* ⊕ *www.lerosier.com* ↩ *6 rooms* ☐ *AE, MC, V* ▯◎▯ *BP.*

$ ▥ **Bayou Teche Guest Cottage.** There could scarcely be a better way to appreciate the Queen City of the Teche than to spend a night in this refurbished 18th-century cottage right on the bank of the bayou, only four blocks from downtown attractions. You can explore the 3 acres of quiet grounds or sit in the front-porch rocking chairs and watch towboats ply the waters. The two-room cottage, which sleeps four, is simply furnished;

you can prepare meals in the kitchen. ⊠ *100 Teche St. 70560* ☎ *337/364–1933* ↩ *1 cottage* ▭ *No credit cards.*

Shopping

Books Along the Teche (⊠ 106 E. Main St. ☎ 337/367–7621), a prime destination for Louisiana bookworms, specializes in titles of regional interest. The store is occasionally visited by local literary legend James Lee Burke, whose Cajun detective Dave Robichaux prowls the streets of New Iberia and New Orleans. You will find not only signed copies of Burke's novels but also a free map of local sites mentioned in his books, paired with relevant quotations.

Konriko Company Store (⊠ 310 Ann St., adjacent to the Conrad Rice Mill ☎ 337/367–6163) sells Cajun crafts and foods. It's open Monday–Saturday 9–5.

Avery Island

⑱ *9 mi southwest of New Iberia.*

The Louisiana coastline is dotted with "hills" or "domes" that sit atop salt mines, and Avery Island is one of these. They are covered with lush vegetation, and because they rise above the surface of the flatlands, they are referred to as islands.

Avery Island is the birthplace of Tabasco sauce, which pleases the Cajun palate and flavors many a Bloody Mary. Tabasco was invented by Edmund McIlhenny in the mid-1800s, and the **Tabasco Factory** is presided over by the fourth generation of the McIlhenny family. You can take a factory tour here. The Jungle Gardens and Bird City are adjacent. ⊠ *Rte. 329* ☎ *337/365–8173* ⊕ *www.tabasco.com* 🎟 *Tour is free; 50¢ toll to enter Avery Island* ⊙ *Daily 9–4.*

Ⓒ The 200-acre **Jungle Gardens**, on Avery Island, have trails through stands of wisteria, palms, lilies, irises, and ferns. Birdlife includes ducks and geese, and there's also a 1,000-year-old statue of the Buddha. These gardens belonged to Edward Avery McIlhenny, who brought back flora from his travels: lotus and papyrus from Egypt, bamboo from China. Bird City, a bird sanctuary on the southeast edge of Jungle Gardens, is sometimes so thick with egrets that it appears to be blanketed with snow. The largest egret colony in the world (20,000) begins nesting here in February or March, and offspring remain until winter. Herons and other birds find refuge here as well. ⊠ *Rte. 329* ☎ *337/369–6243* 🎟 *Jungle Gardens and Bird City $6.25, plus 50¢ toll onto Avery Island* ⊙ *Daily 8–5.*

Erath

⑲ *9 mi west of Jefferson Island.*

The little town of Erath is a quintessential tiny Cajun village. The several rooms of the **Acadian Museum** are filled to the rafters with memorabilia donated by local folks—everything from antique radios and butter churns to patchwork quilts and yellowed newspaper clippings.

✉ *203 S. Broadway* ☎ *337/937–5468* 🎟 *Free; donations suggested* ⊙ *Weekdays 1-4, weekends by appointment.*

"Factory" conjures up images of assembly lines and high-tech equipment, but **D. L. Menard's Chair Factory** (☎ 337/937–5471) fits no such description, and the chairs made by Mr. Menard are very much in demand in this part of the country. Mr. Menard is also a songwriter, a musician (he plays the guitar and has been touring the world with his Cajun band since 1973), a raconteur, and a *traiteur*, or healer. Ladderbacks, old-fashioned rockers, stools, and Early American kitchen chairs are made by hand. The factory is a family business, with Mr. Menard's son making porch swings and his wife and daughter doing the weaving for the rush-seat chairs. Call for directions.

Nightlife

Wilbert "Smiley" Menard operates the most popular dance hall—**Smiley's Bon Ami** (✉ 2206 Rte. 14, between Erath and Delcambre ☎ 337/937–4591)—in coastal Louisiana. On a warm Saturday night, cars park on the moist meadow outside this 1950s-style hall. An older crowd fills the dance floor, gliding in the way that only the elder generation of Cajun dancers seems to have mastered. There are jam sessions on Friday and an early show especially popular with senior citizens on Sunday after mass.

Abbeville

㉑ *5 mi west of Erath, 15 mi south of Lafayette.*

Abbeville has a number of historic buildings and two pretty village squares anchoring the center of downtown. The town sponsors the annual Giant Omelette Festival each November, when some 5,000 eggs go into the concoction. At other times, oysters are the culinary draw.

You can pick up a self-guided walking-tour brochure at the **Abbeville Tourist Office** (✉ 1905 Veterans Memorial Hwy. ☎ 337/898–4264). Many buildings in the 20-block Main Street district are on the National Register of Historic Places. **St. Mary Magdalen Catholic Church** (✉ N. Main and Père Megret Sts.) is a fine Romanesque Revival building with stunning stained-glass windows.

Where to Eat

$-$$ ✕ **Richard's Seafood Patio.** Richard's (pronounced *ree*-charz) is a family-style place. It's well known in these parts for superb boiled crawfish, shrimp, crabs, and great coffee. ✉ *1516 S. Henry St.* ☎ *337/893–1693* ▤ *MC, V* ⊙ *No lunch.*

$-$$ ✕ **Shucks!** To folks throughout Cajun Country, Abbeville means oysters, and the owners at Shucks! have been serving cold bivalves longer than any of the other purveyors in town. The buttery oyster stew, spiked with oyster juice and stuffed oysters, is recommended. Oysters are ridiculously inexpensive in this part of Louisiana, and two dozen of them with a cold beer make a perfect Cajun three-course meal. ✉ *701 W. Port St.* ☎ *337/898–3311* ▤ *AE, MC, V* ⊙ *Closed Sun.*

Cajun Country A to Z

To research prices, get advice from other travelers, and book travel arrangements, visit ⊕ www.fodors.com

BUS TRAVEL

Greyhound has numerous daily departures from New Orleans to Lafayette. The trip takes 3–3½ hours because of frequent stops along the way.

🛈 Bus Information **Greyhound** ☎ 800/231-2222.

CAR TRAVEL

I–10 runs east–west across the state and through New Orleans. Take I–10 west to the Lafayette exit, 128 mi from New Orleans. The interstate route will take about two hours. If you wish, return to New Orleans via U.S. 90, down through Houma, to take advantage of many scenic stopovers. This route will take more than three hours.

EMERGENCIES

Dial **911** for assistance. The Medical Center of Southwest Louisiana has an emergency room.

🛈 Hospital **Medical Center of Southwest Louisiana** ✉ 2810 Ambassador Caffery Pkwy., Lafayette ☎ 337/981-2949.

🛈 Pharmacy **Eckerd** ✉ 4406 Johnston St., Lafayette ☎ 337/984-5220 ☼ Weekdays 7-10, weekends 8-10.

TOURS

Allons à Lafayette provides guides for escorted customized tours.

🛈 Tour Operator **Allons à Lafayette** ☎ 337/269-9607.

TRAIN TRAVEL

Amtrak connects New Orleans and Lafayette. Trains make the three- to four-hour scenic trip each way three times a week.

🛈 Train Information **Amtrak** ☎ 800/872-7245 ⊕ www.amtrak.com.

TRANSPORTATION AROUND CAJUN COUNTRY

The best way to travel around Cajun Country is by car, as other options are very limited.

VISITOR INFORMATION

The Lafayette Convention and Visitors Commission is open weekdays 8:30–5 and weekends 9–5. La Remise, the St. Martinville visitor center, is across the street from the Evangeline Oak park, just behind the church square. It's open daily 10–4.

🛈 **Lafayette Convention and Visitors Commission** ✉ 1400 N. W. Evangeline Thruway [Box 52066], Lafayette 70505 ☎ 318/232-3808 or 800/346-1958. **La Remise** ✉ 215 Evangeline Blvd. ☎ 337/394-2233.

UNDERSTANDING NEW ORLEANS

A CULTURAL GUMBO

NEW ORLEANS IS like no other place in the world. It is often referred to as the most European of American cities, but it is much more than that: start with Amsterdam, stir in some Caribbean, add dashes of Cartagena and Memphis, and you've just begun the recipe. If you become even passably familiar with the city's character and history, it will seem perfectly natural that this one culture produced people as different as Louis Armstrong, Richard Simmons, and Anne Rice.

But then, the original population of New Orleans was not exactly cobbled together on the basis of pragmatism. Soon after its founding in 1718, the fledgling French colony of La Nouvelle Orléans—a swampy, stiflingly hot outpost wrestling with hurricanes, floods, mosquitoes, and cholera and yellow fever epidemics—needed residents. French convicts were shipped over, joining volunteers from Brittany and other French provinces seeking adventure and fortune, and "working girls" were sent to marry the lot and populate the town. Native peoples mixed with former backwoods dwellers and French aristocrats. Also in the mix were African slaves, free people of color, pirates, German farmers, Italian masons, and Irish canal diggers. French Acadians, ejected from Nova Scotia when they refused to convert to Protestantism at the command of the British, wound up outside New Orleans and became known as Cajuns.

Today, traces of these roots enrich the city's heritage: Oktoberfest is observed with gusto; Cajun food and music insinuate themselves into local clubs and homes; African traditions inform jazz funerals and Mardi Gras Indian practices; the St. Patrick's Day parade is a major event (in the place of beads and trinkets, riders throw produce, particularly cabbage); and Italian New Orleanians celebrate Columbus Day and reputedly maintain ties to the Mafia. Meanwhile, Catholics, ever determined to party as hard as they pray, have provided us with the materials of New Orleans's most famous celebration, Mardi Gras.

But like every dynamic city, New Orleans nurses a feisty love-hate relationship with its citizens. The relationship is made more complicated by a circumstance whereby the very sources of discontent—crumbling infrastructure, widespread political corruption, poverty and its attendant crime—sustain the very objects of deepest love. The wealthiest districts rub shoulders with the poorest, a legacy of the once-convenient proximity of slaves' and servants' dwellings to the main house. An approaching hurricane is cause for a theme party with incautious amounts of the notorious namesake beverage. And the hottest club in town is in a shack—not a building renovated to look like a shack, but an honest-to-goodness, occasionally leaky, late-on-the-rent-payments shack. Many cities might regard vulnerability to one of the world's largest rivers, held back only by a man-made hill, as reason for anxiety and humility. New Orleanians, however, point to the Mississippi River levee as a source of civic pride.

The unpolished, haphazard, slightly seedy feel of the city has nothing in common with the sparkling American business centers that most metropolitan areas seem to idealize; visitors often regard the unkempt pockets of downtown New Orleans either with confused—and perhaps spontaneously scheming—bewilderment or with appreciative relief. Some politicians misguidedly campaign to "clean up" New Orleans or to "attract big business." Although voters might nod in unanimous support of these seemingly unassailable goals, when push comes to shove they don't really want this city to become like so many chain-infested others.

Over the years, the Crescent City (named for the crescent-shape curve of the Mississippi) has boomed and ebbed and the city's economy has gone up and down according to the vagaries of such businesses as shipbuilding and oil. Trade once brought money as goods passed through town on the way to Europe. Today the mouth of the Mississippi is nearly as valuable a tourist attraction as it is a port. And with tourism driving the city's economy, New Orleans strives to treat its visitors well.

In New Orleans you can hear some of the best traditional jazz in the world, much of it played by musicians brought up through the legacy of families who have been playing the music since the earliest years of the 20th century. Other musical genres are played at an equally high level, including funk, Latin music, and contemporary jazz. The association of New Orleans music with Louis Armstrong is nearly automatic, but the city has also produced such notables as Dr. John, Professor Longhair, Harry Connick Jr., and the Marsalis and Neville

clans. The most exciting music here always blends influences—African with European, urban with folk—with a dash of island sway often just beneath the surface. A similar range of influences can be detected in New Orleans's celebrated cuisine, which bears the traces of the city's early population: African, French, Spanish, Choctaw Indians, Acadians.

Many visitors spend their entire New Orleans stay in the French Quarter. Although entertaining and fun, a trip limited to the French Quarter will not leave you with a feel for the city as a whole. Uptown, Mid-City, the Warehouse District, the Faubourg Marigny and Bywater districts, and the Garden District all provide a glimpse into the daily routines, coffee shops, and lush cityscapes that New Orleanians treasure, in addition to sights you will not find in the French Quarter. Renting bikes or hopping on the streetcar are excellent ways to experience the city beyond the Quarter.

— Baty Landis

CloseUp

SPEAKING LIKE A LOCAL

NEW ORLEANS, like many other cities, has its own peculiarities of speech. Because it was founded by the French, the city has many street names that a visitor might be inclined to pronounce true to the French. In fact, local pronunciation is quite different. There are also some local terms that can be confusing if you're not familiar with them. For vocabulary specifically referring to local cuisine, see Chapter 3.

One thing that always sets visitors apart is their reference to the trolley. It's a streetcar in New Orleans, not a trolley. And many locals say New-ah-yuns, not New Or-lenz, N'aw-lins, or New Or-leenz. Still, you'll probably fit in fine with the easier-to-pronounce New Or-lenz; the key things to avoid are placing the emphasis on "new" rather than "Or" and using a long "e" sound in "leans." But—here's a curveball—it is pronounced Or-leenz Street.

You need to forget any French you've studied when pronouncing street names. This is where the Texan in the back of class whom everybody snickered at gets his revenge. If you ask what direction Freret (said as Frer-ay, as in French) Street is, you will be met by a blank stare. (The correct pronunciation is Fer-et.) Burgundy Street is Bur-gun-dee; Carondelet is Cahr-ahn-duh-let; Chartres is Chart-ers; Conti is Kon-tie; Iberville is Eye-berville; and Tchoupitoulas is Chop-a-tool-us. And if someone asks you, "Where y'at?," he or she is saying howdy, not asking where you are.

Bayou (pronounced by-you). Stemming from the Indian word bayouk or bayuk, a marshy inlet.

Banquette (pronounced ban-ket). Sidewalk.

Beaucoup (pronounced boo-coo). Very; lots of.

Cold drink. Soda with ice.

Doubloons (pronounced dub-loons, or dub-loons, depending on your upbringing). Aluminum coins, often colored, which Mardi Gras krewes emboss with the theme and date of their parades and throw out to crowds.

Fais-do-do (pronounced fay-doh-doh). Country dance. A Cajun expression derived from the French verbs faire (to make or do) and dormir (to sleep): mothers wanted children to go to sleep so they could dance.

Gallery. Porch or balcony of a certain depth.

Gris-gris (pronounced gree-gree). Voodoo charm; often a small bag filled with several ingredients.

Krewe (pronounced crew). A club that parades at Mardi Gras.

Metairie (pronounced Met-a-ree or Met-tree). Sprawling district of Greater New Orleans. Old Metairie has some streets and homes as beautiful and exclusive as those uptown.

Parish. County.

Where y'at? How are you doing? Correct response is "Hey, where y'at?" or "Alright."

Vieux Carré (pronounced View kah-ray). French Quarter; translated directly as Old Square.

NEW ORLEANS: A HISTORY

KNOWN TO GENERATIONS AS THE CRESCENT CITY AND THE BIG EASY, New Orleans is a city whose magical names conjure up images of a Gallic-Hispanic and Caribbean heritage in a predominantly Anglo-Saxon culture, an amalgamation that forms a unique city and people. It was founded by the French on the banks of the Mississippi River in 1718, taken over by the Spanish in 1762, regained by Napoléon in 1800, and sold to the United States in 1803.

During its nearly 300 years of history, New Orleans has survived yellow fever and cholera epidemics, Indian wars, slave uprisings, economic depressions, revolts, conspiracies, hurricanes, floods, the American and French revolutions, the Civil War and Reconstruction, race riots, and political corruption. It stands like a curious island of Roman Catholicism (of the Mediterranean variety) in a southern sea of hardshell Protestantism that looks upon New Orleans as "Sin City." Perhaps journalist A. J. Liebling characterized it best when he described New Orleans as a cross between Port-au-Prince, Haiti, and Paterson, New Jersey, with a culture not unlike that of Genoa, Marseilles, Beirut, or Egyptian Alexandria. Colonial New Orleans was very much a part of the economic, political, and social sphere of the French and Spanish Caribbean; its earliest population consisted of lesser French and Spanish gentry, tradesmen, merchants, prostitutes, criminals, clergy, farmers from the fields of France and Germany, Acadians from Canada, Canary Islanders, Indians, Africans, English, Irish, and British-Americans. Later came the Italians, Greeks, Cubans, Vietnamese, Central Americans, and others from the Earth's four corners who have made New Orleans one of the nation's most cosmopolitan cities.

It all began on Mardi Gras day in 1699, when a small French-Canadian expedition dropped anchor near the mouth of the Mississippi to explore and colonize "La Louisiane." Over the next few years the expedition built a series of posts and fortifications along the river and the Gulf Coast, including what are today Mobile, Alabama, and Biloxi, Mississippi. By 1718, a permanent settlement was deemed necessary to hold France's claim to the Mississippi; the British and Spanish had their eyes on the vast Mississippi Valley. When French-Canadian Jean Baptiste le Moyne, sieur de Bienville, established that settlement, it must have seemed only natural (and politically wise) to name it after Philippe, Duc d'Orléans, who was ruling France as regent for young Louis XV.

New Orleans has had its glories and problems over the years, with two major standouts—hurricanes and politics. Contrary to orders from France, Bienville insisted upon building his settlement where New Orleans still stands today. He claimed the site was high and dry and protected from hurricanes, but during its first four years the little village was wiped out four times by hurricanes. Politics have been an equally stormy art form here since the city's beginning; even the naming of the first city streets was a stroke of diplomatic genius. As historian John Chase notes in his delightful book on the origins of New Orleans street names, *Frenchmen Desire Good Children* (each name in the title is a street name), Bourbon, Orleans, Burgundy, and Royal streets were so named in honor of the royal families of France. Also honored were the Conti, Chartres, and Condé families, cousins to the Bourbons and Orleanses. (Condé Street was once a section of Chartres Street from Jackson Square to Esplanade Avenue before the name was dropped in 1865; Chartres now extends from Canal Street to Esplanade.) St. Peter Street was named for an ancestor of the Bourbon family;

Louis IX, the Saint-King, was honored with St. Louis Street; Louis XIII's widowed Queen Ann got St. Ann Street; and Toulouse and Dumaine streets were named for Louis XIV's politically powerful royal bastard children.

The best place to get a real feel for the city's unique history is Jackson Square, the heart of the French Quarter, where you are surrounded by the river, St. Louis Cathedral, the colonial Cabildo and Presbytére, and the Pontalba Apartments. Called the Place d'Armes by the French and Plaza de Armas by the Spanish, this was the town square where the militia drilled and townsfolk met. It also was where public hangings, beheadings, "breakings at the wheel," and brandings were carried out.

The Place d'Armes, site in 1803 of the Louisiana Purchase ceremony, was renamed Jackson Square in the 1850s in honor of Andrew Jackson, the hero of the Battle of New Orleans in the War of 1812 and seventh president of the United States. In the center of the square is an equestrian statue of Jackson erected in 1856, one of three cast: a second stands in Lafayette Park in front of the White House in Washington, D.C., and a third in Nashville, Tennessee, Jackson's hometown.

The history of New Orleans is also inseparable from the port of New Orleans. The port is why the city was founded and why it survived. France wanted to colonize Louisiana and built New Orleans to reap imagined riches from the vast interior of North America. Despite the expectations of the first explorers and the French crown, gold and silver did not come pouring out of the North American wilderness; different treasures waited. Quantities of tobacco, lumber, indigo, animal hides, and other indigenous products were floated downriver on flatboats to the new city, where ships from France, Spanish Florida, the West Indies, and the British colonies waited to trade for them with spices, cloth, cutlery, wine, utensils, foods, and other such goods. New Orleans became a commercial center, connecting Europe and the West Indies with the backcountry and upper regions of the Mississippi.

Trade was not without its difficulties. Storms, poorly built ships, privateers, colonial wars, and financially shaky entrepreneurs all added risks to commerce. There were other troubles as well; by the mid-18th century serious international problems were brewing.

In 1754 the long-running dispute between France and England over who owned what in America erupted into war. Dubbed the Seven Years' War in Europe and the French and Indian War in the British colonies along the Atlantic seaboard, it ultimately eliminated France as a colonial power in America. Despite an alliance with Spain (organized in the war's last years), France was defeated, and in 1763 it ceded to England all French territory east of the Mississippi River, keeping for itself just two small islands in the St. Lawrence Seaway.

Not included in the package, however, was New Orleans. Along with all the Louisiana territory west of the Mississippi River, the port had been signed over to Louis XV's cousin, King Carlos III of Spain, in the secret Treaty of Fontainebleau in 1762. (Perhaps that's where the long tradition of backroom deals got its start in Louisiana.) Louis gladly turned Louisiana over to his Spanish cousin. The colony was costing him his royal shirt, and the merchant class in France wanted nothing more to do with it. Carlos III, for his part, accepted the unprofitable holding as a buffer to keep the British away from nearby Mexico.

The Louisiana French, however, generally opposed the change to Spanish rule. When the first Spanish governor, Don Antonio de Ulloa, arrived, he did little to court their favor. After a few breaches in local etiquette and several commercial edicts that hurt the colony's already sagging economy, the settlers drove Ulloa out in a bloodless coup in October 1768. (Local historians, trying to upstage the British colonies along the Atlantic, claim this was the first revolution on American soil against a foreign monarch.)

Retaliation from the mother country was quick and complete. In July 1769 the Spanish fleet dropped anchor at the mouth of the Mississippi, with 2,600 Spanish soldiers under the command of General Alexander O'Reilly, an Irishman in Spanish service. O'Reilly quashed the short-lived rebellion, set up a new government in the colony, and executed the ringleaders of the rebellion.

The American Revolution afforded two of O'Reilly's successors, Unzaga and Galvez, the opportunity to attack their British colonial rival. Through the Louisiana colony, the Spanish sent supplies and munitions to the American rebels and allowed American raiding parties to launch forays into British West Florida. Galvez attacked and captured the British forts at Pensacola, Mobile, and Baton Rouge, and while the British were kept busy with the rebellious colonies, the Spanish took the opportunity to regain West Florida, which they had lost to the British during the French and Indian War.

The Spanish governors of Louisiana opened New Orleans's gates to a great variety of peoples by establishing an open-minded immigration policy that welcomed British-Americans escaping the Revolution as well as French Acadians (whose descendants are Louisiana's famous Cajuns) fleeing the British in Canada. (The Cajuns later moved on to south-central and southwest Louisiana.) Canary Islanders came and settled just below New Orleans, where their descendants still live and speak their ancient language today.

Spanish New Orleans weathered several storms during the last decades of the 18th century, including the French Revolution. Mobs roamed the streets calling New Orleans governor Carondelet a *cochon de lait* (suckling pig) and shouting, "Liberty,

Equality, and Fraternity." Carondelet brought in troops and outlawed publications concerning the Revolution in France. Diplomatically, he also gave refuge to French aristocrats fleeing the carnage, which won him back some favor with the Louisiana French.

Carondelet also had problems upriver with the westward-expanding Americans (usually Kentuckians, called Kaintocks). During the American Revolution, the rebels had assured the Spanish that they had no designs on Louisiana. But by the 1790s their assurances had begun to carry less weight; Americans' use of the river had grown, and so, too, had American desire for free navigation along its length.

As time passed, the situation worsened. Spanish officials in New Orleans occasionally seized American flatboats; the Americans responded by rattling sabers, urged on by the Kaintocks, who called for an invasion of the Louisiana colony. War between the United States and Spain over Louisiana was narrowly averted in 1795 upon the signing of the Pinckney Treaty.

By the end of the 18th century, New Orleans had become a major North American port, handling cargo from all over the world, with a population close to 10,000 and a well-earned reputation as a vibrant colorful city. Mardi Gras was celebrated (though it wasn't yet the extravagant carnival of parades seen today), and Creole food—that unique combination of French, Spanish, West Indian, and African cuisines for which New Orleans is so famous—had found its place on local palates. Unfortunately, much of the old colonial city was destroyed by fire in 1788 and 1794, but each time it was quickly rebuilt; most of the French Quarter of today was constructed during the Spanish colonial days and after the Louisiana Purchase in 1803. The oldest building in the French Quarter, and the only one remaining from French colonial years, is the former Ursuline Convent on Chartres Street, constructed in the 1730s.

For all the changes of the 18th century, the opening of the 19th was to bring even more. In France, Napoléon had reestablished the country as a formidable military force on the Continent. In 1800 he forced Spain to retrocede Louisiana to the French; New Orleans was back in the hands of its first colonial parent, though Spanish officials continued to run the colony for the next three years.

This news sat poorly with U.S. president Thomas Jefferson, who feared that war with France had become inevitable. The issue that concerned him was free navigation along the Mississippi River. To solve the problem, he resolved to buy New Orleans and a portion of West Florida bordering the Mississippi, including Baton Rouge. Napoléon, eager for money to finance his imminent war against England (and reasonably sure that he would lose the land to England or the United States when war came), went Jefferson one better: he offered to sell the entire Louisiana colony.

On April 29, 1803, American emissaries agreed to pay $11,250,000 for Louisiana and, at the same time, to write off $3,750,000 in French debts, setting the territory's cost at $15 million. Short on cash, the United States borrowed the money to buy the territory from banking houses in London and Amsterdam. After the sale, Napoléon commented: "This accession of territory affirms forever the power of the United States, and I have just given England a maritime rival that sooner or later will lay low her pride."

The Americanization of New Orleans moved quickly during the first decade of the 19th century. The city's first suburb, Faubourg St. Mary (today's Central Business District), sprang up and bustled with construction and commerce; this was the American Section. Mississippi flatboatmen made their way downriver from the Missouri and Ohio rivers to sell their cargoes in New Orleans, then made their way home overland along the Natchez Trace.

The year 1812 brought statehood to Louisiana and, almost equally important, the arrival of the first steamboat, the *New Orleans*, captained by Nicholas Roosevelt, ancestral kinsman of the two presidents; 1812 also brought war against Britain. Though its first effects on New Orleans were slight, the War of 1812 eventually came hard to the city. In 1815 Andrew Jackson, with a ragged army of Louisianans and the assistance of Jean Lafitte, Lafitte's Baratarian pirates, and Tennessee and Kentucky volunteers, fought the British and stopped them in a bloody battle at Chalmette Plantation, a few miles downriver from the city. Although casualty estimates for the Battle of New Orleans conflict somewhat, reports placed American losses at 13 killed and 39 wounded, and British losses at 858 killed and 2,468 wounded. Ironically, the battle took place two weeks after the United States and Britain signed a treaty ending the war. Every January 8, local history groups reenact the victory at Chalmette Battlefield, which is now a national park.

The years between the Battle of New Orleans and the Civil War were the city's golden era. By 1820 the population had reached 25,000; during the next 10 years it doubled. By 1840 it had doubled again, with a census count of 102,000 people within New Orleans; about half were black, both free and slave. The city was a major center for slave auctions. The burgeoning port was choked with seagoing ships and riverboats laden with sugar, molasses, cotton, raw materials from upriver, and refined goods from Europe and the Northeast.

The golden age also gave birth to one of New Orleans's most famous pastimes: the Mardi Gras parade. Mardi Gras had been celebrated on the European continent, one way or another, for centuries. The parades originated in Mobile, Alabama, but later moved to New Orleans, where the custom flourished. Begun in the 1820s when bands of maskers marched through the streets throwing confetti and flour (and sometimes lye) in the faces of on-lookers, the parades were first staged by Americans in the American Section and not by the French or Spanish populace, who preferred their gala balls. Vehicles were first used in 1839, and the first carnival organization, the Mistick Krewe of Comus, was formed in 1857.

Through the years of prosperity and celebration, disease continued to stalk the city. The almost yearly visits of yellow fever, cholera, and typhus—encouraged by widespread poverty—took thousands of lives; 8,000 fell to yellow fever in 1853 and another 2,700 in 1856. In that same year cholera claimed the lives of more than 1,000 people, and tuberculosis killed 650. New Orleans was known as one of the unhealthiest cities in the Northern Hemisphere.

If the 18th century can be seen as New Orleans's childhood, then the antebellum period was its adolescence and young adulthood; by its end, the city had reached full maturity. Prosperous and growing, it had an international personality that distinguished it from every other city on the North American continent.

But the Civil War was to change that. On January 26, 1861, Louisiana seceded from the Union. It was a difficult choice for New Orleanians, many of whom had strong commercial and family ties with the Northeast and Midwest. Less than three months after secession, the war began when Southern troops, under the command of New Orleans's own General Pierre Gustave Toutant Beauregard, opened fire on Fort Sumter in Charleston harbor. A month later a Union fleet blockaded the mouth of the Mississippi River, causing severe economic hardship in the city.

The Confederate flag waved barely a year over New Orleans before it fell to Union forces under "Damn the Torpedoes" Admiral David Glasgow Farragut in April 1862. When the Union fleet arrived and trained its guns on a panicked city, the mayor refused to surrender; Farragut threatened to bombard the city but backed down. After a brief standoff, a naval squad went ashore and lowered the Confederate flag. New Orleans, the Confederacy's largest city, had fallen, and Reconstruction had begun.

New Orleans had the dubious distinction of being under Reconstruction longer than any other place in the Confederacy—from May 1862 to April 1877. The city's port and nearby fertile plantations were sources of immense profits for corrupt politicians under Reconstruction; the social and political upheaval it brought on was often violent, with bloody street battles between New Orleans natives and factions of the military-backed Reconstruction government. Withdrawal of federal troops in 1877 brought an end to 15 years of Reconstruction; it also ended a flicker of hope that blacks in New Orleans would enjoy the same constitutional rights and protections as whites. With the end of Reconstruction came home rule and New Orleans's gilded age.

The last two decades of the century saw an era of economic booms and busts, corruption and reform, and labor unrest. With a population of more than 216,000, New Orleans was still the largest city in the South. Large and elaborate Victorian homes, decorated with mass-produced gingerbread frills, sprang up along major avenues and thoroughfares.

New Orleans entered the 20th century with an air of optimism. North and South put aside their differences to defeat the Spanish in the Spanish-American War in 1898. Uptown continued to grow with mansions along St. Charles Avenue, and skyscrapers in the Central Business District hovered over the early-19th-century buildings of the old American Section. The New Orleans World Cotton Exposition of 1884 clearly forecast a century of new promises.

The prosperity continued until the Great Depression of the 1930s as skyscrapers towered even higher above the old city. World War II, however, was a turning point. Although the city prospered during the war years, its population began to fall behind that of other American and southern cities. By 1950 it was no longer the South's largest city, falling to second place behind Houston. By 1970 the Crescent City had dropped to fifth place in the South, and the 1980 and 1990 censuses showed it slipping even further behind.

Census returns those years also showed a decline in the urban population, while surrounding suburbs grew dramatically. Since the early 1960s, tens of thousands of middle-class white and black families have moved to the sprawling communities surrounding the city; thousands of acres of soupy marshlands have given way to tract housing and shopping centers.

The construction of the Louisiana Superdome in the early 1970s, spurred by a booming oil industry, signaled an era of growth that lasted into the mid-1980s. Office high-rises appeared above the Central Business District, and luxury hotels went up throughout downtown. The following decade, however, brought a period of stagnation, as the oil industry experienced a crisis, prompting oil companies to consolidate, mainly in Houston. From the mid-1980s to mid-1990s, expansion for the most part was limited to the Warehouse District: the 1984 World's Fair had paved the way for developers, who moved into the now-renovated old warehouses. In the late 1990s, downtown saw renewed growth, largely thanks to the Warehouse District's Ernest N. Morial Convention Center, developed over the course of the 1990s and now one of the largest spans of contiguous exhibi-

tion space in the country. Once again, luxury hotels are exploding downtown, though construction of office buildings has remained at a standstill. Increasingly, major events such as the Essence Music Festival, sponsored by *Essence* magazine, and the Super Bowl are favoring New Orleans, where the downtown hotels, sights, Convention Center, and Superdome all are within walking distance.

Meanwhile, a restoration trend is sweeping the city. Many young professionals and families are choosing to buy and renovate old houses in the heart of the city. Developers, as well, are rediscovering the riches buried in older architecture. During the 1960s and 1970s, they thought everything old had to be razed to make way for the new; scores of buildings dating from the 1850s and earlier gave way to the wrecker's ball. In more recent years, however, developers have found it profitable to adapt pre–Civil War buildings and warehouses to modern use, with magnificent results, especially in the Warehouse District.

More than 280 years have passed since Bienville's engineers and work crews built the first palmetto huts at the crescent in the Mississippi River. Today New Orleans—the Crescent City, the Big Easy—is scarred and somewhat decayed, but it can be the most beautiful and charming of hostesses. Its people, history, cuisine, and alluring 19th-century mystique and Caribbean-like culture make it like no other city in the nation.

— John R. Kemp

John R. Kemp has written several books about the city, including New Orleans: An Illustrated History.

THE CRADLE OF JAZZ

MUSIC IS THE SOUL OF NEW ORLEANS. Since the 1890s her melodies, rhythms, and musicians have enriched America's artistic heritage, and today the city's musical texture is an interweaving of jazz, rhythm and blues, gospel, rock and roll, Latin beat, and then some.

The sound of New Orleans extends from the classic jazz of the early 1920s through the sterling sound of Louis Armstrong and his mates; from the mid-century dancehall beat of Fats Domino, Professor Longhair, and a legion of rhythm-and-bluesmen to the polished modern improvisations of Wynton Marsalis and the young jazz lions of the 1980s.

As a distinctive sound, New Orleans music is marked by a parade-time backbeat on drums; rocking, vocally suggestive horns; and a percussive piano style with liberal shadings of the blues.

The root of this sound is called the "second line"—the waves of marching dancers who engulf the brass bands with a dazzling body language of gyrating steps, following the musicians as they parade through the streets. Above all, it's music to make you clap your hands and move your feet.

The power of New Orleans music has always come from the neighborhoods. Like Brazilian samba and the Beatles' Liverpool rock, jazz polyrhythms rose like a vox populi from working-class environs of this port city. Louis Armstrong in his memoir, *Satchmo: My Life in New Orleans,* recalled with a measure of tenderness the Back-o'-Town streets where he was raised. "The toughest characters in town used to live there," he wrote, ". . . as did church people, gamblers, hustlers, cheap pimps, thieves, prostitutes, and lots of children."

But the seedbed of jazz music and its later offshoots lay in distant reaches of the past, at Congo Square, the early-19th-century grassy plain (in what is now Louis Armstrong Park) where each Sunday slaves gathered for drum-and-dance celebrations that drew crowds of varied onlookers, including landed gentry.

Congo Square was the cultural transfer point where African percussions and tribal dance steps, akin to those developing across the Caribbean map, began the long, slow march into European instrumentation and melody that would culminate a century later in the birth of jazz.

By the 1930s Armstrong had given the music a grand voice, with lovely lyrical flourishes and gritty blueslike voicings. Since then, New Orleans has produced a continuing line of distinguished musicians. On October 22, 1990, the cover of *Time* featured trumpeter Wynton Marsalis, a virtuoso superstar and eloquent advocate of jazz, as a metaphor of democracy. As Armstrong had done two generations earlier, the 29-year-old Marsalis became the spokesman of America's indigenous art form.

The seeds of New Orleans jazz first took root in the 1890s. New Orleans was then legally segregated but was a town where rare degrees of social intercourse prevailed. It was a society of many layers—Creole descendants of European settlers, Italians, Irish, Germans, blacks, Native Americans, and Creoles of color (or *gens de couleur*).

Music was a common currency among these peoples. Outdoor festivals and indoor dances followed the calendar of Catholic feasts, the biggest of which was Mardi Gras, "Fat Tuesday," ushering in 40 days of Lent. The society orchestras and smaller ensembles that performed for parties and other events were playing syncopated rags; French quadrilles and polkas were popular, too.

A more potent influence, at least for the development of jazz, was the brass bands—

groups that marched in uniforms, playing parade music with rhythmic flavorings that reflected an African percussive tradition.

The musicianship of black Creoles was a primary factor in the emergence of jazz. They were a distinct caste, descendants of African mothers and fathers of French or Spanish ancestry; many first arrived from Haiti in the early 1800s, settling in the Tremé neighborhood (behind what is now Louis Armstrong Park) and, in later years, the Seventh Ward, which lies downtown, well beyond the French Quarter. The lines of racial intermixture were perpetuated by New Orleans aristocrats who kept mulatto mistresses and often supported second, "shadow" families.

Some Creoles amassed great wealth before the Civil War and even owned slaves. They were generally better educated than the blacks who lived upriver from the French Quarter. By the end of Reconstruction and with the tightening of racial laws, the sturdy familial lines and artisan skills of the downtown Creoles had produced a burgeoning tradition of families who taught music and performed professionally.

One such "professor," James Brown Humphrey, played a variety of instruments and was a catalyst for jazz. In 1887 he began regular trips to outlying plantation communities to teach poor blacks, a number of whom moved to town to join brass bands. In the late 20th century two of his grandsons, Willie and Percy Humphrey, were regular performers in Preservation Hall.

A more legendary figure—universally deemed the first great jazzman—was Buddy Bolden, who played cornet (a smaller version of the trumpet) with strong, bluesy currents. Though his music was popular, Bolden suffered a mental breakdown in 1907 and never recorded.

In time, the musical division between blacks, who learned to play by ear—listening to songs, replicating what they heard—and Creoles, who read sheet music,

began to blur. Meanwhile, a red-light district called Storyville gave piano "professors" like Jelly Roll Morton quite a venue until its closure in 1917.

The year 1917 was a milestone for another reason: in New York, a group of white New Orleans musicians led by Nick LaRocca, the Original Dixieland Jazz Band, recorded the first jazz disk. Though jazz was an idiom rooted in African improvisational traditions, many white practitioners, whose style became known as Dixieland, began to flourish in New Orleans as well.

The first generation of New Orleans jazzmen produced three brilliant artists— Louis Armstrong, Jelly Roll Morton, and Sidney Bechet—each of whom left the city to establish his reputation. Morton, a Creole with great talent as a composer-pianist, was a peripatetic figure who died in 1941, down on his luck. Bechet, also a Creole, was a virtuoso clarinetist who left behind a string of memorable recordings. He settled near Paris, where he became a celebrity, and died in 1959.

Armstrong's life was a rags-to-riches odyssey. Records show that Armstrong was born August 4, 1901—however, he preferred the more romantic, fabricated birthday of July 4, 1900. He grew up in the Back-o'-Town ghetto and, after a stint in the Colored Waifs Home, found an early mentor in Papa Joe Oliver, the popular cornetist and bandleader also known as King Oliver. In 1918 Armstrong began traveling the Mississippi, playing on riverboats, refining his technique. In 1922 he left New Orleans to join Oliver's band in Chicago, and for the next half century he traveled the globe, elevating jazz to an international art form.

The music stylizations and recordings of Armstrong, Morton, and Bechet had an enormous influence, yet to all but aficionados of jazz, the historical sensibility they shared is frequently overlooked. Each man worked hard on a biography; their books are solid works of literature as well as classics of jazz history—Armstrong's *Satchmo: My Life in New Orleans,* Bechet's *Treat It Gentle,* and Morton's *Mister Jelly Roll* (written by Alan Lomax, but based on long interviews with Morton).

The sounds of jazz continued to flow in New Orleans through the '30s and '40s. The tidal shift toward a new idiom came after World War II: rhythm and blues.

A blues sensibility ran deep in New Orleans, and the many lyrics about love lost, love found were fashioned into a style, enhanced by gospel techniques, the soaring choirs and drums of the churches, and saxophones and trumpets that blasted like preachers and moaned like bluesmen.

Fats Domino put R&B on the map. In 1949 "The Fat Man," with his rocking piano style and rolling, mellifluous voice, triggered a line of golden records that made teenagers put on their dancing shoes.

Domino had the advantage of a highly skilled producer, trumpeter-bandleader Dave Bartholomew, who molded Fats's sound for the Imperial label. His biggest hit, "Blueberry Hill," was a country boy's song that wedded Fats's appeal to an audience of blue-collar workers and rural folk.

The other influential early rhythm-and-bluesman was Henry Roeland Byrd, who took the stage name Professor Longhair in 1949 and who played in Domino's shadow most of his life. Fess, as he was fondly known among locals, was quite a ticket. A tap dancer in his youth, he made the rounds of Rampart Street honky-tonks in the depression, studying the blues piano of Champion Jack Dupree and Sonny Boy Williamson.

Professor Longhair called his own style "a mixture of mambo, rumba, and calypso." He infused the dance steps of his youth into an intricate, percussive keyboard style, and he sang with the deep heart of a bluesman. He simulated the street pace of Carnival in "Mardi Gras in New Orleans" and "Go to the Mardi Gras," which became local anthems. "Big Chief" was his homage

to the Mardi Gras Indians, groups of blacks who create grand Native American costumes and still parade in neighborhood tribes through New Orleans's backstreets.

In a sense, Professor Longhair's death in 1980 marked the end of the postwar R&B era. His unique style never caught on as a national chart buster, but he had enormous influence on younger musicians. Even before his death, younger jazzmen in the brass bands had begun performing his Carnival tunes.

Domino and Longhair divided New Orleans R&B into two stylistic camps—one a building block of rock and roll, the other a more improvisational, Afro-Caribbean beat. Between these styles was a generation of exceptional musicians.

Allen Toussaint harnessed the talents of a stable of singers in the 1960s. A skilled pianist with a seasoned lyrical touch, Toussaint composed songs for Irma Thomas ("Queen of the Blues"); Aaron Neville, a brawny balladeer with a falsetto reach that chills the spine; Ernie K-Doe, an extravagant stage performer and blues shouter who scored a hit with "Mother-in-Law"; and Benny Spellman, a hefty ex-football player for whom Toussaint penned the memorable "Fortune Teller."

The music of the 1950s fit a new urban groove. White teenagers were the big market; of the many New Orleans artists who reached the kids, Huey "Piano" Smith did it with a colorful entourage known as the Clowns. Drawing on nursery rhymes, Huey wrote uncomplicated, if offbeat, lyrics—"I got the rockin' pneumonia and the boogie-woogie flu"—and the dancers loved it.

When the Beatles and Rolling Stones swept America in the 1960s, the New Orleans R&B scene fell into decline. In the early 1970s the annual Jazz Fest ignited a revival.

One of the most talented 1950s session artists, Mac Rebennack, played piano and guitar and penned dozens of compositions before hitting pop stardom in 1968 as Dr. John. James Booker, who dubbed himself the Piano Prince, also had commanding talent; he could jump from classical chords into R&B bounces with sizzling heat and witty lyrics. Booker, Dr. John, and Art Neville were prime exponents of a piano idiom that roamed the bridge between the Longhair–Domino styles. Booker's death in 1983 was greatly felt in New Orleans's jazz community.

Professor Longhair and Art Neville were also among local musicians exploring a new musical feel: funk. During the late 1960s, Art Neville joined up with Zigaboo Modaliste, George Porter, and Leo Nocentelli to form the Meters, one of the most influential early funk bands in the United States. The real breakthrough here was the rhythm section, which had a solid exciting pulse that clung to the end of the beat. Though the group never hit it really big nationally, they inspired reverence in the music industry around the country and beyond. The Rolling Stones, for example, have always acknowledged their admiration of the Meters, and they invited the Meters to open for them on their 1975 tour.

In 1977 Art joined his brothers to form the Neville Brothers band, which became the city's preeminent pop group. Charles plays saxophone; Cyril sings and plays congas; Aaron, whose 1966 hit "Tell It Like It Is" is still a showstopper, sings and plays hand percussions. The Nevilles' four-part harmonies, set against Afro-Caribbean lines, gave R&B a warm new shading. At the same time, the Nevilles wrote a new chapter in popular music through their association with the Wild Tchoupitoulas, a Mardi Gras Indian tribe led by their uncle, George Landry.

There are approximately 25 black neighborhood groups that masquerade as Indians each Mardi Gras; the folk tradition dates from Reconstruction. As Big Chief Jolley, Landry founded the Wild Tchoupitoulas in the uptown neighborhood where he and his nephews lived. A 1976 LP, *The Wild Tchoupitoulas*, combined the instrumental prowess of the Nevilles and the Meters bands with Jolley's hearty vocals, based on the old a cappella tribal chants, to become a classic. By the time Landry passed away in 1980, Mardi Gras Indian music was emblematic of the Neville sound.

The Nevilles hit their stride in 1990, winning a Grammy for "Yellow Moon." The following year, Aaron Neville took another Grammy for his vocal duet with Linda Ronstadt "All My Life," and in 1992 won his first gold record, "Warm Your Heart," which sold 500,000 copies. His odyssey from stevedore work on the river docks of the Mississippi to musical celebrity is one of the most poignant artistic careers in New Orleans.

In the 1980s New Orleans experienced a jazz renaissance led by the brilliant trumpet work of a young Wynton Marsalis, the product of yet another musical family. As high school students, Wynton and his brothers studied at the New Orleans Center for the Creative Arts, where Ellis Marsalis, their father, directed the jazz program. With brother Branford on saxophone, Wynton emerged as a national star by the time he was 20, and in 1984 won two Grammy awards. Though Branford does not have Wynton's name recognition, he has earned at least an equal portion of respect within the jazz world for his stunning work on sax. His mainstream recognition has included work with Sting and several film scores, among them Spike Lee's *Do the Right Thing*.

A gifted composer-pianist in his own right, Ellis Marsalis has molded at least three other young talents who have achieved national recognition: trumpeter Terence Blanchard, saxophonist Donald Harrison, and pianist Harry Connick Jr. Connick began dazzling audiences with a polished blend of jazz piano and a golden mellifluous singing voice that drew comparisons with Frank Sinatra. He also became a heart-throb in the youth market, a rare feat for a jazz artist. Connick has now emerged as a superstar vocalist, touring with a big band known for its lush arrangements. He has also acted in such films as *Memphis Belle, Little Man Tate,* and *Independence Day.*

The young lions of the 1980s are products of a teaching tradition and a society rooted in musical families. Their myriad innovations draw from a large canvas of sounds. The Dirty Dozen and Rebirth bands have led the brass-band resurgence, a fourth generation of young musicians improvising with blues, bebop, R&B, and jazz.

Yet a new line of young jazz talents emerged in the 1990s—trumpeter Nicholas Payton, son of esteemed bassist Walter Payton; drummer Brian Blade, who learned music in a Shreveport gospel church; trumpeter Kermit Ruffins, who came up through the Rebirth brass band and is now a beloved solo performer; the youngest Marsalis, drummer Jason; Clarence Johnson III, a soulful saxophone player with a personal sound drawing on everything from the church to the avant-garde; Roland Guerin, a versatile bassist who plays with just about everyone in town; and bassist Chris Thomas, a University of New Orleans (UNO) jazz student, among others. Lately, local brass bands have again updated their sound, incorporating hip-hop techniques into the traditional brass format, demonstrating the flexibility that keeps New Orleans music so vibrant, generation in and generation out.

Although a full-blown recording industry has yet to emerge, New Orleans is mak-

ing dramatic strides as a music city. New Orleans in no way rivals Nashville as a production and song-publishing center. Yet tourists flock here by the millions each year, especially for the annual Jazz Fest, which runs from late April to early May. There's a heightened activity in local studios, and a sturdy club circuit signals growth in the entertainment economy. The main obstacle to building a bona fide music industry is capturing a record distribution base.

Artists who make it big often head for New York, as did Armstrong, Dr. John, Wynton Marsalis, and Harry Connick Jr. Yet for all those who moved, many more choose to live here—including some of the city's best talent, such as Fats Domino, the Nevilles, and younger groups such as the Dirty Dozen and Rebirth brass bands—while playing long stretches on concert tours each year.

Despite its drawbacks, a distinctive cultural sensibility—more Latin and African than Anglo-American—has endowed New Orleans with a unique musical society. As saxophonist Harold Battiste, a pioneer of 1950s heritage jazz that came out of small clubs around the Magnolia housing project, once put it: "Musicians come and go, and their creations always seem directed at the city. Because after all is said and done, *New Orleans* is the star."

— Jason Berry

Jason Berry is the author of Amazing Grace: With Charles Evers in Mississippi *and the coauthor of* Up from the Cradle of Jazz: New Orleans Music Since World War II.

VOODOO & THE LIFE OF SPIRITS IN NEW ORLEANS

IMAGINE NEW ORLEANS IN THE COLONIAL ERA. Rain-sodden, prone to yellow fever epidemics, it is a remote port whose plantation economy turns on the toil of African slaves. Indian communities dot swampy woodlands that are well removed from the great estates where Creole aristocrats, their society wedded to interests of the Church, eat sumptuously and party well.

Voodoo charges the territory with powerful impulses, bewildering planter and priest. Away from the plantation house, in the secluded woods near river and bayou, booming drums summon slaves to torch-lighted ceremonies in the night. Men and women gyrate to the percussive rhythms as a cult priest chants. Slap goes his knife, slicing through a chicken's neck—up gushes the blood, covering his hands. Around and around the worshippers dance, shouting in response to the priest's African chants.

Voices pulsate to the beat of hands and sticks on drums, on and on until the spirit hits and a woman is possessed by a current of psychic energy. Her shoulders shake, her body twists, her tongue speaks words no white man understands. The cultists gather round, calming her until the possession passes and she is released from her spell. Now the drumbeats become more insistent and the ceremony resumes.

In the nearby mansion, a Creole planter does not like what he hears; he tells himself he treats his slaves well. But what do those cries mean? A foreboding seeps into his night.

In the 18th century, voodoo was the most dramatic symbol of division between master and slave, and it loomed as a sinister threat to the ruling class. In 1782 the governor of Louisiana, fearing rebellious uprisings of the cults, put a clamp on voodoo-worshipping slaves imported from the Caribbean island of Martinique. But by then it was too late—voodoo had taken root.

Voodoo was a religion that had journeyed to the New World in the hearts and minds of African slaves uprooted from the animist culture of their homeland. Its origins lay in West Africa, particularly in the ancient kingdom of Dahomey (today the People's Republic of Benin) and in neighboring Yorubaland (what is now Nigeria).

In the 1720s, millions of Africans were captured by West African kings and sold as slaves to foreign merchants. Chained and hungry, the hostages were shipped in the holds of large ships that crossed the ocean. The Africans, as beheld by Caribbean and southern planters, were people without religion, redeemed from the savage world they had left behind.

In reality, they came from large, extended families. Many African cultures revolve around communal ceremonies that honor the spirits of departed ancestors. Music and dance rituals recognize the dead as real presences; devotees wear masks and other accessories to embody ancestral figures, deities, animals, and forces of nature.

The Yoruba believe that existence consists of three interconnected zones: the living, the dead, and the unborn. In rituals, masked figures dance to percussive rhythms that evoke the ancients, or *orishas*.

The "talking drum," a percussion instrument that produces multiple tones under the manipulations of highly skilled drummers, is critical to these rituals. The tones of the drum "voice" and the dancer's mask form a continuum—one gives language through music, the other a visual representation of the spirit. Voodoo is the faith, the center of gravity for a tribe. During the slave trade, voodoo, along with its followers, crossed the Atlantic Ocean in the overloaded slave holds. However, the masks would now lie buried in the savannas of the mind: communications with the orishas in the white man's land would be dangerous and difficult.

The deepest implanting of voodoo occurred on the island of Saint Domingue, as Haiti was known before 1804. The Fon, natives of Dahomey, cast a large influence over the island's slave communities. Just as the Yoruba evoked their orishas, the Fon summoned their spirits, called *loa*. To the Fon, "vodun" meant "god" or "protective spirit."

Indoctrinated as Catholics, slaves on Haiti used the Mass in melding African spirits with visages of Christian saints. The Mass provided a New World ritual for voodoo's elastic reach; cultists could forsake the knife from chicken or goat and transform their worship in a less bloody rite while maintaining its inner core, complete with sacrificial gods and drumbeats.

On the night of August 22, 1791, while a storm raged through Saint Domingue, a cult priest named Boukman led a voodoo incantation, drank blood from a pig, and, as reported by historian C. L. R. James, told his followers: "The gods of the white man inspire him with crime. . . . Our god who is good to us orders us to revenge our wrongs." Boukman was killed, but his revolt was one in a succession of slave rebellions culminating with the overthrow of French forces in 1804 and the founding of the Republic of Haiti.

During the next decade, waves of planters, free Creoles of color, and slaves reached New Orleans, many via Cuba, scattering seeds that sprouted new voodoo cults. By then nearly a century had passed since the first slaves had arrived in Louisiana; the vocabulary of African drum voices had been effectively erased, but the religious sensibility had found a new cultural passageway.

Meanwhile, New Orleans was fast becoming a culture *métissage*—a mixture of bloodlines. Segregation was the law, but social intercourse was fluid among the peoples, especially between Creole planters and the mistresses they found among the mulatto women. As the antebellum era wore on, the voodoo sensibility—adaptive to the culture in which it found itself—worked its way into the thoughts and culture of aristocratic white society.

In the 1820s voodoo queen Marie Laveau (believed to have been of black, Indian, and white blood) worked as a hairdresser in white homes, where she gathered secrets of the Creole elite by utilizing domestic servants to spy on whites, many of whom sought her advice as a spiritual counselor. A practicing Catholic, she nevertheless frequently prescribed the sticking of a pin into a voodoo doll to provoke trouble for someone's nemesis, or magical gris-gris dust (spell-casting powder) as a curative or protective hex. Her influence with blacks was greater by virtue of her sway over whites.

Marie made quite a living as a spiritual guide, selling her hexes and charms; she also made regular visits to the local prison. She groomed her daughter Marie to carry on the voodoo tradition; it was the second Marie whose exotic ceremonies of the night became legendary. Sex orgies reportedly occurred during voodoo rites of the late 19th century.

Dr. John, another important voodoo legend, was a towering black man (reputed to be a Senegalese prince in his former life) who owned slaves and was apparently a polygamist. He cultivated his own network of informants among slaves and servants who worked for whites. Aristocrats are said to have sought his advice, making him a legendary figure to blacks, but an outright cult priest he apparently was not.

In New Orleans today, voodoo is a bare whisper of its former self, a shadow along the margins of a different spirit world, grounded in the folkways of black Christian churches. As voodoo waned with

early-20th-century urbanization, spiritualistic religions took root in New Orleans's churches. In these mostly small
chapels, blacks honored the presence of St.
Michael the Archangel, Black Hawk the
Indian, Leith Anderson, and other benevolent figures. Although the base religion
was Christianity, Haitian voodoo had
turned African deities into images of
Catholic saints; the spiritualistic churches
transformed the faces once again, finding
North American spirits to fit the visages
of the new pantheon. Spirits may change
as culture goes through upheavals, but
the coil of memory springs the imagination, triggering messages in music and
dance, myth and symbol.

American Indian tribes shared this imaginative process. Black Hawk was a powerful Sauk chief in Illinois who died in
1838. As Yoruba and Fon spirits resurfaced
in Haiti, so the spirit of Black Hawk
coursed through the mental chambers of
people with Native American heritage. In
1919 the consciousness of Black Hawk
reached New Orleans's spiritualistic
churches through Leith Anderson, a
woman of black and Indian ancestry who
had come from Chicago.

In a WPA interview conducted during the
Depression, Mother Dora, another spiritualistic leader, recalled Leith Anderson:
"She wanted us to pray to Black Hawk because he was a great saint for spiritualism
only. . . . Ah think he came to her one time
and said dat he was de first one to start
spiritualism in dis country way before de
white men come heah."

A Black Hawk cult flourishes in spiritual-
ist churches today. Mother Leith Anderson—also called Leafy—is memorialized as
well. The trancelike possessions are powerful testimony to the belief system—a
benevolent Christian vision of spirits as seed
carriers of culture across space and time.

In 1967 a crusty rock-and-roller named
Mac Rebennack adopted the stage name
and persona of Dr. John. He sported bone
and teeth necklaces, face paint, and a tur-
ban with billowing colored feathers. Con-
fronting this bizarre persona, Mac's
mother, a good Catholic lady, fretted, "I
didn't want him for his soul's sake to be
doing this. But actually, I could see the cre-
ativeness of what he was doing."

In "Gris-Gris Gumbo Ya-Ya," Mac sang
as Dr. John: "Got a satchel of gris-gris in
my hand / Got many clients that come
from miles around."

Perhaps the most visible emblem of
voodoo's hold on the popular imagination
today is the number of visitors who flock
to the tomb of Marie Laveau in St. Louis
Cemetery No. 1 and to the Voodoo Museum in the French Quarter. There is no
dearth of voodoo walking tours during
which a guide will go into further detail
about the history of the religion while
pointing out Marie Laveau's house and
grave, Congo Square, and other places
of interest.

— Jason Berry

BOOKS, MOVIES & MUSIC

Books

New Orleans has long proved an inspiration to writers. They have moved here, set their novels here, drawn the city's spirit into their styles and into their stories. A handful of fiction works are commonly regarded as having captured that spirit with particular insight and poignancy, and any or all of these provide reading that can enrich a trip here.

Local writer Walker Percy wrote many novels based on New Orleans and Louisiana culture. Perhaps his most successful is *The Moviegoer* (1961), full of details about the city as it follows a charming, neurotic native. The brilliant, bitingly funny *A Confederacy of Dunces* (1980), by John Kennedy Toole, is a Pulitzer prize–winning novel about another neurotic New Orleanian—this time, though, he is not so charming. Kate Chopin's *The Awakening* (1899) is a serious story about the life of a New Orleans woman in the mid-1800s, moving and sad in its depiction of the oppressive atmosphere that social privilege can generate. Tennessee Williams's classic play *A Streetcar Named Desire* (1947) provides another portrait of a southern belle, this time in the confused context of Mid-City, working-class New Orleans. Robert Penn Warren's semi-fictional *All the King's Men* (1946) is a thinly veiled story of Huey Long and a beautifully written, insightful look at southern-fried politics. Huey's brother Earl Long, also a onetime governor of the state, is remembered in equally vivid colors in *The Earl of Louisiana* (1961), by A. J. Liebling. Another of the city's great legends is the 1927 flood, considered by some the greatest natural disaster ever to hit this country. That event and its many repercussions—racial, financial, and agricultural to name a few—are captivatingly depicted in the pages of John M. Barry's *Rising Tide: The Great Mississippi Flood of 1927 and How It Changed America* (1997). William Faulkner lived in New Orleans during his early days as a writer; his youthful *Mosquitos* (1927) parodies his fellow French Quarter artistic types.

The eerie romance of New Orleans has given rise to a prevalence of mysteries among local fiction. Frances Parkinson Keyes's *Dinner at Antoine's* (1947) is an early example, a charming murder mystery centered on the grand restaurant and written in the studio behind 1113 Chartres Street. Julie Smith won an Edgar Award for her first murder mystery set in New Orleans: *New Orleans Mourning* introduced policewoman Skip Langdon to readers in 1990; the ensuing series has created many fans of both Smith and Langdon. Tony Dunbar has been turning out highly regarded murder mysteries with a southern twist, most featuring flawed crime solver Tubby Dubonnet. Dunbar's *City of Beads* (1996) and *Shelter from the Storm* (1998) are especially good. For a good mixture of romance and adventure with an eccentric cast of characters, pick up *Bandits* (1999) by Elmore Leonard. In Sarah Shankman's *Now Let's Talk of Graves,* (1990) a journalist-detective travels to New Orleans for a Mardi Gras holiday and investigates a possible murder. Of course, James Lee Burke started all this with his Dave Robicheaux series. Burke's *Neon Rain* (1987) is a good example of the genre.

Superstar author Anne Rice has created an industry by taking the mystical aura of New Orleans (as well as that of a few other cities) in a slightly different direction. Reading at least one of her vampire chronicles will clarify the popularity of Anne Rice–oriented sights in the city. *Interview with the Vampire* (1976), the first of her *Vampire Chronicles* series, is still one of her best. Rice has also penned a novel illuminating the lives of the *gens de couleur* ("free people of color," or free mixed-race Creoles in New Orleans prior to Emancipation). *A Feast of All Saints* (1986) follows the moving story of one young mixed-race Creole boy. Several writers working in New Orleans today also show a gift for capturing the beauties and oddities of the city.

Also in a class of his own is Andrei Codrescu, the transplanted Romanian, National Public Radio commentator, and essayist who happens to call New Orleans home. *The Muse Is Always Half-Dressed in New Orleans* (1993) is a witty collection of droll philosophical essays. Codrescu also has a regular, and generally hilarious, column in the free local weekly *Gambit*.

For an interesting history of the city—through an explanation of New Orleans street names—read *Frenchmen Desire Good Children* (1949), by John Chase. Susan Larson's *The Booklover's Guide to New Orleans* (1999) is filled with information on New Orleans authors and points you to where various writers have lived in the city. Al Rose's *Storyville* (1974) has a good account of the origins of jazz and New Orleans's once-infamous red-light district. Along the same lines, local author Christine Wilkes penned the marvelous *The Last Madame: A Life in the New Orleans Underworld* (2000) about the city's last operating whorehouse. The book is rich with local history and politics, and much of New Orleans's social elite still remembers the book's protagonist fondly. Donald Marquis's *In Search of Buddy Bolden* (1978) makes a valiant effort to balance myth with fact—no light proposition when it comes to New Orleans music—in telling the story of early jazz through the legendary first jazzman, Buddy Bolden. Musical activity in the city is covered in *Up from the Cradle of Jazz* (1986), by Jason Berry, Tad Jones, and Jonathan Foose. The pocket-size history *The Free People of Color of New Orleans* (1994), by Mary Gehman, explains the contributions of that unique group, today often referred to as Creoles.

An invaluable resource for anyone interested in local literature is the informed and enthusiastic staff at the **Maple Street Book Shop** (✉ 7523 Maple St. ☎ 504/ 866–4916 ⊕ www.maplestreetbookshop. com), in uptown New Orleans. A major force in the support and promotion of local writers, Maple Street is where most local authors shop and hold their book signings. In the French Quarter, the staff at **Faulkner House Books** (✉ 624 Pirate's Alley ☎ 504/524-2940) is just as helpful, and the store sells used fine editions of a range of southern and other authors.

Movies

Films set in New Orleans fall into two categories: those that will give you a feel for some of the city's history and living culture and those that are more visually captivating than culturally accurate.

For the former, *Eve's Bayou,* steeped in mystery, betrayal, and voodoo and shot almost exclusively on the north shore of New Orleans, was hailed by critic Roger Ebert as the best movie of 1997. Lynn Whitfield and Samuel L. Jackson shine in the film. *Pretty Baby* (1978), starring Brooke Shields and centering on the tale of Storyville photographer E. J. Bellocq, will inspire you to seek out the landmarks of the notorious red-light district. The film was shot at the Columns Hotel uptown. Elia Kazan's *A Streetcar Named Desire* (1951), starring Marlon Brando and Vivian Leigh, is a beautiful rendering of Tennessee Williams's classic drama, set in Mid-City New Orleans and capturing some of the class tensions that have always tortured the city.

As for the latter, *Interview with the Vampire* (1994), based on the novel by Anne Rice, has vampires Tom Cruise and Brad Pitt appearing around the French Quarter, in Lafayette Cemetery, and at Oak Alley plantation. In *The Pelican Brief* (1993), based on the John Grisham bestseller, Julia Roberts plays a Tulane law school student who discovers why two supreme court justices have been murdered. A more recent Grisham-based film is *Runaway Jury* (2003), starring Gene Hackman, Dustin Hoffman, and John Cusack. This time, a gun company tries to pay off the jury in a high-profile trial. *Sudden Impact* (1983) is a Clint Eastwood Dirty Harry film, largely set in uptown New Orleans. *Double Jeopardy* (1999) stars Ashley Judd and Tommy Lee Jones in an entertaining faux-murder mystery set mainly in the French Quarter and surrounding cemeteries. In *JFK* (1991), New Orleans district attorney Jim Garrison (Kevin Costner) tries to prosecute a city businessman (Tommy Lee Jones) for conspiracy in the assassination of President John F. Kennedy. *The Big Easy* (1987) features Lake Pontchartrain, the Piazza d'Italia, and a catchy zydeco music sound track as it unfolds its tale of a wise-guy police lieutenant (Dennis Quaid) who uncovers corruption in the New Orleans police force.

Two documentaries provide invaluable glimpses into contemporary music culture in New Orleans. Stevenson Palfi's *Piano Players Rarely Play Together* (1982) brings together Allen Toussaint, Toots Washington, and Professor Longhair onto a single stage, shortly before Professor Longhair's death. Les Blank's *Always for Pleasure* (1978) is a penetrating look into Mardi Gras Indian culture. Another documentary, *The Farm* (1998), was produced by inmates at Angola Prison, upriver from New Orleans. The film offers an incisive, at times heartbreaking, look at the corrupted local penal justice system.

Other films shot in New Orleans are: *Hard Target* (1994); *Undercover Blues* (1993); *Storyville* (1992); *Miller's Crossing* (1990); *Tune in Tomorrow* (1990); *Blaze* (1989); *Angel Heart* (1987); *Tightrope* (1984); *Cat People* (1982); *Easy Rider* (1969); and *Panic in the Streets* (1950). For a glimpse of Cajun country, take a look at *The Apostle* (1997), *Passion Fish* (1992), *Belizaire the Cajun* (1986), *No Mercy* (1986), and Les Blank's documentaries on Cajun culture.

Music

It would be impossible to prepare fully for the incredible variety of music you will hear pouring from shops, restaurants, bars, and clubs in New Orleans. Far and away the best source for local and regional music is the Louisiana Music Factory (210 Decatur St., ☎ 504/586–1094), a mecca for musicians passing through New Orleans and an important force in the local music community. The staff will help you identify that great band you heard the night before, and some local CDs are available only here. Saturday afternoons bring live in-store concerts. The store also ships anywhere.

Louis Armstrong laid the foundation of a classic style that New Orleans musicians—and jazz artists worldwide—still draw upon today. Any CD from the series *The Hot 5s and 7s* (CBS Records) is a good bet; the whole set is now available as a four-CD box set (JSP 100). The clarinet playing that seduced Paris is captured on *The Best of Sidney Bechet* (Blue Note 28891). The Preservation Hall Jazz Band still plays each night at Preservation Hall; hear the group's traditional jazz on *Songs of New Orleans, Parts I and II* (Preservation Hall Records 5). Danny Barker's all-acoustic and entertaining *Save the Bones* (Orleans Records 1018) captures the folk element in traditional New Orleans music.

Piano virtuosity has a long and rich history in New Orleans. Good examples of Jelly Roll Morton's ragtime art are found on *The Piano Rolls* (Nonesuch 79363) and *The Pearls* (Bluebird 6588). Professor Longhair, who developed his own unique "rumba-boogie" style and influenced every local pianist to come after him, has a slew of recordings; a couple of the best are *Rock and Roll Gumbo* (Dancing Cat 3006) and *Mardi Gras in Baton Rouge* (Rhino 70736). The dazzling, intensely intellectual playing of James Booker can be sampled on *Junco Partner* (Hannibal 1359) and *The Lost Paramount Tapes* (DJM 10010). In the rhythm-and-blues camp, you'll find many of Fats Domino's jaunty favorites on *The Fat Man* (EMI 52326). More good New Orleans R&B is available on Lee Dorsey's *Working in the Coalmine*.

Some of the best artists to come out of New Orleans are still playing local clubs today. Dr. John's raspy mysticism comes through especially well on *Gumbo* (Atco 7006). The funky Meters (currently playing as "The Funky Meters") have a number of good albums, including *The Very Best of the Meters* (Rhino 72642) and the two-CD *Funkify Your Life* (Rhino 71869). The Neville Brothers have a greatest-hits album, *Uptown Rulin'* (A&M Records 490403), which traces the trajectory of their funk-R&B development. That unique New Orleans genre, Mardi Gras Indian music, gets a good hearing on the Wild Magnolias' *I'm Back at Carnival Time* (Rounder 2094). The Rebirth Brass Band is the local favorite among contemporary brass bands; the group's *Feel Like Funkin' It Up* (Rounder 2092) and *Take It to the Street* (Rounder 2115) provide a good sense of this dynamic, modern sound that falls somewhere between traditional jazz and hip-hop.

Though Cajun country lies upriver from New Orleans, its unique French-language folk music is very popular in town, too. For a good introduction, try *The Balfa Brothers Play Traditional Cajun Music* (Swallow Records 6011) and David Doucet's *Quand j'ai parti* (Rounder 1640) or *"1957"* (Rounder 6088). Zydeco, Cajun's bluesier near-relation, is best exemplified by the classic recordings of Clifton Chenier, including *Louisiana Blues and Zydeco* (Arhoolie 329) and *Bogalusa Boogie* (Arhoolie 347); hot albums by zydeco's newest generation include Geno Delafose's *French Rockin' Boogie* (Rounder 612131) and Nathan and the Zydeco Cha-Chas' *Creole Crossroads* (Rounder 612137).

— Baty Landis

INDEX